The History of Early Christianity

STUDIES IN THE RELIGION AND HISTORY OF EARLY CHRISTIANITY

Edited by Gerd Lüdemann

Vol. 3

PETER LANG

Frankfurt am Main · Berlin · Bern · New York · Paris · Wien

Niels Hyldahl

The History
of Early Christianity

PETER LANG
Europäischer Verlag der Wissenschaften

Die Deutsche Bibliothek - CIP-Einheitsaufnahme

Hyldahl, Niels:

The history of early Christianity / Niels Hyldahl. - Frankfurt am
Main ; Berlin ; Bern ; New York ; Paris ; Wien : Lang, 1997
    (Studies in the religion and history of early
    Christianity ; Bd. 3)
    ISBN 3-631-30404-8

NE: Arbeiten zur Religion und Geschichte des Urchristentums

Original titel: Den Ældste Kristendoms Historie
© Museum Tusculanums Forlag & Niels Hyldahl 1993, 1994
First published by Museum Tusculanums Forlag: Copenhagen.
Translated by: Else Marie Arevad / Helen Dyrbye
Layout: Anders Hyldahl / Mogens Jacobsen

ISSN 0949-3069
ISBN 3-631-30404-8
US-ISBN 0-8204-3197-4

© Peter Lang GmbH
Europäischer Verlag der Wissenschaften
Frankfurt am Main 1997
All rights reserved.

Printed in Germany 1 2 3 4 5 7

PREFACE

The contents of this book are based mainly on a series of lectures I gave to students of theology at the University of Copenhagen in 1988 and 1989. Since then, I have worked intermittently on both the presentation and the subject matter. Several of the students who attended my lectures have been very helpful to me during this time. My colleague Mogens Müller helped me by providing advice, engaging in interesting discussions and by undertaking the time-consuming task of reading draft manuscripts several times. Per Bilde from the University of Aarhus also read an earlier version of the text, and has generously assisted me by offering a great deal of valuable advice and suggested improvements. However, any errors and shortcomings are to be blamed entirely on myself.

My aim was to identify historical links between the early history of Judaism and early Christianity, not only during the period of early Christianity but also between then and now. Far too often, the history of early Christianity is treated only as contemporary New Testament history and reduced to a description of the political, cultural, religious and social conditions of the period. Such a "static" approach neglects one essential point: the dynamics of history. I hope that this book will give the reader the feeling that history is moving and evolving all the time, and that we are moving and evolving along with it.

It was never my intention to present an exhaustive description of the history of early Christianity. Nor have I attempted to present a coherent and comprehensive exposition of the Jewish and Christian apocalyptic and the early history of Judaism as the background of early Christianity, although this would have been useful. In my opinion, this information should be collected and presented by a group of specialists. Such a project will have to wait.

The reference list I have provided is not exhaustive, but includes the titles I consider most important. Readers can then find more literature in the areas that interest them.

Finally, a few parts of the present book (1.1 and 3.6.2) have already been published in other contexts. Sections have also been presented at international congresses in Dublin, Milan and Denmark. But the historical links mentioned above are presented for the first time in this book.

Copenhagen, August 1992   *Niels Hyldahl*

PREFACE TO THE ENGLISH EDITION

I owe rather many persons my sincere thanks for their help in the publication of this English translation of my book. First and foremost Gerd Lüdemann, Göttingen, with whom I have the new Pauline chronology in common, for his keen interest in having the book printed in the series *Studies in the Religion and History of Early Christianity*, and Michael Goulder, Birmingham, whom I owe more than words can tell. Next, the staff of the library in the Department of Biblical Exegesis, Copenhagen, not least Bodil Glenstrup, for procuring English translations of German theological literature. I would also like to thank the two translators, Else Marie Arevad and Helen Dyrbye, for their dedication to this job, and Pia Guldager, Århus, who has made the maps and kindly given permission to re-use them, with English names, in this edition. For covering the expenses of translating I also wish to thank the following Danish institutions, some of which also helped in publishing the Danish edition: G.E.C. Gads Fond, Jens Nørregaards og Hal Kochs Mindefond, Københavns Universitets Almene Fond, and the Theological Faculty at the University of Copenhagen. For all their support I am deeply grateful.

Bible quotations have mostly been taken from the Revised English Bible, and, where not otherwise indicated, modern literature has been translated by the translators.

Copenhagen, August 1996   *N.H.*

CONTENTS

1 EARLY JUDAISM

Bibliography

a) Sources

The Book of Daniel (in the Old Testament).

The Apocrypha of the Old Testament (in Bible editions which include them – and in *Bibelen i kulturhistorisk lys*, edited by Svend Holm-Nielsen and Bent Noack, volume 6: De Apokryfe Skrifter, with introductions by Jes Asmussen, Copenhagen 1970).

De gammeltestamentlige Pseudepigrafer i oversættelse med indledninger og noter, by E. Hammershaimb et al., Copenhagen 1953-1976.

Die Texte aus Qumran. Hebräisch und Deutsch. Mit masoretischer Punktation, Übersetzung, Einführung und Anmerkungen, published by Eduard Lohse, Darmstadt 1971.

Dødehavsteksterne. Skrifter fra den jødiske menighed i Qumran i oversættelse og med noter, by Eduard Nielsen and Benedikt Otzen, Copenhagen 1959.

Die Tempelrolle vom Toten Meer. Übersetzt und erläutert, by Johann Maier (Uni-Taschenbücher, 829), Munich 1978 = *The Temple Scroll. An Introduction, Translation & Commentary* (Journal for the Study of the Old Testament, Supplement Series, 34), Sheffield 1985.

Altjüdisches Schrifttum außerhalb der Bibel. Übersetzt und erklärt, by Paul Rießler, Augsburg 1928, 2nd edition, Darmstadt 1966.

Jüdische Schriften aus hellenistich-römischer Zeit, published by W.G. Kümmel, Gütersloh 1973 ff.

The Mishnah. Translated from the Hebrew with Introduction and brief explanatory Notes, by Herbert Danby, London 1933, and many later reprints.

Josephus. With an English Translation, by H.St.J. Thackeray, Ralph Marcus et al., I-IX (Loeb Classical Library), Cambridge (Mass.) 1926-1965.

Jødernes krig mod Romerne, translated by Alexander Rasmussen, Copenhagen 1905.

Flavius Josephus, De bello Judaico/Der jüdische Krieg. Zweisprachige Ausgabe der sieben Bücher. Herausgegeben und mit einer Einleitung sowie mit Anmerkungen versehen, by Otto Michel and Otto Bauernfeind, I-III, Darmstadt 1959-1969.

Philo von Alexandria. Die Werke in deutscher Übersetzung, published by Leopold Cohn, Isaak Heinemann et al., I-VII, 2nd ed., Berlin 1962-1964 (volume VII first published in 1964).

Philo. With an English translation, by F.H. Colson et al., I-X + Supplementary Volumes I-II (Loeb Classical Library), Cambridge (Mass.) 1929-1962.

The Essenes According to the Classical Sources, ed. by Geza Vermes & Martin D. Goodman (Oxford Centre Textbooks, I), Sheffield 1989.

The Old Testament Pseudepigrapha, edited by James H. Charlesworth, Vol. 1 (Apocalyptic Literature and Testaments), London 1983; Vol. 2 (Expansions of the "Old Testament" and Legends, Wisdom and Philosophical Literature, Prayers, Psalms, and Odes, Fragments of Lost Judeo-Hellenistic Works), London 1985.

Florentino García Martínez: *The Dead Sea Scrolls Translated. The Qumran Texts in English*, Leiden – New York – Cologne 1994.

The Dead Sea Scrolls. Hebrew, Aramaic, and Greek Texts with English Translations, ed. by James H. Charlesworth, Vol. 1 (Rule of the Community and Related Documents), Tübingen – Louisville 1994; Vol. 2 (Damascus Document, War Scroll, and Related Documents), Tübingen – Louisville 1995.

b) General works

Emil Schürer: *Geschichte des jüdischen Volkes im Zeitalter Jesu Christi*, I-III, with index, 4th-5th ed., Leipzig 1907-1921.

Id.: *The History of the Jewish People in the Age of Jesus Christ (175 B.C.–A.D. 135). A New English Version*, published by Geza Vermes, Fergus Millar et al., I-III.1/2, Edingburgh 1973-1987.

J. Wellhausen: *Die Pharisäer und die Sadducäer. Eine Untersuchung zur inneren jüdischen Geschichte*, Greifswald 1874; 2nd ed. Hannover 1924; 3rd ed. Göttingen 1967.

V. Tcherikover: *Hellenistic Civilization and the Jews*. Translated [from Hebrew] by S. Applebaum, 2nd ed., Philadelphia – Jerusalem 1961; repr. 1970.

D.S. Russell: *The Method & Message of Jewish Apocalyptic 200 B.C. – A.D. 100*, London – Philadelphia 1964.

Martin Hengel: *Judentum und Hellenismus. Studien zu ihrer Begegnung unter besonderer Berücksichtigung Palästinas bis zur Mitte des 2. Jh.s v. Chr.* (Wissenschaftliche Untersuchungen zum Neuen Testament, 10), 2nd ed., Tübingen 1973 = *Judaism and Hellenism*, I-II, Philadelphia – London 1974.

E.P. Sanders: *Paul and Palestinian Judaism. A Comparison of Patterns of Religion*, Philadelphia – London 1977.

Per Bilde: *Josefus som historieskriver. En undersøgelse af Josefus' fremstilling af Gaius Caligulas konflikt med jøderne i Palæstina (Bell 2, 184-203 og Ant 18, 261-309) med særligt henblik på forfatterens tendens og historiske pålidelighed* (Bibel og historie, 1), Copenhagen 1983.

Benedikt Otzen: *Den antike jødedom. Politisk udvikling og religiøse strømninger fra Aleksander den Store til Kejser Hadrian*, Copenhagen 1984 = *Judaism in Ant-*

iquity. Political Development and Religious Currents from Alexander to Hadrian (The Biblical Seminar, 7), Sheffield 1990.

Christopher Rowland: *Christian Origins. An Account of the Setting and Character of the most Important Messianic Sect of Judaism*, London 1985, pp. 23-108: "Jewish Life and Thought at the Beginning of the Christian Era".

Per Bilde: *Flavius Josephus, Between Jerusalem and Rome. His Life, his Works, and their Importance* (Journal for the Study of the Pseudepigrapha, Supplement Series, 2), Sheffield 1988.

E.P. Sanders: *Judaism. Practice & Belief 63 BCE – 66 CE*, London – Philadelphia 1992.

Doron Mendels: *The Rise and Fall of Jewish Nationalism. The History of Jewish and Christian Ethnicity in Palestine within the Greco-Roman Period (200 B.C.E.-135 C.E.)* (The Anchor Bible Reference Library), New York 1992.

1.1 Jews and Seleucids

Bibliography

Elias J. Bickermann: *Der Gott der Makkabäer. Untersuchungen über Sinn und Ursprung der makkabäischen Erhebung*, Berlin 1937 = *The God of the Maccabees. Studies on the Meaning and Origins of the Maccabean Revolt* (Studies in Judaism in Late Antiquity, 32), Leiden 1979.

F.-M. Abel: *Les Livres des Maccabées* (Études Bibliques), 2nd ed., Paris 1949.

Otto Mørkholm: *Antiochus IV of Syria* (Classica et Mediaevalia. Dissertationes, VIII), Copenhagen 1966.

Jochen Gabriel Bunge: *Untersuchungen zum zweiten Makkabäerbuch. Quellenkritische, literarische, chronologische und historische Untersuchungen zum zweiten Makkabäerbuch als Quelle syrisch-palästinensischer Geschichte im 2. Jh. v. Chr.*, Bonn 1971.

John R. Bartlett: *The First and Second Books of the Maccabees* (The Cambridge Bible Commentary, New English Bible), Cambridge 1973.

Jonathan A. Goldstein: *I Maccabees. A New Translation with Introduction and Commentary* (The Anchor Bible, 41), New York 1976.

Karl Christ: *Krise und Untergang der römischen Republik*, Darmstadt 1979.

Christian Habicht: *2. Makkabäerbuch* (Jüdische Schriften aus hellenistisch-römischer Zeit, I/3), Gütersloh 1976, 2nd ed. 1979.

Thomas Fischer: *Seleukiden und Makkabäer. Beiträge zur Seleukidengeschichte und zu den politischen Ereignissen in Judäa während der 1. Hälfte des 2. Jahrhunderts v.Chr.*, Bochum 1980.

Klaus-Dietrich Schunck: *1. Makkabäerbuch* (Jüdische Schriften aus hellenistisch-römischer Zeit, I/4), Gütersloh 1980.

Nils Martola: *Capture and Liberation. A Study in the Composition of the First Book of Maccabees* (Acta Academiae Aboensis, ser. A: Humaniora, 63/1), Åbo 1980.

Klaus Bringmann: *Hellenistische Reform und Religionsverfolgung in Judäa. Eine Untersuchung zur jüdisch-hellenistichen-Geschichte (175-163 v.Chr.)* (Abhandlungen der Akademie der Wissenschaften in Göttingen, Philol.-hist. Kl., Dritte Folge, Nr. 132), Göttingen 1983.

Jonathan A. Goldstein: *II Maccabees. A New Translation with Introduction and Commentary* (The Anchor Bible, 41A), New York 1984.

Bezalel Bar-Kochva: *Judas Maccabaeus. The Jewish Struggle against the Seleucids*, Cambridge 1989.

Otto Mørkholm: Antiochus IV, in: W.D. Davies/L. Finkelstein, eds., *The Cambridge History of Judaism*, Vol. II (The Hellenistic Age), Cambridge 1989, pp. 278-291.

Niels Hyldahl: Jøderne og Seleukiderne, in: Troels Engberg-Pedersen/Niels Peter Lemche, eds., *Tradition og nybrud. Jødedommen i hellenistisk tid* (Forum for bibelsk eksegese, 2), Copenhagen 1990, pp. 65-92.

Niels Hyldahl: The Maccabean Rebellion and the Question of "Hellenization", in: Per Bilde/Troels Engberg-Pedersen/Lise Hannestad/Jan Zahle, eds., *Religion and Religious Practice in the Seleucid Kingdom* (Studies in Hellenistic Civilization, 1), Århus 1990, pp. 188-203.

1.1.1 Politics and economics

In order to understand the origins and history of early Christianity, it is necessary first to study the history of the Jewish people during the period from approx. 200 B.C. to approx. A.D. 100. At that time, their situation had remained largely unchanged for several centuries. Since their deportation to Babylon and the destruction of the first temple in 587 B.C., the Jewish people had had no king and no national independence. They had, in fact, been ruled by several great powers. First came the Babylonians, then the Persians, who allowed them to return and rebuild the temple at Jerusalem in about 520 B.C. Next, after 331 B.C., came the Greeks, i.e. the Macedonians, led by Alexander the Great and his Macedonian phalanxes. He conquered the entire Near East, including Egypt and the Persian empire.

From the beginning of Macedonian rule, Greek was the common language, and the culture was Hellenistic. The impact of this on early Judaism and its history can hardly be overestimated.

After Alexander's death in 323 B.C., the power struggles among the Diadochi ("the successors") split his worldwide empire into several parts. In 312 B.C., Syria, with its newly built capital Antioch on the Orontes River, came under the rule of the Seleucids, while the Ptolemies or Lagids assumed power in Egypt, with its capital Alexandria founded by Alexander himself. Since the rule of the Persians, whose administrative system still existed in many ways, Palestine had been a separate region as part of the satrapy Coele-Syria-Phoenicia. As in the earlier history of Israel, Palestine was a bone of contention between two great rival empires, one to the north, the other to the south. For a long time – from 312 until 198 B.C. – Palestine belonged to Egypt and the Ptolemies. But at the battle at Paneas (to the north of the lake of Huleh, by the source of the Jordan and not far from what was later called Caesarea Philippi), the Seleucid ruler of Syria, Antiochus III the Great (223-187) defeated the Ptolemaic commander Scopas, who led the Egyptian forces on behalf of Ptolemy V Epiphanes (203-180). This was how Antiochus III came to rule over Palestine and the Jews. Syrian rule continued in principle until Pompey conquered the country for the Romans in 63 B.C.

It is important to understand the situation of the Jews when their country was conquered by Antiochus III, at the beginning of the second century B.C. Without a king, and without national independence, they were not a nation, but only a people, a small ethnic minority whose territory had been reduced to the mountainous parts of Judea, with Jerusalem and its temple as its centre. Furthermore, Judea had no access to the Mediterranean Sea.

For centuries, there had also been Jews living in the Diaspora ("dispersion") – both in the nearby Diaspora, Galilee and the land on the other side of the Jordan; and in the far Diaspora, Egypt and the area near the Euphrates and the Tigris, as well as in fast-growing Jewish communities in Asia Minor, North Africa (Cyrene – now called Libya), and later also in Greece, Macedonia and Italy. So the Jewish people were divided between the home population in Judea and the majority living in the Diaspora.

The Jews in Judea constituted a temple state governed by the high priest and a council of elders. Since the rule of the Persians, and under Greek rule, the special ethnic character of the Jews had been respected and remained unchallenged. To the outside world they were represented by the high priest, who was responsible for paying an annual tribute to the foreign rulers. At the time in question, the tribute to the Syrian rulers amounted to 300 talents. The population also had to pay several taxes, such as poll tax, salt tax, crown tax etc. In principle, it was of no concern to the Syrian rulers how the high priest managed to collect the money for the annual tribute. There is considerable evidence that this was done by assessing the value of private property. In rural areas, the tax was based on the value of farmers' freeholds, and in the cities – primarily Jerusalem – inhabitants' houses, their private incomes, etc. were assessed. As far back as the Ptolemaic rule, the collection of taxes and duties was farmed out to tax collectors, and there is no reason to believe that the system was changed with the transfer of power. But the new Seleucid rulers may have appointed other local people whom they trusted more to these positions. The original tax collectors had, after all, worked for the Ptolemaic rulers and may have remained loyal to them. At an early stage, the new rulers seem to have introduced a special "temple tax" in Jerusalem. As well as the high priest, there was now also a temple administrator, whose task appears to have been to secure the Seleucid State extra revenues from a tax on the profits of the temple itself. Customs duties, i.e. taxes on exported or imported goods, became another important source of revenue: while the Jewish population of Judea and Jerusalem had little export trade, they needed to import large quantities of goods, since the country had relatively few raw materials, especially metal and wood.

The population in the rural areas of Judea were farmers. They kept oxen, sheep and goats and produced cereals, wine and fruit, while the inhabitants of Jerusalem – and indirectly the whole population of Judea – lived off the temple and the profits it made. The people who benefited from this temple trade were primarily the priests, the Levites, the rich landowners who had houses in Jerusalem, tradesmen and craftsmen.

It is essential to understand the ethnic interdependence between the Jews in Jerusalem and those in the nearby and the far-off Diaspora, because without this interdependence, the temple and the priests in Jerusalem could hardly have subsisted – Judea was too poor a country for that. Moreover, the Diaspora Jews' pilgrimages to Jerusalem and the temple were a vital source of income. This interdependence was the more important, as the Jewish population in Judea was surrounded by Gentile populations; several of these "heathen", i.e. Gentile, cities in Palestine were autonomous and organized on the model of the Hellenistic *pólis*.

It is equally important to recognize the extent of the area covered by the empire when Antiochus III had also conquered Palestine at the turn of that century. In addition to Syria itself with its capital Antioch, the empire included Persia and Media to the east, extended as far as the Indian border, and almost entirely covered the peninsula of Asia Minor, the territory of modern Turkey. Antiochus III truly deserved to be called "the Great". Farthest to the south, next to the then arch-enemy Egypt, lay the small regions of Judea, Samaria and Idumea, whose small populations had had no particular reason to feel dissatisfied with the Egyptian rulers, and whose loyalty to the Seleucid State could therefore not be taken for granted.

Far from being a solid and stable unity, the Seleucid empire consisted of a number of relatively independent regions with widely different populations, cultures and languages. They were loosely connected by the political system and its administration. The head of this system was the autocratic king, whose governors, strategists and officials were employed in the various countries of the empire. They were assisted by stationary garrisons and mobile army groups, mostly mercenaries. The power of the State depended on the ruler and his strength, since the king himself was the only authority common to the different parts of the empire. The king's revenues were enormous, but so were his expenditures: paying the mercenaries and keeping the administration going required an enormous and constant inflow of capital. The money came from conquests, tributes, taxes and duties, as well as from the rich silver mines and other metal mines in Asia Minor, which the king had naturally claimed as his own property.

But Antiochus the Great was not to stay great for ever.

In 190 B.C., during the battle of Magnesia on the River Maeander in the western part of Asia Minor, Antiochus III was finally beaten by the great new power that was to dominate the world for centuries to come: the Romans. At the Peace of Apamea in 188 B.C., Antiochus had to accept a number of extremely strict peace terms which deprived him of his power and led to the ultimate disintegration of the Syrian empire.

Antiochus was forced to give up all of Asia Minor except the province of Cilicia behind the Taurus Mountains. This meant that he lost his silver and gold mines. He also had to give up his entire fleet except for ten ships, so he no longer ruled the waves of the Mediterranean and the Aegean Sea. He had to give up the elephants he had used in battle (the Seleucids used Indian elephants, the Ptolemies had African elephants), and pay enormous reparations to the Romans: several years' provisions for the Roman and Pergamene armies and – the most important part of the peace agreement – he had to pay a total amount of 15,000 talents to the Romans. This enormous amount was to be paid as follows: 500 talents immediately after the peace agreement in 188 B.C.; 2,500 talents at the ratification, and the rest – 12,000 talents – in twelve annual instalments of 1,000 talents each. As Antiochus himself died shortly after – in 187, his successors to the Seleucid throne had to pay the greater part of the debt. The Romans refused to cancel any part of it.

All this money had to be paid by the populations that belonged to the Seleucid empire, now deprived of Asia Minor – a severe taxation that weighed heavily on Judea as well.

To get an idea of the amounts of money involved, it might be useful to take a look at Antiochus' next successor but one: Antiochus IV Epiphanes (175-164 B.C.), who was detested by all his subjects, and with good reason. Although the debt from the Peace at Apamea was paid in his time,[1] he managed to extract enormous amounts of money out of Judea during his short reign of less than ten years.[2]

During the first six years from his accession in 175 until he plundered the temple in 169 B.C., he collected the following amounts: 1,030 talents over the two years when Jason was high priest; 2,960 talents over the next four years when Menelaus was high priest and until the plunder of the temple; 1,800 talents from the plunder of the temple itself in 169 B.C. This amounted to a total of no less than 5,790 talents in just six years, taken from Judea and transferred to the Seleucid treasury! It equals approximately one third of the total reparations demanded by the Romans at the Peace of Apameas. In other words, during the six years between 175 and 169 B.C., an average of almost 1,000 talents a year was extracted from the small country of Judea alone – the same

---

1   See also Mørkholm, *Antiochus IV of Syria*, p. 65.
2   For further information about the following review of the financial situation, see Bringmann, *Hell. Reform u. Religionsverfolgung*, pp. 111-120: "Steuerdruck und Tempelraub".

amount that the Seleucids had been required to pay the Romans in annual instalments. Or three times the amount of 300 talents a year that Antiochus IV's predecessor, Seleucus IV Philopator (187-175) had received in total tributes from Judea during the last six years of his reign, a total of 1,800 talents paid over the same time span: six years. These figures do not include poll tax, salt tax or any other taxes.

We can also get an impression of the enormity of these amounts by looking at them from another point of view. A little less than two hundred years later, during the reign of Archelaus of the Herod dynasty (4 B.C.-A.D. 6), Judea, Samaria and Idumea together had to pay 600 talents a year to the Roman treasury. Judea probably had to pay at least half this amount, as much as the "normal" tribute before Antiochus IV, although Judea was then considerably smaller than at the time of the Herodian dynasty. During the reign of Archelaus, this taxation represented approximately 14 per cent of the entire production of Judea – a heavy taxload considering the country's relatively small production at that time. The taxload must therefore have been impossibly heavy for the small population under Antiochus IV. One need hardly look further in search of a motive for the Maccabean uprising during his reign!

But let us return to the situation in Judea immediately after Antiochus III's assumption of power after the battle at Paneas, when he was at the height of his power.

We have two documents which pinpoint the situation in Judea at that time, both recorded by Josephus, and both considered authentic today: Ant. Jud. XII, 138-144 and 145-146.[3]

The first document is a copy of a letter from the victorious Antiochus to his strategist for Coele-Syria, Ptolemy, son of Thraseas – the name Ptolemy indicates "Egyptian" descent. In the letter, the king orders Ptolemy to carry out certain instructions. The procedure is characteristic of both the Ptolemaic and the Seleucid administrations, and we may assume that it is the original Greek version of the letter:

138 King Antiochus to Ptolemy, greeting. Inasmuch as the Jews, from the very moment when we entered their country, showed their eagerness to serve us and, when

---

3   A thorough discussion with explanations is found in Ralph Marcus, *Josephus. With an English Translation*, VII, 1943, pp. 743-766: "Appendix D: Antiochus III and the Jews (Ant. xii. 129-153)".

we came to their city, gave us a splendid reception and met us with their senate and furnished an abundance of provisions to our soldiers and elephants, and also helped us to expel the Egyptian garrison in the citadel, 139 we have seen fit on our part to requite them for these acts and to restore their city which has been destroyed by the hazards of war, and to repeople it by bringing back to it those who had been dispersed abroad.

140 In the first place we have decided, on account of their piety, to furnish them for their sacrifices an allowance of sacrificial animals, wine, oil and frankincense to the value of twenty thousand pieces of silver, and sacred *artabae*[4] of fine flour in accordance with their native law, and one thousand four hundred and sixty *medimni* of wheat and three hundred and seventy-five *medimni* of salt. 141 And it is my will that these things be made over to them as I have ordered, and that the work on the temple be completed, including the porticoes and any other part that it may be necessary to build. The timber, moreover, shall be brought from Judea itself and from other nations and Lebanon without the imposition of a toll charge. The like shall be done with the other materials needed for making the restoration of the temple more splendid.

142 And all the members of the nation shall have a form of government in accordance with the laws of their country, and the senate, the priests, the scribes of the temple and the temple-singers shall be relieved from the poll-tax and the crown-tax and the salt-tax which they pay.

143 And, in order that the city may the more quickly be inhabited, I grant both to the present inhabitants and to those who may return before the month of Hyperberetaios exemption from taxes for three years. 144 We shall also relieve them in future from the third part of their tribute, so that their losses may be made good. And as for those who were carried off from the city and are slaves, we herewith set them free, both them and the children born to them, and order their property to be restored to them.[5]

The letter begins with a description of the Jews' and especially Jerusalem's friendly reception of the Seleucid army and the Jews' recognition of Seleucid supremacy. It is important to note that the Jewish people was represented by Jerusalem's council of elders, in Greek: *gerousía*. The Jews are granted a

---

4   There is no indication of quantity.
5   Josephus, Ant. Jud. XII, 138-144 (chapter 3.3). Literature: E.J. Bickerman, La charte séleucide de Jérusalem, Revue des Études Juives 100 (1935), pp. 4-35 = Der seleukidische Freibrief für Jerusalem, in: Abraham Schalit, ed., *Zur Josephus-Forschung* (Wege der Forschung, 84), Darmstadt 1973, pp. 205-240 = La Charte séleucide ..., in E.J. Bickermann, *Studies in Jewish and Christian History*, II (Arbeiten zur Geschichte des antiken Judentums und des Urchristentums, IX), Leiden 1980, pp. 44-85; id., *God of the Maccabees*, Leiden 1979, p. 33.

number of privileges as a reward for having recognized the transfer of power, for having helped the Seleucid army to drive the Egyptian garrison away from Jerusalem so that it could be replaced by a Seleucid garrison, and for other services rendered to the Seleucid army.

Looking at the last part of the letter, we notice that the Jews are exempt from taxation for three years, and that this privilege is also granted to the Jews who had left the country because of the war, or because they sympathized with the Ptolemies – provided they return to Judea within a certain time limit. The king is clearly interested in re-establishing a loyal population and a well-regulated country. On the other hand, the population still has to pay tribute. As we saw, the tribute Judea had to pay amounted to 300 talents a year at the time of Antiochus III's successor and son, Seleuchus IV (187-175 B.C.). Only a third of that tribute will be cancelled "in future", as it says – a lenience that proved to be short-lived, as we already know! So the devastated Judea had to pay 200 talents a year to the Seleucid treasury for its "liberation", and full taxes again after three years.

Looking at the middle part of the letter, we can see who would benefit the most from the privileges granted after the transfer of power: the council of elders, the priests, the scribes of the temple and the temple singers. They – the non-productive upper class – would not have to pay any tax at all. Furthermore, materials would be provided for repairing and rebuilding the temple and Jerusalem, and the temple would receive a substantial gift in the form of sacrifices, so that it could resume its normal functions. The king himself would pay the expenses of repairing both the town and the temple and the cost of the gift.

Perhaps the most important concession is that the Jews are allowed to live "in accordance with the laws of their country", as it says. This concession is important because it gives the Jewish people the privilege of internal self-government, and the right to practise their own religion. Legally it means that the Jews' "right" to practise their own religion and to live according to their own law, i.e. the stipulations of the Mosaic law, depended entirely on the permission of the Seleucid ruler. "Jerusalem was thus a holy city, but not because of a sovereign decision on the part of the Jews. It was a holy city on the basis of a royal order which confirmed the "law of the fathers" and thus assured their observance," as E.J. Bickerman writes.[6] In theory, this "right" could be cancelled at any time, and that is precisely what happened in 168 B.C., when Antiochus IV was king and banned the Jewish religion. But in the actual situation after Antiochus III's assumption of power, that contingency may have meant less to the Jews: they probably considered Antiochus III as an instrument of God, somebody who fulfilled His will. As long as Antiochus III fulfilled the will of God, the Jewish people had no reason to complain. But if he did not, then he was disobedient to God and could no longer rely on the loyalty of the Jewish people.

These legal aspects are important for a proper understanding of the later history of the Jewish people, and I suspect a certain connection exists between these aspects and the Maccabean assumption of power which took place when Antiochus IV had banned the Jewish religion and the Jews rebelled against the Syrian authorities. The Hasideans, i.e. the "pious" people, refused to support the Maccabees' assumption of power. But unlike the Hasideans, the Maccabees could no longer accept that foreign rulers should have the power to decide whether or not the Jews should be allowed to practise their own religion and live according to their own laws, because that power belonged to God alone, and no human being, however mighty, could contest it. I shall return to this later in the book.

The other document from the period immediately after Antiochus III's assumption of power is a notice to the public, probably written on a bronze plaque fixed on a wall in Jerusalem. It concerns the temple and Jerusalem:

145 ... It is unlawful for any foreigner to enter the enclosure of the temple which is forbidden to the Jews, except to those of them who are accustomed to enter after purifying themselves in accordance with the law of the country. 146 Nor shall anyone bring into the city the flesh of horses or of mules or of wild or tame asses, or of leopards, foxes or hares or, in general, of any animals forbidden to the Jews. Nor is it lawful to bring in their skins or even to breed any of these animals in the city. But only the sacrificial animals known to their ancestors and necessary for the propitiation of God shall they be permitted to use. And the person who violates any of these statutes shall pay to the priests a fine of three thousand drachmas of silver.[7]

---

6   Bickerman, *God of the Maccabees*, p. 34.
7   Josephus, Ant. Jud. XII, 145-146 (chapter 3.4). Literature: E.J. Bickermann, Une proclamation séleucide relative au temple de Jerusalem, Syria 25 (1946-1948), pp. 67-86

No foreigner, i.e. no Gentile, may enter the temple, but only those Jews who have the right to do so according to custom, i.e. the priests and other temple servants, and first they must clean themselves according to the usual rules, i.e. the stipulations of the Mosaic law. Furthermore, only animals that may be used as sacrifices are allowed into Jerusalem. The penalty for transgression is a fine of 3,000 drachmas payable to the priests of the temple.

These prohibitions were probably written by a Seleucid official, because we know from the time of the New Testament that Gentiles who entered the temple were punished with death – not just with a fine (see also the paragraph referred to in note 51 below). According to the Mosaic law, it was not forbidden to bring domestic animals such as donkeys into Jerusalem (as Jesus did on Palm Sunday). The person who wrote these prohibitions may have used some kind of standard text, which did not quite correspond with the real situation in Jerusalem in the early days of the Seleucid rule. But apart from that, the Seleucid "programma" is based on the existing standards and must therefore be considered authentic. Accordingly, this "programma" reflects the cultic aspects of Antiochus III's acknowledgement of the Jewish people's right to practise their own religion. The prohibition against allowing Gentiles access to the temple in Jerusalem was violently transgressed during the reign of Antiochus IV, when he introduced a heathen religion to this very building in 168 B.C. – as described later in this book. This fact also supports the theory that the Maccabees fought for national independence in order to ensure that the religious practice of the Jewish people did not depend on the good-will of foreign rulers.

1.1.2 Culture

An important detail is linked to one of the documents quoted above, or perhaps both of them. We know from 2 Macc. 4.11 that a man named John, the father of Eupolemus, was the Jew who negotiated peace terms with Antiochus III on behalf of the Jewish people after the transfer of power that took place when the Syrians defeated the Egyptians during the battle of Paneas in 200 B.C. This John must therefore have spoken Greek – the official language in the Near East after the time of Alexander the Great.

= id., *Studies in Jewish and Christian History*, II (see n. 5 above), pp. 86-104; Klaus Bringmann, *Hell. Reform u. Religionsverfolgung*, 1983, pp. 77-78.

We know his son Eupolemus from the history of the Maccabees, since he was one of the two envoys whom Judas "Maccabaeus" sent to Rome in 161 B.C. to negotiate a treaty of friendship and alliance between the Romans and the Jewish people; the other envoy was Jason. The same Eupolemus is known for his literary studies. His historical work "Of the kings of Judea" was written in about 158 B.C., after his return from Rome. We do not not know whether Eupolemus knew Latin as well as Greek; but whatever the case he was undoubtedly one of the better-educated Jews of his time. Although he was a Hellenist himself, he found it right to serve the Jewish cause and to fight the "Hellenistic" Jews who assimilated with the Greek world, which explains why he joined the Maccabees.[8]

The character of Eupolemus, the son of John, illustrates the facts we have to keep in mind in order to understand why the cultural and religious war broke out between the Jews and the Seleucid rulers in Antioch. As mentioned above, Eupolemus was what we would call a Hellenistically minded Jew – open to the Greek culture of his time and able to speak Hebrew, Aramaic and Greek. As the author of a historical work, he must also have possessed the literary knowledge necessary for a man who wanted to assert himself in the cultural world. Nevertheless, there is no doubt about his loyalty in the Maccabean war: he was on the side of the nationalist Maccabees, against the Syrians and their "Greek ways". The same might also be said about Jason.

Jason may well be Jason of Cyrene whose Greek work in five volumes was abridged to one book by the author of 2 Macc.: it is particularly striking that 2 Macc. ends with Nicanor's defeat and death in February 161 B.C., immediately before Eupolemus' and Jason's journey to Rome (2 Macc. 4.11), and shortly before the death of Judas Maccabaeus. The journey and the treaty are described in detail in 1 Macc. 8.17-32.[9] The historical truth of the journey and the treaty is

---

8   About Eupolemos: See Doran Mendels, *The Land of Israel as a Political Concept in Hasmonean Literature. Recourse to History in the Second Century B.C. Claims to the Holy Land* (Texte und Studien zum Antiken Judentum, 15), Tübingen 1987, pp. 29-46: "The Fifties: Eupolemos – City, Temple, the Land and the United Monarchy".

9   In 1855, L. Herzfeld was the first to identify Jason, the son of Eleazar (1 Macc. 8.17), who went to Rome with Eupolemus on behalf of Judas Maccabaeus, as Jason from Cyrene, the author of the work in five volumes abridged to 2 Macc. by the unknown Epitomist. Without any convincing arguments, the identification is contested by most scholars, including Hengel, *Judentum u. Hellenismus*, p. 182 (*Judaism and Hellenism*, p.

confirmed by Josephus, Ant. Jud. XIV, 233 (chapter 10.15): in a letter sent to the island of Cos, Consul C. Fannius Strabo (161 B.C.) says that a treaty has been made between the Senate and the Jews, and requests that the Jewish envoys be guaranteed a safe journey home.[10] Later, Jason's son Antipater participated in a similar diplomatic mission to Rome to renew the treaty between the Romans and the Jews: 1 Macc. 12.16. It is interesting to note that the words *hellenismós* (2 Macc. 4.13) and *ioudaïsmós* (2 Macc. 2.21, 8.1 and 14.38) are mentioned for the first time in the Second Book of the Maccabees, and that they are mentioned as opposites.[11]

There is another reason for using Eupolemus and Jason to illustrate the course of events during the conflict between the Jews and the Greek world in which they lived: in recent research, several scholars have argued rather forcibly that what prompted Antiochus IV to ban the Jewish religion in 168 B.C. was the receptiveness to Greek culture which was prevalent in the higher echelons of the Judean people. The same scholars even maintain that the religious suppression was caused by Greek-minded Jewish reformers – not by Antiochus IV, who cared little about internal Jewish affairs.[12]

Of course Antiochus IV's personal opinion of the matter is of little importance. There is no reason to believe that he was particularly hostile to the Jews, or that he was more interested in suppressing the Jewish religion than the other successive rulers (the Persians, the Ptolemies and later the Romans). In fact, such an interest on his part would be difficult to understand or explain, considering the liberal religious policies of these rulers as a whole.

The first Book of the Maccabees quotes the words which have generally been considered as normative for the interpretation of the course of events: in

---

98), and Bar-Kochva, *Judas Maccabaeus*, pp. 181-182. The fact that the author Jason was from Cyrene does not prove anything: see Mk. 15.21!

10 See Schürer, *History*, I, p. 172, n. 33.

11 See also Liddell & Scott, *A Greek-English Lexicon*, ed. Jones, Oxford 1940, s. v. *hellenismos*, which means "imitation of the Greeks, Hellenism" and also "use of a pure Greek style and idiom" as one of the five stoic *aretaì lógou* attributed to the stoic philosopher Diogenes of Babylon (d. circa 152 B.C.) – and he was a contempory of Jason!

12 This point of view has been strongly defended, especially by Bickerman, *God of the Maccabees*, and by Hengel, *Judentum u. Hellenismus*. On the other hand, it has also been strongly criticized by several scholars, including Tcherikover, *Hell. Civilization and the Jews*, and Bringmann, *Hell. Reform u. Religionsverfolgung*, pp. 11 ff. and pp. 141 ff.

the time of Antiochus IV, a group of renegade Jews, it says, persuaded many people to accept their views by saying, "We should go and make an agreement with the Gentiles round about; nothing but disaster has been our lot since we cut ourselves off from them" (1 Macc. 1.11). We have no way of telling what kind of "disaster" they are referring to. Moreover, this assertion turns the entire history of Israel upside down, since fraternization with non-Jewish communities was regarded as the source of all disasters throughout the history of Israel. But as Klaus Bringmann explained in 1983, this extract from 1 Macc. 1.11 represents the subsequent self-justification of the victorious Maccabean or Hasmonean movement.[13] The First Book of the Maccabees is the "official" history of the Maccabees, which was written in the last third of the second century B.C. Accordingly, the words from 1 Macc. 1.11 in no sense reflect the ideas of people from the upper classes in the early Seleucid period under Seleucus IV and Antiochus IV – they serve to justify the Maccabean struggle for power and the victims it had claimed among the Jews themselves.

To understand the situation properly, we must draw a clear distinction between these two concepts, Greek culture and religious suppression. Eupolemus himself personifies the fact that Jewish openness to Greek culture has its own established limits, and that these limits are transgressed whenever the Jewish religion – or rather the Jewish identity and independence – are threatened. On the other hand, the example of Eupolemus also illustrates that Greek culture and the Jewish religion are not mutually exclusive. Consequently, the Jewish openness to Greek culture was not responsible for the ban on the Jewish religion and the persecution of its adherents during the reign of Antiochus IV. In fact, there was no anti-Semitism at all in the Greek-Roman world – on the contrary, an anti-Semitic attitude did not exist until it developed after the Maccabees or the Hasmoneans began to oppress the Gentile communities within and outside Palestine.[14]

Onias III was the high priest of the Jews during the reign of Seleucus IV. According to the Second Book of the Maccabees, Seleucus sent his chancellor, Heliodorus, to Jerusalem to try to seize some of the riches that were kept in the temple there – normally referred to as the "temple treasure". At the same time, mention is also made of a man called Simon. He and his brother Menelaus, who

---

13 Bringmann, *Hell. Reform u. Religionsverfolgung*, pp. 146-147.
14 See Bringmann, *Hell. Reform u. Religionsverfolgung*, pp. 141 ff.

later became high priest, belonged to the Bilgah priest clan. Simon, who was temple administrator (2 Macc. 3.4 ff.), quarrelled with Onias about the revenues generated by the city market, and when he could not have his own way, he went to the Seleucid authorities and told them about the riches hidden in the temple of Jerusalem. This induced Seleucus to send Heliodorus to Jerusalem, but his mission failed, and he returned to Antioch empty-handed.

Shortly after, Seleucus IV was murdered – by Heliodorus! – and Antiochus IV succeeded him, even though he was not the rightful heir to the throne. A brother of the then high priest Onias, Jason, who at least came from a family of high priests, took advantage of the situation and seized power himself: he offered Antiochus IV a substantial increase of the annual tribute from Judea (of course the population had to pay the increased tribute) and a one-off payment of 150 talents, on condition that Antiochus appointed him high priest and – what is more – allowed Jason himself to change Jerusalem's constitution so that it became more like the Greek *pólis* form of government.

Antiochus IV was not hard to persuade. Onias III, whose Ptolemaic sympathies made him unreliable in the eyes of Antiochus, had to resign from his position as high priest. He went to Daphne, a suburb of the Syrian capital Antioch, and asked for sanctuary in the famous Apollo temple there.[15] This in itself is remarkable: a Jewish high priest asking for sanctuary in a heathen temple! But it shows how complicated the cultural situation really was, and illustrates the fact that the historical events of the time cannot be painted in black and white. Later, a certain Andronicus, who had been bribed by Jason's illegitimate successor to the office of high priest, persuaded Onias to leave the temple, and had him murdered. But that is another story.

It is not quite clear what form of government Antiochus IV allowed Jason to introduce in Jerusalem, and historians have differing opinions on this subject. 2 Macc. 4.9 says that he undertook to "enrol [sc. as citizens] in Jerusalem a group to be known as Antiochenes".[16] At the same time, Jason was allowed to set up a

---

15 According to Tcherikover, *Hell. Civilization and the Jews*, p. 469, it was a Jewish synagogue. Against these apologetics, see: Habicht, *2. Makkabäerbuch*, p. 221.

16 The following translation would also be possible: Jason undertook to enrol the inhabitants of Jerusalem as "Antiochenes"; Tcherikover, *Hell. Civilization and the Jews*, p. 161. But it is more likely that only people from the influential circles were enrolled as "Antiochenes", and not all the inhabitants of Jerusalem. See Bringmann, *Hell. Reform u. Religionsverfolgung*, pp. 84 ff.

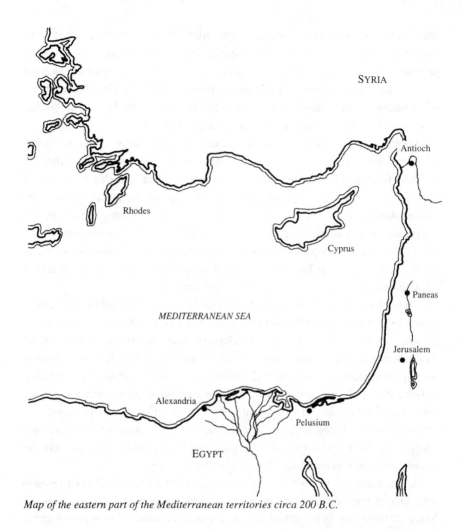

Map of the eastern part of the Mediterranean territories circa 200 B.C.

sports stadium, and to introduce Greek-style education for young men. Jason himself must have decided who should be granted citizenship and vote at the popular assembly, and Jason himself must have received payment for these enrolments.

The purpose of all these measures is unclear. Several scholars have argued that the incentive was financial gain, but their theory is not supported by facts. There is only one occasion on which we know with certainty that the new form of city government functioned in practice: the games held in Tyre every five years (2 Macc. 4.18 ff.). On that occasion, Jason sent envoys there, and gave them 300 drachmas for sacrifices to Hercules of Tyre, also known as Melqart. That was clearly an act of idolatry from a Jewish point of view, and the envoys themselves, who were probably "citizens" of the new *pólis* Jerusalem/Antioch, changed their minds and gave the money to fit out the Seleucid Mediterranean fleet.

In a similar context, the First Book of the Maccabees also mentions that Jews who took part in the athletic games in Jerusalem as if they were Greeks, had operations to remove the marks of circumcision (1 Macc. 1.15 – see also 1 Cor. 7.18). No one knows for sure whether this is true; nor do we know if the Jews practised sports in the nude in Jerusalem, or if they only did so when they took part in sporting events outside Judea – for instance the games in Tyre.

After a couple of years Jason had to admit defeat: he could not procure the money he had promised Antiochus IV. In about 173-172 B.C., another man came forward to succeed him: Menelaus, a brother of Simon, the temple administrator mentioned above. Menelaus was a priest – as we know, his brother Simon was a member of the Bilgah priest clan (see also below, in the paragraph referred to in note 68), but he was not a member of a high priest family. Menelaus was the first Jewish high priest who did not belong to a high priest family. He must have known from the beginning that his power rested on slender foundations, and that he could only continue in office by promising Antiochus IV large amounts of money. Jason fled to the land east of Jordan, which had really always remained pro-Ptolemaic. But the final outrage was yet to come: in 169 B.C., when Menelaus was running short of money to pay Antiochus IV, he helped him to rob the temple in Jerusalem, the very basis of his own existence.

1.1.3 Chronology

When discussing chronology, there are two key factors we have to consider: the Seleucid chronology and the discrepancies that exist between 1 and 2 Macc. as regards the relative chronological order of two events, namely the rededication of the temple and the death of Antiochus IV.

The official chronology of the Seleucid empire dates back to the year 312 B.C., when Seleucus I Nicator (312-280 B.C.) came to power. It is important to note here that the new year began in the autumn. This was the Macedonian calendar, and 312-311 B.C. was its first year. Most of the events in 1 and 2 Macc. are dated according to this calendar. But in 1 Macc., several events seem to be dated according to the Babylonian-Jewish calendar, in which the new year began in spring with its first month called Nisan.

The eastern, Babylonian parts of the Seleucid empire used a chronology whose first year began in the spring and corresponded to year 311-310 B.C. Consequently, only the period from spring to autumn was the same year according to both calendars, and between autumn and spring, there was a difference of one year between the two calendars.

In the past, many scholars believed that 1 Macc. referred to two chronologies: the official Seleucid era (S.E.) beginning in the autumn of 312 B.C., and the so-called Babylonian era, which began in the spring of 311 B.C.[17] This has caused a great deal of discussion and uncertainty. It would seem natural to assume that the western S.E. was used in Palestine, but most scholars have contested this theory, since the Jewish New Year is supposed to have been celebrated in the spring, with Nisan as the first month. But in 1966, Otto Mørkholm began to suspect that this theory might be wrong: "The use of two eras within the same historical work is astonishing."[18]

On the other hand, Klaus Bringmann argues convincingly that there was no "contamination" between two different chronologies which could have caused chronological uncertainty. The Jewish year, which began in the spring, was a typical "religious" year and cannot simply be converted into the Macedonian calendar. For instance, it says in 1 Macc. 10.21 that the Feast of Tabernacles was held in the seventh month (Tishri according to the Jewish calendar) of the year 160. But there is no reason to assume that this refers to the Babylonian chronology. Let me use an example to clarify the situation: no Jew would ever have said that the Feast of Tabernacles was held in the first month, although that would be more or less correct according to the Macedonian calendar. Jewish feasts are dated according to the Jewish calendar and the Jewish method of counting months. Nor is there any reason to believe that the Jews would have

---

17 It is tempting to call this chronology "the Babylonian era" (B.E.), but it was in fact just as "Seleucid" as the one we call S.E. Lester L. Grabbe, Maccabean Chronology: 167-164 or 168-165 BCE, Journal of Biblical Literature 110 (1991), pp. 59-74, suggests the spring of 312 B.C. as the starting point!

18 Mørkholm, *Antiochus IV of Syria*, p. 161.

used the Babylonian chronology, starting from 311 B.C. The "religious" year was only for internal Jewish use, and all dates are easily understood according to the S.E.

This is also confirmed by the existing references to the Jewish sabbatical year, which characteristically spans from Tishri to Tishri (not from Nisan to Nisan!), beginning at the same time as the new year of the Macedonian calendar – the "secular" year. In a sabbatical year, the fields were not sown in the autumn, and since the land had lain fallow, there was no harvest in the following spring and summer, when the stores from the preceding year were used up. We know that the years 164-163 B.C., 143-142 B.C. and 136-135 B.C. were sabbatical years. On the basis of these observations, Klaus Bringmann has dated the following events (the Roman months are approximately indicated):

> The defeat of Nicanor: 151 S.E. = February 161 B.C.
> Jonathan becomes high priest: 160 S.E. = September 152 B.C.
> The murder of Jonathan: 169 S.E. = February 143 B.C.
> The "liberation" of the Jews and the beginning of their own chronology:
> New Year 170 S.E. = October 143 B.C.
> The murder of Simon: February 135 B.C.

(Note that year 1 S.E. = 312-311 B.C. Accordingly, for instance, year 151 S.E. can be converted as follows: $312 - (151 - 1) = 162$, but then "162" is the year 162-161 B.C. from autumn to autumn.)

On the basis of these calculations, it is possible to establish whether Antiochus IV died before or after the rededication of the temple. In 1 Macc. 4.52, we read that the temple was rededicated on the 25th Kislev (a Jewish month!) 148 S.E., and 1 Macc. 6.7 tells us that Antiochus IV knew that Judas Maccabaeus had conquered the temple precinct. This indicates that the temple was rededicated before the death of the king. But 2 Macc. 9.1-29 describes first the death of Antiochus IV and then, in 10.1-8, the conquest of Jerusalem and the temple, followed by the rededication of the temple. Before we accept this at face value, however, we should consider the sentence in 2 Macc. 10.9 which indicates that the two events took place in the opposite order: "We have already given an account of the end of Antiochus called Epiphanes." This leads to the conclusion that 1 Macc. and 2 Macc. 10.9 indicate the correct order of the two events: first the rededication of the temple, then the death of Antiochus IV.

From a list of Babylonian kings, we know with certainty that Antiochus IV died in November 164 B.C. As mentioned above, 1 Macc. 4.52 says that the temple was rededicated on the 25th Kislev 148 S.E. Since this event was dated according to the Jewish calendar, many annotators have linked it with the Babylonian New Year in spring. According to this theory, the temple was rededicated in December 164 B.C., at the same time as news of the king's death reached Jerusalem. It seems to indicate that 2 Macc. reports the events in the correct order and that 1 Macc. is wrong on this point.[19]

But this simply cannot be correct. According to 1 Macc. 6.7, the king knew that the temple precinct had been conquered by Judas Maccabaeus, and 1 Macc. 5.1 ff. describes the Maccabees' acts of retaliation against their Gentile neighbours. In my opinion, Klaus Bringmann suggests the only possible solution to this chronological problem when he points out that the date mentioned in 1 Macc. 4.52 does not refer to the Babylonian chronology, but – here as elsewhere – to the western S.E.[20] If this is true, the temple was rededicated in December 165 B.C. (148 S.E. = 165-164 B.C.), and the king died almost a year later. Since the rededication took place on the third anniversary of the profanation of the temple,[21] we can establish the following dates:

> Profanation of the temple: December 168 B.C.
> Rededication of the temple: 25 Kislev 148 S.E. = December 165 B.C.
> Death of Antiochus IV: November 164 B.C.

---

19 In modern times, e.g. Bunge, *Untersuchungen zum zweiten Makkabäerbuch*, 1971.
20 See Bringmann, *Hell. Reform u. Religionsverfolgung*, p. 25-26.
21 The order of events (first the king's death, then the rededication of the temple) corresponds with the account in 2 Macc. and is defended in Bunge: *Untersuchungen zum zweiten Makkabäerbuch*, p. 409, et al. The solution to the problem of the correct order of these events is linked to 1 Macc. 1.54 and 4.42, according to which three years passed between the profanation and the rededication (cf. Josephus, Ant. Jud. XII, 248; 320), while 2 Macc. 10.3 refers to an interval of two years. See Habicht, *2. Makkabäerbuch*, pp. 249-250, where the author declares himself unable to solve the problem. As we know, Dan. 12.7 – and Josephus, Bell. Jud. I, 19, 32 – refer to an interval of three and a half years, probably because the seer had not yet witnessed the rededication of the temple. In my opinion, the interval of three and a half years in Dan. 12.7 argues in favour of the three-year interval according to 1 Macc. and against the two-year interval according to 2 Macc., because if 2 Macc. is correct on this point, it would be difficult or even impossible to explain the three and a half years mentioned in Dan.

The historical "errors" in 2 Macc. are probably due to the literary composition of the work – the author, i.e. the Epitomist who shortened the work of Jason of Cyrene, dates all four documents in 2 Macc. 11.16 ff. to the time of Antiochus V (164-161 B.C.).[22]

1.1.4 Military and political events

In November 170 B.C., as part of the sixth Syrian war, Antiochus IV began his first Egyptian campaign, which lasted until the autumn of 169 B.C. It was a preventive war, his intention being to prevent the Ptolemies from repossessing Palestine, which they had lost after the battle of Paneas. Judea and the Jewish people were naturally deeply involved in these events, which could very easily revive pro-Ptolemaic feelings among the Jews.

There has been some uncertainty regarding the number of Antiochus' Egyptian campaigns. But the general opinion today seems to be that he engaged in two, not three campaigns: the first between November 170 B.C. and the autumn of 169 B.C., and the second during the summer of 168 B.C.[23] The first campaign ended in an almost complete victory for Antiochus, but the political situation remained unclarified: Antiochus left his army in Pelusium (in the eastern part of the Nile delta) and returned to Antioch. To make a good impression on the Romans and several Greek cities that had not attempted to stop his advance, he sent them large gifts of money – 150 talents in all. We know now where he acquired the money – out of the 1,800 talents he had plundered from the temple of Jerusalem in the late summer of 169 B.C., with the help of his protégé, high priest Menelaus. The second campaign ended outside Alexandria, which Antiochus besieged again. But by then the international situation had changed completely.

---

22 See below, in the paragraph referred to in n. 37.
23 See e.g. Mørkholm, *Antiochus IV of Syria*, pp. 64-101 – an excellent explanation and description of the complicated and interesting events. Habicht, *2. Makkabäerbuch*, p. 224: "Today there is broad agreement that: the king made two (and not three) campaigns to Egypt (cf. Dan. 11.25-26), the first from November 170 to the autumn of 169, the second in 168; that – as hinted in Dan. 11.28 and 11.30 – he visited Jerusalem twice, in 169 and 168; that during his first visit there, he entered and robbed the temple, guided by Menelaus; that during his second visit, he imposed martial law within the city because he saw Jason's attack and the ensuing civil war as an insurrection and a secession, as stated in 2 Macc. 5.11." See also Bringmann, *Hell. Reform u. Religionsverfolgung*, p. 29.

On 22nd June 168 B.C., the Romans ended the third Macedonian war by defeating Perseus at Pydna. On Delos in the Aegean Sea, a Roman delegation led by C. Popilius Laenas had been awaiting the outcome of the battle. On receiving news of the victory, they proceeded to Rhodes, where Popilius harshly upbraided the inhabitants for their "passivity" during the Macedonian revolt. After five days, the delegation left for Alexandria and went to see Antiochus IV in his camp on the beach at Eleusis, outside the capital.

This was where one of the most important events in world history took place.

Antiochus had always been a great admirer of the Romans and knew Rome from his younger days, when he had spent several years there as a hostage. He approached the Roman delegation in a friendly manner, but Popilius handed him an official letter from the Roman senate ordering him and his army to leave Egypt immediately. When Antiochus asked permission to consult his Friends[24] before making his decision, Popilius used his staff to draw a circle in the sand around the king's feet. He then commanded him to reply before he stepped out of the circle. Amazed by this incredible breach of diplomatic conventions, Antiochus gave in on the spot. A time-limit was fixed for evacuation, and Antiochus had to leave with his army and the booty he had already taken. At the beginning of the second Egyptian campaign, Antiochus had conquered Cyprus from the Ptolemies, but Popilius made him give the island back to the Egyptians shortly after. The situation *ante quo* was now re-established.

After the battle of Pydna and the showdown at Eleusis, the Romans were masters of all the Mediterranean territories, and nobody could challenge their position of power. On the other hand, we must not forget that Antiochus had ensured that Palestine remained under Seleucid rule, and that he had – to a certain extent – won the sixth Syrian war.

News of Antiochus' loss of prestige reached Jerusalem in the form of a false report of his death (2 Macc. 5.5). The former high priest Jason seized the opportunity to conquer Jerusalem with a thousand men, and Menelaus had to take refuge in the Seleucid garrison in the city. A civil war broke out, during which many people were killed, including Menelaus' brother, Lysimachus.

---

24 A "Friend" was one of the king's personal counsellors who took part in political and military consultations. See for instance Mørkholm, *Antiochus IV of Syria*, pp. 102 ff., "The Administration".

Seeing Jason's return as a rebellion[25] – which it probably was – Antiochus ordered a detachment of his army, which had returned undefeated from Egypt, to impose martial law within the city: thousands of people were executed (40,000 according to 2 Macc. 5.14), and thousands were sold as slaves. Jason fled the country for ever. A strong Syrian castle, Acra, was built in Jerusalem, and a military governor was put in charge of a large contingent of "Greek" mercenaries, "impious foreigners", as they are called in 1 Macc. 1.34, 3.45, 14.36, or "the people of a foreign god", as they are called in Dan. 11.39. Not until Simon became their leader (143-135 B.C.) did the Maccabees succeed in expelling these Syrians and taking Acra, so that all Jerusalem came into their hands and could be purged of heathens. Menelaus, Antiochus IV's protégé, was reinstated to his former office with Syrian support, but now without a normally functioning temple and without an active body of priests – the temple had, as we know, been robbed the year before – and many foreigners were now living in Judea and Jerusalem.

All this happened in the summer and early autumn of 168 B.C.

1.1.5 Religious suppression

To make the situation even worse for the surviving Jews, Antiochus IV then issued an edict banning the Jewish religion. Circumcision, temple sacrifices (in so far as any sacrifices could be performed as the situation stood), and the observance of the Sabbath and the Mosaic law, were forbidden on penalty of death (1 Macc. 1.41-50, 2 Macc 6.1 ff.). Antiochus IV desecrated the temple by setting up "the abomination of desolation" on the burnt-offering altar (1 Macc. 1.54, Dan. 9.27, 11.31 and 12.11).[26]

When discussing the significance of these events, there are three important factors we have to consider: the chronology, the role of Menelaus and the financial measures which followed the profanation of the temple.

---

25 Other cities also took the opportunity to revolt: Tarsus and Mallus in Cilicia (2 Macc. 4.30), and possibly also Aradus in Phoenicia, although this is contested in Mørkholm, *Antiochus IV of Syria*, pp. 122-124. See also Bringmann, *Hell. Reform u. Religions-verfolgung*, pp. 120-121.

26 Hebr. *shiqqus meshomem*, which is a corruption of *ba'al shamin*, "the Lord of the Heavens". According to 1 Macc. 1.59, it was not a statue of a god, but rather an altar placed on top of the burnt-offering altar. See also Mk. 13.14 = Matt. 24.15.

The religious suppression is traditionally supposed to have been imposed in December 167 B.C., more than a year after the civil disturbances which Antiochus considered as a rebellion and brutally crushed with his troops. The question remains: what happened in the meantime, and what was the real motive for the religious suppression?

As we have already seen, Klaus Bringmann has solved this problem by demonstrating that the religious suppression was imposed in December 168 B.C., a couple of months at the most after the civil disturbances – not more than a year after. This seems to indicate that the religious suppression had nothing to do with enthusiasm for Hellenistic reforms in Jerusalem's upper classes. Jason's reform was already history, he and his adherents were eliminated, and the Book of Daniel, in which the religious suppression plays an important part, says nothing about a Hellenistic reform.[27] According to the established chronology, it is much more likely that the religious suppression is linked to the military and civil situation in Jerusalem – and in Judea as a whole – immediately after the rebellion against Seleucid rule had been quashed: the religious suppression was a simple and logical way of subjugating a rebellious people.[28] So this is a good example of the importance of an accurate knowledge of chronology!

When discussing Menelaus as a person, it is important to realize the impossible situation in which he had placed himself, seen through the eyes of his own people. As early as in 170 B.C., he had arranged the murder of the last legitimate high priest, Onias III, and had sold some gold vessels that belonged to the temple to get money to pay off the killer. His conduct outraged the Jews. The council of elders – or perhaps the council of the new *pólis*, if it had any real power – sent a delegation to Antioch, asking the king to remove Menelaus. But Antiochus IV protected the only Jewish friend he probably had, and was also afraid that a new high priest might have pro-Ptolemaic sympathies. So instead of removing Menelaus, he executed those who had criticized him (2 Macc. 4.43-50). This incident destroyed any remaining relationship between Menelaus and the Jewish priests and people. And the following year, 169 B.C., Menelaus

---

27 Cf. Bringmann, *Hell. Reform u. Religionsverfolgung*, p. 12.
28 Bringmann, *Hell. Reform u. Religionsverfolgung*, pp. 130 ff., sees the high priest Menelaus as "the intellectual instigator of the religious ban" and considers his religious betrayal as a "flight forward" (p. 130). His point of view is not necessarily incompatible with the view expressed above.

himself even helped Antiochus to plunder the temple, so that its normal functions had to be suspended. Menelaus had burnt all his bridges and had to take extreme measures in order to get a minimum of support from his compatriots. He also had to keep paying the annual tribute of 740 talents that he had promised the king in return for the office of high priest[29] – there is no evidence that the king ever cancelled this debt.

The extreme measures referred to above are described in the Book of Daniel: "Those whom he [i.e. Antiochus IV] favours he will load with honour, putting them into authority over the people and distributing land as a reward" (Dan. 11.39). It does not say in so many words that these people were Jews and not foreigners, but it does say that the king gave them land as a reward for their loyalty to him, and so much land could only be provided through confiscation.[30] There is no doubt that the priests were among the victims of the confiscations. And we know that the members of the new upper class were really Jews, and that they were Menelaus' only supporters after the religious suppression. In 163 B.C., about five years after the establishment of the new upper class, and shortly after the Maccabees had recaptured the temple precinct and rededicated the temple in Jerusalem, some members of the new upper class who had survived the Maccabean revolt made a petition to the successor of Antiochus IV, Antiochus V Eupator (164-161 B.C.). They said to the king: "We were happy to serve your father, to follow his instructions and obey his decrees. And what was the result? Our own countrymen turned against us; indeed they put to death as many of us as they could lay hold of, and they robbed us of our property" (1 Macc. 6.23-24; cf. 7.6-7). In other words: the old upper class of priests, Levites and elders had been removed during the religious suppression, and a new upper class had been installed in its place by force.

---

29 See section 1.1.1 above, "Politics and Economics".

30 Cf. Bar-Kochva, *Judas Maccabaeus*, pp. 438-444: "Was a Seleucid military settlement established in Jerusalem?". On p. 441, Dan. 11.39 is interpreted as follows: "The Books of the Maccabees do not explicitly report the confiscation of land and its distribution to the Hellenizers, but probably the later despoilment of their estates (1 Macc. 6.24 and 7.7) should be understood against that background. ... The custom is well known from the Seleucid empire: generally a low price was asked for royal lands which were handed over to people whom the king wished to reward. It may also mean the sale of land not to private individuals, but to the Hellenistic *polis* established in Jerusalem, in order to increase its income."

Menelaus himself came to rather an unfortunate end. Under Antiochus V it was recognized that Menelaus was "reponsible for all the troubles" (2 Macc. 13.4),[31] and the king ordered him to be taken to Beroea (Aleppo in North Syria) and executed there in a tower filled with burning ashes (2 Macc. 13.3-8).[32] The description of Daniel's companions in the furnace is an obvious parallel (Dan. 3). One of the 24 priestly clans, the Bilgah clan (1 Chr. 24.14, Neh. 12.5; cf. Lk. 1.5), whose members included the temple administrator Simon, Menelaus and his brother Lysimachus, was later deprived of its position among the priestly clans of Jerusalem when its slaughter ring was locked.[33]

1.1.6 The Maccabees and their assumption of power

In these circumstances, it is not surprising that the resistance to the religious suppression originated from priests who had lost their means of subsistence, and that prominent priests led the revolt: the priest Mattathias from Modeïn (almost halfway between Jerusalem and Joppa on the Mediterranean coast) and his five sons: Judas nicknamed "Maccabaeus", John "Gaddis", Eleazar "Avaran", Jonathan "Apphus" and Simon "Thassis" (1 Macc. 2.1-5). They were members of the respected Joiarib priest family (Neh. 12.6), which was later awarded the leading position among the priestly clans of the temple (1 Chr. 24.7).[34] This family was called the Maccabees after Judas Maccabaeus. Possibly the name "Hasmoneans", which we find in Josephus (Ant. Jud. XII, 265 i.a.), but not in 1 and 2 Macc., lies behind the observation in 1 Macc. 2.1 that one of Mattathias' forefathers was called Simon.[35]

---

31 Cf. the view of Bringmann, n. 28 above.
32 This method of execution was probably of Persian origin; see Habicht, *2. Makka-bäerbuch*, p. 267.
33 See Hengel, *Judentum u. Hellenismus*, p. 509 (*Judaism and Hellenism*, p. 279). Concerning the slaughter rings which were used when animals were slaughtered in the temple, see Maier, *Tempelrolle*, pp. 91-92 (*The Temple Scroll*, pp. 89-90).
34 See Schürer, *History*, II, 1979, p. 250, n. 50.
35 Wellhausen, *Pharisäer u. Sadducäer*, p. 94, n. 1, assumed that the Hebrew original of 1 Macc. 2.1, where Mattathias' paternal grandfather is said to have been called Simon, used the words *ben hashmon*. See Schürer, *History*, I, 1973, p. 194, n. 14, where this assumption is mentioned, but neither supported nor contested. Fischer, *Seleukiden u. Makkabäer*, p. 57, n. 144, says that the meaning of the name is unknown; but apparently he does not know about Wellhausen's hypothesis. If Wellhausen is right, then the later Maccabees were not the first to be called Hasmoneans. Schürer, I, p. 194, n. 14, is incorrect in saying that "Asamonaios" is mentioned in 1 Macc. as Mattathias' forefather.

Together with large numbers of volunteers, many of whom had been stripped of their properties, Mattathias' sons took to the hills of Judea (cf. Matt. 24.16 = Mk. 13.14 = Lk. 21.20) from where they fought a guerilla war with varying degrees of success against the Syrian government troops.

Soon the Maccabees were joined by a group of Hasideans (1 Macc. 2.42, 7.13; 2 Macc. 14.6; Dan. 11.33), "stalwarts of Israel, every one of them a volunteer in the cause of the law" (1 Macc. 2.42). The fact that the Hasideans, i.e. "the Pious", are mentioned here suggests that they were members of an established movement or group, which had been formed some time before the religious suppression in 168 B.C. There had always been "pious" people in Israel, but apparently it was under the Seleucids that they formed a movement or "assembly" (synagogé: 1 Macc. 2.42). Possibly their organization was a consequence of Menelaus' usurpation of the high priest office in 173 B.C., in which case the original Hasideans were identical to the members of the sect that later emigrated from Jerusalem and went to live in Qumran by the Dead Sea.[36] I shall return to this later in the book. After the execution of Menelaus, when an officially legitimate high priest called Alcimus had been installed, the Hasideans supported him and terminated their association with the Maccabees (1 Macc. 7.13; 2 Macc. 14.6).

During the year 165 B.C., Judas succeeded in capturing Jerusalem and its temple precinct, but not the Syrian castle Acra, which remained a constant threat to the Jews. Judas made great efforts to restore the temple; he had new vessels and utensils manufactured to replace those which Antiochus IV had stolen: the seven-branched candelabrum, the incense altar and the table for shewbread. The burnt-offering altar was pulled down and the stones hidden in a safe place on the temple hill "until there should arise a prophet to give a decision about them" (1 Macc. 4.46; cf. Deut. 18.15; Mal. 4.5), a new burnt-offering altar was built of unhewn stones as prescribed in the Mosaic law (Exod. 20.25; Deut. 27.5-6). Priests who had not chosen the wrong side during the religious persecution were appointed, the temple was rededicated, and

---

36 Bringmann, *Hell. Reform u. Religionsverfolgung*, p. 125, n. 19, refers to the Damascus document 1.5-11 (Lohse, *Die Texte aus Qumran*, p. 67), according to which the "Teacher of Righteousness" appeared twenty years after the congregation of the Hasideans was first established, and Bringmann assumes that the group of Hasideans appeared in about 172-170 B.C. as a reaction against the sins of Menelaus; see also Schürer, *History*, II, 1979, pp. 586-587; Sanders, *Judaism*, pp. 341 ff.

finally the burnt-offering altar was inaugurated on the 25th Kislev 165 B.C. We do not know who acted as high priest on that occasion, but it cannot possibly have been Menelaus (in spite of the observations in letter No. 2 below), nor is there any reason to believe that it was Judas Maccabaeus himself. But it is doubtful whether the rededication could have taken place without the presence of a high priest and with Judas in charge of the ceremonies.

1.1.7 Four documents from the Maccabean time

2 Macc 11.16-38 quotes four letters from this period. They are listed below in the order and with the dates suggested by Klaus Bringmann:[37]

Letter No. 1: October 165 B.C., from Lysias, chancellor of Antiochus IV, who was later to become guardian of Antiochus V:

> 16 From Lysias to the Jewish Community. 17 Greeting. Your representatives John and Absalom have laid before me the document, a copy of which is attached,[38] and have asked me to give my views on its contents. 18 Whatever required to be brought to the king's attention I have communicated to him, and what was within my own competence I have granted. 19 Provided, therefore, you maintain your goodwill towards the government, I for my part shall endeavour to promote your wellbeing for the future. 20 I have charged your representatives and mine to confer with you about the details. 21 Farewell. The twenty-fourth day of Dios<corinthios> in the year 148.[39]

---

37   Bringmann, *Hell. Reform u. Religionsverfolgung*, pp. 40 ff. Another order and other dates are suggested in Habicht, *2. Makkabäerbuch*, pp. 179-185: No. 1: 2 Macc. 11.27-33, No. 2: 2 Macc. 11.16-21, No. 3: 2 Macc. 11.34-38 (all written during the reign of Antiochus IV, between October 165 and October 164), and No. 4: 2 Macc. 11.22-26 (from Antiochus V). From discussions with Habicht, Bringmann proceeded to establish his own order and his own dates, which also reflect his own new theory of chronology. See also Mørkholm, *Antiochus IV of Syria*, pp. 162-165: "Appendix II. The documents in II Maccabees, 11". According to Mørkholm, the letter from the Roman legates is not authentic, but his opinion on this subject is based on a previously common conjecture; otherwise Mørkholm's theory is not incompatible with those of Habicht and Bringmann. Bar-Kochva, *Judas Maccabaeus*, pp. 516-542: "The negotiations between the Jews and the Seleucid authorities during the reigns of Antiochus Epiphanes and Antiochus Eupator" differs on several points from Habicht's and Bringmann's views on the documents.

38   The fact that this document is not quoted in 2 Macc. supports the letter's authenticity.

39   The name of the month is wrong – the Macedonian calendar has no month with this name. *Dios* was the name of the first month of the year. Cf. Mørkholm, *Antiochus IV of Syria*, p. 155 with n. 61.

Letter No. 2: November-December 165 B.C., from Antiochus IV:

27 From King Antiochus to the Senate of the Jews and to the Jewish people. Greeting. 28 We trust that all is well with you; we ourselves prosper. 29 Menelaus has made plain to us that it is your wish to return to your homes. 30 We therefore declare an amnesty for all who return before the thirtieth day of Xanthicus. 31 The Jews may follow their own food-laws as heretofore, and none of them will be in any way victimized for any previous offence committed in ignorance. 32 I am sending Menelaus to reassure you. 33 Farewell. <The fifteenth day of Xanthicus>[40] in the year 148.

Letter No. 3: February-March 164 B.C., from the Roman legates Quintus Memmius and Titus Manlius:

34 From Quintus Memmius and Titus Manlius, envoys of the Romans, to the Jewish people. Greeting. 35 We give our assent to all the concessions that Lysias, the Kinsman,[41] has granted you. 36 Be pleased to examine carefully the questions which he reserved for reference to the king; and then send someone without delay, so that we may make suitable proposals on your behalf, for we are proceeding to Antioch. 37 Send messengers immediately, therefore, so that we also may know what is your opinion. 38 Farewell. The fifteenth day of Xanthicus in the year 148.

Letter No. 4: New Year 164-163 B.C., from Antiochus V:

22 From King Antiochus to his brother Lysias. Greeting. 23 Now that our royal father has joined the company of the gods, we desire that our subjects shall be left undisturbed in the conduct of their own affairs. 24 It has been brought to our notice that the Jews are not prepared to accept our father's policy and adopt Greek ways; they prefer their own mode of life and request that they be allowed to observe their own laws. 25 It is our pleasure, therefore, that this nation like others shall continue undisturbed. We hereby decree that their temple be restored to them and that they be allowed to regulate their lives in accordance with their ancestral customs. 26 Have the goodness, therefore, to inform them of this and to ratify it, so that, appraised of our policy, they may be reassured and manage their affairs to their own satisfaction.

These four documents, whose authenticity is beyond reasonable doubt, illustrate how the relationship between the Maccabees and the Seleucid authorities changed during the period between the autumn of 165 B.C., when

---

40 The date is wrong, and has probably slipped into the text from letter No. 3.
41 Cf. n. 24 above.

the Maccabees captured Jerusalem and the temple precinct (but not Acra), and the beginning of Antiochus V's reign at the end of 164 B.C.

According to letter No. 1, Lysias is now on speaking terms with the Maccabees. "John" is probably John Gaddis, one of Mattathias' five sons (1 Macc. 2.2); he is later killed in one of the battles with neighbouring peoples (1 Macc. 9.36 ff.). In other contexts, Absalom is also mentioned as a Maccabean partisan (1 Macc. 11.70 and 13.11). Lysias clearly wants to put an end to the Maccabean revolt.

According to letter No. 2, unbeknown to Lysias, a now desperate Menelaus goes to see Antiochus IV in South Mesopotamia. The king confirms that he still supports Menelaus, he fixes a time limit for the return of the rebels, and he sends Menelaus back to Jerusalem with the letter – probably in vain, now that Menelaus had lost his influence. The amnesty and the formal repeal of the religious suppression are of little practical value: for instance, the letter does not say that confiscated property will be given back to those who return.

According to letter No. 3, Roman delegates are staying in Syria – even after "the day at Eleusis" in the summer of 168, the Romans were still wary of Antiochus IV, and on several occasions they sent envoys to Syria to assure themselves of his obedience to Rome. A large delegation led by Tiberius Sempronius Gracchus, father of the famous Gracchus brothers,[42] arrived in Antioch in the autumn of 166 B.C. and submitted their report to the Senate of Rome in the summer of 164 B.C. We do not know the names of the other senators, but neither do we know Quintus Memmius and Titus Manlius from any other sources, a fact that tends to indicate that the letter and the names are authentic. The letter is a perfect example of Rome's policy towards the rival empires in the Near East: to weaken them by supporting any rebel movement that might help Rome in its efforts to maintain and increase its own power. Apparently certain peace negotiations have been opened between the Maccabees and Antiochus IV, and the Romans promise the Maccabees their full support. The letter should be seen in connection with letter No. 1 (the contents of which must have been familiar to the writers), and with the Maccabean-Roman treaty which Eupolemus and Jason negotiated with the Romans during their visit to Rome in 161 B.C. (1 Macc. 8.17 ff., 2 Macc. 4.11).

---

42 See Karl Christ, *Krise u. Untergang*, pp. 120-121; Mørkholm, *Antiochus IV of Syria*, pp. 55 and 100.

Letter No. 4 illustrates the situation immediately after Antiochus IV's death in November 164 B.C.: the religious suppression is stopped by the new king. Since Antiochus V is still a child, it is really his guardian Lysias who is responsible for this action according to the plans he made as early as in the autumn of 165 B.C. – and the temple is formally restored to the Jews.

1.1.8 The Jews under the rule of the Maccabees

We do not know how the repeal of the religious suppression and the restoration of the temple were implemented. But they constitute the background for Menelaus' execution, the appointment of Alcimus as the new, formally legitimate high priest, and the split between the Hasideans and the Maccabees. Neither the Maccabees themselves nor all those whose possessions and properties had been confiscated benefited from the reconciliation. That was one of the reasons why the Maccabees continued to fight the Seleucids. Another reason was that – unlike the Hasideans – the Maccabees still refused to accept that the natural right to practise their own religion should be granted to them by the Seleucid ruler, who could rescind this right whenever it suited him.

So the fighting continued. Alcimus quarrelled with his own people, and when he died in about 160 B.C., the Jews had no high priest. At about this time, Judas Maccabaeus was killed while fighting the Seleucid troops. Jonathan succeeded him as the leader of the Maccabees, but it took him some time to accumulate sufficient power and influence and to gain the respect of the successive Seleucid rulers. Unlike Judas, who had been a warrior, Jonathan was more of a politician. In September 152 B.C., during the Feast of Tabernacles, he appointed himself high priest (1 Macc. 10.21).

Apart from revealing the weakness of the Seleucid rulers, Jonathan's self-appointment as high priest was a repetition of Menelaus' fatal mistake some twenty years before: although they were priests, Mattathias and his sons were not members of a high priestly family. That was a serious disadvantage for the high priest, who was the Jewish people's highest representative at home as well as abroad. The high priest himself, who was responsible for upholding the Mosaic law, could not circumvent its stipulations – unless, of course, his position was based on power or, as in this case, based on the weakness of the Seleucids. This was confirmed later when the Seleucid king Alexander Balas appointed Jonathan strategist and meridarch, i.e. military governor, of Judea (1 Macc. 10.51 ff.).

There is little doubt that Jonathan's appointment as high priest was a decisive factor in the establishment of the Qumran sect: some of the law-abiding Hasideans followed their priests and emigrated from Jerusalem to settle in Qumran by the Dead Sea. The Hasideans had broken relations with the Maccabees long ago. But now history was to repeat itself: Jonathan, "the new Menelaus", made them emigrate, just as the appointment of Menelaus had made them form the Hasidean *synagogé* twenty years before. And when the Qumran sect talked about "the wicked priest", for instance in the Commentary on Habakkuk (1QpHab), they were probably referring to Jonathan. This hypothesis is supported by the fact that the name "Hasideans" is assumed to be the origin of the well-known name "Essenes".[43]

Jonathan was succeeded by the youngest of Mattathias' five sons, Simon, who was killed in February 135 B.C. Simon gave the Jews national and political independence – he succeeded in capturing Acra in Jerusalem – and appointed himself both high priest and king. High priest and king rolled into one! Admittedly, Simon only did what several other secular rulers did at that time,[44] but this secularization, which characterized the culmination of the Maccabean rule, was unprecedented in Israel's post-exile history.

In his lifetime, Simon's positions as high priest and king were declared hereditary, and one of his sons, John Hyrcanus I, succeeded him (135-104). The increasing weakness of the Seleucid rulers made it possible for John Hyrcanus to consolidate his own power. In 128 B.C., he captured Shechem, destroyed the Samaritans' temple on Mount Gerizim and subdued the Samaritans; he also subdued the Idumeans to the South and forced them to be circumcised.[45] Circa 108 B.C., he besieged the city of Samaria, captured it after one year and destroyed it completely. During the reign of John, events developed into an open quarrel between him and the Pharisees.

---

43 See Schürer, *History*, II, 1979, pp. 585-590: "The Origin and History of the Essenes". See also n. 36 above.

44 See Schürer, *History*, II, 1979, p. 227, n. 2.

45 A different interpretation of these events is presented by Shaye J.D. Cohen, Religion, Ethnicity, and "Hellenism" in the Emergence of Jewish Identity in Maccabean Palestine, in: Per Bilde et al., eds., *Religion and Religious Practice*, pp. 204-223, in particular pp. 211 ff. (see section 1.1 here above).

After John, came his sons Aristobulus I (104-103), and Alexander Jannaeus (103-76). Alexander once crucified 800 political opponents among the Jews and, while they were still alive, had their wives and children killed in front of them. He was succeeded by his widow, Queen Alexandra (76-67 B.C.), who appointed her son Hyrcanus II high priest, since her sex prevented her from occupying this position herself. She made peace with the Pharisees, and in her lifetime there was peace within Palestine as well as between Palestine and its neighbours. Immediately after her death, however, her two sons, Hyrcanus II and Aristobulus II (67-63), started fighting for the throne.

In 63 B.C., Pompey conquered Palestine and Jerusalem, and the Jewish freedom under Maccabean rule was lost.

1.2 The temple and the priests

Bibliography

Schürer: *History*, II, 1979, pp. 227-236: "The High Priests", and pp. 237-313: "Priesthood and Temple Worship", with bibliography.

Hengel: *Judentum und Hellenismus*, 2nd ed. 1973, pp. 241-275: "Ben-Sira und die Auseinandersetzung mit dem hellenistischen Freigeist in Jerusalem" (*Judaism and Hellenism*, pp. 131-153: "Ben Sira and the Controversy with Hellenistic Liberalism in Jerusalem").

The Mishna Treaty Tamid, in: Danby, *The Mishnah*, pp. 582-589: "Tamid (The Daily Whole-offering)".

Maier: *Tempelrolle*, pp. 25-50: "Das Heiligtum in der Heiligen Stadt und sein Kult" = *The Temple Scroll*, pp. 20-42: "The Sanctuary in the Holy City and its Cult".

Hans Aage Mink: Præsentation af et nyt Qumranskrift: Tempelrullen, Dansk Teologisk Tidsskrift 42 (1979), pp. 81-112.

John Strange: "Tempelvisionen", in: Kirsten Nielsen/John Strange, *Ezekiels Bog* (Det Danske Bibelselskabs Kommentarserie), Copenhagen 1988, pp. 223-272.

Troels Engberg-Pedersen: Erfaring og åbenbaring i Siraks Bog, in: Troels Engberg-Pedersen/Niels Peter Lemche, eds., *Tradition og nybrud* (see section 1.1 above), pp. 93-122.

1.2.1 The temple

After Josiah's reform in 622 B.C., all sacrifices in Israel were performed at the temple in Jerusalem, and all priests were employed there. This made the city prosper and gave power to the priests of the temple.

The pre-exile shrine described in the Old Testament (Exod. 35-40) is assumed to have been the tabernacle constructed during the time of the wanderings in the wilderness. 1 Kgs. 6-7 describes Solomon's temple, which was destroyed in 587 B.C. Ezekiel's description from the time of the exile (Ezek. 40-46) was based on the visions from the years 573-571 B.C., on Ezekiel's own memories of the temple as he had seen it, and on the description in 1 Kgs. 6-7. It is a description of an ideal temple that never existed. Like Ezekiel, the author of the Temple Scroll from Qumran creates a utopian ideal to compensate for the missing temple that Solomon had built or ought to have built.

Little is known about the rebuilding of the temple in about 520-516 B.C. under Persian rule. All we know is what is written in the Books of Haggai and Zechariah, who had encouraged the Jews to start rebuilding the destroyed temple. Apart from the descriptions in the Old Testament, most of our knowledge of the temple, its layout and functions is based on Josephus' description of the situation after Herod the Great had restored it in the time of the New Testament (Ant. Jud. XV, 380-425, chapter 11.1-7). This means that we have to be careful in drawing parallels between that period and the period of the Seleucids and the Maccabees.

According to Jn. 2.20, it took 46 years to build the temple. If we count from the time when work began on rebuilding it in about 20 B.C. during the reign of Herod, the temple was finished in about A.D. 26.

There is, however, another – probably also rather idealized – description from the early Seleucid period, about 180 B.C. We find it in Ecclus. 50, and it takes us back to the period before the upheavals which began in 169 B.C. under Antiochus IV. The author himself, Jesus Sirach, was a scribe and perhaps even one of "the scribes of the temple" mentioned in Antiochus III's letter (Josephus, Ant. Jud. XII, 143).[46] Whatever the case, he did not belong to the Hasideans, who were more likely behind the Book of Daniel, which was written later. Unlike them, he was a Jewish nationalist and believed that the people's political salvation depended on their observance of the law. Jesus Sirach first describes the high priest, Simon the Righteous, the priests "of Aaron's line", the temple singers and the people or "the assembly of Israel" as it says, and then proceeds

---

46   See Hengel, *Judentum u. Hellenismus*, pp. 244 and 274 (*Judaism and Hellenism*, pp. 133 and 153).

to describe the ceremonies of daily temple worship, including the Tamid morning and evening sacrifices, which were often, but not always, performed by the high priest himself, for instance on important feast days and on the Sabbath. In the same context, he also describes the temple house with its curtain, the burnt-offering altar in the priests' court, the burnt-offering and the drink-offering which were part of the daily Tamid sacrificial worship:[47]

1 Greatest among his brothers and the glory of his people was the high priest Simon son of Onias,
in whose lifetime the house was repaired, in whose days the temple was fortified. 2 He laid the foundation for the high double wall, the high retaining wall of the temple precinct. 3 In his day a reservoir was dug, a cistern broad as the sea.

4 He was concerned to ward off disaster from his people and made the city strong against siege.

5 How glorious he was as he processed through the temple, emerging from behind the veil of the sanctuary! 6 He was like the morning star appearing through a cloud or the full moon on festal days; 7 like the sun shining on the temple of the Most High or the light of the rainbow on the gleaming clouds; 8 like a rose in springtime or lilies by a fountain of water; like a green shoot upon Lebanon on a summer's day 9 or frankincense burning in the censer; like a cup all of beaten gold, decorated with every kind of precious stone; 10 like an olive tree laden with fruit or a cypress with its summit in the clouds.

11 When he assumed his resplendent vestments, robing himself in full and proud array, he went up to the holy altar, adding lustre to the court of the sanctuary. 12 While he received the sacrificial portions from the priests, as he stood by the altar hearth with his brother priests around him like a garland, he was like a young cedar of Lebanon in the midst of encircling palms.

13 All the priests of Aaron's line in their splendour stood before the whole assembly of Israel, holding the Lord's offering in their hands.

14 To complete the ceremonies at the altar and adorn the offering of the Most High, the Almighty, 15 he reached out his hand for the cup and made the libation from the blood of the grape, pouring its fragrance at the base of the altar to the Most High, the King of all.

16 Then the priests of Aaron's line shouted and blew their trumpets of beaten silver; they sounded a mighty fanfare as a reminder before the Most High.

---

47 The versification is the one used in Rahlfs' edition of Septuaginta. The complicated versification is described in Holger Mosbech, *Prolegomena til en ny Prøveoversættelse af Siraks Bog*, Copenhagen 1937.

17 At once all the people prostrated themselves to worship their Lord, the Almighty, God Most High.

18 The choir broke into praise, in the full, sweet strains of resounding song,

19 while the people were making their petitions to the Lord Most High, the Merciful One, until the liturgy of the Lord was finished and the ritual complete.

20 Then Simon came down and raised his hands over the whole congregation of Israel to pronounce the Lord's blessing and to glory in his name;

21 and again they bowed in worship to receive the blessing from the Most High.

According to Josephus, this high priest was Simon II, also called "the Righteous", who was high priest when Antiochus III conquered Palestine and Jerusalem in about 200 B.C.[48] We have already heard of him – though indirectly, since his name was not mentioned – because he must have been at the head of the council of elders who received Antiochus III when he came to Jerusalem.[49] The text quoted above refers to the high priest Simon in whose lifetime the temple was repaired and fortified, a high wall was built around the temple precinct, and a reservoir "as broad as the sea" was dug (Ecclus. 50.1-3). This information is in line with the contents of Antiochus III's letter, in which he ordered the city and the temple to be restored after the war between Egypt and Syria.[50] It is important to note that Jesus Sirach speaks about the high priest Simon's lifetime as of a past period he wants to revive. In his own time, under Onias III – or perhaps Jason? – the situation has deteriorated, the temple is no longer the same and does not function as it did in the past. In short, he has experienced a change for the worse. Wisdom, i.e. observance of the law, is the countermeasure he recommends. Apparently the law is no longer observed as it used to be in Simon's time.

The temple court was considerably enlarged during the reign of Herod the Great, but otherwise the temple itself and its immediate surroundings were probably more or less the same as in later times.

The temple building faced east and was provided with giant doors which the doorkeepers opened and closed every day. These doors were so heavy that it required a team of no less than 200 men to open and close them, and the creaking was said to be heard as far away as Jericho! Behind the doors was the

---

48 Josephus, Ant. Jud. XII, 224, 229, 238 and XIX, 298.
49 See section 1.1.1, above n. 5.
50 See n. 49 above.

38

temple curtain, and behind it the sanctuary. The seven-branched candelabrum, which was always burning, was kept there together with the table of shew-bread and the incense altar. At the very back of the temple building was "the Holy of Holies", where the high priest was the only person permitted to enter, and even then, only on the Day of Atonement, the 10th Tishri.

In front of the temple building was the priests' court, where the burnt-offering altar stood in the open. Its groundplan was square, and its south side had a flight of stairs from top to bottom. As we know, these stairs were not smooth, but made of "unhewn stones" like the altar itself,[51] and were used by the temple servants who tended the fire on top of the altar and carried firewood up to it. The fire on top of the burnt-offering altar burnt continually, and when the sacrificial animals had been slaughtered and cut up, the cuts intended for sacrifice were burned there. In Simon's time, the high priest and the priests seem to have mounted the altar when sacrifices were made.[52] Between the temple building and the burnt-offering altar was a large water basin where the priests washed their hands and feet. North of the temple building itself were enclosures for slaughtering and cutting up sacrificial animals.

In front of the priests' court with the burnt-offering altar was the Israelites' court, which was reserved for male Israelites. In front of that was another court called the women's court. This was not reserved for women alone: women were allowed there and nowhere else within the temple precinct. In front of the women's court, facing east, was the richly ornamented gate called "the Beautiful Gate" (Acts 3.2 and 3.10), which was the usual entrance to the temple precinct; this gate was also opened and closed every day, by a team of twenty men.

Around the temple building itself, on its north, west and south sides, were buildings with many rooms. Some of these rooms were used by the priests when they were on duty, others were used for storing temple equipment, tools, priests' robes, sacrificial animals and firewood. There were also rooms for the temple treasure, which consisted mostly of valuables deposited by private individuals.[53] The administration of the temple treasure required great competence and care

---

51   See section 1.1.6 above.
52   According to Aristeas 93, it is more likely that the priests deftly threw the sacrificial cuts onto the top of the altar, but there is no evidence to support this theory.
53   See 2 Macc. 3.10-12.

and was entrusted to certain temple priests who had been appointed guardians of the temple treasure. By virtue of its holiness, the temple was considered to be a good and safe bank, a fact that also tempted several princes to loot it when they needed money.[54] In neither respect did the temple of Jerusalem differ from other contemporary temples. Along the walls of the women's court, thirteen chests were placed to receive people's gifts of money (cf. Mk. 12.41-44 = Lk. 21.1-4). This money was spent on the temple and its management, and there is no indication that any of it was given to the poor – besides, the Jewish community had other institutions to take care of the poor, at least in New Testament times.[55]

As mentioned above, there was one major difference between the temple that had existed before Herod the Great, and the temple he started rebuilding: he extended the temple precinct considerably to the south. This extension probably included the establishment of the "heathens' court", since there is no evidence of such a court before the reign of Herod the Great. It was situated outside the area occupied by the temple building, the priests' court, the Israelites' court and the women's court. During the Seleucid period, there cannot have been any court to which Gentiles had access if only Jews were allowed within the temple precinct.[56] The Temple Scroll from Qumran, which may be dated to 100 B.C., appears to confirm this. In fact it is uncertain whether Antiochus III's notice to the public[57] implies that others than the priests themselves had access to the temple.

We do not know where the Syrian castle Acra (*acra* = castle) lay. According to Schürer, "the site of this Acra is one of the most controversial questions in the topography of Jerusalem".[58] Even before the religious suppression under Antiochus IV, there had been first a Ptolemaic, then a Seleucid garrison with a castle in Jerusalem. According to 1 Macc. 1.35-36, 4.41, 4.60 and 6.18 ff., Acra must have been situated near the temple precinct, because its soldiers were a constant threat to the Jews during and after the rededication of the temple in 165 B.C. This is confirmed by the fictive Aristeas

---

54 See Schürer, *History*, II, 1979, pp. 279-284.
55 See section 3.3.3 below.
56 See Schürer, *History*, III.1, 1986, pp. 415-417.
57 See section 1.1.1, above n. 7.
58 Schürer, *History*, I, 1973, p. 154, n. 39.

letter, which has been dated to approx. 100 B.C. but claims to have been written in the time of Ptolemy II Philaldelphus (285-246 B.C.). It says that two Gentiles, Andreas and Aristeas, were not allowed to visit the temple itself,[59] so they walked up to the castle in Jerusalem, from where they could see everything that happened within the temple precinct. This castle, which was built of large stones and topped with towers, was ostensibly intended to protect the temple, and therefore guarded by "the most reliable men".[60] It must have been situated north of the temple itself, otherwise it would not have commanded the detailed view of the temple precinct mentioned above. In about 134 B.C., not long after the Syrian castle Acra had been taken by Simon (1 Macc. 13.49-52 and 14.7), and shortly after he became king and high priest, John Hyrcanus I is known to have built a castle which was also his residence. It was situated in the north-western corner of the temple precinct and was called Baris.[61] Herod the Great enlarged this castle and the residence in a grandiose style, added tall towers and called it Antonia.[62] This was before the sea battle at Actium in 31 B.C., in which Antony was beaten. Antonia was where Paul was later taken into custody by the Roman commander Claudius Lysias and his men (Acts 21.31 ff.). On these grounds, there is reason to believe that the Syrian castle Acra was also situated in this north-western corner of the temple precinct.[63]

---

59 Cf. Antiochus III's notice, see section 1.1.1, above n. 7.

60 Aristeas 100 ff.

61 See Josephus, Ant. Jud. XV, 403; XVIII, 91. "Baris" comes from the Hebrew *bîra*, "fortress".

62 See Josephus, Bell. Jud. V, 238-245 (chapter 5.8), Ant. Jud. XV, 292, 403, 409. No discussion will be made here as to whether Pilate's "palace", or rather praetorium (Mk. 15.16, Matt. 27.27, Jn. 18.28, 18.33 and 19.9) was identical to Herod's palace in the western part of Jerusalem or the castle Antonia. See also section 3.1.4 below.

63 Cf. John Strange, Jerusalems topografi i hasmonæisk tid. Akra-problemet, Dansk Teologisk Tidsskrift 54 (1991), pp. 81-94. According to another theory, Acra stood *south* of the temple hill, in the area of the City of David: 1 Macc. 1.33, or "in the lower city": Josephus, Ant. Jud. XII, 252, but still on the eastern hill range, where the temple also stood. See also Bar-Kochva, *Judas Maccabaeus*, 1989 (see section 1.1 above), pp. 445-465: "The location and history of the Seleucid citadel (the Acra) in Jerusalem", and Schürer, *History*, I, 1973, p. 154, n. 39. If this is correct, Acra must have been destroyed after the conquest, and therefore the Aristeas letter refers to Baris.

1.2.2 The priests

We have already heard that Simon, Menelaus and Lysimachus belonged to the Bilgah priestly clan, which had been deprived of its slaughter ring in Jerusalem.[64]

Miriam, whose father was a priest, also belonged to the Bilgah clan. We are told that she married a Greek officer, and that when heathens, i.e. Gentiles, forced their way into the temple in 168 B.C., she went in with them and walked up to the burnt-offering altar in the priests' court. There she took off one of her sandals, struck it against the altar and cried: "Wolf, wolf, you have squandered the riches of Israel and did not stand up for her in the time of her need!"[65]

Although the story seems to have the characteristics of a legend, it is undoubtedly true – its details are far too frighteningly precise to be invented. It expresses in a nutshell the main problem during the critical years of Antiochus IV's reign and all the years while the temple stood in Jerusalem: the exploitation of the people.

It has often been said that the Maccabean revolt led by priest Mattathias and his five priest sons originated in the social inequalities that existed between the privileged priests, including the high priestly families in Jerusalem, and poor country priests like Mattathias' family in Modeïn, and that the revolt itself served a just cause.

That is hardly true. There is no evidence that Mattathias and his family were poor; on the contrary, Mattathias himself was highly regarded by the local community: 1 Macc. 2.17-18. And there is no evidence that the Maccabean leadership brought any prosperity to the Jews (1 Macc. 14.25-49 is a virtual piece of propaganda for Simon). On the contrary, it resulted in a reign of terror, especially under Alexander Jannaeus. It is important to remember that the priests started the revolt because the ban on the Jewish religion had deprived them of their livelihood – they fought to defend their own interests. Once the ban was repealed, the Hasideans refused to follow them and made a stand against Jonathan when he had himself appointed high priest in 152 B.C. Many Hasideans followed their own priests when they emigrated to Qumran by the Dead Sea.

---

64 See section 1.1.5 above.
65 See Hengel, *Judentum u. Hellenismus*, pp. 515-516; see also p. 509 (*Judaism and Hellenism*, p. 283; se also p. 279).

There may well have been social and financial inequalities among the priests of the temple in Jerusalem. It could hardly be otherwise, with 24 different priestly clans of varying ranks, probably established according to descent. But these inequalities were negligible compared to the inequalities between the rich and the poor people of the population as a whole. The priests were exempt from tax, and except during the religious suppression, they were always well provided for, unlike the rest of Judea's population. However, Miriam's reproach was not addressed to the most distinguished and privileged priest families, but rather to the temple itself. The costs of running the temple were exorbitant and represented an apparently endless draining of the very lifeblood of the country. This benefited the priests rather than anybody else. If we choose to call the Maccabean revolt a social rebellion, this is only true in so far as the Maccabees succeeded in persuading large sections of the population to support them. Furthermore, the success of the revolt was due less to the participation of the masses than to the fact that it was organized by competent people from the upper class – the priests themselves.

This body of priests included both priests and Levites (cf. Lk. 10.31-32). Deut. makes no distinction between priests and Levites as far as rank and functions are concerned. But Ezek. 44 establishes the priests' precedence over the Levites by stating that only priests – and not Levites – may take part in the altar service, cf. Num. 3.1-4 and 2 Kgs. 23. Before Josiah's reform, the Levites had been priests at various shrines in the country, while the priests, i.e. the descendants of Zadok (Ezek. 44.15-27), had served as priests at the temple in Jerusalem even before the reform. Religious historians have defined the Zadokites as the priests who had always belonged in Jerusalem (and maybe been priests at the Jebusitic shrine in the city; cf. Gen. 14). This put Jerusalem's priests in a superior position, and since they lived in the city, they often acquired the most important temple offices and the privileges that were associated with them – such as the administration of the temple treasure.[66]

According to Old Testament tradition, all male members of Levi's tribe served as priests or temple servants in Israel, while Aaron's descendants, who

---

66 For information on the traditional point of view, see Julius Wellhausen, *Prolegomena zur Geschichte Israels*, 6th ed., Berlin 1905, pp. 115-145: "Die Priester und Leviten". A different point of view is found in J. Gordon McConville, Priests and Levites in Ezekiel: A Crux in the Interpretation of Israel's History, Tyndale Bulletin 34 (1983), pp. 3-31.

also belonged to the tribe of Levi, were (high) priests. According to this genealogy, Aaron had two sons: Eleazar and Ithamar. Out of the Ithamar line came Abiathar, the son of Ahimelech of Nob,[67] where all the other priests were killed during the reign of king Saul (1 Sam. 22). Together with Zadok, he became high priest during the reign of David (2 Sam. 8.17). But when Solomon banished Abiathar (1 Kgs. 2.26-27), Zadok became sole high priest (1 Kgs. 4.2). With Abiathar banished, Eli's priestly line was discontinued or at least reduced (1 Sam. 2.27 ff.), and Eleazar's line prevailed. The priest Phinehas, Eleazar's son, also belonged to this line (Num. 25), and according to a later genealogical theory, Zadok was descended directly from Phinehas (1 Chr. 6.53).

Even when the first temple was destroyed, the Zadokites managed to maintain their influence in Jerusalem. This is emphasized in both 1 and 2 Chr. Both reflect the situation during the relatively late period where these books were written.[68] Nevertheless, it was impossible to disguise the fact that priests belonging to Ithamar's line were also active: according to 1 Chr. 24.1-6, sixteen of the twenty-four priestly clans had heads of families who belonged to the Eleazar line, while the other eight clans had heads of families from the Ithamar line – including Bilgah's division.

Phinehas was of the "true" Eleazar-Zadok line and known for his zeal (Greek: *zêlos*), Num. 25. It is obvious from 1 Macc. 2.26-54 that Mattathias chose Phinehas as his ideal at the beginning of the Maccabean revolt. Of course this also served to justify the Maccabees' claim to the high priest office.

The genealogies of the priests had to be defined and documented. This was necessary because of the restrictions on their choice of wives. Consequently

---

67 As is well known, there is an error on this point in Mk. 2.26, although Wellhausen says in *Prolegomena*, p. 145, n. 2: "The fact that he [Abiathar] is mentioned here instead of Ahimelech is no error; it means: during the period named after Abiathar's pontificate."

68 Cf. Wellhausen, *Pharisäer u. Sadducäer*, pp. 47-50. Schürer, *History*, II, 1979, p. 250, n. 50, raises and discusses the question of whether 1 Chr. 24.7-18 – the list of the 24 priest clans – may have been written during the time of the Maccabees: the Maccabees belonged to Joirarib's clan, which is at the top of the list. For information about the 24 priest clans, see H.G.M. Williamson, The Origins of the Twenty-Four Priestly Courses. A Study of 1 Chronicles xxiii-xxvii, in: J.A. Emerton, ed., *Studies in the Historical Books of the Old Testament* (Supplements to Vetus Testamentum, 30), Leiden 1979, pp. 251-268; Simon J. de Vries, Moses and David as Cult Founders in Chronicles, Journal of Biblical Literature 107 (1988), pp. 619-639, concerning secondary sections of text, including 1 Chr. 24.1-31: p. 629, n. 23.

their genealogies were known and possibly recorded in the temple archives. Indeed, interest in genealogy is one of the characteristics of the "priestly" layers of the Old Testament scriptures. Furthermore, interest in and knowledge of astronomy were necessary requirements for priests, not only because astronomy was used to fix the dates of the annual religious feasts, but also because of its importance to the Jewish apocalyptic of that time.[69] It is important to note, however, that genealogy was only established for priests – not for common Jews. This is indirectly relevant to the evaluation of the two genealogies of Jesus in the New Testament: Matt. 1.1-17 and Lk. 3.23-38.[70] The priests' interest in genealogy, astronomy and chronology is linked to the functions of the scribes, which are described in the next section.

The temple of Jerusalem was a vital element in the history of early Christianity in the days of Jesus and his apostles: it employed large numbers of priests, Levites and other temple staff, it housed extensive transactions in money and goods, and attracted countless Jewish visitors, especially during the important pilgrim feasts, Passover, Pentecost and the Feast of Tabernacles. Later, when the temple was destroyed in A.D. 70, all its functions stopped immediately, and the priests and all the temple staff disappeared. At this point, the Jewish religion began to change into the Rabbinic Judaism we know today. Studies of early Christianity must always take account of the fact that the temple still existed in the time of Jesus. The "cleansing of the temple", which is described by all four Evangelists, can only be understood against this background, and it was probably a decisive moment in the life and works of Jesus as well as an important factor in the accusations against him that led to his crucifixion.

1.3 The religious parties: Essenes, Pharisees and Sadducees

Bibliography

J. Wellhausen: *Pharisäer u. Sadducäer*, 1874 – still an outstanding piece of work on the subject.

---

69 See Otzen, *Den antike jødedom*, pp. 185-186 (*Judaism in Antiquity*, pp. 219-220).
70 See Marshall D. Johnson, *The Purpose of Biblical Genealogies*, 1969 (see section 2.4 below).

(Hermann L. Strack and) Paul Billerbeck: *Kommentar zum Neuen Testament aus Talmud und Midrasch,* IV.1, Munich 1928, 3rd ed. 1961, pp. 334-352: "Die Pharisäer u. Sadduzäer in der altjüdischen Literatur".

Schürer: *History,* II, 1979, pp. 381-403: "The Pharisees and Sadducees", and pp. 555-590: "The Essenes".

E.P. Sanders: *Paul and Palestinian Judaism* (see section 1 above).

Id.: *Jesus and Judaism,* Philadelphia – London 1985.

Jacob Neusner: *Judaism in the Beginning of Christianity,* Philadelphia – London 1984 = *Jødedommen i den første kristne tid* (Relieff Publikasjoner, published by Religionsvitenskapelig institutt, Trondheim University, 21), Trondheim 1987.

Dieter Lührmann: Paul and the Pharisaic Tradition, Journal for the Study of the New Testament 36 (1989), pp. 75-94.

E.P. Sanders: *Judaism* (see section 1 above), pp. 315-494: "Groups and Parties".

Günter Stemberger: *Pharisäer, Sadduzäer, Essener* (Stuttgarter Bibelstudien, 144), Stuttgart 1991.

James C. VanderKam: *The Dead Sea Scrolls Today,* Grand Rapids (Michigan) – London 1994.

Geert Hallbäck: Saddukæerne. En tidshistorisk undersøgelse, in: Lone Fatum/Mogens Müller, eds., *Tro og historie. Festskrift til Niels Hyldahl. I anledning af 65 års fødselsdagen den 30. december 1995* (Forum for bibelsk eksegese, 7), Copenhagen 1996, pp. 118-131.

Gerd Theißen: Sadduzäismus und Jesustradition. Zur Auseinandersetzung mit Oberschichtsmentalität in der synoptischen Überlieferung, ib., pp. 224-245.

1.3.1 Josephus and the religious parties

When Josephus uses the terms "philosophies" or "philosophical schools" to describe the Jewish religious parties that existed before and during the reign of Herod the Great, his contempory Greek readers must have been able to understand these analogies in spite of their inadequacy. He mentions three: the Essenes, the Pharisees and the Sadducees, for example in Bell. Jud. II, 119-166 (chapter 8.14) and Ant. Jud. XVIII, 11-22 (chapter 1.2-5). His knowledge of these three Jewish parties was based partly on his own experience; according to his autobiography, he had attended each of these "philosophical schools" and therefore knew them intimately, cf. Vita 11-12 (chapter 2). However, a considerable part of the historical material, especially material concerning the origins and development of these parties, comes from one of Josephus' most important sources, Nicolaus of Damascus, a historiographer who lived in Herod the Great's time, and whose works we know only indirectly through Josephus' use of them.[71]

In a historical context, Josephus refers to the Essenes, the Pharisees and the Sadducees – in this order – as if they existed as early as in Jonathan's time, in about the middle of the second century B.C.: Ant. Jud. XIII, 171 (chapter 5.9). But his first definite description of the Pharisees and the Sadducees relates to John Hyrcanus I (135-104): Ant. Jud. XIII, 288-298 (chapter 10.5-6). Therefore, the Pharisees must have existed as a party in the time of John Hyrcanus, during the last third of the second century B.C. It says there that John Hyrcanus, who was both high priest and king, belonged to the Pharisees' party himself and was on friendly terms with them. Once when he had invited them to his residence, probably his palace Baris, he told them that he wanted to be righteous (Greek: *díkaios*), and that in all matters he did what pleased God and them. The righteousness mentioned here is the righteousness that is valid in the eyes of God.[72] John Hyrcanus went on to ask the Pharisees to guide him back to the path of righteousness, if he should lose his way. None of them had anything to say to this, except a man called Eleazar, who said: "If you want to be righteous, then give up the office of high priest and be content with your position as king."

When – according to the narrative – John Hyrcanus wanted to know why he should do that, Eleazar gave the following explanation: "We have been told that your mother was a prisoner of war under Antiochus Epiphanes." He was clearly hinting that John Hyrcanus was of dubious descent, and that he was therefore unfit to be a priest, much less a high priest. This explanation is obviously untrue

---

71 See Schürer, *History*, I, 1973, pp. 28-32. Josephus knows a fourth "philosophy", i.e. the party of John the Galilean, which existed at about the beginning of the Christian era: Ant. Jud. XVIII, 23-25 (chapter 1.6). He blames that party for the catastrophe that ended in the war with the Romans in 66-70 and the destruction of the temple. The movement of Judas the Galilean and the Zealots will be described later in connection with Roman rule – we are presently concentrating on the three above-mentioned parties, which emerged and developed during the period of the Seleucids and Maccabees.

72 Cf. Wellhausen, *Pharisäer u. Sadducäer*, p. 18, n. 1. Wellhausen also writes: "Even as early as in the passage where Josephus tells about them for the first time [the text mentioned above], the Pharisees use "righteousness" as a criterion. Since its norm was the Torah, it was a very easy criterion to use and an extremely convenient instrument of judgment: "This man cannot be from God: he does not keep the sabbath". No traits in the Pharisees' character are more conspicuous in the New Testament than their inquisitorial attitude, their perpetual inquiries and criticism" (p. 20).

and anecdotal. The real reason is that the Pharisees disapproved of John Hyrcanus' double role as high priest and king. Furthermore, in case there is some truth in Eleazar's slanderous allusion to John Hyrcanus' ancestry, it obviously refers to the fact that the Maccabees were not members of a high priest family, but had taken this office illegitimately, thereby breaking the Jewish tradition. So what offended the Pharisees was the Maccabees' possession of the office of high priest. To John Hyrcanus, this position consolidated his power, while the royal throne was of secondary value. The order of precedence is obvious: the office of high priest comes before the royal throne.

At the end of the narrative, John Hyrcanus angrily breaks with the Pharisees, bans their party, punishes those who follow their teachings (Ant. Jud. XIII, 296) and joins the party of the Sadducees.[73]

1.3.2 The historical origins of the parties

When looking for the historical origins of the Pharisees and the Sadducees, we must go further back into the second century B.C., since they both existed as regular, established parties at the time of John Hyrcanus. After the exile, in the time of Ezra and Nehemiah, there were hardly any distinctions between priests and scribes. But in about 200 B.C., they split into two independent groups in Judea, and these two groups became the leaders of the Jewish people. This is confirmed by Antiochus III's letter (see the passage referred to in note 5 above), but it is remarkable that he mentions the scribes as a class still closely linked to the temple.

It has been maintained that in the early Maccabean period, the Sadducees emerged from the clan of priests, and the Pharisees from the clan of scribes.[74]

---

73 Cf. the important 4QMMT text (translation in Martínez, *The Dead Sea Scrolls Translated*, pp. 77-85).

74 See Schürer, *History*, II, 1979, p. 388: "The priests and Torah scholars or "scribes" were the two leading influences which determined Israel's internal development after the exile. In Ezra's time they were still essentially identical. During the Greek period they grew further and further apart. At about the time of the Maccabean wars, they evolved into two parties sharply opposed to one another. From the priestly circles emerged the Saducean party, and from those of the Torah scholars came the party of the Pharisees, the lay experts in religious matters."

This rather schematic theory seems plausible and should not be rejected out of hand. But its credibility depends on an explanation of the fact that the Hasideans' *synagogé* – and with it the Essenes – also emerged at almost the same time.[75]

We have seen that Jesus Sirach may have been a temple scribe – but not a Hasidean.[76] On the other hand, there is evidence of a connection between the Pharisees and the people behind the Book of Daniel, i.e. the Hasideans.[77] This connection is the belief they shared, i.e. the belief in the resurrection of the dead and the judgment of the actions of man: this belief was an essential part of the Pharisees' teachings and is also expressed in Dan. 12.2-3. Consequently, there is no direct historical link between the scribes and the Pharisees, and certainly no common identity between the scribes as a clan and the Pharisees as a party.[78] Moreover, it cannot possibly be true that the priests of the temple became Sadducees: the Sadducees were not necessarily priests, they were a party, and some of the priests emigrated together with some of the Hasideans from the temple and settled in Qumran. We must conclude that the real situation was much more complex than the schematic picture of developments would have us believe. One of the most important reasons for the confusion is the unclarified key position held by the Hasideans during this period.

The situation can be briefly illustrated as follows:

Before Antiochus IV, the priests and scribes had separated into two independent clans. Both of them were, together with the country's principal families, represented in the Jewish council of elders, with the high priest as their leader. But during the reign of Antiochus IV, a third group was formed: the Hasideans' *synagogé*. Later the Hasideans joined the Maccabees, but broke away from them again after some time.

The Essenes: When Jonathan became high priest in 152 B.C., some of the priests – probably under the leadership of the genuine Zadokite priest we know

---

75 See section 1.1.6 above.
76 See the passage referred to in n. 46.
77 Cf. Schürer, *History*, II, 1979, pp. 400-401.
78 This is explained in Wellhausen, *Pharisäer u. Sadducäer*, pp. 8-10 and p. 20: the expression "the scribes and the Pharisees", which establishes a clear distinction between these two groups, occurs frequently in the New Testament, and: "As the most faithful disciples, they [the Pharisees] joined the scribes ... In influence, the party [i.e. the Pharisees] was superior to the clan [i.e. the scribes] it had espoused" (p. 20).

from the Qumran documents, which refer to him as "the Teacher of Righteousness" – went to Qumran accompanied by a number of Hasideans. As an Essene party, these Hasideans seem to have had little influence on the Jewish community: unlike the Pharisees and the Sadducees, the Essenes are not mentioned anywhere in the New Testament. The Essenes believed in community of property and practised it among themselves. During Roman rule after 63 B.C., Essenes lived not only in Qumran, but all over Palestine, so their indirect influence on Jesus' movement should not be underestimated.

The Pharisees: The remaining Hasideans formed the Pharisaic party and tried to make the best of the situation by associating themselves with the scribes. Their Hasidean origin manifested itself in their belief in the resurrection of the dead and the judgment of actions, while their association with the scribes was reflected in the oral tradition they maintained as a guiding principle for interpreting the Torah (the Mosaic law). "The Pharisees were relatively few in number, no more than approx. 6,000" (Josephus, Ant. Jud. XVII, 42). They generally tried to observe the purity precepts that applied to the priests, but although they were respected by the people, their movement did not appeal to the masses – unlike Jesus and the movement he started.

The Sadducees: The priests who remained in Jerusalem came to terms with the situation there and entered into an alliance with the Sadducean party, which had been established in the meantime. This party was known for its refusal to acknowledge any rules that were not stated in the Scriptures. It therefore rejected the very strict interpretation and the oral tradition advocated by the Pharisees. The party attached itself to the Maccabean princes, and the name "Sadducees" (derived from the name of high priest Zadok!) seems to be a kind of apologetic-polemic recognition of the Maccabees' usurpation of the high priestly office.

1.3.3 Two distinct problems

When discussing the religious parties in early Judaism, there are two distinct problems that each deserve a commentary.

In the first place, E.P. Sanders has questioned the traditional theory that the Pharisees survived the catastrophe in A.D. 70 as a party, and that it was they who passed on the Jewish tradition which was later written down in the Rabbinic literature – the Mishnah, the Talmud, etc. Sanders questions this theory by maintaining that the Pharisees disappeared during the catastrophe, and rejects the idea of any common identity between Pharisaic Judaism and the Judaism of the Rabbinic literature.[79] Sanders' rejection of the traditional theory is justified in so far as the Pharisees were not scribes; unlike the clan of the scribes, they were not theorists but practicians – Wellhausen may be right in calling them "religious virtuosos".[80] And the Rabbinic literature is really Rabbinic, i.e. written by scribes, and cannot therefore be called Pharisaic. On the other hand, the Rabbinic literature does have unmistakable Pharisaic features, and its contents are incompatible with the views of the Sadducees, who refused to acknowledge "the tradition of the Fathers". And contrary to Sanders' theory, the descriptions of the Pharisees which we find in Josephus and the New Testament may well be true, especially if Sanders is right in saying that there is no Pharisaic literature.

Sanders' dismissal of Pharisaism looks like a defence of Judaism – a quite unnecessary defence if Sanders is right in his general view of Judaism.[81]

Secondly, Sanders is right in drawing attention to a fundamental feature of early Judaism which Christian exegetes and theologians have often ignored or even rejected: early Judaism was fundamentally what Sanders calls "covenantal nomism".[82] This means that the Jews of that time counted above all on God's incredible mercy: He had chosen the Jewish people as His own people and made a covenant with them which also ensured that they would remain within that covenant on the single condition that they observed its stipulations. These were written in the Torah (Greek: *nómos*), which even had stipulations for expiation in case the stipulations of the covenant were violated. God's mercy was above everything – including the law and the stipulations man must observe in order to prove himself worthy of God's mercy. But even if Sanders is right on this

---

79 See Sanders, *Paul and Palestinian Judaism*, for instance p. 426: "It seems to me quite possible that we not only have no Sadducean literature, but also virtually no Pharisaic literature, apart from fragments embedded in the Rabbinic material. Thus I know a good deal less about Pharisaism than has been "known" by many investigators." See also Sanders, *Jesus and Judaism*, for instance pp. 49-50.

80 *Pharisäer u. Sadducäer*, p. 20.

81 Sanders presents a different and more traditional view of the Pharisees and their history in his book *Judaism*, pp. 380-412: "The Pharisees I: History", and pp. 413-451: "The Pharisees II: Theology and Practice".

82 See Sanders, *Paul and Palestinian Judaism*, pp. 422 ff.

point, it is still important to point out that the Pharisees may have used the Torah as a convenient instrument of judgment,[83] and that they may have practised a "law control" that finally left nothing to the mercy of God, because they had given the Torah the status of God.

There are two main arguments against Sanders' definition of Judaism as "covenantal nomism". In the first place, by adhering to the Torah, he actually excludes at least Pauline and Johannine Christianity from the common ground of Judaism, although as a "religious party", the Christians are just as Jewish as the Essenes, the Pharisees and the Sadducees. Secondly, Sanders' definition does not take the Messiah problem into account; if the Messiah comes and makes other rules for his kingdom than the detailed stipulations of the Torah – what then? E.P.Sanders seems to consider Judaism and Christianity as static, separate entities. In the present book, however, early Judaism and early Christianity are seen as dynamic, interactive movements whose evolution can only be explained in the light of history.

1.4 The synagogue and its community

Bibliography

Martin Hengel: Proseuche und Synagoge. Jüdische Gemeinde, Gotteshaus und Gottes-dienst in der Diaspora und in Palästina, in: G. Jeremias/H.-W. Kuhn/H. Stege-mann, eds., *Tradition und Glaube. Das frühe Christentum in seiner Umwelt. Fest-gabe für Karl Georg Kuhn zum 65. Geburtstag*, Göttingen 1971, pp. 157-184 = Joseph Gutmann, ed., *The Synagogue: Studies in Origins, Archaeology and Archi-tecture*, New York 1975, pp. 27-54.

Jørgen Skafte Jensen: Den gudfrygtige Kornelius, in: Niels Hyldahl/Eduard Nielsen, eds., *Hilsen til Noack. Fra kolleger og medarbejdere til Bent Noack på 60-årsdagen den 22. august 1975*, København 1975, pp. 108-117.

Niels Hyldahl: A Supposed Synagogue Inscription, New Testament Studies 25 (1978-79), pp. 396-398.

Schürer: *History*, II, 1979, pp. 423-454: "Synagogue".

Schürer: *History*, III.1, 1986, pp. 150-176: "Gentiles and Judaism: "God-Fearers" and Proselytes", in particular pp. 165 ff.

---

83   See Wellhausen, n. 72 above.

Joyce Reynolds/Robert Tannenbaum: *Jews and God-Fearers at Aphrodisias. Greek Inscriptions with Commentary* (Cambridge Philological Society, Suppl. 12), Cambridge 1987.

J. Andrew Overman: The God-Fearers: Some Neglected Features, Journal for the Study of the New Testament 32 (1988), pp. 17-26.

Helga Botermann: Review of Reynolds/Tannenbaum: *Jews and God-Fearers at Aphrodisias*, Zeitschrift für Rechtsgeschichte 106 (1989), pp. 606-611.

Howard Clark Kee: The Transformation of the Synagogue after 70 C.E.: Its Import for Early Christianity, New Testament Studies 36 (1990), pp. 1-24.

Helga Botermann: Die Synagoge von Sardes: Eine Synagoge aus dem 4. Jahrhundert? Zeitschrift für die neutestamentliche Wissenschaft 81 (1990), pp. 103-121.

Richard E. Oster: Supposed Anachronism in Luke-Acts' Use of *SYNAGOGE*. A Rejoinder to H. C. Kee, New Testament Studies 39 (1993), pp. 178-208.

Howard Clark Kee: Defining the First-Century CE Synagogue: Problems and Progress, New Testament Studies 41 (1995), pp. 481-500.

1.4.1 The historical origins of the synagogue

Until a few years ago, when reference was made to a (Jewish) synagogue in New Testament time, a building would normally be the first idea that came into people's minds. The three first Evangelists say several times in their Gospels that Jesus and his disciples visited Jewish "synagogues"; the story of Jesus' first public appearance in the synagogue of Nazareth in Lk. 4.16-30 is an example of this traditional point of view.

In this context, however, it is necessary to distinguish between a) Palestine and the Jewish diaspora in the Greek-Roman world, b) the different meanings of the word "synagogue", and c) the time before and after A.D. 70, when the temple of Jerusalem was destroyed and the Jewish priestly office ceased to exist.

The fact is that until A.D. 200, Palestine seems to have had no synagogues in the concrete, architectural sense of "meeting houses", although there may have been "meeting places" for worship and law studies in private homes and public buildings. Howard C. Kee wrote in 1990: "there is simply no evidence to speak of synagogues in Palestine as architecturally distinguishable edifices prior to 200 C.E. Evidence of meeting places: Yes, both in private homes and in public buildings. Evidence of distinctive architectural features of a place of worship or for study of Torah: No."[84] This applies to the Theodotus Synagogue in Jerusalem: Adolf Deißmann dated it to New Testament times,[85] but it was in fact built in the second century or early in the third century A.D. This also applies to the "synagogues" excavated on Masada and in Herodium – they are only synagogues in the sense of "meeting places". And "meeting (place)" is precisely what the Greek word *synagogé* means (see for instance James 2.2, Rev. 2.9 and 3.9). Even in the Gospel of Mark, the oldest of the Gospel texts, this word is used twice when referring to "their [sc. the Pharisees' and the scribes'] synagogue" (Mk. 1.23, 1.39, 3.1). According to Kee, this seems to imply that the disciples of Jesus had their own meeting places (not buildings!) which may have been similar to – but not identical to – those of the Pharisees and scribes.

In the Diaspora, the Greek word *synagogé* seems to have been the name for the local Jewish congregation. The word *proseuché* (prayer place) was the name for the building where the congregation met (see for instance Acts 16.13 and 16.16). The fact that the word *proseuché* was used especially often in Egypt, suggests that the synagogue as an institution and the building where the congregation met were first established in Egypt. If this is true, the model can hardly have been the Greek school with its physical training, but rather the Egyptian school, which was connected to the temple and devoted itself to studies of old sacred texts.

According to Mark 13.9-11, those who believed in Christ would be "handed over to the courts" and "beaten in synagogues". This text was written in about A.D. 70, the year when the temple of Jerusalem was destroyed, and it shows, as Kee rightly points out, that by then the synagogue was about to develop from a

---

84 Kee, NTSt 36 (1990), p. 9.

85 Adolf Deißmann, *Licht vom Osten. Das Neue Testament und die neuentdeckten Texte der hellenistisch-römischen Welt*, 4th rev. ed., Tübingen 1923, pp. 378-380 (*Light from the Ancient East: The New Testament Illustrated by Recent Discovered Texts of the Graeco-Roman World*, New York 1927 – has not been available): "Die Synagogen-Inschrift des Theodotos zur Jerusalem". It says there: "Any Jewish inscription found in Jerusalem which is written in Greek with the characters used in the early period of the Roman empire can immediately be dated to the period before A.D. 70. For a long time after, no Jew was allowed within the city boundary, much less allowed to build anything there or establish a synagogue" (p. 380). In 1995, Kee dates the Theodotus inscription to the mid- to late third century: NTSt 41 (1995), pp. 499-500.

simple community or congregation into a sociopolitical structure with its own procedures for interpreting the law.[86]

It follows from what is said above that there were no proper synagogue buildings in Palestine until the end of the second century C.E. It has simply been taken for granted that synagogue buildings, such as Luke and the other Evangelists knew them from their own time, already existed in Palestine in the time of Jesus and his disciples. This is obviously an anachronism. In fact the synagogue buildings have been misdated: several early synagogue buildings are now dated to later periods than previously, or their remains are explained in new ways. A well-known example is the inscription "The Hebrews' Synagogue" found in Corinth in 1898.[87]

1.4.2 Proselytes and "God-fearers"

Besides the Jews themselves, both in Palestine and in the Diaspora, two other groups of different ethnic origins, neither of them Jewish, had joined early Judaism: proselytes and "God-fearers". How many of them there were, both relatively and absolutely, remains an open question which is still being discussed. "Proselyte" (from Greek: *prosélytos*, i.e. "one who joins [Judaism])" is the name for a Gentile who has rejected his own religion (the idols), and fully adopted the Jewish religion, including the obligation to observe the Mosaic law and its requirement of circumcision. At some point, we do not know exactly when, but it was probably about A.D. 100, baptism of proselytes was included in the rituals during which the the proselytes were received into Judaism. We do not know if the male proselytes were circumcised before or after the ceremony; there may also have been different local traditions for this. Out of the seven "overseers of the poor" named in Acts 6.5, Nicolas of Antioch (who is not surprisingly mentioned after all the others) is said to be a proselyte, and the Jew Tryphon's companions in the dialogue with Justin immediately after the Jewish-

---

86 Kee, NTSt 36 (1990), p. 14.
87 See Kee, NTSt 36 (1990), p. 18, n. 29. The marble block bearing the inscription probably dates from the second century C.E., but the place where it was found, the market street which led down to the sea port of Lecaeum, bears evidence of both Jewish and Christian meetings and their distinctive character of informal gatherings in people's homes, shops and workshops.

Roman war in A.D. 132-135 must have been Gentiles about to convert to Judaism.[88]

But it is not quite clear whether Tryphon's companions were proselytes or God-fearers. "God-fearers" are traditionally defined as Gentiles who had not converted completely to Judaism, but had joined the Jewish religion in so far as they had rejected their heathen religion and attended the Jewish worship on the Sabbath, from which they acquired some knowledge of the Old Testament. Although they were neither circumcised nor baptized as proselytes, they were more than just symphathizers: by supporting the Jewish community financially, they helped to improve its social status and reputation (see Lk. 7.3-5;[89] Acts 10.1-2). Whether and to what extent the early Christian mission also benefited from the support of God-fearers remains an open and controversial question.

The way in which the word is used in the Acts led to the assumption that it was unproblematic to regard "God-fearers" as a *terminus technicus* for Gentiles like those described above. Since about 1950, however, it has been discussed whether the Acts present a historically correct picture of the "God-fearers" as a separate, non-Jewish group, and whether it is right or wrong to regard the term "God-fearers" as a *terminus technicus*. The terms used in the Acts are respectively *foboúmenoi tòn theón* (up to and including Acts 13.26) and *sebómenoi tòn theón* (as from Acts 13.50); the term "Jews and God-fearing proselytes" also occurs (Acts 13.43). Some Jewish inscriptions might suggest that this really means "pious and God-fearing Jews".

But new light was shed on the problem in 1976, when an inscription from about A.D. 200 was found in Aphrodisias in the south-western part of Asia Minor. This inscription shows that "God-fearers", here in the form *theosebeîs*

---

88 See Theodor Zahn, Studien zu Justinus Martyr, Zeitschrift für Kirchengeschichte 8 (1886), pp. 1-84, see pp. 57-61 there.

89 It says here that the centurion whose servant is ill is praised by the Jewish elders for being "a friend of our nation" and for having "built our synagogue" (Lk. 7.5). This passage (which is not found in the parallel story in Matt. 8.5 ff.) explicitly refers to a synagogue building as if such a building existed in Palestine at the time of Jesus, which is contrary to the historical evidence. It is also the only explicit reference to a synagogue building in the New Testament. As Kee remarks, it confirms the impression of Luke/Acts as "a document from a hellenistic centre, where (as the archeological evidence we have examined suggests) Jews in the Diaspora had begun to modify houses or public structures in order to serve more effectively the needs of the local Jewish community" (Kee, NTSt 36 (1990), p. 17).

(corresponding to the Latin form *metuentes*), was a current term and, like *foboúmenoi/sebómenoi tòn theón*, used to describe Gentiles who had adopted the Jewish religion, but – unlike the proselytes – without submitting to circumcision and committing themselves to satisfying all the requirements of the Mosaic law.

The inscription is sensational because it proves that a considerable number of the citizens of Aphrodisias were willing to demonstrate their association with Judaism by publishing their names and the fact that they were *theosebeîs*. The inscription lists the names of a large number of persons who had contributed to the establishment of a Jewish "soup-kitchen" that supplied food to indigent Jews (and others?); so in this case it was not a synagogue. As one of the editors of the inscription points out, there is no evidence of anti-Semitism in Aphrodisias in about A.D. 200, when the building and inscription were made.[90]

1.4.3 Summing up

The few selected – and by no means exhaustive – comments above were meant to give an idea of the Jewish institutions during the time of Jesus. Besides the temple, the priestly clans and the religious parties, there were synagogue communities and – presumably – proselytes and God-fearers. With its widely ramified but well-coordinated institutions, the Jewish community was un-doubtedly one of the most stable social structures known in the world of anti-quity. Some of its institutions may have broken down or been destroyed, and yet Judaism continued to exist – it even attracted large numbers of Gentiles and was able to add new values to their lives.

The selected comments were also meant to stimulate a critical attitude to several traditional views on early Judaism. It was, above all, a complex and diverse religious culture that varied from place to place; Palestinian Judaism was strongly influenced by Hellenism, and there were distinct differences and conflicts of interests between Jews in Palestine and Jews in various parts of the Diaspora. Furthermore, recent research has shed new light on the traditional "Biblical history": it is surprising to learn that there were probably no synagogue buildings in Palestine before A.D. 200, and that the synagogues

---

90 Tannenbaum, *Jews and God-Fearers*, p. 126: "there seem to be no signs here of strong, or at least of open, antisemitism in Aphrodisian society at this date – which is not, of course, to say that Jews might not sometimes be the subject of tensions."

which existed in the Diaspora are now generally dated to a later period than previously – some of them to a much later period. This means that as institutions, the Synagogue and the Church developed in parallel with each other, and that the Church did not "take over" an existing established institution.

It would be interesting to know, however, to what extent Christianity expanded at the expense of Judaism, for instance among God-fearers and proselytes who were already connected with Judaism and its monotheism. This question will be one of the subjects for further research into the history of early Christianity.

1.5 Provisional conclusions

As explained above, *Judaism emerged in the Seleucid and Maccabean period of the Jewish people's history.* The Maccabean revolt saved the Jewish people and the Jewish religion from certain extinction.[91] If we look at the situation from a historical point of view, it also saved Christianity, which emerged from Judaism (cf. Jn. 4.22) and would otherwise have perished with it. And how should we look at the situation if not from a historical point of view?

To the Jews, the preservation of national independence was inseparably linked to history: they wanted to revive and relive the great period of David. The Maccabean revolt and the subsequent restoration of the Jewish nation, which also prevented the extinction of the people and their religion, were part of history and its changing pattern, a fulfilment of the people's hope for national rebirth. It was a period that called for constant reflection on Israel's history – the history that was stopped – or at least suspended for many years – when the Romans took control of the country in 63 B.C.

---

91 Bickerman writes: "It was the steadfastness of the martyrs, the courage of the Maccabeans, which saved for the Jews, and thus for mankind, the principle of monotheism. It was they who led the people back to the God of Abraham, Isaac, and Jacob" (*God of the Maccabees*, 1979, p. 2). But these observations are open to criticism on several points.

2 JESUS

Bibliography

a) Sources

The New Testament.

Josephus (see section 1 above).

Erich Klostermann: *Apocrypha, I-III* (Kleine Texte für Vorlesungen und Übungen, 3, 8 and 11), Berlin – Bonn 1904 ff.

Montague Rhodes James: *The Apocryphal New Testament being the Apocryphal Gospels, Acts, Epistles, and Apocalypses with other Narratives and Fragments newly translated*, Oxford 1924, repr. 1953.

Wilhelm Schneemelcher, ed.: *Neutestamentliche Apokryphen*, 5., völlig neubearbeitete Aufl., I: Evangelien, II: Apostolisches, Apokalypsen und Verwandtes, Tübingen 1987-89 = *New Testament Apocrypha*, translated by R. McL. Wilson, I: Gospels and related writings, II: Writings relating to the apostles; Apocalypses and related subjects, Cambridge 1991-1992.

J.K. Elliott, ed.: *The Apocryphal New Testament. A Collection of Apocryphal Christian Literature in an English Translation based on M.R. James*, Oxford 1993.

b) General works

Albert Schweitzer: *Geschichte der Leben-Jesu-Forschung*, orig. 1906, 2. Aufl. Tübingen 1913, 6. Aufl. 1951 (see also below, n. 113) = *The Quest of the Historical Jesus. A Critical Study of its Progress from Reimarus to Wrede* (1st ed. 1910), 3rd ed., London 1954 (a translation of the German 1906 edition).

Frederik Torm: *Forskningen over Jesu Liv. Tilbageblik og Fremblik*, Københavns Universitets Festskrift, Copenhagen 1918.

James M. Robinson: *Kerygma und historischer Jesus*, Zürich – Stuttgart 1960.

Mogens Müller: *Jesus-opfattelser – i den nytestamentlige forskning* (Religion: Tekster og temaer), Copenhagen 1978.

2.1 Historical and political developments

Bibliography

Kirsopp Lake, in: F.J. Foakes Jackson/Kirsopp Lake, eds., *The Beginnings of Christianity*, Part I, Vol. I, Prolegomena, London 1920, pp. 421-425: "Appendix A – The Zealots".

Abraham Schalit: *König Herodes. Der Mann und sein Werk* (Studia Judaica. Forschungen zur Wissenschaft des Judentums, IV), Berlin 1969.

Christ: *Krise und Untergang der römischen Republik* (see section 1.1 above), pp. 424-466: "Octavians Aufstieg und die Begründung des Principats".

Martin Hengel: *Die Zeloten, Untersuchungen zur jüdischen Freiheitsbewegung in der Zeit von Herodes I. bis 70 n. Chr.* (Arbeiten zur Geschichte des Spätjudentums und Urchristentums, 1), 1. Aufl. Leiden 1961, 2. verbesserte u. erweiterte Aufl., Leiden – Cologne 1976 = *The Zealots. Investigations into the Jewish Freedom Movement in the Period from Herod I until 70 A.D.*, Edinburgh 1989.

C.T.R. Hayward, in: Schürer: *History* (see chapter 1 above), II, 1979, pp. 599-606: "Appendix B: The Fourth Philosophy: *Sicarii and Zealots*".

B. Otzen: *Judaism in Antiquity* (see chapter 1 above), pp. 33-39: "The Romans and Herod the Great", and pp. 39-45: "The Sons of Herod, the Procurators, and the two Rebellions".

Richard A. Horsley: *Jesus and the Spiral of Violence. Popular Jewish Resistance in Roman Palestine*, San Francisco 1987.

Niels Willert: *Pilatusbilledet i den antike jødedom og kristendom* (Bibel og historie, 11), Århus 1989.

2.1.1 A short review

After Syria's collapse and Pompey's conquest of Palestine in 63 B.C., the Romans took control of the country. The new relationship that was now established between the Jews and the Romans was of course very different from the relationship that had existed between them during the time of the Maccabees (see sections 1.1.2 and 1.1.7 above). Herod the Great – who was an Idumean, not a Jew (see section 1.1.8) – was king of Palestine from 37 to 4 B.C. and ruled the country in accordance with the terms of the Roman senate, later the Roman emperor. During this period, Palestine enjoyed a relatively high degree of independence, though the Jewish people were not so fortunate. However, in the time of Caesar (died 44 B.C.), the Jews in the Diaspora were in principle allowed to practise their own religion in synagogue congregations. The restoration of the temple in Jerusalem began during the reign of Herod the Great, and the Maccabean castle Baris was rebuilt and renamed Antonia. But Herod installed and removed the high priests at his own discretion, and the Jewish synedrium, which had replaced the previous *gerousía* even in the time of John Hyrcanus, had relatively little influence.

During the reign of Herod the Great, the Roman civil wars which had followed the death of Caesar ended with the battle at Actium in 31 B.C., and Octavian, who also conquered and subjected Egypt in 30 B.C., abolished the republic and introduced the principate in 27 B.C. As Roman emperor, now under the name of Augustus, he ruled the vast Roman empire until A.D. 14.

In about 25 B.C., Augustus reorganized the Roman provinces; this reorganization still applied in New Testament times. The old senatorial provinces remained under civil administration, each of them governed by a proconsul, while the new provinces in the remoter parts of the Roman empire came under direct military administration, governed by the emperor himself through the legates, i.e. military governors, he had appointed. Roman legions were stationed in all the imperial provinces to defend them against external enemies, and to control any internal rebel movements. Except during the reign of Herod the Great, whose status as a (vassal) king was tolerated by the emperor, Palestine was governed by the legate of Syria, who resided in the capital Antioch – one of the richest cities of the empire along with Rome, Ephesus and Alexandria.

Herod's kingdom included the whole of Palestine, and after his death in 4 B.C., his sons obtained the emperor's permission to divide it into tetrarchies (i.e. "quarter principalities", each governed by a tetrarch, or "quarter prince"), but as the country was divided among only three of Herod's sons, they were not tetrarchs in the literal sense of the word. Archelaus (deposed in A.D. 6), who was in fact given the title of ethnarch, "prince of the people", was allocated Judea, Idumea and Samaria. Philip (died A.D. 33/34) was allotted Trachonitis east and northeast of the Lake of Galilee. And Herod Antipas (exiled in A.D. 39) received Galilee and Perea east of the River Jordan. Another son called Herod lived as a private citizen in Caesarea: see section 2.3.1 below.

When Archelaus was deposed in A.D. 6, his territory (Judea, Idumea and Samaria) was placed under the authority of the Roman prefects (later called procurators). They resided in Caesarea on the Mediterranean coast, but visited Jerusalem often, especially during the Jewish pilgrim feasts. The best known among them was Pontius Pilate (A.D. 26-36), who was prefect during the time of emperor Tiberius (A.D. 14-37). Although invested with considerable authority, the prefects were formally responsible to the legate of Syria; incidentally, Pontius Pilate was dismissed by Vitellius shortly after the latter was appointed legate.

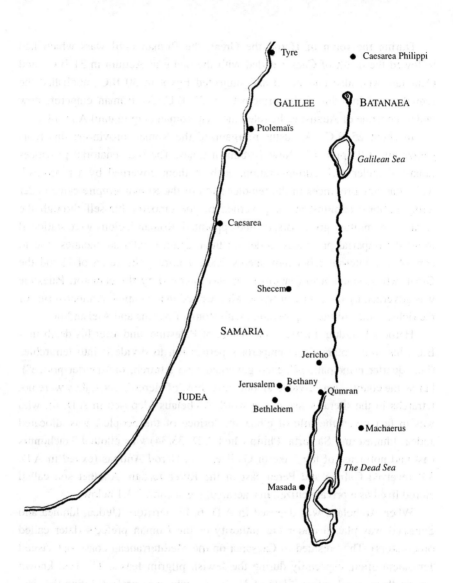

Map of Palestine at the time of Jesus

John the Baptist and Jesus lived and worked during the reign of the emperor Tiberius and the tenure of Pontius Pilate, and while Herod Antipas and Philip were tetrarchs in Galilee, Perea and Trachonitis.

Not until the end of the apostolic era did opposition to Roman foreign rule become so strong that it led to rebellion and war: the Jewish-Roman war that broke out in A.D. 66 and ended in the capture of Jerusalem and the destruction of the temple in A.D. 70. These upheavals, which have no immediate relevance to the discussion of Jesus and the apostolic era, will be described later in this book. At this stage, it is more relevant to describe one of the religious and political parties which has been considered very important, also for the time of Jesus: the Zealots (see section 1.3.1 above, n. 71).

2.1.2 Who were the Zealots?

In the historical literature of the New Testament, Judas the Galilean is specifically mentioned as a rebel figure who made his first appearance at the time of the census, and who was, at least theoretically, regarded as a parallel figure to Jesus himself (Acts 5.37). Furthermore, the Sicarii are mentioned as a rebel movement that existed during the tenure of the prefect Felix in about A.D. 55; for a short time at least, Paul was suspected of being one of them (Acts 21.38). Finally, we also know that one of Jesus' disciples, Simon, was nicknamed "the Zealot" (Lk. 6.15; Acts 1.13).[1] According to Martin Hengel, his nickname is the first evidence of the Zealots' party name.[2] It is interesting to note that all references to the Zealots are found in Lk.-Acts.

Judas the Galilean allied himself with a Pharisee called Saddok when Archelaus was deposed in A.D. 6 and Judea, Samaria and Idumea came under direct Roman administration. Quirinius, the Roman legate for the province of Syria, then organized a census for tax purposes (cf. Lk. 2.2), which provoked a rebellion, led by Judas, against the Romans. Naturally this rebellion took place in Judea: Judas' nickname "the Galilean" indicates that his activities did *not* take place in Galilee, and as we know, the census did not include Galilee.[3]

---

1   Cf. Mk. 3.18 and Matt. 10.4: "Canaanite" is the Semitic equivalent of the Greek word *zelotés*.
2   Hengel, *Die Zeloten*, 2nd ed., p. 344 (p. 338 in *The Zealots*).
3   Cf. Hengel, *Die Zeloten*, pp. 342-343; p. 409, n. 2 (pp. 336 and 401, n. 58 in *The Zealots*).

According to Josephus, Judas was the leader of "the fourth philosophy", which had nothing in common with the three others (the Essenes, the Pharisees and the Sadducees – see section 1.3.1. above); yet Josephus adds rather inconsistently that Judas agreed with the Pharisees in every respect – cf. his association with the Pharisee Saddok – except on one important point: Judas' followers had "an almost invincible passion for freedom, since they maintained that God alone was their leader and master."[4] Their refusal to acknowledge any other masters than God himself must have been the single most important "Zealotic" feature of the movement initiated by Judas the Galilean.

This movement continued to exist even after the Romans had quashed the revolt which broke out in A.D. 6; it remained more or less constantly active until and after the capture of Jerusalem and the destruction of the temple in A.D. 70, and it survived even until the Romans finally (re)captured the fortress Masada in A.D. 74. Judas the Galilean had a son called Menahem, and when the war against the Romans broke out in A.D. 66, he and his men took possession of Masada and its arsenal. When other rebel Jews in Jerusalem had captured the temple precinct and the castle Antonia, Menahem went to Jerusalem with some of his supporters and took charge of the defence of the city and the temple.

However, shortly after the outbreak of the war, Menahem and some of his supporters were murdered in the temple court while he was on his way to worship in the temple, dressed in royal robes and "surrounded by armed Zealots".[5] As a result, his own and his supporters' active participation in the revolt in Jerusalem was limited to a few weeks. The murder was committed by a group of priests led by the commander of the temple guard, a priest called Eleazar, who was the son of the moderate high priest Ananias[6] – the Eleazar who was responsible for suspending the two daily sacrifices for the emperor.

---

4   Josephus, Ant. Jud. XVIII, 23 (chapter 1.6).
5   Bell. Jud. II, 444 (chapter 17.9): "attended by his suit of armed fanatics" is H.St.J. Thackeray's translation in: *Josephus. With an English Translation*, II, 1927, p. 497, though the term "fanatics" is explained in a note as "Greek zealots". Cf. C.T.R. Hayward, in: Schürer, *History*, II, 1979, p. 602, n. 28. But in *Die Zeloten*, 2nd ed. 1976, pp. 398-399 (pp. 390-391 in *The Zealots*), Hengel makes it clear that they were not "fanatics" or "zealous followers", but genuine Zealots. Incidentally, the first reference to them is found in Josephus. The relationship between the Zealots and the Sicarii is a different matter.
6   In Schürer, *History*, II, pp. 600-601, Hayward calls him Eleazar, son of Simon. This is wrong – they are two different persons.

Menahem's murder can be explained as blood vengeance, since Menahem had previously murdered Eleazar's father Ananias and Ananias' brother Hezekiah to satisfy his own aspiration to become high priest.[7] Whether this explanation is correct or not, Menahem's murder eliminated any possibility of unity among the initiators of the rebellion against the Romans. A few of Menahem's supporters escaped after his murder, most of them to Masada, but their participation in the rebellion in Jerusalem was finished.

Josephus mentions a number of rival factions that fought among themselves while participating in the rebellion against the Romans in A.D. 66-70:[8] 1) the "Sicarii", whose origins can be traced back to Judas the Galilean, though they did not use his name; 2) the Galilean John of Gischala, who defended the temple to the end together with his supporters; 3) Simon bar Giora and his supporters, who were the last group of rebels to force their way into Jerusalem – they represented the majority of the rebel forces and took charge of the main defence of the city; 4) the Idumeans, who had joined various factions and finally fought together with Simon bar Giora; and 5) the "Zealots", who had established their headquarters in the temple; they were dominated by the priests of the temple and defended it together with John of Gischala.

Such an enumeration is open to a great deal of theoretical discussion, also on the subject of terminology, including the use of the terms "Zealots" and "Sicarii". In his important book *Die Zeloten* of 1961, Martin Hengel maintains that when used in its absolute sense, the term "Zealots" refers to a religious-political party whose existence is first established during the rebellion of Judas the Galilean in A.D. 6, and whose distinctive ideology – God alone is our master – was unique in the early history of Judaism. On the other hand, C.T.R. Hayward in his study of 1979 picks up the thread of Kirsopp Lake's theory of 1920 by arguing that it was Judas the Galilean who founded the party of the Sicarii, and that there is no evidence of the Zealots as a party until the outbreak of war in A.D. 66. He also points out that the Zealots were a priestly party unlike the Sicarii, who counted Menahem among their members.

In this context, I do not intend to concentrate on details of terminology. Strictly speaking it is not correct to speak of "Zealots" until the movement was

---

7   Cf. Hengel, *Die Zeloten*, p. 407 (p. 399 in *The Zealots*).
8   Cf. Hengel, *Die Zeloten*, p. 390 (pp. 382-383 in *The Zealots*), and Hayward, in Schürer, *History*, II, 1979, p. 601.

dominated by priests, and in the rebellion against the Romans, this did not happen until the outbreak of war in A.D. 66. According to this definition, neither Judas the Galilean nor his son Menahem were Zealots: they were not priests but laymen, and since Judas' movement was later to be known under the name of "Sicarii" (from Latin *sica,* a dagger with an upturned point), it would hardly be correct simply to call them Zealots.

On the other hand it is obvious that Judas and Menahem belonged to the Zealotic movement. But Zealotism was not a new phenomenon that emerged suddenly in the time of Judas the Galilean as a result of his activities. The Zealotic idea that God alone is the master of man dates from the time of the Maccabees, who were priests and recognized Phinehas as their ideal (see section 1.1.1 and the passage referred to in note 6, and section 1.2.2). The fact that scholars have found it difficult to reach this seemingly obvious conclusion should, at least to a certain extent, be ascribed to the influence of Josephus' terminology and his way of writing history. Josephus is not interested in describing his people's latest history and the final catastrophe in A.D. 70 as logical consequences of the preceding events; on the contrary, by insisting on blaming all those who participated in the rebellion against the Romans and calling them robbers, murderers, bandits and (sic!) "Sicarii", he cuts them off from any connection there might have been between them and the Jewish tradition.

However, Martin Hengel unintentionally recognizes the Zealots' connection with the Jewish tradition, past and future. This is evident from his convincing analysis of the relationship between Eleazar, Ananias' son, and Menahem, Judas' son, which he sees in the light of the knowledge we have about the Essenes and the later Bar Kokhba rebellion (A.D. 132-135): the "dual role" which the priestly Messiah and the royal Messiah shared between them.[9] I shall return to this subject later in the book (see section 2.4.3 below).

---

9   See Hengel, *Die Zeloten,* pp. 300-301, including n. 5 (p. 294, including n. 353 in *The Zealots*); and p. 371 (p. 364 in *The Zealots)*: "It is possible that Eleazar and Menahem may originally have thought of a priestly and royal dual role of the kind that was practised by the Essenes and is suggested later during the period of Bar Koseba. Menahem's military successes, however, point with increasing clarity to his attempt to achieve unrestricted total rule for himself."

The Zealots' connection with the tradition of early Judaism as a whole – and Hengel is not blind to this, either[10] – clearly shows that "the fourth philosophy" was far from being an independent "party" like the other three. Martin Hengel wants the Zealots, "the fourth philosophy" to be a party whose history dates back to Judas the Galilean. Kirsopp Lake, and after him, C.T.R. Hayward even maintain that there is no evidence of the Zealots as a historical party until the outbreak of war in A.D. 66. But Josephus' description of the Zealots as "a fourth party" reveals his desire to reduce the entire rebel movement to a well-defined and relatively short-lived phenomenon that was an exception in the early history of Judaism: once defeated and eliminated by the Roman military power, the rebel movement could be described as an isolated phenomenon which had nothing in common with Judaism as such; and the rebels could be described as fanatics and robbers, who quarrelled and fought among themselves like other rebel movements and even oppressed the Jewish people and led them to disaster. Martin Hengel and other historians have let themselves be misled by Josephus' description and have not really seen through the motives for his description of the situation. The Zealots – to use the name Josephus gives them – actually represented the consistent development of fundamental ideas and principles from the previous part of early Judaism's history, even the part that gave birth to Judaism: the time of the Maccabees and the Hasmoneans.

2.1.3 A general assessment

The interpretation of early Judaism and its origins behind this description of historical events is based on the recognition of the unique importance of the Maccabean/Hasmonean period. Over a period of a hundred years, the Maccabees succeeded in gaining political power and maintaining the people's right to national independence. During this period, Judaism came into existence, and a number of its important institutions were developed and consolidated. Admittedly, the Roman rule established in 63 B.C. deprived the Jewish people of their recently acquired national independence, but their struggle for freedom had made them aware of their own strength and restored their belief in their common identity as a people. They were willing to make the necessary sacrifices whenever an opportunity presented itself for regaining political and

---

10 Hengel, *Die Zeloten*, pp. 151-234: "Der Eifer" (pp. 146-228 in *The Zealots*: "Zeal").

national independence. Obviously discussions on ways and means were inevitable in the circumstances: policies of collaboration and resistance never go hand in hand. Other considerations also influenced the process of deciding how far they could go, especially the expected reactions of the surrounding Gentile world, which always kept a close watch on all Jewish activities inside and outside Palestine. And yet a distinct continuity can be observed throughout the course of history, a continuity that was still very much in evidence even after the Romans had seized power and introduced prefect and procurator administration in Judea, Samaria and Idumea in A.D. 6: Judaism still remained the same as it had been in the time of the Maccabees and the Hasmoneans.

Such was Judaism in the time of Jesus.

2.2 Problematics regarding the historical Jesus

Bibliography

William Wrede: *Das Messiasgeheimnis in den Evangelien. Zugleich ein Beitrag zum Verständnis des Markusevangeliums,* first published in 1901, 3rd ed. Göttingen 1963 = *The Messianic Secret* (Library of Theological Translations), Cambridge – London 1971.

Julius Wellhausen: *Einleitung in die drei ersten Evangelien,* Leipzig 1905, 2nd ed. 1911.

Martin Dibelius: *Die Formgeschichte des Evangeliums,* first published in 1919, rev. 2nd ed. 1933, 3rd ed. Tübingen 1957 – all quotations are from the 2nd or latest ed. = *From Tradition to Gospel* (Library of Theological Translations), Cambridge 1971.

Karl Ludwig Schmidt: *Der Rahmen der Geschichte Jesu. Literarkritische Untersuchungen zur ältesten Jesusüberlieferung,* Berlin 1919, repr. Darmstadt 1964.

Rudolf Bultmann: *Die Geschichte der synoptischen Tradition* (Forschungen zur Religion und Literatur des Alten und Neuen Testaments, 29), first published in 1921, 2nd rev. ed. 1931, 3rd ed. Göttingen 1957 = *The History of the Synoptic Tradition,* Oxford – New York 1963.

Rudolf Bultmann: Zur Frage der Christologie, first published in 1927, in: id., *Glauben und Verstehen. Gesammelte Aufsätze,* I, Tübingen 1933, pp. 85-113.

Nils Alstrup Dahl: Problemet "Den historiske Jesus", in: id., *Rett lære og kjetterske meninger,* Oslo 1953, pp. 156-202 = The Problem of the Historical Jesus, in: id., *Jesus the Christ. The Historical Origins of Christological Doctrine,* ed. Donald H. Juel, Minneapolis 1991, pp. 81-111.

Hans Conzelmann: *Die Mitte der Zeit. Studien zur Theologie des Lukas* (Beiträge zur historischen Theologie, 17), first published in 1954, 5th ed. Tübingen 1964 = *The Theology of St Luke*, London 1960, New York 1961.

Ernst Käsemann: Das Problem des historischen Jesus, first published in 1954, in: id.: *Exegetische Versuche und Besinnungen*, I, Göttingen 1960, p. 187-214 = The Problem of the Historical Jesus, in: id., *Essays on New Testament Themes* (Studies in Biblical Theology), London 1964, pp. 15-47: "The Problem of the Historical Jesus".

Willi Marxsen: *Der Evangelist Markus* (Forschungen zur Religion und Literatur des Alten und Neuen Testaments, 67), first published in 1956, 2nd ed. Göttingen 1959.

Rudolf Bultmann: *Das Verhältnis der urchristlichen Christusbotschaft zum historischen Jesus* (Sitzungsberichte der Heidelberger Akademie der Wissenschaften, Philol.-hist. Kl., 1960, 3.), Heidelberg 1960 = id., *Exegetica. Aufsätze zur Erforschung des Neuen Testaments*, ed. Erich Dinkler, Tübingen 1967, pp. 445-469 = The Primitive Christian Kerygma and the Historical Jesus, in: C.E. Braaten/R.A. Harrisville, eds., *The Historical Jesus and the Kerygmatic Christ*, Nashville 1964, pp. 15-42.

Helmut Ristow/Karl Matthiae, eds.: *Der historische Jesus und der kerygmatische Christus. Beiträge zum Christusverständnis in Forschung und Verkündigung*, Berlin 1961.

Ernst Käsemann: Sackgassen im Streit um den historischen Jesus, in: id., *Exegetische Versuche und Besinnungen*, II, Göttingen 1964, pp. 31-68 = Blind Alleys in the "Jesus of History" Controversy, in: id., *New Testament Questions of Today*, London 1969, pp. 23-65.

Rudolf Bultmann: Antwort an Ernst Käsemann, in: id., *Glauben und Verstehen. Gesammelte Aufsätze*, IV, Tübingen 1965, pp. 190-198.

Mogens Müller: Historikerens Jesus, den historiske Jesus og kirkens Kristusforkyndelse, Dansk Teologisk Tidsskrift 38 (1975), pp. 81-104.

Heikki Räisänen: *The "Messianic Secret" in Mark* (Studies of the New Testament and Its World), Edinburgh 1990.

E.P. Sanders: *The Historical Figure of Jesus*, London 1993.

2.2.1 William Wrede

When William Wrede's book about "the Messianic Secret" was published in 1901, it heralded a new epoch in the history of New Testament exegesis. The fact that the Gospel of Mark must be regarded as the oldest of the four Gospel books had been established as early as in 1838.[11] Now, however, Wrede's study of the Gospel of Mark demonstrated that it was far from objective in its description of Jesus' life and work and belonged in the history of dogmatics exactly like the other books of the New Testament. Indeed, Mk. was dominated by the Christian view of the belief in Jesus as Christ to such an extent that it had to be disregarded as a source of information on the historical Jesus. As early as at the turn of the century, Wrede's investigation of this Gospel text (cf. the subtitle of his book) paved the way for the redaction critical analysis of the Gospel texts which was to be developed much later, after the end of the second world war – see section 2.2.3 below.

With regard to his main subject, the Messianic Secret, Wrede advanced the theory that the text of Mk. was characterized by an overlap of two different strata of the Jesus tradition. According to Wrede, the enigmatic request to keep Jesus' identity as Messiah or Christ secret until his resurrection (cf. in particular Mk. 9.9) can be explained by the fact that the historical Jesus was not considered to be Messiah, and that Jesus himself did not claim to be Messiah. On the other hand, the earliest congregation believed him to be Messiah. This contradiction in the Jesus tradition is resolved through the theory of the Messianic Secret: Jesus was Messiah, but this was not revealed until his resurrection.

With this theory, Wrede also drew attention to a factor that proved vital to research on the Gospel texts during the following decades: the Jesus tradition as it was during the period *before* the Gospel texts existed in writing, but *after* the time of the historical Jesus himself.

As soon as Wrede had pointed out the necessity of analyzing the Gospel texts themselves, it was suddenly understood that there were no less than three strata of problematics concerning Jesus and the Gospel texts: 1) the historical Jesus himself, 2) the oral tradition of this historical Jesus and 3) the Evangelists' literary adaptation of this oral tradition.

The publication of Wrede's book in 1901 had the effect that all studies of the historical Jesus in theology and exegesis were abandoned almost immediately: if even the Gospel of Mark – the oldest and therefore presumably the most reliable description of the life and work of Jesus – could no longer be

---

11 Through Weiße's and Wilke's independently formulated hypotheses on Mark as a partial solution to the synoptical problem.

used as a source, it was better to give up studying a subject which could not be based on any reliable evidence. At the same time, the effect of Wrede's book was intensified to an almost uncanny extent by Albert Schweitzer's demonstration that all descriptions of the life of Jesus since the Age of Enlightenment – especially those which claimed to be based on objective scholarly studies of the subject – proved to reflect their authors' own contemporary ideas and views much more than anybody would have expected, and were also characterized by the authors' arbitrary use and selection of Gospel texts. Paradoxically, Schweitzer's own attempt at a description of the historical Jesus proved to be just as dependent on its own period as the descriptions he had so perspicaciously criticized.[12]

So the studies of the historical Jesus – stratum 1 – were abandoned by the theological scholars and left to amateurs. Instead exegetes concentrated their attention on the tradition of the historical Jesus – stratum 2. If you cannot have the best, you must settle for the second-best![13]

2.2.2 Form criticism
This type of criticism was practised most intensely during the period between the two world wars, and as early as in 1920, the school of form criticism was established by Martin Dibelius, Rudolf Bultmann and others. Its influence on theological research was considerable. It can be defined briefly as follows: exegetic studies of the Jesus tradition concentrated on the spoken word, the sermon and the preaching of the Gospel, because: "In the beginning was the sermon."[14] This point of view was also reflected in the contemporary dialectic

---

12 Cf. Dahl, *Rett lære*, pp. 184-185 (*Jesus the Christ*, p. 98): "... Schweitzer's own theory, which did not proceed from the beginning but rather from the climax of Jesus' public life, found the key for understanding the history of Jesus in the delay of the parousia at the time the seventy were sent out (Matt. 10:23) and rested on an entirely arbitrary combination of the sources."

13 Cf. Hyldahl, Træk af den nytestamentlige eksegeses historie i Danmark i det 20. århundrede, in: Kirkehistoriske samlinger 1979, pp. 127-150, see p. 134.

14 "Im Anfang war die Predigt" – this famous observation of Martin Dibelius does not come from his *Formgeschichte*, but from his earlier treatise, Die alttestamentlichen Motive in der Leidensgeschichte des Petrus- und Johannesevangeliums, in: *Abhandlungen zur semitischen Religionsgeschichte und Sprachwissenschaft* (Beihefte zur Zeitschrift für die alttestamentliche Wissenschaft, 33), Gießen 1918, pp. 125-150, see p. 146; reprinted in:

theology and in the research on Luther, which was enjoying a renaissance at that time. While focusing on the congregation as the place where the Jesus tradition belonged and was kept alive, theologians also became aware of the sociological aspects of this tradition and the congregation itself. Studies of the literary peculiarities of the individual scriptures led to an acknowledgment of the connection between form ("Gattung") and function – "Sitz im Leben", as it was called in German. Since the question of the historical Jesus had been abandoned, it was no longer relevant to ask whether anything was historically correct. Now the functions of the tradition and its components became subjects for studies and discussions. As a result of this new thinking, Karl Ludwig Schmidt and others found it necessary to establish a clear distinction between "redaction" (editing) and "tradition", a process during which "redaction" was treated with little respect and often dismissed as relatively unimportant, because this made it so much easier to concentrate on the study and discussion of "tradition". At the time, few people realized the negative consequences of this attitude. According to the prevailing exegetic conviction, the Evangelists could not always have understood the substance of the material they had edited so poorly. As a result, the Evangelists' careful adaptation of the texts was often neglected, and the texts themselves were used only as a window through which the spectator looked at the tradition behind the text. This way of thinking remained unchallenged until after the Second World War, when the newly established school of redaction criticism attempted to redress the balance. It is interesting to note that the question of the historical Jesus was taken up again at the same time.

As already mentioned, the link between exegesis – in this context the work of the school of form criticism – and theology was obvious. To some exegetes and theologians, this link was so self-evident and natural that they made a theological *virtue* of the *necessity* of dismissing the question of the historical Jesus. This applied to Rudolf Bultmann, who not only maintained that Jesus had disappeared behind the smoke of the fire he had lit himself, but declared himself happy with this: from a theological point of view, the historical Jesus was of no

Martin Dibelius: *Botschaft und Geschichte. Gesammelte Aufsätze, I: Zur Evangelien-forschung*, published by Günther Bornkamm, Tübingen 1953, pp. 221-247, see p. 242.

importance and only served to safeguard the Christian faith, which need not and should not be safeguarded in any way.[15]

But making a theological virtue of historical necessity had its price: when the question of the historical Jesus was abandoned, the fact that Jesus was a Jew and therefore belonged in early Judaism was turned into a triviality of no relevance either to theology or to the Church itself. From a christological angle, Bultmann's point of view was in line with docetism (from Greek *dokeîn*, "to appear" – see also section 2.5.1 below): the question of Christ had been reduced to one single point in the mathematical sense of having no extension, i.e. the belief in his death and resurrection. It was not "das Was" but "das Daß"[16] that counted, and the problem of the historical Jesus was not solved, but simply ignored. In principle, this was what the gnostics, including Marcion, had done in the days of the early church.

2.2.3 Redaction criticism and the question of the historical Jesus

It is interesting to note that two different important events took place at almost the same time, in the middle of the 1950s: the school of redaction criticism was established, and the question of the historical Jesus was taken up again.

While form criticism had dominated research into Gospel texts during the period between the two world wars, redaction criticism, which was introduced by Hans Conzelmann in 1954, was to dominate a considerable part of the German research on the Gospel texts after the Second World War. It is true that redaction criticism represented a legitimate reaction against form criticism in as far as it recognized the importance of the Evangelists' contribution to the Gospel texts we know from today's New Testament. On the other hand, since the analysis of redaction criticism was limited to stratum 3, it represented yet another step away from the principal subject: Jesus himself. From a historical as

---

15 Bultmann, *Glauben und Verstehen*, I, p. 101: "My critical radicalism has never made me uncomfortable, on the contrary, quite comfortable. But I often have the impression that my conservative colleagues among New Testament scholars seem rather uncomfortable, for I always find them busy with their rescue work. I just let the fire burn, for I can see what it burns: all the illusions of the life-of-Jesus theology, the *Christòs katà sárka* itself." The use of this quotation from 2 Cor. 5.16 is questionable in this context.

16 A play on the German words "was" (= the interrogative pronoun *what*) and "daß" (= the conjunction *that*).

well as theological point of view, it would be almost impossible to stray further from the original subject!

In 1954, however, Ernst Käsemann, who was a disciple of Bultmann, pointed out the necessity of returning to the question of the historical Jesus. Contrary to his own teacher, he maintained that if the question of the historical Jesus was not placed on the agenda of theology, Christianity and the Church itself would eventually be left with a myth that had nothing whatever to do with reality. Clearly the life-of-Jesus research, which Wrede and Schweitzer had exposed as an illusion at the beginning of the century, could not and should not be revived: neither the external nor the internal (psychological) development of Jesus could be reconstructed and described. However, the fact remained that the Evangelists – especially the author of Lk.-Acts – had the historical Jesus in mind when they wrote the Gospel texts, and had tried to present what purported to be historical, chronological descriptions of events. This has compelled modern theology to take the question of the historical Jesus seriously, and to ask who and what he was.

Strange as it may seem, however, theology has made no real progress since then as far as the question of the historical Jesus is concerned. Several attempts have been made to answer this question, including Günther Bornkamm's book about Jesus dated 1956 and Ed Parish Sanders' book from 1985 (see section 2.5.1 below). Some of the answers concentrate on the preaching of Jesus (Bornkamm), but in such a way that the reader cannot always be sure whether they refer to the preaching of Jesus or the theology of the Evangelists. Others only confirm that we know very little, and that the little we know tends to indicate that Jesus did not break with the Judaism of his own time (Sanders). It is important to note that none of the authors are interested in the question of whether Jesus was Messiah before his death and resurrection, although this particular question cannot possibly be regarded as immaterial from a christological point of view.

Nevertheless, the question of the historical Jesus still requires an answer. As Nils Alstrup Dahl said: "If we theologians ignore this task, others will undertake it."[17] Admittedly, any idea of reforming Christianity on the basis of critical research into Jesus would be unrealistic, but on the other hand, such research would at least be a worthwhile piece of work which somebody has to

---

17 Dahl, *Rett lære*, p. 173 (*Jesus the Christ*, p. 91).

undertake in the spirit of Paul (1 Cor. 7.29), "as one who does not undertake it".[18] After all, there are certain things we do know. I will just mention two indisputable facts which mark the beginning and end of the work of Jesus: in the first place, we know that Jesus was baptized by John the Baptist, and secondly, we know that Jesus was executed as the king of the Jews according to the inscription on his cross. The baptism of Jesus immediately involves another person, John the Baptist. It seems as if these two persons, John and Jesus, represent a "priest" and a "king" respectively, and perhaps this idea will make it possible to find a new way of formulating the question of Jesus as Christ or Messiah – the christological question.

2.3 John the Baptist

Bibliography

Martin Dibelius: *Die urchristliche Überlieferung von Johannes dem Täufer* (Forschungen zur Religion und Literatur des Alten und Neuen Testaments, 15), Göttingen 1911.

Harold W. Hoehner: *Herod Antipas* (Society for New Testament Studies, Monograph Series, 17), Cambridge 1972, especially pp. 110-171: "Antipas and John the Baptist".

W. Schenck: Gefangenschaft und Tod des Täufers. Erwägungen zur Chronologie und ihrer Konsequenzen, New Testament Studies 29 (1983), pp. 453-483.

Gerd Theißen: Das "schwankende Rohr" in Mt. 11,7 und die Gründungsmünzen von Tiberias. Ein Beitrag zur Lokalkoloritforschung in den synoptischen Evangelien, Zeitschrift des Deutschen Palästina-Vereins 101 (1985), pp. 43-55 = id.: *Lokalkolorit und Zeitgeschichte in den Evangelien. Ein Beitrag zur Geschichte der synoptischen Tradition* (Novum Testamentum et Orbis Antiquus, 8), Freiburg (Schweiz) – Göttingen 1989, pp. 26-44 = The "Shaken Reed" in Mt 11:7 and the Foundation Coins of Tiberias, in: id., *The Gospels in Context. Social and Political History in the Synoptic Tradition*, Edinburgh 1992, pp. 26-42.

Rainer Riesner: Bethany beyond the Jordan (John 1:28). Topography, Theology and History in the Fourth Gospel, Tyndale Bulletin 38 (1987), pp. 29-63.

Joseph Ernst: *Johannes der Täufer. Interpretation – Geschichte – Wirkungsgeschichte* (Beiheft zur Zeitschrift für die neutestamentliche Wissenschaft, 53), Berlin – New York 1989.

---

18 Cf. Dahl, *Rett lære*, p. 173 (*Jesus the Christ*, p. 92).

2.3.1 The tradition

One of the strangest features of the New Testament's description of the life of Jesus is the special relationship that existed between Jesus himself and another person, John the Baptist. It must be regarded as an indisputable fact that Jesus let John the Baptist baptize him in the River Jordan. This shows us that Jesus established a bond between himself and John the Baptist, and Jesus' assertion that the baptism performed by John was from God (Mk. 11.30) makes it clear that Jesus believed that John had been sent by God. It seems as if Jesus was in some way "dependent" on John the Baptist. On the other hand, we cannot be sure that John the Baptist saw Jesus as somebody sent by God, or that it was Jesus he referred to when he said: "After me comes one mightier than I am" (Mark 1.7). According to the Gospel texts, he was referring to Jesus, and John was his "forerunner". But this may be second-hand knowledge. It appears that disciples of John the Baptist had established their own movement, independently of Jesus (see Mk. 2.18; Lk. 1.76 ff. – in the "Benedictus" – and 3.15, 11.1; Jn. 1.6-8, 15, 20 ff.; cf. Acts 19,1 ff. – in Ephesus?!). This seems to indicate that while Jesus himself and his work would have been inconceivable without John, John the Baptist and his work are both historically and theologically quite conceivable without Jesus.

As well as the New Testament descriptions of John the Baptist, we have a remarkable narrative from Josephus, Ant. Jud. XVIII, 109-126 (chapter 5.1-3). It describes the imprisonment and execution of John and can therefore be regarded as a parallel to Mk. 6.17-29. The text is as follows:[19]

> 109 In the meantime, a quarrel, whose origin I shall relate, arose between Aretas, king of Petra,[20] and Herod.[21]
>
> The tetrarch Herod had taken the daughter of Aretas as his wife and had now been married to her for a long time. When starting out for Rome, he lodged with his half-

---

19   English translation: Louis H. Feldman, in: *Josephus. With an English Translation*, IX, 1965, pp. 77 ff.
20   Aretas IV, king of the Arabian Nabateans (9 B.C.-A.D. 40); cf. 2 Cor. 11.32. Petra (cf. § 120), the capital of the Nabateans, was situated about halfway between the south end of the Dead Sea and the north end of the Gulf of Aqaba. The Nabateans controlled the areas south and south-east of Palestine, cf. the name "Arabia" in Gal. 1.17.
21   Herod Antipas, son of Herod the Great and tetrarch of Galilee and Perea 4 B.C.-A.D. 39.

brother Herod[22] [probably in Caesarea by the Sea], who was born of a different mother, namely, the daughter of Simon the high priest. 110 Falling in love with Herodias, the wife of this half-brother – she was a daughter of their brother Aristobulus and sister to Agrippa the Great[23] – he brazenly broached to her the subject of marriage. She accepted and pledged herself to make the transfer to him as soon as he returned to Rome. It was stipulated that he must oust the daughter of Aretas. 111 The agreement made, he set sail for Rome.

On his return after transacting his business in Rome, his wife, who had got wind of his compact with Herodias, before any information reached him that she had discovered everything, asked him to send her away to Machaerus, which was on the boundary between the territory of Aretas and that of Herod. She gave no hint, however, of her real purpose. 112 Herod let her go, since he had no notion that the poor woman saw what was afoot. Some time earlier she herself had dispatched messengers to Machaerus, which was at that time subject to her father,[24] so that when she arrived, all preparations for her journey had been made by the governor. She was thus able to start for Arabia as soon as she arrived, being passed from one governor to the next as they provided transport. So she speedily reached her father and told him what Herod planned to do.

113 Aretas made this the start of a quarrel. There was also a dispute about boundaries in the district of Gamala.[25] Troops were mustered on each side and they

---

22 Little is known about this Herod – he was, like Herod Antipas, a son of Herod the Great and originally destined to inherit the throne, but seems to have lived as a private individual in Caesarea on the coast of the Mediterranean Sea; cf. section 2.1.1. In Mk. 6.17, Herodias' first husband is called Philip, which is not correct (contrary to Hoehner, *Herod Antipas*, pp. 133-136). According to Josephus, there is no evidence that this Herod was also named Philip. But the tetrarch Philip was the son-in-law of the Herod mentioned here and his wife Herodias, since he was married to their daughter Salome, and was half-brother of both Antipas and this Herod.

23 Agrippa I, king 37-44; cf. Acts 12.1-23.

24 The castle Machaerus did not belong to Aretas, but to Antipas. It was situated in Perea and was used as a frontier fortress against the Nabateans; but the written tradition is uncertain, and Feldman's translation is based on a correction of the text.

25 This place name is often corrected by editors, including Feldman, IX, pp. 80-81. But see Gerd Theißen, *Lokalkolorit u. Zeitgesch.*, pp. 85-102: "Die Legende vom Tod des Täufers – eine Volksüberlieferung mit Nachbarschaftsperspektive", n. 56 on p. 86 (= The Legend of the Baptizer's Death: A Popular Tradition Told from the Perspective of Those nearby? in: id., *The Gospels in Context*, pp. 81-97, n. 56 on p. 82): "Gamala was in Philip's territory, thus precisely in the region that the Nabateans had bought in 21 or 20 B.C.E., but had not been able to take possession of. Now they could make their demands effective. Probably they raised the claim only after Philip's death in 34 C.E. The war with

were now at war, but they dispatched others as commanders instead of going themselves. 114 In the ensuing battle, the whole army of Herod was destroyed when some refugees, who had come from the tetrarchy of Philip[26] and had joined Herod's army, played him false.

115 Herod sent an account of these events to Tiberius.[27] The latter was incensed to think that Aretas had begun hostilities and wrote to Vitellius[28] to declare war and either bring Aretas to him in chains, if he should be captured alive, or, if he should be slain, to send him his head. Such were the instructions of Tiberius to his governor in Syria.

116 But to some of the Jews, the destruction of Herod's army seemed to be divine vengeance, and certainly a just vengeance, for his treatment of John, surnamed the Baptist. 117 For Herod had put him to death, though he was a good man and had exhorted the Jews to lead righteous lives, to practise justice towards their fellows and piety towards God, and so doing to join in baptism. In his view this was a necessary preliminary if baptism was to be acceptable to God. They must not employ it to gain pardon for whatever sins they committed, but as a consecration of the body implying that the soul was already thoroughly cleansed by right behaviour. 118 When others too joined the crowds about him, because they were aroused to the highest degree by his sermons, Herod became alarmed. Eloquence that had so great an effect on mankind might lead to some form of sedition, for it looked as if they would be guided by John in everything that they did. Herod decided therefore that it would be much better to strike first and be rid of him before his work led to an uprising, than to wait for an upheaval, get involved in a difficult situation and see his mistake.

119 Though John, because of Herod's suspicions, was brought in chains to Machaerus,[29] the stronghold that we have previously mentioned, and there put to death, yet the verdict of the Jews was that the destruction visited upon Herod's army was a vindication of John, since God saw fit to inflict such a blow on Herod.

120 Vitellius got himself ready for war against Aretas with two legions of heavy-armed infantry and such light-armed infantry and cavalry as were attached to them as auxiliaries. Proceeding from the kingdoms that were under the Roman yoke, he pushed toward Petra and occupied Ptolemaïs. ...

Antipas took place in 36 C.E. The large number of deserters from Philip's territory shows that not everyone was convinced of the superiority of Antipas' claims."

26 For information on the tetrarch Philip: see n. 21 above.
27 The emperor Tiberius (14-37) – he died on 15th March 37, cf. § 124.
28 Vitellius, military governor of Syria (35-39).
29 See § 112.

124 On the fourth day [of Vitellius' and Antipas' visit to Jerusalem during the feast of Passover or Pentecost in A.D. 37[30]], when he received a letter notifying him of the death of Tiberius,[31] he administered to the people an oath of loyalty to Gaius.[32] He now recalled his army, ordering each man to go to his own home for the winter, for he was no longer empowered as before to make war abroad now that the government had fallen into Gaius' hands. ... 126 Vitellius accordingly withdrew to Antioch.

In this context, it might be relevant to quote Josephus' observations on Herodias and Salome in Ant. Jud. XVIII, 136-137 (chapter 5.4):

136 Herodias was married to Herod, the son of Herod the Great by Mariamme, daughter of Simon the high priest. They had a daughter Salome, after whose birth Herodias, taking it into her head to flout the way of our fathers, married Herod [Herod Antipas], her husband's brother by the same father [Herod the Great], who was tetrarch of Galilee; to do this she parted from a living husband. 137 Her daughter Salome was married to Philip, Herod's [Herod the Great's] son and tetrarch of Trachonitis. When he died childless,[33] Aristobulus, the son of Agrippa's [Herod Agrippa's] brother Herod, married her. Three sons were born to them – Herod, Agrippa, and Aristobulus.

By way of comparison, Mk. 6.14-29 is quoted below:

14 Now King Herod[34] heard of Jesus, for his fame had spread, and people were saying, "John the Baptist has been raised from the dead, and that is why these miraculous powers are at work in him." 15 Others said, "It is Elijah." Others again, "He is a prophet like one of the prophets of old." 16 But when Herod heard of it, he said, "This is John, whom I beheaded, raised from the dead."
17 It was this Herod who had sent men to arrest John and put him in prison at the instance of his brother Philip's[35] wife, Herodias, whom he had married. 18 John had

---

30 Passover, i.e. 14th Nisan, fell on 19th April in A.D. 37. Regarding the question of whether it was the feast of Passover or Pentecost, see Hoehner, *Herod Antipas*, pp. 256-257 and pp. 313-316: "The Date of Pilate's Return to Rome".

31 See n. 27 above.

32 Gaius Caligula, emperor 37-41.

33 Circa A.D. 33/34.

34 i.e. Herod Antipas, who was not a king, but only tetrarch of Galilee and Perea. The fact that he is called "king" may be due to popular idioms, unless he is mistaken for Herod the Great, who was a king. A different explanation is given in Theißen, *Lokalkolorit u. Zeitgesch.*, p. 92 (p. 87 in *The Gospels in Context*), namely that the later Herodians acquired the title of king: "The fact that Antipas appears as "king" in Mk 6:17ff. could well be a trace of narrators in whose environment Herodians were "kings" quite as a matter of course."

35 The name is wrong – see n. 22 above.

told him, "You have no right to take your brother's wife." 19 Herodias nursed a grudge against John and would willingly have killed him, but she could not, 20 for Herod went in awe of him, knowing him to be a good and holy man; so he gave him his protection. He liked to listen to him, although what he heard left him greatly disturbed.

21 Herodias found her opportunity when Herod on his birthday gave a banquet to his chief officials and commanders and the leading men of Galilee. 22 His [Herod Antipas'] daughter Herodias[36] came in and danced, and so delighted Herod and his guests that the king said to the girl, "Ask me for anything you like and I will give it to you." 23 He even said on oath: "Whatever you ask I will give you, up to half my kingdom." 24 She went out and said to her mother, "What shall I ask for?" She replied, "The head of John the Baptist." 25 The girl hurried straight back to the king with her request: "I want you to give me, here and now, on a dish, the head of John the Baptist." 26 The king was greatly distressed, yet because of his oath and his guests he could not bring himself to refuse her. 27 He sent a soldier of the guard with orders to bring John's head; and the soldier went to the prison and beheaded him; 28 then he brought the head on a dish, and gave it to the girl; and she gave it to her mother.[37]

29 When John's disciples heard the news, they came and took his body away and laid it in a tomb.

---

36 In v. 22 there is a difficult problem of textual criticism. The best variant which is found in Nestle, Nestle/Aland, 26th ed., and *The Greek New Testament*, 3rd. ed., has *autoû* [masc.], while textus receptus has *autês (tês)* [fem.]. According to the latter variant (Herodias' daughter), the girl must be Herodias' daughter Salome (whom we know from Josephus), but this raises the problem of Salome's age. If it is true that she was born in A.D. 6 – cf. Schenk, NTSt 29 (1983), p. 465 – she was too old to be called a (young) girl, in Greek *korásion* (Mk. 6.22-28); in Mk. 5.42, Jairus' daughter is also called a *korásion*, and she was only twelve years old, as it says there. According to the first variant (his daughter Herodias), the girl was called Herodias and was a child of the marriage between Herod Antipas and Herodias – the girl calls Herodias "mother". If this is correct, the marriage must of course have taken place a number of years before this event, and Aretas' daughter's flight to Arabia even earlier (see also the passage referred to in n. 43 below). A third point of view is found in Theißen, *Lokalkolorit u. Zeitgesch.*, pp. 94 ff. The author "defends" the historical inaccuracies in Mk. 6.14 ff., which he regards as the result of a later popular and anti-Herodian tradition.

37 In NTSt 29 (1983), pp. 466-467, Schenk rightly points out: "There is no evidence in the text of Mark that the daughter is aware of her mother's cunning plan. Any suggestions to that effect are unfounded: the girl seems embarrassed and does not know what to demand, so she asks her mother and tragically becomes a passive tool in her mother's hands. And finally – after the nefarious deed – she immediately hands the dish with the head of the Baptist to her mother. This gesture reveals who was really behind the request [the mother]. Commentators who ignore this, misinterpret Mark's description of the daughter's role and character."

There are both similarities and differences between the descriptions given by Josephus and Mark. One of the similarities is that the story of John the Baptist's execution is told "in past perfect". In the light of other events (in Josephus, the war between Antipas and Aretas; in Mark, the miracles performed by Jesus), they both describe how Antipas had *on a previous occasion* ordered the execution of John the Baptist. In either case, the description of the execution is an explanatory postscript to a description of another event, and is as such *of secondary importance:* §§ 116-119 in Josephus and vv. 17-29 in Mark, both give the impression of being appendages to the main stories.

It is also important to note that the two descriptions have similar functions: in Josephus, Antipas' defeat in the war against Aretas is seen as a divine rehabilitation of the executed John the Baptist,[38] and in Mark, the executed John the Baptist now confronts his slayer Antipas as a rehabilitated and exalted figure that forces Antipas to acknowledge and confess his own guilt (Mark 6.16).[39]

Furthermore, both descriptions recognize John the Baptist as a righteous person (Josephus: § 117; Mark: 6.20).

Another similarity between Josephus and Mark is that they both – from their different points of view – clearly condemn the marriage between Antipas and Herodias as an immoral relationship. There is no hard evidence that their moral condemnation of the marriage should be seen in the light of the fact that it represented a violation of the Mosaic Law (and according to Mk. 2.23 ff. and 7.1 ff., Mark does not defend the observance of this), but rather in the light of the fact that both Herodias and Antipas had had no scruples about breaking their marriage vows.

Among the differences between Josephus' and Mark's descriptions, it is important to note that Josephus explains the execution of John the Baptist as the result of a political decision, while Mark holds Herodias morally responsible for the execution. There need be no objective contradiction between these explanations, since Antipas was already responsible for imprisoning John the Baptist. On the other hand, the reasons for his imprisonment are moral according to Mark, and political according to Josephus.

---

38 Cf. Schenk, NTSt 29 (1983), pp. 460 and 463.
39 Cf. Schenk, ib., pp. 471-472.

Another and more important difference lies in the fact that only Mark mentions a connection between the marriage of Antipas and Herodias and the execution of John the Baptist. Josephus does not connect these events, but only refers to political motives; according to him, John the Baptist is imprisoned and executed for political reasons, and the marriage between Antipas and Herodias results in the war between Antipas and Aretas, but he does not say that the marriage had been condemned or even mentioned by John the Baptist.

Apparently Mark is not aware of the political complications, including the fact that Antipas had been married to Aretas' daughter.

It is also important to note that the banquet during which John the Baptist was executed seems to have been held in Galilee according to Mark (but if that is correct, why was only John's head brought to the banquet? – Mogens Müller, and cf. Josephus, § 115), while Josephus says he was executed in the castle Machaerus in south Perea. The only reasonable explanation is that Josephus is right on this point, and that Mark's knowledge of the course of events is incomplete.

All things considered, Josephus' description is to be preferred, while Mark's description with its obvious errors – he calls Herodias' previous husband Philip and implies that the execution took place in Galilee (?) – is probably based on various popular legends about the death of John the Baptist but not on a reliable tradition which could otherwise have reached the Evangelist through Baptist congregations.[40]

2.3.2 Three problems

Three problems each deserve a commentary here.

In his above-mentioned treatise of 1983, Wolfgang Schenk argues for the establishment of a new chronology concerning John the Baptist. According to Schenk, Antipas did not marry Herodias until after the death of Philip the tetrarch in A.D. 33/34, and there was a political motive behind the marriage: Antipas wanted to control Philip's tetrarchy east and north-east of the Lake of Galilee. However, the emperor Tiberius then decided to place the area under the direct administration of Syria's military governor. When Caligula became emperor (A.D. 37-41), the area was finally entrusted to Agrippa I, Herodias' brother. Schenk also maintains that John the Baptist was not executed until

---

40 Cf. Schenk, ib., p. 470.

A.D. 35, and that he therefore outlived Jesus by several years.[41] But both arguments are untenable. Josephus himself does not establish any connection between the marriage of Antipas and Herodias and the execution of John the Baptist. Furthermore, nothing in the texts as much as hints that the marriage took place after the death of the childless Philip.[42] And finally, John the Baptist may have been imprisoned and executed well before the war between Antipas and Aretas in A.D. 36 (according to Josephus, § 113, a boundary dispute between Antipas and Aretas was certainly one of the motives for this war). In this context, it may be relevant to note that Hegesippus saw a connection between the execution of Jesus' brother James in A.D. 62 and Jerusalem's fall eight years later in A.D. 70,[43] and that according to Matt. 22.7, there was a connection between Jesus' death and Jerusalem's destruction 40 years later.

In 1985, Gerd Theißen argued that the words of Jesus about "the swaying reed" in the desert (Matt. 11.7-9; Lk. 7.24-26) should be seen as an example of "local colour" – despite the fact that the same expression is used in other contexts, for instance in 3 Macc. 2.22. Coins from the reign of Herod Antipas also show the reed as his emblem.[44] These coins date from the period after A.D. 19, when Antipas founded his new capital Tiberias (named after the emperor) on the western shore of the Lake of Galilee. Moreover, the above-mentioned

---

41 Cf. Schenk, NTSt 29 (1983), pp. 463-464, where he refers to Karl Theodor Keim's historical research from the second half of the 19th century, according to which John the Baptist was executed in the mid-thirties. Keim also quite consistently dated the death of Jesus to Passover A.D. 35 or 36, but Schenk rejects this with reference to the latest chronology, and maintains that John the Baptist must have survived Jesus! I fail to understand why a relatively late dating of Jesus' death would be unacceptable. If Paul's conversion took place in A.D. 40 – see my book *Die paulinische Chronologie* (Acta Theologica Danica, XIX), Leiden 1986, pp. 120 ff. – there is no valid reason for excluding the possibility that Jesus died at a later date than usually supposed. The only real time limit is the tenure of Pilate, A.D. 26-36. See also my arguments against Harald Riesenfeld in my article, Otto Møller og astronomien, in: *Teologi og tradition. Festskrift til Leif Grane*, Århus 1988, pp. 66-84, especially pp. 76 ff. But it is important to note that Schenk's late dating of the Baptist's death is unfounded, and that the tradition of the New Testament is quite clear on the point that Jesus survived the Baptist; cf. Theißen, *Lokalkolorit u. Zeitgesch.*, pp. 94-95.

42 See also n. 36 above.

43 Eusebius, Hist. eccl. II, 23.18.

44 See Hoehner, *Herod Antipas*, p. 99, n. 2; Theißen, ZDPV 101 (1985), pp. 45 ff. = id., *Lokalkolorit u. Zeitgesch.*, pp. 26 ff.

words of Jesus clearly emphasize the contrast between "the prince" and "the ascetic". Reeds grew in the desert along the banks of Jordan. Theißen writes: "The Baptizer's protest against Antipas and his marriage to Herodias is thus part and parcel of a popular reaction against the advance of "foreign" customs in the Herodian upper classes: their conformist behaviour, their luxury, and their family life meet with rejection among the common people. John the Baptist is a mouthpiece of this native opposition and reaction."[45] He maintains that the words of Jesus in Matt. 11.7-9 are of Palestinian origin and must be authentic: the early Christians believed that the Baptist was the prophet of Jesus, his forerunner, but here Jesus places him above all prophets, saying that he is "more than a prophet".

In 1987, Rainer Riesner convincingly identified "the place at Bethany beyond Jordan, where John was baptizing" (Jn. 1.28; cf. 10.40-42). We know that according to Jn., there were two "Bethanies", one near Jerusalem and another beyond the River Jordan, and that John also baptized in other places, for instance at Aenon near Salim, "because water was plentiful in that region" – on the west bank (Jn. 3.23). But "Bethany beyond Jordan" seems to have been the place he preferred. After an impressive summary of the entire research history on this subject, Riesner concludes that Bethany was not a town but a region (Greek *tópos*: Jn. 10.40), and that "Bethany" is identical to "Batanaea" (the phonetic resemblance is unmistakable), or Bashan, as it is called in the Old Testament – east and north-east of the Lake of Galilee.[46] In other words: a considerable part of John the Baptist's activities must have taken place in Philip's tetrarchy, near Bethsaida-Julias and Caesarea Philippi, at the source of Jordan in North Palestine. Jesus himself took refuge there and found many disciples (Jn. 10.40-42) – a fact that should also be seen in the light of Jn. 1.35 ff., according to which Jesus' first disciples had been disciples of John, who told them to follow Jesus. Furthermore, this text also says explicitly that Jesus found his first disciples in the region of Bethsaida-Julias, which was the capital of Philip the tetrarch and – according to Jn. 1.44 – the native town of the

---

45 Theißen, ZDPV 101 (1985), p. 55 = *Lokalkolorit u. Zeitgesch.*, pp. 43-44 (p. 42 in *The Gospels in Context*). Cf. id., Jesusbewegung als charismatische Wertrevolution, New Testament Studies 35 (1989), pp. 343-360, in particular p. 345.
46 Cf. also Klaus Wengst, *Bedrängte Gemeinde*, 3rd ed. 1990 (see section 4.2 below), p. 172.

disciples Andrew, Peter and Philip. It was there (despite Jn. 12.21, they were not in Galilee yet!) that Jesus and his first disciples gathered before they went on to Galilee (Jn. 1.43; cf. 2.1: Cana in Galilee); Jesus himself was from Nazareth in Galilee (Jn. 1.45).

Unlike Schenk's unsuccessful attempt to establish an alternative chronology, both Theißen's and Riesner's investigations show that John the Baptist was active during the period before the death of Philip the tetrarch in A.D. 33/34, and that he spent most of his time in the areas that belonged under the tetrarchs Philip and Antipas.

2.3.3 Three observations

In this context, I find it relevant to add three observations of my own.

First, it is important to note that John the Baptist was of priestly descent. According to Lk. 1.5 ff., this is an indisputable fact, since his father Zechariah was a priest of Abijah's clan, and his mother Elisabeth was descended from Aaron, cf. Exod. 6.23.[47] The truth of this observation is confirmed by the fact that the priests of Jerusalem's temple had to establish their genealogies.[48] By all accounts, John the Baptist himself was not a priest at the temple of Jerusalem, nor is there any reason to believe that he had ever been a priest. On the contrary, he lived as an ascetic prophet preaching conversion and penance. On the other hand, the fact that he baptized his followers and disciples can be seen as a priestly element in as far as the baptism he practised was a symbolic cleansing (cf. Josephus's description in § 117) and therefore appears to have had a certain connection with the established cult.[49]

Secondly, it is important to note that unlike the contemporary Jewish cleansing rituals, John's baptism in water was performed only once on each individual: it represented an initiation into a "new" community that differed essentially from the traditional Jewish community. (In early Judaism, there is only one possible parallel to the baptism of John, i.e. the Jewish baptism of

---

47 Cf. Ernst, *Johannes der Täufer*, p. 122 with n. 32; and pp. 269-272: "Die Abstammung des Johannes aus priesterlichem Geschlecht". Michael Goulder rejects John's priestly origin: *Luke. A New Paradigm* (Journal for the Study of the New Testament, Suppl. Series, 20), I-II, Sheffield 1989, pp. 212 ff.

48 See the passage referred to in n. 69, section 1.2.2 above.

49 On the other hand, any idea that John the Baptist may have belonged to the Essene Qumran community by the Dead Sea must be rejected as pure conjecture.

proselytes through which Gentiles were received into Judaism; but there is no evidence of proselyte baptism being practised before A.D. 70 and the emergence of Rabbinic Judaism.) John's baptism was aimed at Jews. But the fact that John invited Jews to let themselves be baptized by him clearly indicates that the Jewish religion was in a sense regarded as "insufficient". It is therefore logical to assume that Gentiles also had access to John's baptism – although there is no evidence that others than Jews were baptized by John. In John's words, God could "make children for Abraham out of these stones" (Matt. 3.9 = Lk. 3.8); this indicates that John the Baptist was the first to break through the "covenantal nomism"[50] which Sanders defined as a characteristic feature of early Judaism.[51]

Finally, it must be established that John's baptism in water was the natural model for Christian baptism. To be more explicit: Jesus himself did not practise baptism – only his disciples, the original Church, did this (cf. Jn. 4.2). But the fact that Jesus let himself be baptized by John the Baptist (Mk. 1.9-11 = Matt. 3.13-17 = Lk. 3.21-22; cf. Jn. 1.29-34) represents the institution of Christian baptism, because what Jesus had done, every Christian must do. Christian baptism is Christian because Jesus submitted to the same baptism. What John's twelve or so disciples in Ephesus achieved by being baptized again in the name of Jesus (Acts 19.1-7) is a literary rather than a historical question.[52]

2.4 The relationship between John the Baptist and Jesus

Bibliography

Benedikt Otzen: Die neugefundenen hebräischen Sektenschriften und die Testamente der zwölf Patriarchen, Studia Theologica 7 (1953), pp. 125-157.
Marshall D. Johnson: *The Purpose of the Biblical Genealogies with special Reference to the Setting of the Genealogies of Jesus* (Society for New Testament Studies,

---

50 See section 1.3.3 above.
51 Cf. Dale C. Allison, Jesus and the Covenant: A Response to E.P. Sanders, Journal for the Study of the New Testament 29 (1987), pp. 57-78, in particular pp. 58-61; and my own article: E.P. Sanders' Jesusbog, Dansk Teologisk Tidsskrift 51 (1988), pp. 104-111, in particular p. 110.
52 In this context it is interesting to read in the preceding chapter (Acts 18.24-28) that Apollos was not baptized in the name of Jesus, "although the only baptism he knew was John's."

Monograph Series, 8), Cambridge 1969 (2nd ed., 1989), pp. 115-138: "Genealogical Speculation on the Ancestry of the Messiah".

Anders Hultgård: *L'eschatologie des Testaments des Douze Patriarches, I. Interprétation des textes* (Acta Universitatis Upsaliensis, Historia Religionum, 6), Uppsala 1977.

id.: *L'eschatologie des Testaments des Douze Patriarches, II. Composition de l'ouvrage; textes et traductions* (Acta Universitatis Upsaliensis, Historia Religionum, 7), Uppsala 1981.

Schürer: *History* (see section 1 above), III.2, 1987, pp. 767-781: "The Testaments of the Twelve Patriarchs".

Matthias Klinghardt: *Gesetz und Volk Gottes. Das lukanische Verständnis des Gesetzes nach Herkunft, Funktion und seinem Ort in der Geschichte des Urchristentums* (Wissenschaftliche Untersuchungen zum Neuen Testament, 2., 32), Tübingen 1988, pp. 71-77: "Die Konzeption der beiden Messias in Qumran und TestXII".

2.4.1 A seemingly one-sided relationship

There is no reliable evidence that John the Baptist ever confirmed the existence of a special relationship between himself and Jesus, or even expressed an opinion on the things Jesus said and did.[53] On the other hand, Jesus spoke of John the Baptist several times and was baptized by him. On these premises I see no reason to go further into the question of whether John the Baptist was the forerunner of Jesus in the traditional sense of the word. Instead I shall try to investigate, first the relationship between John the Baptist and Jesus in a wider sense, and secondly Jesus' explicit references to John the Baptist, knowing that such an investigation may well be incomplete and provisional. In the past, this relationship was often seen as a simple relationship between "the forerunner" and "Messiah". When this point of view was abandoned as historically unsound, the relationship – unique though it is from any point of view – was either shelved as an insoluble problem, or John the Baptist was simply regarded as a prophet who – like Jesus himself, and perhaps even as a kind of rival to him – preached God's impending coming.

---

53 The only hint of such evidence is the passage in which the imprisoned John the Baptist instructs his disciples to ask Jesus: "Are you the one who is to come, or are we to expect someone else?" (Matt. 11.2-3 = Lk. 7.18-20). Even if this passage could be attributed to the oral tradition (which is hardly the case), and not simply to the process of editing, it only tells us that John the Baptist was considering *the possibility* that Jesus might be someone special, not that he was convinced of this.

As I said above, the words of John the Baptist that God could "make children for Abraham out of these stones" indicates that he had broken through the covenantal nomism that characterized early Judaism (cf. the second paragraph of section 2.3.3 above). In so far as this theory is based on John's statement, it depends on the interpretation of this statement. Another possible interpretation is a prophecy or "threat" of judgment: since God himself chose the children of Abraham, i.e. the Jews, as his own people, he can also reverse his decision and reject them – unless they repent and turn to God. According to this interpretation, there is nothing unusual in the statement from a Jewish point of view.

On the other hand, the statement certainly implies at least a latent possibility that others than Jews may become "children for Abraham". Moreover, the baptism of John – and the fact that each individual submits to this event only once – seem to indicate that Judaism in itself is "insufficient", and that more is expected of the future than that which Judaism can offer with all its priests and institutions. Sanders is wrong to overlook this possibility.[54]

All things considered, it must be concluded that in his work and preaching – his "words and deeds" – John the Baptist represented a strong criticism of contemporary Judaism because he did not refer to the existing institutions, but introduced a new institution: the baptism of John. By introducing baptism as a cultic innovation and by practising it himself, he – a priest's son – performed a priestlike function. At the same time, however, the difference between the Maccabean priests and the priest's son John the Baptist is obvious. And he was not alone in criticizing Jerusalem's temple and its body of priests.[55] Admittedly, John's criticism of the temple and the priests was quite different from the criticism expressed by the Qumran congregation by the Dead Sea. They – and especially their priests! – criticized the temple and its priests because the temple had temporarily ceased to function as it should,[56] while John the Baptist turned his back on the temple and the priests through his preaching and baptism. In fact, his critical attitude is reminiscent of the prophets' criticism of the cult and

---

54 See n. 51.

55 Cf. the passage about the priest's daughter Miriam in section 1.2.2 above.

56 Cf. Maier, *Tempelrolle*, 1978, p. 68: "Hence the harshest criticism of the current Temple was quite consistent with the strongest affirmation of the Temple cult" (*The Temple Scroll*, p. 59).

the temple in the Old Testament. However, it is difficult to draw such distinctions, especially since the historical developments during the period since the establishment of the Qumran congregation in about 152 B.C. may have obliterated specific motives for criticizing the temple and the priests. In one sense, the Qumran congregation also turned its back on the temple and the priests, and who knows whether a radical reform of Jerusalem's temple cult might not have satisfied even John the Baptist?

Whatever the case, John the Baptist has the characteristics of both a prophet and a priest – Jesus called him a prophet, or rather "more than a prophet" – and he institutionalized and practised a cultic and therefore priestly act which was approved by Jesus.

In this connection, it is important to note that Jesus recognized John's baptism, not only by letting John baptize him, but also by referring to it in a specific context, namely the synoptic tradition concerning the question about Jesus' authority (Mark 11.27-33 = Matt. 21.23-27 = Lk. 20.1-8). Jesus answers this question by asking a counter-question: "The baptism of John, was it from Heaven (i.e. from God) or from men?" There can be no doubt about Jesus' own opinion: the baptism of John was not a human invention, but a divine act: God himself was behind John's baptism. But the opponents could not find words to answer Jesus' counter-question, because if they said "from Heaven", they would have to admit that they had not acted accordingly, and they could not answer "from men" for fear of the consequences, since people believed that John the Baptist was a prophet sent by God.[57] So they said nothing, and therefore Jesus did not answer their question about his authority.

This confirms that the leaders of the people – the high priests, the scribes and the elders[58] in Jerusalem (Mk. 11.27 = Matt. 21.23 = Lk. 20.1) – did not recognize the baptism of John as a divine act, but rejected it. In this sense, the baptism of John was a criticism of the leaders' attitude, since they rejected it.

It is even more important to note that the question of Jesus' authority appears in a specific context that is still recognizable in the synoptic text: in connection with and immediately after the cleansing of the temple (Mk. 11.15-17 = Matt. 21.12-17 = Lk. 19.45-48). When the opponents ask by what authority Jesus does "this" (Greek *taûta*: Mk 11.28 = Matt. 21.23 = Lk. 20.2),

---

57 Cf. Josephus §§ 116 and 119 in section 2.3.1 above.
58 In fact, representatives of the synedrium that had replaced the previous *gerousía*.

they are referring specifically to the recent cleansing of the temple. That the cleansing of the temple was really a criticism of the temple and the priests is beyond doubt. The essential point is that when challenged by his opponents, Jesus does not take the opportunity to question them about their interpretation of the scriptures; he asks a counter-question about the baptism of John. In doing this, Jesus himself establishes a link between the baptism of John and the cleansing of the temple, which confirms that the baptism of John should also be seen as a criticism of the temple and the priests.

2.4.2 John as a priestly Messiah

John the Baptist was an eschatological figure. This appears from his preaching about God's impending judgment. For the purpose of gaining an insight into the relationship between John the Baptist and Jesus, there is not much point in referring to other eschatological or Messianic movements or figures. It is far more relevant to study certain features of early Judaism which have been much discussed since the discovery of the Qumran documents, and which also shed light on facts that we need to take into consideration in order to understand the problems we are dealing with in the present context.

The Damascus Document (now called CD), which was discovered in 1896 and published in 1910, was proved to be Essene after the discovery of the Qumran documents (among which it belonged). In this document, there are several singular references to "Aaron's and Israel's Messiah" or "Messiah from Aaron and Israel" (CD 12.23-24; 14.19; 19.10-11; 20.1). It has been much debated whether this expression refers to one Messiah or two different Messiahs. Now, however, the discovery of the Qumran documents has finally established that it refers to two Messiahs: one from Aaron and one from Israel – i.e. a priestly Messiah and a royal Messiah. This appears from "the Rule of the Community" (1QS), which makes it quite clear that there are two Messiahs: "... until a prophet and Ahron's and Israel's (two) Messiahs come" (1QS 9.11). It is confirmed in "the Rule of the Congregation" (1QSa), which is almost as clear on this point: "This is the session of the men of the name who are invited to the feast for the Council of the Community when God leads forth the Messiah [sc. the royal Messiah] to be with them: The Priest [sc. the Messiah of Aaron] shall enter at the head of all the Congregation of Israel and all his brothers, the Sons of Aaron, the priests who are invited to the feast, the men of the name. And they shall sit before him each man according to his glory. And after them the Messiah of Israel shall enter. And the heads of the thousands of Israel shall sit before him each man according to his glory" (1QSa 2.11-15).[59] This confirms the appearance of two eschatological Messianic figures, a priestly and a royal Messiah, and the priestly Messiah ranks above the royal Messiah.

The discovery of this astonishing fact also sheds new light on other texts from the period of early Judaism which have been – and still are – much discussed: the Testaments of the Twelve Patriarchs.[60] A few extracts are quoted below:

From TJud.:

21.1 And now, children, love Levi so that you may endure. Do not be arrogant toward him or you will be wholly destroyed. 2 To me God has given the kingship and to him [sc. Levi], the priesthood; and he has subjected the kingship to the priesthood. 3 To me he gave earthly matters and to Levi, heavenly matters. 4 As heaven is superior to the earth, so is God's priesthood superior to the kingdom on earth, unless through sin it falls away from the Lord and is dominated by the earthly kingdom. 5 For the Lord chose him over you to draw near to him, to eat at his table, to present as offerings the costly things of the sons of Israel. ... 24.1 And after this there shall arise a Star from Jacob in peace: And a man shall arise from my posterity [sc. from the tribe of Judah] like the Sun of righteousness, walking with the sons of men in gentleness and righteousness, and in him will be found no sin. 2 And the heavens will be opened upon him ...

From TReub.:

6.5 For this reason, I say to you, you will vie with the sons of Levi and will seek 6 to be exalted above them, but you will not be able: For God will perform vengeance in their behalf, and you will die an evil death, 7 since God gave Levi the authority, and to Judah with him [as well as to me and to Dan and to Joseph], to be rulers. 8 It is for this reason that I command you to give heed to Levi, because he will know the law of God and will give instructions concerning justice and concerning sacrifice for Israel until the consummation of times; ... 10 Draw near to Levi in humility of your hearts in order that you may receive blessing from his mouth. 11 For he will bless Israel and Judah, since it is through him [sc. Judah] that the Lord has chosen to reign in the presence of

---

59 Translation: James H. Charlesworth, ed., *The Dead Sea Scrolls. Hebrew, Aramaic, and Greek Texts with English Translations*, Vol. 1, p. 117.
60 Translation by Howard C. Kee, in: James H. Charlesworth, ed., *The Old Testament Pseudepigrapha*, Vol. 1, pp. 775-828.

all the people. 12 Prostrate yourselves before his [sc. Judah's] posterity, because ...
And he shall be among you an eternal king.

From TSim.:

7.1 And now, my children, be obedient to Levi and to Judah. Do not exalt
yourselves above these two tribes, [because from them will arise the Saviour come
from God]. 2 For the Lord will raise up from Levi someone as high priest and from
Judah someone as king ...

These texts make it quite clear that Levi and Judah have the highest ranks in
Israel, and that the high priest and the king shall come from these two tribes.

It is not my intention to go into the complicated literary origins of the
Testaments of the Twelve Patriarchs or give an opinion on the widely divergent
assessments of the original Jewish composition and the Christian editing of the
work. There seems to be a tendency towards general agreement that the extent
of Christian editing is relatively limited, and that it is in fact a work from the
period of early Judaism, probably the first half of the last century B.C. The work
– in particular the Levi-Judah texts – argues against the Maccabean-Hasmonean
combination of the positions of priest and king in one and the same person, so it
must have been written before the Romans conquered Palestine in 63 B.C.[61]

In his book of 1977 about the eschatology in the Testaments of the Twelve
Patriarchs, Anders Hultgård emphasized the importance of Levi's precedence
over Judah, and saw the eschatological high priest, "the priest-saviour",
prefigured in Levi. What is more: Anders Hultgård was among the first to point
out certain striking points of resemblance between this priestly Messiah figure
and John the Baptist.[62] The fact that John the Baptist was of priestly descent[63] is
confirmed in Lk. 1.5 ff., which seems to have originated partly from disciples of
John the Baptist, as many exegetes have already observed. From this, Hultgård
immediately draws the conclusion that "the concept of a priestly Messiah could

---

61 Cf. Otzen, in: *De gammeltestamentlige Pseudepigrafer*, II, p. 684; Schürer, *History*, III.2,
1987, pp. 774 ff. It is particularly difficult to appraise Marinus de Jonge's studies from
1953 ff., and his assertion that the Testaments are really a Christian work centred on
Israel's obligation to accept the belief in Christ.

62 Hultgård, *L'eschatologie*, I, pp. 376-378. For information on previous studies on the
same subject, see also Ernst, *Johannes der Täufer*, pp. 123-124.

63 See section 2.3.3 above.

therefore be applied to him [i.e. John the Baptist] without any difficulties."[64] However, this is nothing but a theory that can only be used in so far as it is supported by the texts. Now, Lk. 1.17 attributes a Messianic function to John when it says that he will "prepare a people that shall be fit for the Lord" – but according to Hultgård, this corresponds with the function attributed to the Levitical "priest-saviour" of the Testaments: TJud. 18.8-9 and TDan. 5.11. Both TDan. 5.11 and Lk. 1.17 mention the "rebellious" or "disobedient" (Greek: *apeitheîs*). Hultgård identifies these as pagans, which must be considered to be pure conjecture. According to Hultgård, the last part of the "Benedictus" (Lk. 1.68-79), where Zechariah speaks directly to the child John, is consistent with both TNapht. and TLevi as far as the functions of the eschatological, priestly saviour are concerned. All things considered, the analogies pointed out by Hultgård should not be rejected, although they do not say a great deal; in particular, they fail to show that the Testaments had the influence Hultgård maintains they had. On the other hand, these analogies emphasize the connection between the texts of Luke mentioned above and the Messianic ideas of early Judaism.

In his eagerness to prove the importance and influence of the work, Hultgård tends to underestimate two facts: 1) it is not Levi, but Levi-Judah, i.e. the dual concept of "priest and king", which constitutes a fundamental principle in the Testaments; and 2) the "priest and king" theme should be seen in the context of early Judaism as a whole, and not as a distinctive feature of the Testaments of the Twelve Patriarchs that differentiates the eschatology of this work from the prevailing ideas of the period. Perhaps Hultgård's main error is that his reconstruction of the traditions behind the Testaments and his analysis of the work lead him to believe that the Levitical "priest-saviour" is the absolute key figure and originally the only Messiah, and that some time later, when the Maccabees/Hasmoneans had also taken possession of the royal throne, this figure was "supplemented" with the royal Messiah of Judah's tribe.[65] But as we already know, the Pharisees did not blame John Hyrcanus I for his possession of

---

64 Hultgård, *L'eschatologie*, I, p. 377.
65 Hultgård rightly points out that the Maccabean or Hasmonean assumption of power was illegitimate, since the Maccabees as priests were not of Judah's tribe. However, the Jewish literature has no examples of criticism of the Maccabees or Hasmoneans for their non-Judean descent.

the royal power, which was relatively unimportant in his time, but rather for his illegitimate possession of the office of high priest,[66] or for being both high priest and king at the same time. It may be correct – as Hultgård points out[67] – that after Pompey's assumption of power, the Jews declared that they did not want to have a king, since they were accustomed to obeying their priests, provided the priests honoured God (Josephus, Ant. Jud. XIV, 41). However, this does not prove that the Testaments of the Twelve Patriarchs turned against the Maccabean/Hasmonean kings in particular – it was much more likely a natural reaction in the situation when the Romans had seized control of the country: the Jews had had enough of the reign of the Maccabees.

2.4.3 Old Testament and Jewish background

In order to understand the references to the two Messiahs, a priestly Messiah of Levi's tribe and Aaron's line, and a royal Messiah of Judah's tribe and David's line, it is necessary to take Israel's history during the post-exile period into consideration – although Hultgård finds this pointless as regards the eschatology of the Testaments.[68]

According to the Book of Ezekiel, the land should be governed by the Zadokite priests[69] and by "the ruler" (Ez. 44.15 ff.; 45.7 ff.), i.e. the cultic and the political government respectively – in this order of precedence! The Books of Haggai and Zechariah from the period when the temple was being rebuilt in about 520 B.C. refer to the high priest Joshua and the Davidic king Zerubbabel as "the two anointed ones" (in a sense, they are two "Messiahs", although this name is not used), who are the leaders of the country (Zech. 4.1 ff.). In Zech. 6.11, however, the original text, which must have covered the coronation of Zerubbabel, has been changed into a description of the high priest Joshua. This should be seen in the light of the fact that the Davidic kingship was not restored after the exile. See also Hag. 1.1 ff.; 2.20 ff. and Zech. 3.8 ff.

During the following period, Israel had no king. When the Seleucids assumed power in about 200 B.C. under Antiochus III, the high priest was the

---

66 See section 1.3.1 above.
67 Hultgård, *L'eschatologie*, I, p. 61.
68 Hultgård, *L'eschatatologie*, I, pp. 65 ff.
69 Cf. section 1.2.2 above.

country's supreme leader, or ethnarch.[70] But the Davidic kingship was not forgotten. Both Ecclus. from about 175 B.C. and 1 Macc. from about 100 B.C. refer to it, but clearly give it second priority, after the office of high priest. It says in Ecclus. 44-50 (Heroes of Israel's past):

45.23 Phinehas, son of Eleazar, ranks third in renown for being zealous in reverence towards the Lord, and for standing firm with noble courage when the people defected; by so doing he made expiation for Israel.[71] 24 Therefore a covenant was established with him, assuring him charge of the sanctuary and the people, conferring on him and on his descendants the high-priesthood for ever. 25 As by a covenant with David, son of Jesse of the tribe of Judah, the royal succession should always pass from father to son, so the priestly succession was to pass from Aaron to his descendants.[72]

And similarly, the priest Mattathias says in his valedictory speech to his five sons (1 Macc. 2.49 ff.; the "valedictory speech" as a literary genre recurs in The Testaments of the Twelve Patriarchs):

2.54 Phinehas, our forefather, never flagged in his zeal,[73] and his was the covenant of an everlasting priesthood. ... 57 David was a man of loyalty, and he was granted the throne of everlasting kingdom.[74]

These historical, prophetic and eschatological texts, which together span more than 400 years of Israel's history, leave no room for doubt that during the period of early Judaism, the ideal leaders are still a high priest of Aaron's line and Levi's tribe, and a king of David's line and Judah's tribe. In the light of this tradition, there is really nothing strange in the fact that independently of each other, both the Testaments of the Twelve Patriarchs and the Qumran documents mention two Messiahs, although this may initially appear strange. The idea of a

---

70 Cf. section 1.1.1 above.

71 Num. 25; cf. section 1.2.2 above.

72 Ecclus. 45.23-25.

73 Cf. n. 71! The invocation of Phinehas is characteristic of the pro-Maccabean literature: it apparently serves the purpose of legitimizing the later Maccabean usurpation of the high priest office; cf. n. 74 below.

74 1 Macc. 2.54 ff. The reference to the everlasting *Davidic* kingdom in 1 Macc. – the Maccabean propaganda literature! – is astonishing. It should probably be ascribed to the tradition, which appears to have been firmly established at the time.

Messiah of Levi's tribe and another Messiah of Judah's tribe was characteristic of the period and closely linked to Israel's post-exile history and development.[75]

On these grounds, it must be established that the theme "priest and king" – in this order! – played a central role in the eschatology of early Judaism. This also explains the far-reaching *political* consequences of the Jewish people's expectations of the future in relation to the ruling powers, whether they were Persians, Syrians, Maccabees/Hasmoneans or Romans.

According to Josephus, John the Baptist was imprisoned and executed for *political* reasons.[76] The same probably applies to Jesus; I shall return to this question later in the book. In this context, however, it is more important to bear in mind that the eschatology of early Judaism centred around the expected appearance of the priestly Messiah of Levi's tribe and Aaron's line and the royal Messiah of Judah's tribe and David's line, and that John the Baptist and Jesus represented the priestly and the royal Messiah, for whom Israel was waiting.[77]

---

75 Cf. a Rabbinic text quoted in (Hermann L. Strack and) Paul Billerbeck, *Kommentar zum Neuen Testament aus Talmud und Midrasch*, I, Munich 1926, p. 87: "You sent salvation to that generation (in Egypt) through two saviours only, see Ps. 105.26: "He sent his servant Moses and Aaron whom he had chosen." And also to this generation (in the Messianic time) he sends two who are like those (two): "Send out your light and your truth" Ps. 43.3; "your light" is the prophet Elijah of the house of Aaron [n. 1: Elijah is here identified with Phinehas, who is expected to return as the Cohen Sedek, or high priest of the Messianic time; "the light" is here the symbol of priesthood], of whom it says in Num. 8.2: "When you put the seven lights in position, see that they shed their light forwards;" and "your truth" is the Messiah ben David, see Ps. 132.11: "The Lord has sworn in truth unto David; he will not turn from it." And in Mal. 3.23 it says: "Look, I shall send you the prophet Elijah;" look, that is one of them; and the other: "Here is my servant, whom I uphold" Isa. 42.1." See also section 2.1.2, the passage referred to in n. 9. Concerning Jewish Messianic expectations, see now e.g. J. H. Charlesworth et al., eds., *The Messiah: Developments in Earliest Judaism and Christianity* (The First Princeton Symposium on Judaism and Christian Origins), Minneapolis 1992; John J. Collins, *The Scepter and the Star: The Messiahs of the Dead Sea Scrolls and Other Ancient Literature* (Anchor Bible Reference Library), New York 1995.

76 See § 118 in section 2.3.1 above.

77 In his book *Johannes der Täufer*, 1989, pp. 122-125, Josef Ernst investigates the question of whether John the Baptist and Jesus should – as presumed by a few exegetes – be considered as the priestly and the royal Messiah respectively. He comes to the conclusion that John is not described as a Messianic figure in Lk. 1 (which may be correct), and that even the theory of an expected appearance of two Messiahs of royal and priestly origins is not supported by any historical facts (p. 124). Naturally this critical attitude cannot be

2.4.4 John, not just a "forerunner"

Among the several attempts that have been made to explain the relationship between John the Baptist and Jesus, I have chosen to comment on E.P. Sanders' explanation – not because it is particularly convincing, but because he is one of the few who have an eye for the relationship and recognize the need to explain it. Furthermore, Sanders makes it quite clear that it is impossible to explain the relationship between these two persons without explaining the intentions of Jesus – in other words, the christological problem (cf. section 2.5 below).

Sanders first repudiates the view suggested by others, including Martin Hengel, that Jesus was executed by mistake because both the Romans and Jesus' own disciples had misunderstood his preaching and believed it to be political, whereas it was in fact harmless and should therefore not have led to his crucifixion: if the kingdom of Jesus was not of this world, but was completely apolitical, as Martin Hengel believes, then there was no reason to kill him.[78] (This theory also raises the question of how it is possible, from a theological point of view, to attribute any idea of salvation to the death of Jesus if his execution was a mistake and therefore nothing but a regrettable judicial murder – but that is a different matter.) Hengel argues, however, that the Sadducees stage-managed the crucifixion, and that they alone did *not* misunderstand Jesus any more than they later misunderstood his brother James when they had him stoned to death in A.D. 62 (see chapter 3). Sanders rightly points out that: "There are obviously difficulties with this view. How could the Sadducees have understood what the disciples did not?"[79] Sanders therefore suggests a solution which implies that Jesus "saw his work as bearing on the fate of Israel as a people,"[80] and it is in this context that Sanders discusses the relationship between John the Baptist and Jesus.[81]

John the Baptist had preached conversion and penance with a view to the impending judgment; Jesus did not (cf. the observations below on Matt. 11.16-19 = Lk. 7.31-35). Sanders writes: "It may well be that, in Jesus' view, he [Jesus] did not himself have to do it *all*. Although we all know that we should

---

ignored, but I feel that it expresses a scepticism which is refuted by the Old Testament and Jewish tradition. See Klinghardt, *Gesetz und Volk Gottes*, pp. 69 ff.

78 For information on Hengel's view, see Sanders, *Jesus and Judaism*, 1985, pp. 223 ff.
79 Sanders, ib., p. 225.
80 Sanders, ib., p. 226.
81 Sanders, ib., pp. 227-228.

not follow the Gospels and relegate John to the status of an intentional forerunner of Jesus, we often fail to explore the possibilities inherent in Jesus' positive relationship to John. He may have seen himself as supplementing and thus completing John's work. John had called on Israel to repent and had warned of a coming general judgment, but too few had responded. Jesus then set out to promise inclusion to the most obvious outsiders. It is not that he did not "believe in" repentance and a general judgment, but that he left the basic proclamation of them to his great predecessor. ... His special mission was to promise inclusion in the coming kingdom to the outsiders, the wicked, if they heeded to his call."[82]

There is certainly some truth in these mostly very precise arguments of Sanders, although he himself is aware that the solution as a whole is "obviously speculative".[83] The truth in Sanders' observation lies in the precision with which he places Jesus in relation to John (not the other way round!), and in his suggestion that Jesus supplements or completes the work John had started and been doing. The wrong or "speculative" part of Sanders' solution is his suggestion that 1) John's preaching of penance is directed towards Israel, whereas 2) Jesus invites "the outsiders", "the wicked", to follow him.[84] This point of view makes it impossible to see how Jesus can have supplemented or

---

82 Sanders, ib., p. 227.

83 Sanders, ib., p. 227. In his book *The Historical Figure of Jesus*, 1993, pp. 230-37, Sanders offers a clearer explanation of the same difficulties: "Jesus was conscious of his differences from John, and he commented on them more than once. The prostitutes repented when John preached – not when Jesus preached. John was ascetic; Jesus ate and drank. And Jesus was a friend of tax collectors and sinners – not of former tax collectors and sinners, which is what Zacchaeus was after he met Jesus [Lk. 19.1-10], but of tax collectors and sinners. Jesus, I think, was a good deal more radical than John. Jesus thought that John's call to repent should have been effective, but in fact it was only partially successful. His own style was in any case different; he did not repeat the Baptist's tactics. On the contrary, he ate and drank with the wicked and told them that God especially loved them, and that the kingdom was at hand. Did he hope that they would change their ways? Probably he did. But 'change now or be destroyed' was not his message, it was John's. Jesus' was, 'God loves you'" (p. 233).

84 "Sinners" are not Jews in general, *am ha-ares*; according to Sanders, even the Pharisees did not consider other Jews as "sinners"; cf. Sanders, *Paul and Palestinian Judaism*, 1977, pp. 152-157: "The amme ha'arets"; id., *Jesus and Judaism*, pp. 174-211: "The Sinners". It can hardly be denied that there is a real conflict between Sanders' and Wellhausen's views (see section 1.3.1 above, n. 72). However, Sanders does not mention Wellhausen's work from 1874 on the Pharisees and Sadducees.

completed the work of John the Baptist. In fact, there appears to be no connection, but rather a contradiction, between the work of John and the work of Jesus. Nor does Sanders see John the Baptist and Jesus in the light of the eschatology of early Judaism and its Messianic traditions. In short, Sanders' "solution" is no solution at all.

It is interesting to note that by emphasizing how Jesus "promised inclusion" to "the outsiders" and "the wicked", Sanders really sees Jesus as one who breaks with the traditional "covenantal nomism". In another context, Sanders recognizes that "Jesus ... looked to a new age, and therefore he viewed the institutions of his age as not final, and in that sense not adequate".[85] As we have seen,[86] the covenantal nomism was already broken when John said that God could "make children for Abraham out of these stones," and with the baptism of John, all the existing Jewish institutions were declared insufficient or "not adequate". It is through such an observation, and not through Sanders' definite solution, that it may be possible to perceive a connection or agreement between the preachings of John and Jesus.

2.4.5 What Jesus said about their relationship
Apart from the Gospel of John, which is ambivalent if not even negative in its view of John the Baptist – including the view of him that is reflected in the rendering of the things Jesus said about him[87] – there are, in the Gospels of Matthew and Luke, several statements made by Jesus about John the Baptist which deserve to be mentioned here.

The first of these is difficult or even impossible to understand – also because it is rendered differently by the two synoptists and in different contexts: Matt. 11.12-14 and Lk. 16.16. In Matt. it says: "Since the time of John the Baptist, the kingdom of Heaven [the kingdom of God] has been subjected to violence (Greek: biázetai) and violent men (Greek: hoi biastaí) are taking it by force. For until John, all the prophets <and the law> foretold things to come;

---

85   Sanders, *Jesus and Judaism*, p. 269; see my commentary on this, DTT 51 (1988), p. 110.
86   See section 2.3.3 above.
87   John the Baptist was *not* the light, but just a man (Jn. 1.6-8); John came before Jesus, but ranked below him (1.15); John was *not* the Messiah, *not* Elijah, *not* the Prophet, but just a voice crying in the wilderness (1.20-23); John must become less, Jesus must become greater (3.30); John was just a lamp that burned for a time (5.35). See also Ernst, *Johannes der Täufer*, pp. 186-216: "Johannes der Täufer im vierten Evangelium".

and John is the destined Elijah, if you will but accept it." In Luke it says: "The law and the prophets were until John: since then, the good news of the kingdom of God is proclaimed, and everyone forces (Greek: *biázetai*) a way in." The problem is whether these texts refer to John the Baptist as one of the prophets, and that he therefore belongs to the era *before* the kingdom of God is proclaimed and "taken by force", or whether he belongs to the new era, which, in one sense, he introduces. The assertion that he was Elijah (Matt. 11.14; cf. Mk. 9.11-13 = Matt. 17.10-12) is not mentioned in Lk., which on the other hand seems to consider Jesus himself as a prophet.[88] This unconditionally awards John a position of high rank and importance and certainly seems to indicate that he belongs to the new era, in which the Gospel is being preached. Whatever the case, the words about the kingdom of God being "taken by force" are so obscure that I shall refrain from any attempt at an interpretation.

The other statement made by Jesus which I wish to mention here is much clearer and apparently unambiguous: Matt. 11.16-19 = Lk. 7.31-35. It is related almost identically by both synoptists, and in the same context. It is therefore sufficient to quote the text in Matt.: "How can I describe this generation? They are like children sitting in the marketplace and calling to each other, "We piped for you and you would not dance. We lamented, and you would not mourn." For John came, neither eating nor drinking, and people say, "He is possessed;" the Son of Man [i.e. Jesus himself][89] came, eating and drinking, and they say, "Look at him! A glutton and a drinker, a friend of tax-collectors and sinners!"" With these words, Jesus creates a graphic, almost three-dimensional image of John the Baptist and himself which seems to represent them as an ascetic and an epicure respectively, or at least as opposites. At the same time, however, it is clear that there is a link between them, a task they both have to perform for the sake of the people. The meaning is that they are both rejected because people refuse to listen to them.

It is important to note that the rejection of both John the Baptist and Jesus which is expressed in these words applies only to those who *did* reject them:

---

88 Cf. Johnson, *The purpose of the Biblical Genealogies*, 1969, pp. 240-252: "Jesus as Prophet".

89 The expression "the Son of Man" is *not* a title, and certainly not another name for Messiah, but – at least in this context – simply a paraphrase for Jesus. See Mogens Müller, *Der Ausdruck "Menschensohn" in den Evangelien. Voraussetzungen und Bedeutung* (Acta Theologica Danica, XVII), Leiden 1984.

"the children", i.e. Israel, not those who accepted them. Moreover, there is hardly any reason to date the words to a (late) phase in the work of Jesus, when he is supposed to have admitted both John the Baptist's and his own defeat; this would be a psychologization which the words do not justify, and which would be more in line with the old life-of-Jesus research from the time before Wrede. On the contrary, the words about John who neither eats nor drinks, and Jesus who eats and drinks, are meant to characterize these two persons and the relationship between them as Jesus saw it, and people's negative reaction is precisely the reaction of those who rejected them both.

It is also interesting to note that the reference to "children" who call to other "children" implies that Jesus does not place John the Baptist and himself in a position above or apart from the people, but on an equal footing with the people and as part of them.

But should the contrast between "the lamenter" and the "piper" really be interpreted as a contrast between the ascetic and the epicure? It seems to give no meaning. John was hardly an ascetic in the sense that he saw asceticism as an object in itself – it is more likely that his asceticism was a reaction against the luxury of the royal family (Matt. 11.7-8 = Lk. 7.24-25).[90] The idea of Jesus as an epicure who thought of nothing but himself is simply absurd. On the other hand, the character sketch is perfectly in line with the traditional priest-and-king theme discussed above: here are the priest and the king, the ideal leaders of Israel – but the majority of the people reject them.

This emphasizes once more the political and social character of the relationship and its critical attitude towards society, and shows how deeply it is rooted in Israel's history.

2.5 Christological problematics

Bibliography

Ernst Käsemann: Das Problem des historischen Jesus, 1954 – see section 2.2 above.
Günther Bornkamm: *Jesus von Nazareth* (Urban-Bücher, 19), Stuttgart 1956, 8th ed. 1968 = *Jesus of Nazareth*, London 1960.

---

90   Cf. Theißen: see the passage referred to in n. 45, section 2.3.2 above.

Oscar Cullmann: *Die Christologie des Neuen Testaments*, first published in 1957, 3rd rev. ed., Tübingen 1963 = *The Christology of the New Testament*, Revised Edition, Philadelphia 1963.

Ferdinand Hahn: *Christologische Hoheitstitel. Ihre Geschichte im frühen Christentum* (Forschungen zur Religion und Literatur des Alten und Neuen Testaments, 83), first published in 1963, 3rd ed., Göttingen 1966.

Martin Hengel: Christology and New Testament Chronology. A Problem in the History of Earliest Christianity, first published in German in 1972, in: id., *Between Jesus and Paul. Studies in the Earliest History of Christianity*, London 1983, pp. 30-47.

Ragnar Leivestad: *Hvem ville Jesus være?* Oslo 1982.

E.P. Sanders: *Jesus and Judaism*, 1985 – see section 1.3 above.

P.M. Casey: *From Jewish Prophet to Gentile God. The Origins and Development of New Testament Christology* (The Edward Cadbury Lectures at the University of Birmingham, 1985-86), Cambridge – Louisville (Kentucky) 1991, pp. 57-77: "Jesus of Nazareth".

Villy Sørensen: *Jesus og Kristus*, Copenhagen 1992.

2.5.1 The problems of modern research

It is important to keep in mind that the present exercise is an attempt to understand Jesus in the light of his own time and the social and political conditions that existed during the era of early Judaism, and not in the light of *later* dogmatic and ecclesiastical doctrines about Jesus as Christ, Son of God – doctrines which have been used in an unscholarly and anachronistic way to create a retrospective image of Jesus and his work. Such an attempt cannot be made without thorough studies and critical assessments of the branch of modern New Testament theology called christology.

During the period after the publication of Wrede's book about the "Messianic Secret" in 1901, the christological problems in the New Testament were often seen from a chronological point of view. This was a natural consequence of the theory of the "Messianic Secret", according to which neither the historical Jesus himself nor his disciples believed him to be Messiah. In fact, this theory served to explain how the earliest congregations could believe in Jesus as Messiah at a time when there was still evidence that Jesus himself was not Messiah. The explanation was that Jesus did not reveal his identity as Messiah or Christ until his resurrection – until this point, he had kept his true identity secret.

At the turn of the century, the Religio-Historical School, which counted Wrede, Bousset and Gunkel among its adherents,[91] propounded the theory of the "Messianic secret" in the form that became generally known during the following decades through the work of Bultmann and others, and deservedly acquired great influence on New Testament exegesis and theology. In 1913 – after Wrede! – Bousset published his book *Kyrios Christos*, in which christology is perceived as a religio-historical phenomenon that first appeared in Hellenistic, Greek-speaking congregations when they began to worship the Lord Christ as a cult hero and, in fact, established a completely new religion.[92] This also explains why one of the main sections of Rudolf Bultmann's *Theologie des Neuen Testaments* is a description of the Hellenistic congregation's kerygma as it was before and during the time of Paul.[93] In 1922, Holger Mosbech, who had joined the Religio-Historical School and become acquainted with Bousset in Göttingen, expressed the same view of Christology in two articles published in Danish encyclopedias. They attracted considerable attention among theologians as well as laymen due to their contents and wide propagation.[94] In one of these articles he writes:

[Historical research] has to undertake the task of investigating the existing sources, partly in order to provide a biography of Jesus which in every respect remains within the limits of the view that he was a man like other men, one of the giants of humanity,

---

91   For information on the Religio-Historical School established at the faculty of theology in Göttingen (not to be confused with the Liberal Theological School established in Berlin under Adolf Harnack), see Gerd Lüdemann, Die Religionsgeschichtliche Schule, in: Bernd Moeller, ed., *Theologie in Göttingen. Eine Vorlesungsreihe* (Göttinger Universitätsschriften, Serie A: Schriften/Band 1), Göttingen 1987, pp. 325-361; Gerd Lüdemann/Martin Schröder, eds., *Die Religionsgeschichtliche Schule in Göttingen. Eine Dokumentation,* Göttingen 1987.

92   Wilhelm Bousset, *Kyrios Christos. Geschichte des Christusglaubens von den Anfängen des Christentums bis Irenäus,* first published in 1913, 5th ed. (with preface by Rudolf Bultmann), Göttingen 1965.

93   Rudolf Bultmann, *Theologie des Neuen Testaments,* 2nd ed., Tübingen 1954, §§ 9-15: "Das Kerygma der hellenistischen Gemeinde vor und neben Paulus".

94   Holger Mosbech, art. "Jesus Kristus", in: *Salmonsens Konversationsleksikon,* 2nd ed., vol. XIII, Copenhagen 1922, pp. 76-86; and in *Hagerups illustrerede Konversationsleksikon,* 3rd ed., vol. V, Copenhagen 1922, pp. 393-395. See my commentary in: Kirkehistoriske samlinger 1979, pp. 140-141.

a religious genius, but still only a man; but also to explain how it could happen that this man was honoured and worshipped as a deity a relatively short time after his death.[95]

Either you can try to prove that Jesus as a person became the object of a number of supernatural ideas that were characteristic of his time, especially ideas connected with mystic redeemer deities ...; or you may assume that during his life on earth, Jesus himself claimed and was believed to be more than a man; but from a liberal point of view it will then be very difficult to avoid coming to the conclusion that he was a deranged fanatic.[96]

Assuming that Jesus was nothing but a man, whom both Paul and the Evangelists nevertheless considered as a divine being, the question remains: how could it happen that a mortal man was worshipped as a god only twenty or thirty years after this death, or perhaps even earlier?[97]

So from this point of view, christology – the doctrine about Jesus as Christ – turns into a *chronological* problem: Jesus himself was not Messiah (or Christ in Greek), but very soon the earliest congregations came to believe that he was Messiah, and this happened in such a short time that it constitutes a chronological problem which historians of religion or psychologists must try to solve.

Ferdinand Hahn was confronted with the same problem in his book *Christologische Hoheitstitel*, which was published in 1963, and Martin Hengel took it up again in 1972 when he wrote his treatise about Christology and New Testament Chronology, in which he discusses "the enormously rapid christological development of the first years."[98] However, this particular branch of research now seems to have come to a dead end. Although some of the representatives of this christology can accept that certain features of early Judaism and the historical Jesus may have been of vital importance to the subsequent christological development, the christological problem still remains a chronological problem: there was simply not enough time for the development

---

95 Mosbech, in *Salmonsen*, XIII, p. 77.
96 Mosbech, ib., p. 79; the reference to the "liberal point of view" should be understood in the light of Mosbech's association with the Liberal Theology – he had met Harnack in Berlin.
97 Mosbech, ib., p. 79.
98 Hengel, *Between Jesus and Paul*, p. 42. Cullmann's *Christologie* represents a strange apologia for the traditional ecclesiastical christology; but New Testament christology needs no apologia, and I shall therefore refrain from any further comments on this.

of such a christology. So the Religio-Historical School failed in its attempt to explain the origins of christology.

Another and quite different explanation was inspired by the emergence of the Dialectic Theology shortly after the First World War. In Denmark, it was represented by Bent Noack and others. In 1956, he published an article about the Messiah image in the Gospel of John and its christology, in which he claims that "messianology" and "christology" are two different phenomena which have little in common.[99] According to this distinction, the "Messiah image", including any Messianic concepts, is a phenomenon that belongs in early Judaism and reflects the Jews' expectations of the Messianic king they were waiting for and their ideas of his nature, origins and work, whereas christology is a Christian concept based on various Christian descriptions of the person of Jesus Christ, his origins, nature and work.[100] In short, messianology is a Jewish doctrine concerning the Jewish expectations of Messiah, while christology is a Christian doctrine concerning Jesus Christ.

However, such a distinction between messianology and christology does not take account of the fact that the words "Messiah" and "Christ" (Greek: *christós*) mean the same thing: "the Anointed One". Moreover, the distinction creates an immense distance between Judaism and Christianity – a distance which must be regarded as unhistorical, since we know that Christianity originated from Judaism itself and can only be understood in the light of Israel's history. Moreover, the distinction between messianology and christology seems to harbour a cryptic Marcionism, which can be ascribed to the German theological tradition, or more specifically Liberal Theology, the Religio-Historical School and Dialectic Theology, and which has certain anti-Semitic characteristics as well as suggestions of a docetic christology with gnostic features.[101] It was

---

99 Bent Noack, Johannesevangeliets messiasbillede og dets kristologi, Dansk Teologisk Tidsskrift 19 (1956), pp. 129-155; see also my commentary in: *Udenfor og indenfor. Sociale og økonomiske aspekter i den ældste kristendom* (Tekst & Tolkning, 5), Copenhagen 1974, pp. 99-100.

100 Noack, DTT 19 (1956), p. 129.

101 In 1920, the liberal theologian Adolf Harnack published his famous book about the heretic Marcion: *Marcion. Das Evangelium vom fremden Gott*, 2nd ed., Leipzig 1924 (see section 4.5 below), p. 217, in which he wrote: "the rejection of the Old Testament in the second century [ascribed to Marcion] was a mistake which the great church rightly avoided; to maintain it in the sixteenth century [during the Reformation] was a fate from which the Reformation was not yet able to escape; but still to preserve it in Protestantism

reasonable to expect that the revival of the life-of-Jesus research in 1954 would result in a new approach to the christological problem, but this did not happen. On the contrary, the approach to the problem continued to follow the old course that was originally set by the Religio-Historical School. This is confirmed by Günther Bornkamm's book on Jesus of 1956 and – in spite of all the differences between them – E.P. Sanders' book of 1985. As early as in 1926, Rudolf Bultmann himself wrote in the introduction to his book on Jesus:

> Personally I am of the opinion that Jesus himself did not believe that he was Messiah, ... In the following presentation, however, I shall not discuss this question at all, not only because nothing definite can be said about it, but mainly because I consider it an irrelevant question.[102]

The same applies to his pupil Bornkamm, who only discusses "the Messianic question" in chapter VIII of his Jesus book and answers it negatively: Jesus used no Messianic names for himself; the early church alone conferred the Messianic dignity on him after his resurrection, which also inspired them to believe that he was everything the Messianic titles implied.[103]

Sanders' approach to the problem is somewhat different: it is based on the idea that Jesus proclaimed a new kingdom in which his disciples would be given central positions, so it was an obvious conclusion that Jesus himself was a king – or rather a viceroy under the true king, God himself. "If Jesus taught his disciples that there would be a kingdom and that *they* would have a role in it, he certainly, at least by implication, gave himself a role also. "Messiah" will do perfectly well for the person who is superior to the judges of Israel, even if he was not a warrior."[104] But then he also says: "I do not doubt that ... he was

---

as a canonical document since the nineteenth century is the consequence of a religious and ecclesiastical crippling" (p. 134 in *Marcion. The Gospel of the Alien God*, 1990). Rudolf Bultmann was rightly accused of being a (modern) docetist: cf. Regin Prenter, *Skabelse og genløsning. Dogmatik*, III, Copenhagen 1953, pp. 375-381; this is due to Bultmann's distinction between Judaism and Christianity: to him, the historical Jesus was a Jewish rabbi and unimportant from a theological point of view, whereas the death and resurrection of Christ is the central point in Christianity and Christian theology.

102 Rudolf Bultmann, *Jesus* (first published in 1926 in a series called "Die Unsterblichen. Die geistigen Heroen der Menschheit in ihrem Leben und Wirken"!), Tübingen 1951, p. 12.

103 Bornkamm, *Jesus von Nazareth*, pp. 155-163.

104 Sanders, *Jesus and Judaism*, p. 234.

unique; in some way or other everyone is unique. ... What is unique is the result. But, again, we cannot know that the result springs from the uniqueness of the historical Jesus."[105] So the result is still the same.

But what does Ernst Käsemann himself have to say? After all, he was the one who in 1954 reopened the discussion about the historical Jesus and rightly pointed out that since the evangelists wrote about the historical Jesus, it was clearly not their intention to let a myth take the place of history, nor to allow a celestial being to supplant Jesus of Nazareth.[106] And at least Käsemann makes the following observation under the heading of "The distinctive element in the mission of Jesus": "The only category which does justice to his claim (quite independently of whether he used it himself and required it of others) is that in which his disciples themselves placed him – namely, that of the Messiah."[107]

But is this cautious and basically non-committal answer really worthy of this important issue? Does it give the issue its proper weight?

2.5.2 Jesus as Christ and Messiah

Perhaps the time has come for theology and New Testament exegesis to finally acknowledge the fact that the man the earliest congregation believed to be Christ saw himself as Messiah, *christós*, "the Anointed One", and was regarded as such by his disciples. Any other theory which in one way or another seeks to avoid this identification leads to nothing but confusion.

The old life-of-Jesus research with its studies of the psychological life of Jesus and his Messianic "self-awareness" has been abandoned, and rightly so. Instead, research has – in as far as it has approached the question of the historical Jesus – concentrated on the preaching of Jesus (cf. Bultmann and Bornkamm) or on his work (cf. E.P. Sanders), in short, *either* the things Jesus said *or* the things he did. Characteristically, the question of Jesus as a person has been left out of the debate – presumably due to a general feeling that this

---

105 Sanders, ib., p. 240.
106 Käsemann, *Exeg. Versuche u. Besinnungen*, I, p. 196 (*Essays on New Testament Themes*, p. 25): "For if primitive Christianity identifies the humiliated with the exalted Lord, in so doing it is confessing that, in its presentation of his story, it is incapable of abstracting from its faith. At the same time, however, it is also making it clear that it is not minded to allow myth to take the place of history nor a heavenly being to take the place of the Man of Nazareth."
107 Käsemann, ib., p. 206 (*Essays on New Testament Themes*, p. 38).

question was too reminiscent of the old life-of-Jesus research and its interest in the psychology of Jesus – a question which must remain unanswered for many good reasons.

But the question of Jesus as a person is not a psychological question; it is a question of his functions, of who he wanted to be.[108] Or, to be more explicit, the question of Jesus as a person is not an uninteresting question of secondary importance (as Bultmann and Bornkamm in particular maintained); it is nothing less than the christological question itself, which no theologian or exegete can afford to ignore.

In fact, it was the exact question which Jesus himself asked his disciples at Caesarea Philippi in Northern Palestine:[109] "And you, who do you say I am?" (Mk. 8.27-33 = Matt. 16.13-23 = Lk. 9.18-22), and Peter replied on behalf of the disciples: "You are the Anointed One (Greek: *christós*)" (Mk. 8.29), "You are the Anointed One, the Son of the living God" (Matt. 16.16), or "You are God's Anointed" (Lk. 9.21). These words can hardly be understood except in the sense of the words of the Old Testament psalm about "the Lord (i.e. God) and his Anointed" (Ps. 2.2), and "You are my son, this day I became your father" (Ps. 2.7).

2.6 Jesus as Messiah (the reason for the trial and death of Jesus)

Bibliography

Albert Schweitzer: *Geschichte der Leben-Jesu-Forschung*, 6th ed. 1951 (see section 2 above), pp. 390-443: "Die Lösung der konsequenten Eschatologie".
Josef Blinzler: *Der Prozeß Jesu. Das jüdische und das römische Gerichtsverfahren gegen Jesus Christus auf Grund der ältesten Zeugnisse dargestellt und bearbeitet*, 3rd ed. Regensburg 1960, 4th ed. 1969.
Nils Alstrup Dahl: Der gekreuzigte Messias, in: Ristow/Matthiae, eds., *Der historische Jesus und der kerygmatische Christus*, 1961 (see section 2.2 above), pp. 149-169;

---

108 Cf. Leivestad, *Hvem ville Jesus være?* 1982.
109 This location was not chosen at random: during the era of the old northern kingdom, Jeroboam I built a shrine in Dan (1 Kgs. 12.28 ff.), and the battle of Paneas was fought there (see section 1.1.1 above). See also Rainer Riesner, section 2.3.1 above; and George W.E. Nickelsburg, Enoch, Levi, and Peter: Recipients of Revelation in Upper Galilee, Journal of Biblical Literature 100 (1981), pp. 575-600. The conversion of Paul took place in the same area, on the road to Damascus.

also in English: The Crucified Messiah, in: Nils A. Dahl: *Jesus the Christ* (see section 2.2 above), 1991, pp. 27-47.

Olof Linton: Processen mod Jesus. Kilder, kildevurdering og teorier i den nyere debat, Dansk Teologisk Tidsskrift 25 (1962), pp. 1-35.

E.P. Sanders: *Jesus and Judaism*, 1985 (see section 1.3), pp. 294-318: "The Death of Jesus".

Christopher Rowland: *Christian Origins*, 1985 (see section 1 above), pp. 164-174: "The Arrest and Trial of Jesus"; pp 174-187: "Jesus' Personal Claim".

2.6.1 The crucified Messiah

The Norwegian New Testament exegete Nils Alstrup Dahl is also aware of the fact that no substantial progress has been made even after the debate on the historical Jesus was reopened in 1954 (or, to be precise, in 1953, when Dahl published his article concerning the historical Jesus) and that this debate remains firmly embedded in questions of method without making much headway: "From time to time the great and fundamental questions must be asked; in this way blind alleys are exposed, false questions and alternatives are unmasked, and new ways are opened for further research. But it is seldom fruitful to dwell too long on discussion of methodology and principles. It was necessary and very useful that, in the last decade, the problem of the historical Jesus was raised anew [a reference to Käsemann, 1954]. Now we would do better to turn again to work with specific questions."[110]

Dahl also shares my opinion that the lack of progress should be ascribed to the risk of repeating the mistakes of the old psychologizing life-of-Jesus research. This reluctance is not justified, however, considering the important problems that remain unsolved: "... in reality little has been done with these questions in the last decades. This is a result of misgivings about the nineteenth-century biographies of Jesus but is not a legitimate consequence of the reaction against them."[111]

Dahl agrees with Käsemann that it is impossible to reconstruct either the external or the internal life of Jesus, but he rightly points out: "But from this it does not follow that historical questions about causal relationships neither can nor ought to be asked at all. There is certainly some purpose in asking about the

---

110 Dahl, in: *Der historische Jesus*, p. 151 *(Jesus the Christ*, p. 29).
111 Dahl, ib., p. 157 *(Jesus the Christ*, p. 35).

causes and effects of Jesus' death; moreover, questions must be asked, whether we find the task pleasant or not."[112]

With these ideas in mind, Dahl energetically throws himself into the task of answering one specific question: the meaning and justification of the assertion that Jesus was executed as Messiah.

2.6.2 Wrede or Schweitzer?

In order to understand Dahl's investigation, it is important to keep in mind that he deliberately goes back into the history of research and rightly points out – in Schweitzer's own words – that when the old life-of-Jesus research came to an end at the turn of the century, it was replaced by a new problem with two alternative solutions, one suggested by William Wrede (1859-1907), and the other by Albert Schweitzer (1875-1965). In the book in which he presented and explained his own point of view, Schweitzer also discussed Wrede's book of 1901 about the "Messianic Secret".[113]

Albert Schweitzer belonged neither to the Liberal nor to the Religio-Historical School, but established his own School of Consistent Eschatology, although this was inspired by Johannes Weiß' *Die Predigt Jesu vom Reiche Gottes*, 1892. Nevertheless, the only part of the heritage from Schweitzer which the next generation of New Testament scholars could accept was the eschatological problem: the fact that God's kingdom had failed to materialize in the way it was expected to appear. Otherwise, they chose to ignore Schweitzer's demonstration of the main problem concerning the question of the historical Jesus: the non-Messianic nature of Jesus' public work versus his Messiahship

---

112 Dahl, ib., p. 165 *(Jesus the Christ*, p. 42).
113 At the same time as Wrede published his book in 1901, Schweitzer published his own *Das Messianitäts- und Leidensgeheimnis. Eine Skizze des Lebens Jesu* (Das Abendmahl im Zusammenhang mit dem Leben Jesu und der Geschichte des Urchristentums, 2nd vol.), Tübingen – Leipzig 1901. A few years later, Schweitzer himself wrote a summary of this and a discussion with Wrede in: *Geschichte der Leben-Jesu-Forschung* (1st ed. published in 1906 under the title *Von Reimarus zu Wrede. Eine Geschichte der Leben-Jesu-Forschung*), 2nd ed. 1913, pp. 368-443: "Die Kritik der modern-historischen Anschauung durch Wrede und die konsequente Eschatologie" (pp. 368-375 = English translation, pp. 328-395: "Throughgoing Scepticism and throughgoing Eschatology"), "Darstellung und Kritik der Konstruktion Wredes" (pp. 376-389), and "Die Lösung der konsequenten Eschatologie" (pp. 390-443). In the present context, I refer to Schweitzer's summary and discussion.

according to the existing sources, i.e. the texts of the New Testament. Dahl writes: "Recent research has unjustly taken from Schweitzer's work only the problem of eschatology and the "delay of the parousia" and has ignored the chief problem with regard to Jesus' life, namely, the problem of the non-Messianic character of Jesus' public ministry in relation to his Messiahship affirmed by the sources."[114]

In fact, Schweitzer himself defined the new problem that had replaced the old life-of-Jesus research when he pointed out that the apparent contradiction between the non-Messianic character of Jesus' public work and the unquestionable Messiahship which the New Testament sources conferred on him, was due *either* to the contemporary Jewish Messiah tradition (Schweitzer's own theory) *or* to the interpretation of Mark the Evangelist (Wrede's theory).[115] Schweitzer wrote: "The inconsistency between the public life of Jesus and His Messianic claim lies either in the nature of the Jewish Messianic conception, or in the representation of the Evangelist. There is, on the one hand, the eschatological solution, ... and there is, on the other hand, the literary solution, ... *Tertium non datur.*"[116]

So the situation is this: The unique nature of Jesus' Messiahship can be understood on the basis of the eschatology of early Judaism, as Schweitzer himself maintained. The alternative solution is that the belief in Jesus as Christ first appeared in the Greek, Hellenistic world, which was the theory of the Religio-Historical School. (At the beginning of the century, Palestinian Judaism had not been discovered to be Hellenistic itself.)

In other words: Either "the Messianic Secret" belongs historically to the historical Jesus himself (Schweitzer), or "the Messianic Secret" – and christology itself – are theological and literary products of the earliest Christianity (Wrede).

---

114 Dahl, in: *Der hist. Jesus*, p. 158 (*Jesus the Christ*, p. 35).

115 It is not quite correct to say that Wrede maintained that "the theory of the Messianic secret" was the *literary* solution of Mark the Evangelist; Wrede himself pointed out that "the theory" was already part of the tradition before Mk. was written and could therefore not be ascribed to the Evangelist. In the present context, however, this detail is not very important.

116 Schweitzer, *Gesch.*, p. 375 (*The Quest of the Historical Jesus*, p. 335); cf. the quotation in Dahl, *Der hist. Jesus*, p. 158 (*Jesus the Christ*, p. 35).

111

2.6.3 Consistent Eschatology

In the view of Albert Schweitzer,[117] Jesus was really of royal, Davidic descent. He was Messiah. Of course his Messiahship cannot be not inferred from his Davidic descent alone, but only when this is seen in the light of early Jewish eschatology, which predicted the coming of God's kingdom and the glorification of Messiah (cf. 1 Cor. 15.51-52). But the time had not yet come to reveal that Jesus was Messiah. God's kingdom would not come until enough people believed in the prediction of its imminence, so Jesus sent his disciples out with instructions to spread the message that God's kingdom was about to come (Matt. 10.5 ff.) With the words of Matt. 10.23: "... before you have gone through all the towns of Israel, the Son of Man [i.e. Jesus himself in a transformed shape] will have come", Jesus explained to his disciples that he did not expect them to come back during the time of the present world, but only when God's kingdom had come, and then as Jesus' co-regents in this new kingdom of God – which shows how quickly it was all supposed to happen.

The prediction that God's kingdom was near failed to come true, however, and the disciples returned safe and sound from their travels. Then Jesus saw that *he* must go alone through suffering and death to prepare the way for the kingdom of God. Jesus explained this at Caesarea Philippi, where his disciples, with Peter as their spokesman, had come to believe that Jesus was Messiah. With this object in mind – to force God's kingdom to come through his own suffering and death – Jesus went up to Jerusalem with his disciples. In short glimpses he allowed his Messiahship to reveal itself, for instance when he entered Jerusalem, but people did not really understand what it meant. During the interrogation before the high priest, the crucial question was asked: "Are you the Messiah, the Son of the Blessed One?" (Mk. 14.61), and Jesus confirmed this. How did the high priest know that Jesus was Messiah? Schweitzer's famous answer was: The high priest knew this from Judas' betrayal.

In his own view, Albert Schweitzer's historical or eschatological solution was the only alternative to William Wrede's "literary" solution to the problem of Jesus' Messiahship. *Tertium non datur*, as he wrote. Admittedly, there are several questionable points in Schweitzer's explanation. Above all, Schweitzer himself, who ought to have known better, made the fundamental error of writing

---

117 See Schweitzer, *Gesch.*, pp. 390-443, "Die Lösung der konsequenten Eschatologie".

about the external and internal life of Jesus. Still, he is quite clear on one important point: Jesus was of royal, Davidic descent and believed himself to be the Messiah firmly rooted in the eschatology of early Judaism. This view represents an absolute difference between Schweitzer and Wrede. The question remains whether this difference also proves that we are dealing with two alternative solutions.

2.6.4 The royal Davidic descent of Jesus

In this context, it is also relevant to note that Albert Schweitzer is one of the very few New Testament exegetes who believed in the royal Davidic descent of Jesus – not that this belief in itself has any value as evidence (only the texts themselves can have this) but because he drew attention to facts which might otherwise have been forgotten.

As we know, Jesus' royal and Davidic descent is described in the genealogies in Matt. 1.1-17 and Lk. 3.23-38 (cf. 2.4) and confirmed by Paul in Rom. 1.3. Whatever else may be said on this subject, the fact that he was the first-born remains undisputed. Schweitzer writes: "There is no reason to doubt the two first Gospels[118] and Paul on this subject. The fact that the Davidic genealogies in Matthew (1.1-17) and Luke (3.23-38) were constructed later and cannot be regarded as authentic does not disprove the royal descent of Jesus' family. With Zerubbabel, a branch of the house of David had returned from exile. His role as a political leader, which inspired the Messianic hopes expressed by the prophets Haggai (2) and Zechariah (3 and 4), soon came to an end. Nevertheless, it is inconceivable that his descendants would forget their ancestry. Whether they were also able to prove it through a well-established genealogy is another question."[119]

Furthermore, Schweitzer also mentions Hegesippus' well-known reference to an event involving two relatives of Jesus, both descendants of his brother

---

118 See for instance Matt. 3.16-17 and Mk. 1.10-11, which both describe the baptism of Jesus and the revelation that told him that he was Messiah – according to Schweitzer.

119 Schweitzer, *Gesch.*, pp. 393-394. Cf. Cullmann, *Christologie*, pp. 128 ff. (*Christology*, pp. 127 ff.). For further information on the genealogies in Matt. and Lk., see Johnson, *Biblical Genealogies*, 1969 (cf. section 2.4 above), pp. 139-228: "The Genealogy of Jesus in Matthew", and pp. 229-252: "The Genealogy of Jesus in Luke". Regarding the relationship between the high priest Joshua and the king Zerubbabel (cf. Lk. 3.27!), see section 2.4.3 above.

Judas (Mk. 6.3), who were interrogated by the emperor Domitian (A.D. 81-96) about the rumours of their alleged political claims.[120] Contrary to the view of Schweitzer, Hegesippus' description of this event shows that the Roman rulers did not regard royal descent as a politically harmless matter.

Finally, Julius Wellhausen made an interesting observation which deserves to be mentioned in this context. It refers to a passage in Josephus, Ant. Jud. XVII, 41-45 (chapter 2.4) concerning the Pharisees and their Messianic belief: Towards the end of the reign of Herod the Great (37-4 B.C.), the Pharisees had gained influence at his court, especially with his brother Pheroras, whom Herod had made tetrarch of Perea, east of Jordan. The Pharisees predicted that God would deprive Herod the Great and his descendants of their royal power and give it to Pheroras and his children, and they informed not only Pheroras and his wife of this, but also members of Herod's court. Furthermore, they told a eunuch named Bagoas, who belonged to Herod's staff, that the people's future king would one day call him Father and Benefactor and also make him able to marry and have children – this seems to be a Messianic interpretation of Isa. 56.2-5 concerning the "barren tree". In his rage, Herod ordered the guilty to be executed, not only the Pharisees and Bagoas, but all members of his household who had listened to the Pharisees (Ant. Jud. XVII, 44). Wellhausen's conclusion is: "The Pharisees were expecting Messiah to come soon, before the death of Herod. ... It is the Messianic movement which the Pharisees, assisted by women and courtiers, bring into the palace of the usurper of David's throne, and the suspicious old man [i.e. Herod the Great] is so frightened that he kills everybody in his house who has heard what the Pharisees said. Cf. Matt. 2 [the slaughter of the innocents]."[121]

2.6.5 A third point of view?

Nils Alstrup Dahl refuses to accept that there is no other solution to the Messianic problem than the alternatives which seem to have constituted a barrier to any real progress in research ever since the time of Wrede and

---

120 Schweitzer, *Gesch.*, p. 395. Hegesippus' description of this event is found in Eusebius, Hist. eccl. III, 19-20; see also section 3.2.5 below.
121 Wellhausen, *Pharisäer u. Sadducäer*, 1874, pp. 25-26. See also Schürer, *History*, II, 1979, p. 505.

Schweitzer.[122] He maintains that there is a third point of view, and that it offers a solution based on facts, not conjecture.

Dahl is referring to the following facts: a) the inscription on the cross, "The King of the Jews", and b) the New Testament's general use of the name Christ, which is inseparably linked to the name of Jesus.

In Dahl's view, these two facts prove two things: 1) that Jesus was really crucified as the king of the Jews, and that this historical fact had a decisive influence on the formulation of the first Christian dogma: Jesus is Messiah; and 2) that the belief in Jesus as Messiah does not represent a "re-Judaization" of Jesus himself and his preaching; on the contrary, it represents a fundamental, radical Christianization of the Jewish Messiah title: "First, that Jesus was crucified as King of the Jews is not a dogmatic motif that has become historicized in the passion narratives; precisely to the contrary, it is a historical fact that became centrally important for the formulation of the first Christian dogma: Jesus is the Messiah. Second, the confession of Jesus as the Messiah is not to be understood as a "re-Judaizing" of the preaching and person of Jesus but, on the contrary, as a thorough, radical Christianizing of the Jewish title of Messiah."[123]

However, Dahl is rather evasive in his reply to the question of why Jesus was crucified as Messiah. Jesus and his preaching *might* have encouraged both his adherents and his opponents to raise the question of whether he wanted to be Messiah, and his personal authority would have made this question seem quite natural and understandable. But according to Dahl, it must have been his opponents who made a vital issue out of this question and turned it into a matter of life or death for him. "The inscription of charge presupposes that Jesus was accused before Pilate on the ground that he made a royal-messianic claim. If so, one may further infer that Jesus, confronted with the charge that he thought himself to be the Messiah, accepted the accuracy of the charge by his silence, if not in any other way."[124] And: "The claim to be the Messiah was thus extorted from Jesus. He did not raise it on his own initiative – at least not expressly and directly. However, before the accusation made in the face of impending death,

---

122 Dahl, in: *Der historische Jesus*, p. 158 (*Jesus the Christ*, p. 35): "Contemporary research [1961!] has scarcely gone beyond these alternatives."
123 Dahl, ib., p. 163 (*Jesus the Christ*, p. 40).
124 Dahl, ib., p. 166 (*Jesus the Christ*, p. 43).

he did not deny he was the Messiah."[125] And finally: "It is quite probable that the title "Messiah" was first brought forth as an expression of false expectation, as an accusation and as a mockery of Jesus. Only later, after the appearance of the risen Lord, was it taken up as a unifying expression of confession and preaching."[126]

Through his suggested third solution, Dahl attempts to circumvent Schweitzer's alternatives by maintaining that although Jesus himself, in all the things he said and did, never specifically claimed to be Messiah, he was nevertheless crucified as Messiah. The fact that he did not reject the accusation when it was made against him became decisive in the preaching of Christianity: the end of the life of Jesus became the essence of Christianity. Both the historical Jesus and the proclaimed Christ are the crucified Messiah.[127]

Is Nils Alstrup Dahl's theory, which has been adopted by several others,[128] really a solution which will – as he claims – make it possible to break through the barrier of the alternatives formulated by Albert Schweitzer?

Unfortunately the answer is No.

In the first place, Dahl still faces precisely the same chronological difficulty regarding christology as other New Testament exegetes have met when trying to avoid Schweitzer's eschatological theory: there was not enough time for the formation of a christology, although the existence of such a christology is an established fact (see section 2.5.1 above). Dahl himself admits that "... *from the beginnings of Greek-speaking Christianity (within a few years of the crucifixion)*, the name "Christ" as applied to Jesus [the fact that Jesus was called Christ, Messiah] must have been firmly established. This presupposed that Jesus was *already* designated "the Messiah" and "Jesus the Messiah" *in Aramaic-speaking regions.*"[129] In 1972 – after Dahl – Martin Hengel faces the same problem.[130] Generally speaking, both Dahl's and Hengel's comments on

---

125 Dahl, ib., p. 167 (*Jesus the Christ*, p. 43).
126 Dahl, ib., p. 168 (*Jesus the Christ,* p. 44).
127 Cf. Dahl, ib., pp. 167-168 (*Jesus the Christ*, pp. 43-44).
128 E.g. Hengel, *Between Jesus and Paul*, 1983, p. 36 and n. 34 on p. 162; Sanders, *Jesus and Judaism*, 1985, p. 406, n. 2. It is interesting to note how much – even in detail – Sanders' view corresponds with Dahl's, even when Sanders does not mention it specifically: Sanders, ib., pp. 294 ff.: "The Death of Jesus".
129 Dahl, in: *Der hist. Jesus*, pp. 160-161 (*Jesus the Christ*, pp. 37-38 – my italics).
130 See n. 98 above.

Aramaic- and Greek-speaking Christians, which are inspired by hypothetical ideas based on the passage concerning Hellenists and Hebrews in Acts 6.1 ff., are far from convincing – I shall return to this later in the book.[131] Nor is it obvious that the belief in the resurrection of Jesus must necessarily change into a belief in the resurrection of the crucified *Messiah*, just because he had been crucified as Messiah, and only because of this, as Dahl maintains.[132]

Secondly, it is impossible to understand, from Dahl's description and his own point of view, why Jesus was crucified as Messiah. According to Dahl, Jesus had not said in so many words that he was Messiah, and Dahl maintains that the confession at Caesarea Philippi (Mk. 8.29 with parallel texts), the question of the son of David/the Lord of David (Mk. 12.35-37 = Matt. 22.41-46 = Lk. 20.41-44), and other potential indicators are insufficient as evidence that Jesus himself and others believed him to be Messiah – or at least they are so ambiguous as to be useless.[133] According to Dahl's own explanation, the theory that Jesus' opponents turned the assertion that he was Messiah into an accusation against him is untenable – such an accusation would imply that there was some truth in this, and that Jesus really claimed to be Messiah, but it cannot be considered as something which Jesus had been "forced" to admit *in statu confessionis*.

Nils Alstrup Dahl's third point of view is risky. He balances precariously between Schweitzer on one side and Wrede on the other, poised on a knife-edge between the historical Jesus and the proclaimed Christ, believing to have found in the description of Jesus as "the king of the Jews" the single point where the incompatible alternatives can meet. But they cannot. There is no room for compromise on the razor-sharp ridge between two vertiginous abysses, and anybody who deals with the problems of christology has to choose one side or the other.

---

131 See section 3.3 below.

132 Dahl, in: *Der hist. Jesus*, p. 161 (*Jesus the Christ*, p. 38): "If he was crucified as an alleged Messiah, then – but only then – does faith in his resurrection necessarily become faith in the resurrection of the crucified Messiah." But what if Jesus was *unjustly* crucified as Messiah ("as an alleged Messiah")? Would the disciples and the earliest congregation then have allowed their belief in the resurrection of Jesus to be coloured by this? After all, they must have known better and not let themselves be influenced by the high priest or the procurator!

133 See Dahl, in: *Der hist. Jesus*, pp. 163 ff. (*Jesus the Christ*, pp. 40 ff.).

2.6.6 Sanders' solution

Although he may not be the first or the only one to have done so, Sanders has in my opinion found the right reason why the Jewish authorities, i.e. the high priest, the leading priests and the scribes, wanted to eliminate Jesus: it was the temple cleansing (Mk. 11.15-18 with parallel texts).[134] Sanders writes: "the temple scene is the last public event in Jesus' life: he lived long enough for it, but not much longer. In this case it seems entirely reasonable to argue *post hoc ergo propter hoc*."[135]

Unlike Sanders, however, I am of the opinion that this public act – no matter what was precisely said and done on this occasion – presupposes that Jesus was Messiah, that he proclaimed this in public, and that his cleansing of the temple was a criticism of the temple and the cult, just like the baptism of John (cf. section 2.4.1 above).

Furthermore, the cleansing of the temple implies that Jesus had come to Jerusalem and was staying there – in other words, that Jesus' entry into Jerusalem had taken place (Mk. 11.1-11 = Matt. 21.1-11 = Lk. 19.28-40 = Jn. 12.12-19). To Sanders, the entry into Jerusalem is "one of the most puzzling [passages] in the Gospels", and he is inclined to consider the event as inauthentic: "Perhaps the event took place but was a small occurrence which went unnoticed. Perhaps only a few disciples unostentiously dropped their garments in front of the ass ..., while only a few quietly murmured 'Hosanna'."[136] If that is not fantasizing, I do not know what fantasizing is! Albert Schweitzer also found the entry into Jerusalem problematic: "To Jesus himself, the entry is a Messianic act, by which he shows his self-awareness [sic!], ... But those who join the cheering crowd have no idea of its meaning to Jesus"[137] – in other words, those who watched the entry saw Jesus as a prophet only (Matt. 21.10-11), and not as the one he wanted to be. But then Schweitzer has to say this because of his theory that it was Judas who betrayed Jesus' Messiahship to the Jewish leaders.

Unlike Schweitzer and Sanders and all others who remain doubtful about the significance of the entry into Jerusalem, I maintain that it took place, that it

---

134 Sanders, *Jesus and Judaism*, pp. 61-71: "The "cleansing" of the temple", and pp. 301 ff.
135 Sanders, ib., p. 302.
136 Sanders, ib., p. 306; see also pp. 306-308 and n. 43 on p. 408.
137 Schweitzer, *Gesch.*, p. 440.

118

can only be understood as a clearly Messianic act, and that everybody immediately understood what was happening:

> Daughter of Zion, rejoice with all your heart;
> shout in triumph, daughter of Jerusalem!
> See, your king is coming to you,
> his cause won, his victory gained,
> humble and mounted on a donkey,
> on a colt, the foal of a donkey.
> He will banish the chariot from Ephraim,
> the war-horse from Jerusalem;
> the warrior's bow will be banished,
> and he will proclaim peace to the nations.
> His rule will extend from sea to sea,
> from the River to the ends of the earth (Zech. 9.9-10).

Sanders maintains that outside the Christian movement there is no evidence of the combination of "Messiah" and "Son of God".[138] Really? What about Ps. 2.2, 7? Wilhelm Bousset maintained that at first "the Lord" (cf. 1 Cor. 12.3) was only conceivable as a christological title in Greek and Hellenistic regions, not in Palestine.[139] Is that so? What about 1 Cor. 16.22, where the exclamation "Come, Lord!" (cf. Rev. 22.20) is also written in Aramaic: *marána thá*, and what about the numerous passages in the Gospels where Jesus is addressed as "Lord" and referred to as "the Lord"?

Indeed he was the Son of God, the Lord, the Lord's Anointed, Messiah (Jn. 1.41; 4.25), Christ and Israel's king!

2.7 The resurrection of Jesus

Bibliography

Hans Frhr. von Campenhausen: *Der Ablauf der Osterereignisse und das leere Grab* (Sitzungsberichte der Heidelberger Akademie der Wissenschaften, Philos.-hist. Kl., Jahrgang 1952, 4. Abhandlung), first published in 1952, 3rd ed. Heidelberg 1966.

Hans Graß: *Ostergeschehen und Osterberichte*, first published in 1956, 4th ed. Göttingen 1970.

---

138 Sanders, *Jesus and Judaism*, p. 298.
139 Bousset, *Kyrios Christos*, 1913 – see n. 92 above.

Johannes Lindblom: *Gesichte und Offenbarungen. Vorstellungen von göttlichen Weisungen und übernatürlichen Erscheinungen im ältesten Christentum* (Acta Reg. Societatis Humaniorum Litterarum Lundensis – Skrifter utgivna av Kungl. humanistiska Vetenskapssamfundet i Lund, LXV), Lund 1968, pp. 78-113: "Christophanien und Christusepiphanien".

H.C.C. Cavallin: *Life After Death. Paul's Argument for the Resurrection of the Dead in 1 Cor 15. Part I: An Enquiry into the Jewish Background*, Lund 1974.

Niels Hyldahl: Auferstehung Christi – Auferstehung der Toten (1 Thess. 4,13-18), in: Sigfred Pedersen, ed., *Die Paulinische Literatur und Theologie. Anlässlich der 50.jährigen Gründungs-Feier der Universität von Aarhus* (Teologiske Studier, 7), Århus – Göttingen 1980, pp. 119-135.

Christopher Rowland: *Christian Origins*, 1985 (see section 1 above), pp. 187-193: "The Resurrection Narratives".

Andrew T. Lincoln: The Promise and the Failure: Mark 16:7, 8, Journal of Biblical Literature 108 (1989), pp. 283-300.

Gerd Lüdemann: *Die Auferstehung Jesu. Historie, Erfahrung, Theologie*, Göttingen – Stuttgart 1994 = *The Resurrection of Jesus*, London 1994.

Adela Yarbro Collins: Apotheosis and Resurrection, in: Peder Borgen/Søren Giversen, eds., *The New Testament and Hellenistic Judaism*, Århus 1995, pp. 88-100.

2.7.1 The belief in the king risen from the dead

To the believers, the resurrection of Jesus meant that God supported him and approved of his preaching and actions, and confirmed his identity as Israel's king.

Therefore the question of the resurrection of Jesus Christ does not allow us to ignore the question of the historical Jesus, or to start a completely new project about the proclaimed Christ. On the contrary, it calls for inquiries concerning the nature of God's justification of him; the proclaimed Christ was not an unknown person, but Jesus, whose words and deeds the historical tradition preserved for posterity.

This brings us to the point in Nils Alstrup Dahl's treatise (see section 2.6.5 above) which seems to represent a real step towards the solution of the old problems concerning the historical Jesus and christology. The subject of the treatise was "the crucified Messiah". We do not know exactly what the entry into Jerusalem meant to Jesus himself and his disciples – but we do know that it was an unquestionably Messianic act, and that Jesus was a king who did not instigate rebellion and war; on the contrary, he made peace among the nations.

When this king was crucified, the continued belief in him was based on the assumption that the new kingdom he had proclaimed would come some time in the future. At the same time, however, this kingdom should also be realized there and then, according to the existing circumstances – not through the establishment of a secret and invisible church which could avoid persecution, but through the establishment of open and visible congregations which functioned as communities, politically and socially as well. This is what belief in "the crucified Messiah" meant, and in my opinion it is the central point in Nils Alstrup Dahl's treatise. Paul's widely spread congregations were not established in order to provide the framework for a purely "spiritual" community of people who shared the same belief; they were meant to create a new world order recognized by everyone, including those in power.

This was precisely what happened immediately, at first among the Jews in Palestine, then among the Jews in the Diaspora, and then also among Gentile nations within and outside the Greek-Roman world. What is most surprising is the speed with which it happened, and the naturalness with which it was carried out. The admission of Gentiles caused no problems until some time later, during the emergence of what is termed Judaization, in the middle of the first century, and there were specific reasons for this – see section 3.4 below.

I shall go no further into these matters in the present context. Instead, I shall attempt to make a historical study of the questions concerning the resurrection of Jesus, the appearances of the resurrected Jesus, and the empty tomb.

2.7.2 The Easter events

Nobody witnessed the resurrection of Jesus, but many bore witness to it. Nobody can rightly maintain that the appearances of Jesus after his resurrection or the empty tomb prove that Jesus rose from the dead: these appearances could have been hallucinations, and the empty tomb can also be explained in other ways (cf. Matt. 28.11 ff.). The resurrection of Jesus cannot be regarded as a historical event in a normal sense, and has therefore no importance from a purely historical point of view.

This is confirmed by two separate facts.

In the first place, Jesus appeared after his resurrection only to those whom Paul mentions in 1 Cor. 15.5-8: Cephas (Peter), the Twelve, the over five hundred brothers (and sisters?) who saw him at the same time, Jesus' brother

James, and all the apostles, including Paul as the last of these. Apart from Paul – who was familiar with the Christian faith and its meaning from his own persecution of Christians – all these people probably already believed that Jesus was Messiah.

Secondly, there is no evidence that the resurrection of Jesus was immediately understood in the light of "the resurrection of the dead" as a general principle which also included the resurrection of Jesus. If that had been the case, then the resurrection of Jesus would have been only one instance of the resurrection of the dead – although his resurrection was unique in the sense that it had already taken place, whereas the resurrection of the dead in general was to take place some time in the future. On the contrary, the resurrection of Jesus was not linked with the resurrection of the dead – or rather, the resurrection of the Christians – until this became necessary, so to speak. This happened when several members of Paul's Christian congregation in Thessalonica died in about A.D. 50 (1 Thess. 4.13 ff.), and when Christians from Paul's congregation in Corinth expressed doubt about the resurrection of the dead in about A.D. 54 (1 Cor. 15.12 ff. – see also note 141 below). In either case, the resurrection of the dead is inferred from the resurrection of Jesus – not from a general belief in resurrection such as the Pharisees also cherished (and Paul had been a Pharisee!).

Regarding the question of the Easter events and the empty tomb, it is useful to consult Hans von Campenhausen's book from 1966, the first edition of which was published in 1952. In the 1966 edition, he comments on Hans Graß' more traditional, but instructive book from 1956, which refers in turn to the 1952 edition of Campenhausen's book. The 1966 edition of Campenhausen's book also submits Willi Marxsen's redaction critical analysis of the Gospel of Mark from 1956[140] to a severe but well-deserved criticism. Furthermore, Campenhausen's work is the work of a true historian, eminently suitable for illustrating the problems connected with a historical description of the events of the resurrection and the empty tomb.

Paul is the author of the earliest and most reliable description of the resurrection and subsequent appearances of Christ (1 Cor. 15.1-11):

---

140 See section 2.2 above.

3. ..., that Christ died for our sins, in accordance with the scriptures; 4 that he was buried; that he was raised to life on the third day, in accordance with the scriptures; 5 and that he appeared to Cephas, and afterwards to the Twelve. 6 Then he appeared to over five hundred of our brothers at once, most of whom are still alive, though some have died. 7 Then he appeared to James, and afterwards to all the apostles. 8 Last of all he appeared to me too; it was like a sudden, abnormal birth. ... 11 But no matter whether it was I or they! This is what we all proclaim, and this is what you believed.[141]

There can be no doubt that these events are mentioned in chronological order: the death of Christ, his burial, and his resurrection on the third day – "in accordance with the scriptures". On the latter point, no one has so far been able to find a suitable passage in the Old Testament which could explain this reference to the resurrection "on the third day".[142] According to Campenhausen, we should consider the possibility that "the third day" may have existed as a fact before a corresponding passage could be discovered in the Old Testament and referred to in the confession [sc. in 1 Cor. 15.3 ff.].[143] "At least this leaves the possibility open that "the third day" was mentioned as a historical date. Naturally this historical date cannot be directly connected with the resurrection itself, since nobody witnessed this according to all the earliest canonical Gospel texts.[144] On the other hand, it could refer to the day when it was first known or "discovered" that the resurrection had taken place. However, this discovery ...

---

141 1 Cor. 15.1-11 is about the common basis of the Christian faith which could not be questioned: the resurrection of Christ. 1 Cor. 15.12-58 is about the resurrection of the dead, which was questioned by the Corinthian congregation. In other words, it was not self-evident that the resurrection of Christ and the resurrection of the dead were two aspects of the same issue. See my own: Auferstehung Christi – Auferstehung der Toten, 1980, in particular p. 121.

142 Many exegetes have suggested Hos. 6.2, but this is certainly far from convincing. In his treatise: And that he rose on the third day according to the scriptures, Scandinavian Journal of the Old Testament 2 (1990), pp. 101-113 (= Opstanden på den tredje dag efter skrifterne, Dansk Teologisk Tidsskrift 51 (1988), pp. 91-103 = id., *Menneskesønnen. En bibelteologisk studie* (Bibel og historie, 19), Århus 1996, pp. 91-102), Jens Christensen suggests that this enigmatic reference in 1 Cor. 15.4b should be understood in the light of an old Jewish tradition which combined Gen. 1.11-13 and Isa. 11.10: the tree of life was planted on the third day of the creation and symbolizes the resurrection of Christ on the third day. But Jens Christensen's attempt at an explanation is not convincing, and apparently he is unaware of Campenhausen's argumentation.

143 See Campenhausen, *Ablauf der Osterereignisse*, p. 12.

144 As already mentioned, nobody witnessed the resurrection, although many bore witness to it.

can hardly be ascribed to the first appearances of the resurrected Christ, since the date [sc. "the third day"] is never connected directly with any of these. By all accounts, these [sc. the appearances of the resurrected Christ] did not take place in Jerusalem, but in Galilee, and the length of time is simply too short compared with the distance between Jerusalem and Galilee, especially if one of the days in question was a sabbath."[145]

In other words: the indication "on the third day" in 1 Cor. 15.4 has nothing to do with the appearances of Christ. They all took place in Galilee, and none of them is dated to any particular day; "the third day" refers to the "discovery" of the recent resurrection: the fact that the resurrection had taken place was *discovered* on the third day. "The third day" was a historical date, which was *later* connected with a passage in the scriptures which is unknown to us today.

According to Mk. 14.28 and 16.7, it had been clearly *predicted* that Christ would appear to the disciples in Galilee, not in Jerusalem, and this appearance is described in Matt. 28.16 ff. and Jn. 21.1 ff. On the other hand, Lk.-Acts and Jn. 20.19 ff. say that the appearances of Christ took place in – or near – Jerusalem. From a historical point of view, there can be no doubt that Mk. and Matt. are telling the truth: "Jesus and many of his supporters originally came from Galilee, and later large congregations, which were independent of Jerusalem, established themselves in Galilee and carried out missionary work there."[146]

Matt., Lk. and Jn. also mention other appearances of Christ, including his appearances to the women by the tomb and to the two disciples on the road to Emmaus near Jerusalem. Yet the earliest Gospel text, Mk. 16.1-8, mentions no appearances of Christ at all (it is an angel the women see by the empty tomb).

---

145 Campenhausen, *Ablauf der Osterereignisse*, p. 12. On p. 59, he refers to F. Scheidweiler's argument formulated in 1959 that fit young men could have walked the distance in two and a half days, and admits that this could weaken his own argument on p. 12 that the distance was too long. But those who know Campenhausen will also know that it takes more to make him change his point of view than an allegation that fit young men could walk from Jerusalem to Galilee in two and a half days!

146 Campenhausen, *Ablauf der Osterereignisse*, p. 15. The appearance to more than 500 brothers at the same time (1 Cor. 15.6) can hardly have taken place in Jerusalem, and can therefore not be identified with the Pentecost event in Jerusalem (Acts 2.5 ff.); cf. Campenhausen, ib., pp. 13-14, p. 18, n. 58, and p. 60. This is also confirmed by the fact that Christ did not appear during the Pentecost event. But see also the passage at the end of this section.

This indicates that the appearances described in the other Gospel texts should be considered as legends – even fantastical legends in the apocryphal Gospels. According to Paul's description in 1 Cor. 15.1-11, he himself was the last to see the resurrected Christ (1 Cor. 15.8 – other, later "visions" of Christ, such as those mentioned in 2 Cor. 12.1 ff., are written on another leaf). Of course it could be argued that Paul's knowledge of later appearances to other persons was incomplete, but this is unlikely, and it must therefore be reasonable to conclude that there had simply not been any appearances during the period of approximately fifteen years between Paul's conversion and his composition of 1 Cor.[147]

While the appearances of Christ mentioned in 1 Cor. 15.5 ff. seem to have taken place in northern Galilee according to the geographical indications,[148] Paul himself does not say anything specific about the Easter events in Jerusalem. He knew that Christ died and was buried, but whether this also led him to believe that the tomb was empty remains an open question – he may have used the words "died" and "was buried" to emphasize the reality of the death of Jesus.[149]

As far as the Easter events in Jerusalem are concerned, our best source is the earliest of the Gospels, i.e. Mark, which is on the whole reliable on this

---

147 Cf. Campenhausen, ib., p. 19-20. Campenhausen even mentions "approximately two decades" (p. 19), but in my opinion, Paul's conversion has generally been dated too early; see n. 41 above.

148 See the passage referred to in n. 146 above; cf. also n. 109.

149 Cf. Campenhausen, *Ablauf der Osterereignisse*, pp. 20-21 and 60-61. On this point Campenhausen disagrees with Graß: originally Campenhausen was almost convinced that Paul's description of the burial of Jesus (1 Cor. 15.4) implied that the tomb was empty, whereas Graß in his book *Ostergeschehen und Osterberichte*, pp. 146 ff., firmly rejects this idea: he regards the traditions of the discovery of the empty tomb as "absolutely secondary in connection with Paul's Easter testimony" (ib., p. 309); cf. Graß, Zur Begründung des Osterglaubens, Theologische Literaturzeitung 89 (1964), col. 405-414: "Paul has not yet adopted the massive realism of the evangelical account of the Easter events. He reveals no knowledge of the empty tomb, and as far as the physical resurrection is concerned, he emphasizes the *totaliteraliter*" (col. 411). On the whole, Campenhausen sticks to his own point of view and emphasizes the Jewish concepts of resurrection, which imply the *physical* resurrection: *Ablauf der Osterereignisse*, p. 20, n. 67, and p. 60. Yet he admits that Paul gives no precise details about the Easter events in Jerusalem (including the empty grave), and that as far as these events are concerned, we have no other sources than the Gospels, in particular Mk. 16.1-8.

point according to Campenhausen. The crucifixion was only seen from a distance by some women who had followed Jesus from Galilee, and who also attended the entombment: Mk. 15.40 ff. The disciples were absent. "Therefore the congregation would have no other Christian eyewitnesses who could tell what had happened than the women who had also attended the entombment."[150]

The narrative in Mk. 16.1-8 about the women who came to the open grave on Easter morning, which ends the Gospel of Mark, runs as follows:

1 When the sabbath was over, Mary of Magdala, Mary the mother of James, and Salome bought aromatic oils, intending to go and anoint him; 2 and very early on the first day of the week, just after sunrise, they came to the tomb. 3 They were wondering among themselves who would roll away the stone for them from the entrance to the tomb, 4 when they looked up and saw that the stone, huge as it was, had been rolled back already. 5 They went into the tomb, where they saw a young man sitting on the righthand side, wearing a white robe; and they were dumbfounded. 6 But he said to them, "Do not be alarmed; you are looking for Jesus of Nazareth, who was crucified. He has been raised; he is not here. Look, there is the place where they laid him. 7 But go and say to his disciples and to Peter: He is going ahead of you into Galilee: there you will see him, as he told you."[151] 8 Then they went out and ran away from the tomb, trembling with amazement. They said nothing to anyone, for they were afraid.

Apart from the inconsistency that the women buy oils and go to the tomb although they do not know how to open it, this is a very simple narrative: the tomb is already open, and an angel, an *angelus interpres*, explains what has happened and tells the women to go to the disciples and remind them of the event which has been foretold: that Jesus is now going ahead of them to Galilee and that they will see him there. Apparently Jesus has already left Jerusalem, so there is no possibility that anybody can see him there, least of all the women, nor is such an appearance mentioned.[152] The angel's behaviour is quiet, he only acts as an *angelus interpres*, and no dramatic events are described.[153]

---

150 Campenhausen, *Ablauf der Osterereignisse*, pp. 22-23.
151 This is a reference to Mk. 14.28.
152 This is unlike Matt. 28.8 ff., in which the women meet Jesus himself after they have left the tomb, and he instructs them to go to the disciples and tell them to go to Galilee, where they will see him. The text does not explain why the disciples could not see Jesus in Jerusalem, if the women had seen him there.
153 Again, this is unlike Matt. 28.2 ff., according to which there was a violent earthquake, and the women saw the angel descend from heaven and roll away the stone. Then Jesus must have passed through the stone as a cloud of atoms! Cf. Campenhausen, *Ablauf der*

The surprising part of the narrative in Mk. is the end: the women do not follow the angel's instructions, but remain silent, saying nothing to anyone (Mk. 16.8). They disobey the angel's command, and it remains unexplained how the disciples, who were still in Jerusalem, were told to go to Galilee. Nor is there any reference to a later meeting between Jesus and the disciples.[154]

In 1903, Julius Wellhausen attempted to solve this mystery through an explanation which was later adopted by many exegetes. He wrote: "The contradiction [i.e. between the angel's command and the women's disobedience] is obvious, but since 16.8 is necessary as a conclusion, it was probably the author himself who unconsciously [sic!] made this contradiction: he tries to explain why the women's account of the resurrection was not known until some time later. In fact, Paul knows nothing about it."[155]

According to this explanation, the tradition of the empty tomb is a late, inauthentic legend, and the Evangelist himself knows this and tries to forestall any objections by implying that the women's silence was the reason why news of the empty tomb did not reach the disciples until much later.

Campenhausen argues convincingly that such an explanation is improbable and clumsy: why would the Evangelist use a legend which he knows is late and inauthentic? Furthermore, Campenhausen rightly points out that news of the resurrection cannot possibly have been kept secret for several years: the women would have had to say what they had seen and heard, at least as soon as the appearances of Christ in Galilee became known and the first congregation was established – certainly not years or decades after the resurrection![156]

Campenhausen's own explanation[157] is more convincing than Wellhausen's. Campenhausen points out how unlikely it is that the women should disobey the angel's instruction and remain silent about their knowledge and ignore the

---

Osterereignisse, p. 30: "This leads to the strange conclusion that Jesus must already have left the closed tomb by passing through the stone."
154 Again, this is unlike Matt. 28.16 ff., according to which the resurrected Jesus appears on a mountain in Galilee to all the eleven disciples and commands them to go to all nations and make them his disciples and baptize them.
155 Julius Wellhausen, *Das Evangelium übersetzt und erklärt*, Berlin 1903, pp. 145-146; cf. the quotation from Graß in n. 149 above. Part of the quotation is also to be found in Campenhausen, *Ablauf der Osterereignisse*, p. 26.
156 Campenhausen, *Ablauf der Osterereignisse*, pp. 26-28.
157 Campenhausen, ib., pp. 37-39.

command they had been given: the Evangelist must have "bent" the tradition for apologetic reasons, that is, in order to prevent any suspicions that the women themselves or others had had the body removed. According to the way in which the Evangelist ends the Gospel text, the appearances of Christ in Galilee (Mk. 14.28 and 16.7) must have taken place with no intervention on the part of the women.

This is a "necessary" solution chosen by the Evangelist himself,[158] which shows that the question of the empty tomb was already being discussed at the time when the Gospel of Mark was written. Naturally the original tradition – which is rendered faithfully in Mk. 16.1-7, right up to the one exception in verse 8 – must then have described how the women carried out the instructions the angel had given them by the empty grave. Furthermore, this takes us so far back in time as to make it probable that the tradition of the empty tomb is really old and may claim to be historical. At the same time, this explanation also provides a convincing explanation of the date called "the third day": it is a historical date and refers to the women's discovery of the empty tomb on the third day; on the other hand, this date has nothing to do with the appearances of Christ to the disciples in Galilee.[159] And finally, there is every indication that the tradition of Joseph of Arimathea (Mk. 15.42 ff.) is historically reliable.[160]

It goes without saying that even if the tradition of the empty tomb is historical, it is no proof of the resurrection of Christ – in fact, the resurrection could be a complete swindle. Campenhausen writes: "Those who believe in the possibility of a removal, a mix-up or any other accidents, are of course free to use their imagination – on this point, anything is possible, and nothing can be proved." But he goes on to say: "However, this has nothing to do with critical research. Having investigated what can be investigated, we have in my opinion no option but to accept the news of the empty grave and its early discovery at face value. There is much evidence for it, and no decisive and certain evidence against it, so it is probably authentic."[161]

---

158 Campenhausen, ib., p. 39.
159 Cf. n. 143 and n. 145 above.
160 Campenhausen, *Ablauf der Osterereignisse*, pp. 41-42.
161 Campenhausen, ib., p. 42. Independently of Campenhausen, Rowland, *Christian Origins*, pp. 189 ff., maintains that the discovery of the empty tomb is of great historical value.

An important point in Campenhausen's historical account of the Easter events is that the disciples are still in Jerusalem – and hiding there – when the women discover the empty tomb; otherwise the angel's instructions would be meaningless: "All the Evangelists make it clear that the disciples stayed in Jerusalem for some time and were still there when the empty tomb was discovered. There is no reason at all to doubt this."[162] And further: "that the news [i.e. of the empty tomb] reached the disciples can ... hardly be seriously doubted; the contradictory, biased statement in Mark [Mk. 16.8] which comes after the angel's command [Mk. 16.7] is secondary and deserves to be ignored, just as it is ignored by the other Evangelists."[163]

Campenhausen also confirms that the resurrected Christ never appeared in Jerusalem, but only later, and in northern Palestine.

Furthermore, Campenhausen maintains that there was no "flight" from Jerusalem – on the contrary, he maintains it was Peter (cf. Mk. 16.7) who made the disciples go to Galilee in order to meet Jesus there. In my view, this is a questionable assumption; in fact, we know nothing about this. The obvious, rational explanation would be that these people, who had made a pilgrimage to Jerusalem, would sooner or later return to the place where they came from.[164]

In Campenhausen's view, however, the most important question in this context is what made the disciples return to Jerusalem shortly after, to preach the Gospel openly and publicly (cf. Acts 2.5 ff.): "What calls for an explanation

---

162 Campenhausen, *Ablauf der Osterereignisse*, p. 44.
163 Campenhausen, ib., p. 49.
164 Cf. Campenhausen, ib., p. 44, n. 175 (on p. 45). On p. 37, n. 147 (cont. on p. 38), Campenhausen argues convincingly against Marxsen's redaction critical view as expressed in his book *Der Evangelist Markus*, 1956: Marxsen understands "Galilee" as a theological concept rather than a historical and geographical name, namely as the place of Jesus' parousia; in this context Marxsen refers to the tradition in Eusebius about the Christians' exodus from Jerusalem to Pella during the Jewish-Roman war in A.D. 66-70 and maintains that this exodus is connected with the parousia expected in Galilee. It seems to me that this view is self-contradictory. Why should the second coming of the Lord take place in Galilee, when it is clear according to Mk. 13.21 ff. that this will be a *universal* event? And is it reasonable to interpret the entire Gospel of Mark as an apocalyptic pamphlet intended to exhort the Christians to emigrate – not to Galilee, but to Pella east of Jordan? See also the detailed explanation in Lincoln, JBL 108 (1989), p. 285, who rightly points out that Mk. 16.7 refers to a resurrection appearance of Jesus, not to the parousia; and Räisänen, *The "Messianic Secret"*, pp. 207-211.

is not the return to Galilee, but the second journey to Jerusalem."[165] Campenhausen's own explanation is that the resurrection appearances of Jesus, which took place in Galilee, inspired the disciples to go back to Jerusalem and preach the new Christian faith there.

On the latter point, however, it is important to bear in mind that the New Testament says nothing about the disciples' "second journey" from Galilee to Jerusalem. The assumption that they went back to Jerusalem is based entirely on the narratives in Lk.-Acts which describe the appearances and the ascension which took place in or near Jerusalem, but these narratives do not say that Jesus and the disciples went back to Galilee; they just describe these events.[166] Nor do the Gospels or the Acts say that the disciples made a second journey from Galilee to Jerusalem; again, our assumption that this must have happened comes from a natural desire to establish harmony between the narratives – a harmony which cannot be established. In other words, we do not know how or when the belief in the resurrection of Christ was first proclaimed and preached in Jerusalem. A traditio-historical consideration would indicate that the appearance to more than 500 brothers at the same time mentioned by Paul (1 Cor. 15.6), which for geographical reasons can hardly have taken place in Jerusalem, may after all be the original source of the narrative of the miracle on the day of Pentecost related in Acts 2.5 ff.

2.7.3 Final observations

To Campenhausen, only one question remains enigmatic from a historical point of view: what started the Easter events, or, in plain words, what happened to the body of Jesus? There were no eyewitnesses who could tell how the tomb was opened and what became of the body. The Christians know the answer to this question, and so do the sceptics. "The situation is only difficult for those who want to believe in the resurrection, but who find the physical resurrection unnecessary or even unacceptable. They are left with a rather embarrassing alternative: to follow the early Christians as far as the belief in the resurrected

---

165 Campenhausen, *Ablauf der Osterereignisse*, p. 44, n. 175 (on p. 45).
166 See Mikeal C. Parsons, *The Departure of Jesus in Luke-Acts. The Ascension Narratives in Context* (Journal for the Study of the New Testament, Supplement Series, 21), Sheffield 1987.

Jesus Christ is concerned, but to follow the Jews as far as the consequences of this belief are concerned."[167]

This brings us back to the old question of Judaism ("the Jews") versus Christianity ("the early Christians") or the historical Jesus versus the proclaimed Christ. I therefore find it fitting to end this section and this chapter with a reference to the so far undisputed fact that Jesus was entombed by Joseph of Arimathea, a respected member of the Council (Mk. 15.42 ff.). Would he have done this if he had not believed that Jesus was Israel's king?

---

167 Campenhausen, *Ablauf der Osterereignisse*, p. 52.

3 THE APOSTOLIC ERA

Bibliography

a) Sources

The New Testament, in particular Paul's letters and the Acts of the Apostles.

Josephus – see section 1 above.

Philo – see section 1 above.

Hugh Jackson Lawlor/John Ernest Leonard Oulton, eds.: *Eusebius, Bishop of Caesarea, The Ecclesiastical History and the Martyrs of Palestine. Translated with Introduction and Notes*, I-II, London 1927-28, reprinted in 1954.

Eduard Schwartz, ed.: *Eusebius, Kirchengeschichte. Kleine Ausgabe*, 5th ed., Berlin 1955.

Knud Bang, ed.: *Eusebs Kirkehistorie* (Skrifter udgivet af Selskabet til historiske Kildeskrifters Oversættelse, 12. Række, 4 and 8), Copenhagen 1940-1945.

b) General works

Eduard Meyer: *Ursprung und Anfänge des Christentums*, I (Die Evangelien), II (Die Entwicklung des Judentums und Jesus von Nazareth), III (Die Apostelgeschichte und die Anfänge des Christentums), Stuttgart 1923-25 (I-II: 4th and 5th ed., III: 1st-3rd ed.), reprinted in 1962.

F.J. Foakes Jackson/Kirsopp Lake, eds., *The Beginnings of Christianity, Part I: The Acts of the Apostles*, Vol. I-V, London 1920-33 (nothing but "Part I" has been published).

Maurice Goguel: *Jésus et les origines du christianisme: La naissance du christianisme*, Paris 1946.

Id.: *Jésus et les origines du christianisme: L'église primitive*, Paris 1947.

Leonhard Goppelt: *Die apostolische und nachapostolische Zeit* (Die Kirche in ihrer Geschichte. Ein Handbuch, published by Kurt Dietrich/Ernst Wolf, I, A), Göttingen 1962.

Bo Reicke: *Neutestamentliche Zeitgeschichte. Die biblische Welt 500 v. – 100 n. Chr.* (Sammlung Töpelmann, II, 2), Berlin 1965 = *Kristendomens historiska bakgrund. Den bibliska världen 500 f.Kr. – 100 e.Kr.*, Stockholm 1967.

Hans Conzelmann: *Geschichte des Urchristentums* (Grundrisse zum Neuen Testament. Das Neue Testament Deutsch, Ergänzungsreihe, 5), Göttingen 1969.

Gerd Lüdemann: *Das frühe Christentum nach den Traditionen der Apostelgeschichte. Ein Kommentar*, Göttingen 1987 = *Early Christianity according to the Traditions in Acts. A commentary*, Philadelphia – London 1988.

François Vouga: *Geschichte des frühen Christentums* (Uni-Taschenbücher, 1733), Tübingen – Basel 1994.

3.1 Chronology. Paul's Letters – the Acts of the Apostles

Bibliography

John Knox: *Chapters in a Life of Paul*, New York – Nashville 1950 = London 1954; Revised Edition by the author and introduced by Douglas R.A. Hare, Macon (Georgia) 1987 = London 1989.

John Coolidge Hurd: Pauline Chronology and Pauline Theology, in: W.R. Farmer/C.F.D. Moule/R.R. Niebuhr, eds., *Christian History and Interpretation: Studies Presented to John Knox*, Cambridge 1967, pp. 225-248.

Niels Hyldahl: *Die paulinische Chronologie* (Acta theologica Danica, XIX), Leiden 1986.

Lars Aejmelaeus: *Die Rezeption der Paulusbriefe in der Miletrede (Apg 20:18-35)* (Annales Academiæ Scientiarum Fennicæ, B/232), Helsinki 1987.

Dixon Slingerland: Acts 18:1-18, the Gallio Inscription, and Absolute Pauline Chronology, Journal of Biblical Literature 110 (1991), pp. 439-449.

3.1.1 A conservative or radical approach?

The traditional question of the historical credibility of the Acts cannot be answered until we have clarified the relationship between the Acts and Paul's letters – the two most important sources of knowledge of the apostolic era, i.e. the period spanning approximately 40 years between the death of Jesus in about A.D. 30[1] and the capture of Jerusalem, and the destruction of the temple in A.D. 70.

The text of the Acts is subject to endless debates regarding its historical value and credibility, and usually the conclusion will simply reflect the debaters' original points of view.

If they are conservative, they will value the Acts for its wealth of knowledge and detail, and maintain that without this book, it would be impossible to present a *coherent* description of early Christianity. Referring to the undeniably striking "we" passages in the Acts (16.10-17, 20.5-8, 20.13-15; 21.1-18 and 27.1-28.16), they will maintain that "we" stands for the author of the Acts and indicates that he was an eyewitness to important parts of the story

---

1   See also section 2.3.2, n. 41.

134

he tells. They will also invoke the preface of the Gospel of Luke and maintain that its reference to "eyewitnesses" supports their own view. Furthermore, they will emphasize specific details which have apparently been proved historically correct by other sources, such as the Gallio episode (Acts 18.12 ff.) and the discovery of the Gallio inscription in Delphi which dates Gallio's tenure as proconsul of Achaia (Greece) to the early 50s.

On the other hand, radical scholars will emphasize the general *secondary* character of the Acts, which was written relatively late in the post-apostolic era. Furthermore, they will argue that there is no evidence that the author himself was an eyewitness to the events he describes – on the contrary, the reference to "eyewitnesses" in Lk. 1.2 makes it quite clear that the author of Lk. and Acts (who must be the same person) was not an eyewitness himself, but wrote an account based on the traditions handed down by original eyewitnesses. Furthermore, radical scholars will point out obvious historical errors, such as the fact that Theudas came *before* Judas the Galilean (Acts 5.36-37 – cf. section 2.1.2 above), and certain discrepancies between the Acts and Paul's letters, including the number of Pauls visits to Jerusalem, on which point the Acts must be rejected in favour of Paul's letters. Finally, they will maintain that the "we" passages in the Acts cannot be used as evidence of its historical credibility as long as the identity of the "we" in these passages remains unknown.

In these circumstances, an assessment of the historical value or credibility of the Acts must be made on the basis of a comparison with Paul's letters, including the almost rhetorical question of whether the primary evidence of Paul's letters – which are unquestionably the earliest Christian documents we have – should simply have priority over the Acts.

3.1.2 The "new" chronology

The "new" Pauline chronology as represented by Ernst Barnikol (1929), John Knox (1936 and later) Donald W. Riddle (1940), John Hurd (1967), Robert Jewett (1979), Gerd Lüdemann (1980), myself (1986) and several others, is gaining ground internationally, especially in American, German and Scandinavian theology, and has attracted increasing attention and acceptance, in spite of a certain amount of opposition.[2]

---

2   Ernst Barnikol, *Die drei Jerusalemreisen des Paulus. Die echte Konkordanz der Paulus-briefe mit der Wir-Quelle der Apostelgeschichte* (Forschungen zur Entstehung des

This new chronology is characterized by two distinctive points of view. Firstly, as far as Paul and his work and theology are concerned, Paul's letters are considered to be of absolute prime importance compared to the Acts. Secondly, the Jerusalem Conference, which Paul describes in Gal. 2.1-10, is seen in the context of Acts 18.22 – not for instance Acts 15.4-35, much less Acts 11.27-30 and 12.25.

These two points of view represent a potential criticism of the Acts as far as its passages about Paul are concerned. According to Paul's letters, which are, as mentioned above, primary texts compared to the Acts, the apostle visited Jerusalem three times after his conversion – and only three times: 1) Gal. 1.18-19; 2) Gal. 2.1-10; and 3) Rom. 15.25-27, 31. According to the author of the Acts, however, Paul goes to Jerusalem no less than five times: 1) Acts 9.26-30; 2) 11.27-30 and 12.25; 3) 15.4-35; 4) 18.22;[3] and 5) 21.17 ff. Two of the five visits which Paul paid to Jerusalem after his conversion at Damascus according

---

Urchristentums, des Neuen Testaments und der Kirche, 2), Kiel 1929; John Knox, "Fourteen Years Later": A Note on the Pauline Chronology, Journal of Religion 16 (1936), pp. 341-349; id., The Pauline Chronology, Journal of Biblical Literature 58 (1939), pp. 15-29; Donald W. Riddle, *Paul. Man of Conflict. A Modern Biographical Sketch*, Nashville 1940; John Knox, *Chapters*, 1950 = London 1954 (Revised Edition, Macon (Georgia) 1987 = London 1989); John Coolidge Hurd, *The Origin of 1 Corinthians*, London 1965 (Reprinted with Corrections and a New Preface, Macon (Georgia), 1983), pp. 3-42: "Pauline Biography and Pauline Theology"; id., Pauline Chronology and Pauline Theology, in: *Christian History and Interpretation*, 1967, pp. 225-248; id., The Sequence of Paul's Letters, Canadian Journal of Theology 14 (1968), pp. 189-200; Robert Jewett, *A Chronology of Paul's Life*, Philadelphia 1979 = *Dating Paul's Life*, London 1979 (German translation: *Paulus-Chronologie. Ein Versuch*, Munich 1982); Gerd Lüdemann, *Paulus, der Heidenapostel, Band I: Studien zur Chronologie* (Forschungen zur Religion und Literatur des Alten und Neuen Testaments, 123), Göttingen 1980 (English translation: *Paul, apostle to the Gentiles. Studies in Chronology*, Philadelphia 1984); Bruce Corley, ed., *Colloquy on New Testament Studies: A Time for Reappraisal and Fresh Approaches*, Macon (Georgia) 1983, pp. 263-364: "Seminar on Pauline Chronology"; Hyldahl, *Chronologie*, 1986; John Knox, On the Meaning of Galatians 1:15, Journal of Biblical Literature 106 (1987), pp. 301-304; id., On the Pauline Chronology: Buck – Taylor – Hurd revisited, in: Robert T. Fortna/Beverly R. Gaventa, eds., *The Conversation Continues: Studies in Paul & John In Honor of J. Louis Martyn*, Nashville 1990, pp. 258-274.

3   The suggestion that Acts 18.22 does not refer to a visit to Jerusalem because the city is not mentioned specifically in the text is contradicted by the unequivocal use of the verbs *anabaínein* and *katabaínein* – the fact that Jerusalem is not mentioned specifically is due to the editorial adaptation of the text; cf. n. 37 below.

to the Acts must therefore be regarded as unauthentic, and the fact that they are mentioned must be ascribed to the editorial adaptation of the texts about Paul.

It is appropriate – or even necessary – to compare Gal. 1.18-19 and Acts 9.26-30, which both describe the first visit to Jerusalem. The same applies to Rom. 15.25 ff. and Acts 21.17 ff., which describe the last visit to Jerusalem. Last, but certainly not least, Gal. 2.1-10 should be compared to Acts 18.22. According to Paul's letters, the "remaining" passages in the Acts are then Acts 11.27-30 and 12.25, which refer to one visit, and 15.4-35, which refers to another. The contents of these two "remaining" passages in the Acts should be "transferred" to the places where they originally belong: Acts 21.17 ff. and 18.22 respectively. In schematic form, it looks like this:

Gal. 1.18-19 = Acts 9.26-30
Gal. 2.1-10 = Acts 18.22 (and 15.4-35)
Rom. 15.25 ff. = Acts 21.17 ff. (and 11.27-30/12.25)

This immediately allows us to draw four interesting conclusions:

1) According to Philem. 24 and Col. 4.14 (and 2 Tim. 4.11), the physician called Luke, who is not mentioned in the Acts or anywhere else in the New Testament other than in these passages, was one of Paul's closest collaborators (not just a fellow traveller!). Unlike Luke the physician, who must have known Paul very well, the author of the Gospel of Luke appears to have had no personal knowledge of Paul's life; otherwise it would be impossible to explain why he would have "invented" two extra visits made by Paul to Jerusalem, when he must have known that these two visits never took place. The fact that the author had no personal knowledge of Paul's life is confirmed by the post-apostolic tradition of the twelve – and only twelve – apostles, each of whom the author of the Acts calls by name without mentioning the apostle Paul, thus excluding him from being an apostle (Rom. 1.1; 1 Cor. 1.1 etc.) according to the Acts![4] On these grounds it must be concluded that Luke the physician cannot be the author of the Gospel of Luke and the Acts of the Apostles.

2) The author of the Gospel of Luke and the Acts did not himself take part in the events he describes (cf. Lk. 1.2, which makes it quite clear that the author himself was not one of "the original eyewitnesses and servants of the Gospel"). Accordingly, even if the preface (Lk. 1.1-4) is understood as an introduction to

---

4   See also section 3.2.4 below.

both the Gospel of Luke and the Acts, it in no way supports the theory that the author participated as an eyewitness in the events he describes[5]. We must always bear this in mind when discussing the authorship of the Acts.

3) The author cannot be identical to the "we" mentioned in certain passages of the Acts (Acts 16.10-17; 20.5-8; 20.13-15; 21.1-18 and 27.1-28.16). These "we" passages clearly indicate the existence of some eyewitnesses, of whose identity we know nothing except that none of them is the author of Lk.-Acts. The fact that Paul's collaborator Luke is not identical to the "we" is confirmed by the following observation.

4) Finally, the "we" must represent fellow travellers, not collaborators of Paul such as Luke the physician (Col. 4.14; Philem. 24).[6]

These four conclusions constitute a valuable source of information as far as the composition of the Acts is concerned.

According to the new chronology, Paul's letters represent the key to all the passages about Paul in the Acts, not the other way round. Naturally this results in a critical attitude towards the historical credibility of the Acts as far as Paul is concerned; in fact it turns the question of the historical value of the Acts into a question of how to read and understand the Acts correctly.

---

5   The theory according to which Lk. 1.1-4 shows that the author of Lk.-Acts was present at the scene of some of the events he describes – primarily the "we" passages in the Acts, through which the author seems to indicate that he himself took part in these events – has been propounded by several scholars, including Henry J. Cadbury, in: Foakes Jackson/Kirsopp Lake, eds., *The Beginnings*, Part I, Vol. II, 1922, pp. 489-510: "Commentary on the Preface of Luke"; id., "We" and "I" passages in Luke-Acts, New Testament Studies 3 (1956-57), pp. 128-132. Since then, however, the discussion on Lk. 1.1-4 has changed after the publication of the works of Loveday Alexander, Luke's Preface in the Context of Greek Preface-Writing, Novum Testamentum 28 (1986), pp. 48-74, and id., *The Preface to Luke's Gospel. Literary convention and social context in Luke 1.1-4 and Acts 1.1* (Society of New Testament Studies, Monograph Series, 78), Cambridge 1993.

6   Cf. Hans Conzelmann, *Die Apostelgeschichte* (Handbuch zum Neuen Testament, 7), Tübingen 1963, p. 6 = *Acts of the Apostles. A Commentary on the Acts of the Apostles* (Hermeneia. A Critical and Historical Commentary on the Bible), Philadelphia 1987, p. xl: "These passages do not portray the reporter as a co-worker of Paul, but rather as a companion ..." Unlike Paul's collaborator Luke (Philem. 24; Col. 4.14; 2 Tim. 4.11), neither the author of the Acts nor this "we" were collaborators: "we" stands for fellow travellers or companions at the most, and the author of the Acts was not even one of these.

The traditional view of the Acts was completely different; indeed, it used to be considered as a central and indispensable historical text which represented the backbone of untold generations' understanding of the earliest Christianity, and which in essence described the historical events truly and convincingly. Normally it was only when the Acts said nothing about a subject that Paul's letters were used to fill the gap, a practice which served to consolidate the position of the Acts as a primary text.

Considering how widespread and predominant this attitude towards the Acts has been and still is, it goes without saying that a critical and convincing review of the Acts which helps to clarify its origins and further our understanding of its historical elements will inevitably lead to radical changes in the traditional view of the Acts' historical credibility. We must remember, however, that these changes are not essential in themselves; the important part is to gain an insight into the origins and editorial adaptation of the Acts, which prove to be far more complicated than previously expected. Ultimately, we can then achieve a better and more reliable understanding of the beginnings of Christianity than we have today. In other words, we must try to get as close as possible to the author of the Acts and form a well-documented theory on the process of creation.

If researchers could agree on the construction of the new Pauline chronology, it would be relatively easy to establish a method for submitting the Acts to a critical review. Contesting the new chronology is one thing,[7] applying

---

7   See e.g. Ernst Haenchen, *Die Apostelgeschichte* (Kritisch-exegetischer Kommentar über das Neue Testament, III), 13th ed., Göttingen 1961, p. 60 = *The Acts of the Apostles. A Commentary*, Oxford 1971, p. 67; Udo Borse, *Der Standort des Galaterbriefes* (Bonner Biblische Beiträge, 41), Cologne 1972, p. 14; id., Paulus in Jerusalem, in: Paul-Gerhard Müller/Werner Stenger, eds., *Kontinuität und Einheit. Für Franz Mußner*, Freiburg (Breisgau), 1981, pp. 43-64; Hengel, *Between Jesus and Paul*, 1983, p. 157, n. 5; F.F. Bruce, Chronological Questions in the Acts of the Apostles, Bulletin of the John Ryland University Library of Manchester, Vol. 68, No. 2, Manchester 1986, pp. 273-295, in part. pp. 290 ff.; Edvin Larsson, *Apostlagärningarna 13-20* (Kommentar til Nya Testamentet, 5B), Uppsala 1987, pp. 409-411; id., Claudius, judarna och den nya Pauluskronologin, in: Peter Wilhelm Bøckman/Roald E. Kristiansen, eds., *Context. Festskrift til Peder Johan Borgen/Essays in Honour of Peder Johan Borgen* (Relieff. Publikasjoner utgitt av Religionsvitenskapelig institutt, Trondheim University, No. 24), Trondheim 1987, pp. 107-120; Alfred Suhl, Theologische Literaturzeitung 113 (1988), col. 186-191; Barclay, JSNT 47 (1992) (see n. 142 below), p. 67, n. 32. Whereas Haenchen's, Hengel's, Suhl's and Barclay's comments are mostly in the nature of ridicule, Bruce and Larsson pick out

it to the Acts is another. The new chronology must be applied in such a way that it is proved correct, not by the Acts or the traditions behind this text, but simply because this chronology is practicable and can be used in such a way that the analysis of the Acts is convincing precisely because it can be carried out.

This has been attempted, most notably by Gerd Lüdemann, both in the first volume of his Pauline trilogy, *Studien zur Chronologie* from 1980,[8] and in his commentary on the Acts, *Das frühe Christentum nach den Traditionen der Apostelgeschichte* from 1987. Lüdemann's fundamental view is that while the Acts as such cannot claim historical authenticity, it is quite a different matter for the tradition behind the Acts: if it is possible to separate editorial adaptation from tradition, the reconstructed tradition or substance of tradition will prove to contain valuable and reliable historical material, the credibility of which can then be confirmed by Paul's letters.

From the viewpoint of the new Pauline chronology, there can hardly be any doubt that in principle, Lüdemann's method is correct: first, to establish a chronology based on Paul's letters alone, and then to come to a decision concerning the Acts.[9] But the question is how Lüdemann carries out his investigation in practice, and whether the investigation can prove its own correctness. And this question raises doubts.

In the first place, it is surprising and rather suggestive that Lüdemann's investigation into the Acts was really made twice: both in 1980 and in 1987 – as if the investigation from 1980 was not sufficient in itself. Admittedly, the commentary from 1987 includes not only the passages about Paul, but the entire

---

certain details which they find unacceptable, and use these as a pretext for a complete but unjust rejection of the fundamental principles of the new chronology in favour of an apologetic acceptance of the traditional chronology of the Acts, according to which Gallio's proconsulate (Acts 18.12 ff.) is still the main point. Regarding Borse, who presents a completely new chronology of his own, see my *Chronologie*, p. 69, n. 10, and pp. 118-119. Apparently Gerhard Schneider, *Die Apostelgeschichte* (Herders Theologischer Kommentar zum Neuen Testament, V), 1-2, Freiburg – Basel – Wien 1980-82, does not comment on the new Pauline chronology; the same applies to Jürgen Becker: *Paulus. Der Apostel der Völker*, Tübingen 1989, pp. 17-32: "Chronologische Fragen zum Leben des Apostels", and in Taylor, *Paul, Antioch and Jerusalem*, 1992 (see section 3.5 below), pp. 51-59, it is dismissed in an appendix.

8   See n. 2 above; I am referring to pp. 152-206: "Die Einpassung der Traditionen der Apg in den allein aufgrund der pln. Briefe gewonnenen Rahmen" (pp. 139-194 in *Paul, apostle to the Gentiles*).

9   Cf. my *Chronologie*, p. 17 with n. 36.

text of the Acts, which is, of course, a considerable benefit. Nevertheless, Lüdemann's commentary is undeniably, at least to a certain extent, intended to confirm or even defend the correctness of his own Pauline chronology. This applies for instance to the early dating of the Pauline mission in Macedonia and Greece to circa A.D. 40, the division of the narrative about Paul in Corinth in Acts 18.1-17 into two "tradition blocks",[10] and the fact that the episode in Antioch is dated before the Jerusalem Conference, and presumed to be the occasion of this.[11] All three examples are really nothing but improbable assumptions.[12] Having said that, it is important to note that this does not affect the validity of the new Pauline chronology – except in the eyes of its opponents![13] Regardless of its final construction, the new Pauline chronology will not need to be confirmed by external evidence such as an analysis of the Acts; it will be convincing in itself, otherwise it would not be "new" at all. Lüdemann seems to ignore this. In other words, it is doubtful whether a reasonably clear distinction between the tradition and the editorial adaptation of the Acts can be established solely on the basis of the text of the Acts – as Lüdemann tries to do – and whether such reconstructed traditions can be used to confirm the correctness of the new chronology.

In this context, it is also surprising to note that Lüdemann's analysis of the Acts makes very little use of the facts revealed by means of the new chronology. Instead of drawing inspiration from the central and really new insight provided by the Pauline chronology, he makes a rather traditional investigation into the Acts with reference to early Christianity, but seems less interested in finding out to what extent and in what ways the author of the Acts adapted his material. In fact, his distinction between editorial adaptation and tradition seems mostly to

---

10 Lüdemann, *Chronologie*, pp. 174-203: "Zur Frage der in Apg 18.1-17 enhaltenen Einzeltraditionen" (pp. 157-177 in *Paul, apostle to the Gentiles*); pp. 213-271: "Die eschatologischen Aussagen in 1Thess 4.13ff und 1Kor 15.51f als Bestätigung der frühen mazedonischen Wirksamkeit Pauli" (pp. 201-261 in *Paul, apostle to the Gentiles*); id., *Das frühe Christentum*, pp. 17-20 and 202-212 (pp. 10-12 and 195-204 in *Early Christianity*).

11 Lüdemann, *Chronologie*, pp. 77 ff. and 101 ff. (pp. 57 ff. and 75 ff. in *Paul, apostle to the Gentiles*). See also n. 22 and n. 96 below.

12 See my *Chronologie*, p. 82, n. 16, and pp. 123-124; see also Udo Schnelle, Der erste Thessalonicherbrief und die Entstehung der paulinischen Anthrolopogie, New Testament Studies 32 (1986), pp. 207-224, in part. pp. 208-209.

13 See n. 7 above.

serve the purpose of dismissing the editorial adaptation as secondary evidence. It is true that his procedure gives a certain guarantee that no details are overlooked. On the other hand, the coherence and general lines are in danger of disappearing; the material falls apart and becomes fragments of tradition. These may of course contain valuable historical information, but their contribution to a total understanding of the history and development of early Christianity is necessarily limited. This is probably due to the atomizing effect of the method of investigation, which submits each section of the Acts to a four-stage analysis including: 1) organization, 2) editorial adaptation, 3) tradition, and 4) history. In other words, a general commentary on the Acts based on an attempt to distinguish between editorial adaptation and tradition in section after section of the entire text of the Acts can hardly be used to reconstruct the earliest history of Christianity. Such a reconstruction must be based on the Pauline chronology, and the text of the Acts must then be brought into line with this.

3.1.3 The possible use of Paul's letters in the Acts?

Perhaps the problems mentioned above are linked to the question of the relationship between the Acts and Paul's letters. During the nineteenth century, most scholars took it for granted that the author of Lk. and Acts knew and used Paul's letters, but that point of view changed completely during the twentieth century. In 1963, Hans Conzelmann stated laconically Luke's failure to use Paul's letters for the account of his life.[14] And in his book about the Pauline passages in the Acts, *Der dreizehnte Zeuge*, Christoph Burchard maintains that the author must have known that Paul's letters existed, but had not read them and regarded them as "unimportant" compared to the other material he had.[15] In 1980, Gerhard Schneider maintained that if the author of the Acts did not use Paul's letters, it was because he did not intend to present Paul as a letter writer,

---

14 Conzelmann, *Die Apostelgeschichte*, p. 2 (p. xxxiii in *Acts of the Apostles*). On the other hand, he also says, ib.: "The individual points of contact between Acts and the letters [Act 9,21 – Gal. 1,13.23; Act 9,25 – II Cor 11.33] rest upon traditions in the Pauline churches. ... It is almost inconceivable, however, that the author of Acts knew nothing at all about the letters. Did he purposely ignore them?"

15 Christoph Burchard, *Der dreizehnte Zeuge. Traditions- und kompositionsgeschichtliche Untersuchungen zu Lukas' Darstellung der Frühzeit des Paulus* (Forschungen zur Religion und Literatur des Alten und Neuen Testaments, 103), Göttingen 1970, pp. 155-158: "Lukas' Verhältnis zu dem Paulusbriefen".

or to describe his theology, but wanted to emphasize how Paul had spread the Gospel "even in the farthest corners of the earth" (Acts 1.8).[16] In 1987, Gerd Lüdemann pointed out that none of the known similarities between Paul's letters and the Acts prove that the author of the Acts used the letters, and he concludes: "The question, therefore, is whether the evidence is not explained better by the hypothesis that Luke used traditions from the Pauline mission territories, individual items in which may have come from reading the letters. In what follows, by way of a test I have presupposed the "tradition hypothesis"."[17]

Lüdemann compares Paul's letters to the Pauline passages in the Acts, which are the product of a combination of tradition and editorial adaptation. Of course Paul's letters are not – and cannot be – identical to the tradition behind the Pauline passages in the Acts; otherwise the Acts would have been nothing but a combination of Paul's letters and an editorial adaptation such as we find in the Acts. Lüdemann even rejects any direct or close connection between Paul's letters and the tradition behind the Acts, or between Paul's letters and the editorial adaptation of the Acts. Considering the uncertain premises, this rejection is hardly reasonable. It also implies that the distinction between tradition and editorial adaptation in the Pauline passages in the Acts is (apparently) made without any use of Paul's letters – which is neither practicable nor desirable.

Finally, Lars Aejmelaeus, in his valuable investigation from 1987, *Die Rezeption der Paulusbriefe in der Miletrede*, has attempted to prove that the author of the Acts knew and used several of Paul's letters.[18] The question of dating Lk.-Acts has also been raised again: in 1990, C.F. Evans suggested that Lk. was written during the period A.D. 75 – 130, probably even in the last part of this period.[19] It goes without saying that the later Lk.-Acts are dated, the more likely it becomes that the author knew and used Paul's letters.

---

16 Schneider, *Die Apostelgeschichte*, 1, pp. 116-118.
17 Lüdemann, *Das frühe Christentum*, pp. 14-16; the quotation is taken from pp. 15-16 (p. 8 in *Early Christianity according to the Traditions in Acts*).
18 In his book *Luke. A New Paradigm*, 1989 (see section 2 above, n. 46), pp. 132-146: "Did Luke know any of the Pauline Letters?", Michael Goulder also comes to the conclusion that the author of Luke knew and used 1 Cor. and 1 Thess.
19 C.F. Evans, *Saint Luke* (TPI New Testament Commentaries), London – Philadelphia 1990, p. 14: "All that can be suggested ... as the date for Luke-Acts is between AD 75 and 130," and p. 111: "... that Luke wrote an apologia, in the fullest sense of the word, for

However the relationship of Paul's letters with the tradition behind the Acts and the adaptation of the Acts should be understood – and this relationship remains unclarified to this day – it is not reasonable to analyse the Pauline passages in the Acts without using Paul's letters, as for instance Lüdemann has done. On the contrary, instead of being left out of the investigation, Paul's letters should form the basis of any analysis of the Pauline passages in the Acts. Perhaps this method will even enable us to acquire more knowledge than we have today about the relationship between the letters on one side and the tradition and the editorial adaptation on the other side, so that we can avoid the risk of formulating doubtful hypotheses which can too easily prove to be wrong.

3.1.4 New insight

It soon appears that the Pauline chronology can readily provide quite a lot of information about the narrative of the Acts, although most of this information is "negative" in the sense that on certain points and in certain respects, the narrative proves to be wrong and therefore not historical. However, even "negative" knowledge – the knowledge that certain parts of the text are *not* true – is valuable, because when we know on which points and in what respects the narrative is notoriously wrong, we can begin to analyse them!

One of the most important discoveries is the fact that the three missionary journeys we know from the Acts and have seen indicated by different dotted lines on countless Bible maps, and which have dominated New Testament history to this day, originate in the adaptation of the Acts and are clearly unauthentic. They are not substantiated by any of Paul's letters.[20] There was no pause or interval between the "first" and "second" journeys,[21] because the

---

a non-Christian readership, and that, like Justin's *Apology*, it became by some route part of Christian literature."

20 Cf. Conzelmann, *Die Apostelgeschichte*, p. 7 (p. xliii in *Acts of the Apostles*): "The most important stylistic means used to achieve this picture of unilinear development is the schematization of Paul's work into missionary journeys. This has dominated the historical picture to the present day;" p. 72 (p. 98 in *Acts of the Apostles*): "Luke has created the conception of "journeys."" See also the passage referred to in n. 23 below.

21 See my *Chronologie*, p. 83, n. 19. Cf. Joachim Jeremias, Untersuchungen zum Quellenproblem der Apostelgeschichte, Zeitschrift für die neutestamentliche Wissenschaft 36 (1937), pp. 205-221, in part. pp. 217-218 = id., *Abba. Studien zur neutestamentlichen Theologie und Zeitgeschichte*, Göttingen 1966, pp. 238-255, according to which the description of the Jerusalem Conference in Acts 15 is an "addition" to the "Antiochian"

contents of Acts 15.4 ff. should really be "transferred" to 18.22, and Paul simply made no stop in Antioch before going to Jerusalem to attend the conference there (Acts 14.26-15.2); cf. 18.22.[22] The journey to Jerusalem in 18.22, which comes between the "second" and the "third" journey according to the "rectilinear"[23] representation of the Acts, was only a short break during the three years which Paul spent in Ephesus, not an interval between two "missionary journeys" – although it is true that he went to Jerusalem in order to attend the conference there.

As already mentioned, the journey to Jerusalem in Acts 11.27-30 and 12.25 is not a historical fact, but must be ascribed to the editorial adaptation of the Acts.[24] Finally, Paul's two visits to Galatia (Acts 16.6 and 18,23) are apparently confirmed by Gal. 4.13, but only apparently; in fact Paul went to Galatia only

---

source. It is important to note, however, that Jeremias considered Acts 15.1-33 and 11.30/12.25 as duplicates and therefore dated the Jerusalem Conference *before* "the first missionary journey".

22 Cf. Lüdemann, *Chronologie*, p. 167 (p. 151 in *Paul, apostle to the Gentiles*). See also my own *Die paul. Chronologie*, p. 82, n. 16; p. 83, n. 19; and Lüdemann, *Das frühe Christentum*, pp. 170 and 171, where he rightly says: "that ... the return to Antioch [Acts 14.26] gives a link back to 13.1-2 and shows the hand of the redactor Luke. That journey therefore must be excluded as an element of the tradition" (p. 171 – p. 164 in *Early Christianity*). On pp. 214-215 (p. 207 in *Early Christianity*), however, Lüdemann maintains that Acts 18.21b-23 refers to a journey to Antioch which took place before the Jerusalem Conference (the episode in Antioch, Gal. 2.11 ff., which he believes determined the Jerusalem Conference, Gal. 2.1-10 – note the reverse order!). This is contrary to all indications; cf. the passage referred to in n. 11 above. See also the passages referred to in n. 38 and n. 96.

23 The terms "Geradlinigkeit" and "Einlinigkeit" are used by Conzelmann in *Die Apostelgeschichte*, p. 7.

24 Cf. Georg Strecker, Die sogenannte Zweite Jerusalemreise des Paulus (Acts 11,27-30), first published in 1962, in: id., *Eschaton und Historie. Aufsätze*, Göttingen 1979, pp. 132-141. Cf. Schneider, *Die Apostelgeschichte*, 1, p. 113 with n. 54: "The reference to Paul's second journey to Jerusalem in Acts 11.27-30 is contradicted by Gal. 1.18 and 2.1. It is the result of an inference drawn by the author. Between his conversion and the Jerusalem Conference (Gal. 2.1-10; Acts 15.1-35), Paul was only in Jerusalem *once*" – but the reference to Acts 15.1-35 is irrelevant and confusing, and when Schneider comments on the dating of the Jerusalem Conference in *Die Apostelgeschichte*, 2, pp. 116 and 191, he seems inclined to believe that it took place *before* "the first missionary journey" (Acts 13-14) – i.e. just what he had previously called an inference drawn by the author of the Acts!

once, and since this visit corresponds with Acts 16.6, Acts 18.23 must be disregarded as evidence of a second visit.[25]

Having said that, we must not forget that apart from these discrepancies between the Pauline passages in the Acts and Paul's letters, there are also important similarities which cannot be dismissed as accidental, and which can therefore complicate the task of clarifying the relationship between tradition and editorial adaptation.

One of the most important problems in this context concerns the "Geradlinigkeit" ("rectilinearity") or "Einlinigkeit" ("unilinearity") which Hans Conzelmann and subsequently others identify as a distinctive feature of the narrative style of the Acts, and which also characterize the Pauline passages of the text.[26] The "rectilinear" character of the narrative can be seen from two contradictory points of view: from a "negative" point of view, it represents a distorting simplification of the history which the text attempts to describe, and from a "positive" point of view, it shows that the narrative of the Acts is on the whole true and correct. In fact, neither point of view is right. Probably the truth is that in several respects, the narrative of the Acts – or the tradition behind it – is in fact precisely as "rectilinear" as the historical order of events indicated in Paul's letters.

---

25 Cf. my *Chronologie*, pp. 78 ff. with n. 7 and n. 9; see also Michael Wolter, Apollos und die ephesinischen Johannesjünger (Act 18,24-19,7), Zeitschrift für die neutestamentliche Wissenschaft 78 (1987), pp. 49-73, in part. pp. 55 ff.: "lukanische Fiktion". Referring to Gal. 4.13, Wolter assumes (p. 55, n. 42) that Paul made only one visit to Galatia, when the congregations were being established there, but on this subject he refers to Lüdemann, *Chronologie*, pp. 124-125, which is not correct (see my *Chronologie*, p. 79, n. 9). See also n. 88 below.

26 Cf. n. 23 above. See also e.g. Lüdemann, *Das frühe Christentum*, pp. 214-215 (pp. 206-207 in *Early Christianity*). Th.H. Campbell, Paul's "Missionary Journeys" as Reflected in His Letters, Journal of Biblical Literature 74 (1955), pp. 80-87, maintained that the chronological order of the Pauline mission stations in Acts was confirmed by Paul's letters. W.G. Kümmel used this to defend the historical reliability of the Acts in his *Einleitung in das Neue Testament*, 14th ed., Heidelberg 1965, p. 177 = id., *Introduction to the New Testament*, New York – Nashville 1975, p. 254. A different view on this subject is presented by Hurd, in: *Christian History and Interpretation*, 1967 (see section 3.1 above), pp. 230-231. See also Alfred Suhl, *Paulus und seine Briefe. Ein Beitrag zur paulinischen Chronologie* (Studien zum Neuen Testament, 11), Gütersloh 1975, p. 81, n. 7; and Hare, in: Knox, *Chapters*, 1987/89 (see section 3.1 above), pp. xii-xiii.

This applies for instance to the chronological order of the various places where Paul lived: Philippi – Thessalonica – Corinth – Ephesus, and also to the lengths of time he spent in Corinth (eighteen months: Acts 18.11[27]) and Ephesus (three years: Acts 20.31[28]). On these points, the text proves to be historically correct, even according to the strictest critical investigations. However, on another point it is quite wrong, i.e. the short duration of Paul's stay in Thessalonica (only three weeks according to Acts 17.2), which is contradicted by Paul's letters, in particular Phil. 4.16.[29]

The same also applies to the number of visits Paul made to the places where he had lived and founded congregations. For instance, when he wrote his letters to the Corinthian congregation, he had visited Corinth only once (when he founded the congregation there). The visit to Greece (i.e. Corinth) mentioned in Acts 20.2-3 was really only his second visit, a fact which is fully confirmed by the Corinthian correspondence.[30] So in this case, the "rectilinear" narrative of the Acts has not sacrificed the truth for historical and literary simplification by leaving out an extra visit to Corinth. Similarly, when Paul wrote 1 and 2 Thess., he had visited the Macedonian congregations in Philippi and Thessalonica only once, i.e. when he founded the congregations there, and the visits in Macedonia mentioned in Acts 20.1 and 20.4 ff. are really his first visits in the area since he founded these congregations. On the other hand, the Acts says nothing about his imprisonment in Ephesus, where he wrote the captivity letters, Phil., Col. and Philem.[31] Furthermore, the description of Paul's three years in Ephesus: Acts

---

27 For information on Lüdemann's interpretation of Acts 18.1-17, see n. 10 above.
28 For information on the references to three months (Acts 19.8) and two years (Acts 19.10) in Ephesus, see the passage referred to in n. 32 below.
29 See my *Die paul. Chronologie*, p. 109.
30 See my *Die paul. Chronologie*, especially pp. 34-41 and 102-106. Since then I have become acquainted with Eduard Golla, *Zwischenreise und Zwischenbrief*, 1922 (see section 3.6 below) – an investigation which also rejects the idea of an "intermediate journey" and an "intermediate letter". Unfortunately, it was completely overshadowed by Hans Windisch' commentary on 2 Cor. from 1924.
31 The fact that Phil. – and Col. and Philem. – were written during a term of imprisonment in Ephesus is established in my *Die paul. Chronologie*, pp. 18-26: "Die Gefangenschaft des Paulus in Ephesus". Unlike many other exegetes who share my theory, but for the most part only support it with circumstantial evidence, I believe that I have substantiated it: the double travelling plan for Timothy and Paul himself respectively in Phil. 2.19 and 2.23-24 recurs in 1 Cor. 4.17 and 4.18-21 (cf. the passage referred to in n. 33 below); note also that the word *tachéos* in Phil. 2.24 and 1 Cor. 4.19 expresses a promise in the

18.19-20.1[32] is, on the whole, completely misleading, although it is correct on a few points, such as Paul's dispatch of Timothy (and Erastus) from Ephesus to Macedonia: Acts 19.22, which is identical to Timothy's (and the brothers': 1 Cor. 16.11!) journey from Ephesus to Philippi and Corinth: Phil. 2.19-23 and 1 Cor. 4.17.[33] Another point on which this description is correct is Apollos' ministry in Corinth, where he worked independently of Paul: Acts 18.24-28, which corresponds to 1 Cor. 3.6.[34]

The Acts says nothing about Paul's letters – it only mentions the letters which are quoted in the text: James' letter with the apostolic decree, Acts 15.23-29, and Lysias' letter to Felix, 23.26-30.

---

former case and a threat in the latter case; 1 Cor. was written in Ephesus (1 Cor. 16.8), so Phil. must have been written during a term of imprisonment in Ephesus and, what is more, before 1 Cor. In his review of my book in Journal of Theological Studies 38 (1987), pp. 505-507, F.F. Bruce asked how there could be a *praetorium* (Phil. 1.13) in the proconsular province Asia, which was under civilian administration (see section 2.1.1 above): "Anyone who assigns an Ephesian provenance to Philippians should explain what a *praitórion* was doing in Ephesus" (p. 506). For the time being, I can only refer to Martin Dibelius, *An die Thessalonicher I/II. An die Philipper* (Handbuch zum Neuen Testament, 11), 3rd. ed., Tübingen 1937, in which Dibelius also maintains that Phil. was written during Paul's imprisonment in Ephesus, and writes that *praitórion* can mean "the residents (cf. the parallel *toîs loipoîs*) of the governor's palace ..., in Ephesus also the praetorians stationed there, cf. the epitaph in Wood's Discoveries at Ephesus, the epitaphs in appendix No. 2, p. 4" (p. 65). Dibelius refers to J.T. Wood, *Discoveries at Ephesus including the Site and Remains of the Great Temple of Diana*, London 1877, appendix (Inscriptions from Tombs, Sarcophagi, etc.), p. 4, No. 2: "DIS MANIBVS/T. VALERIO. T. F. SECVNDO. MILITIS. COH/ORTIS VII/ PRAETORIAE. CENTVRIAE. SEVERI/T. VALERIVS. T. F. SECVNDVS. MILES./ COHORTIS. VII. PRAETORIAE. CEN/TVRIAE. SEVERI. DOMO. LIGVRIAE/ MILITAVIT. ANNIS VIII. STATI/ONARIVS. EPHESI. VIXIT/ ANNOS. XXVI. MENSES VI." It is important to note, however, that Dibelius' interpretation of the inscription (which really consists of two inscriptions) is incorrect. I hope to be able to return to the whole question with the help of Bengt Malcus, so that it can be finally established that Paul's letter to the Philippians was in fact written during his imprisonment in Ephesus. On praetorium, see section 1.2.1, n. 62.

32   For information on this subject, see Walter Grundmann, Paulus in Ephesus, Helikon 4 (1964), pp. 46-82; Francis Pereira, *Ephesus. Climax of Universalism in Luke-Acts. A Redaction-Critical Study of Paul's Ephesian Ministry (Acts 18.23-20.1)* (Jesuit Theological Forum Studies, 1), Anand (India) 1983.

33   See n. 31 above.

34   See my *Die paul. Chronologie*, p. 8, n. 17, p. 17, n. 37, p. 85, n. 24.

Another very important point which needs to be clarified is the question of the Judaists and the scant reference to them in the Acts.

The Acts says nothing about the Judaists' activities in the Pauline congregations; we shall return to this later, in section 3.4. However, from Paul's letter to the Galatians we know that the Judaists were active in Paul's congregations, but that they did not assert themselves until Paul came to Ephesus. We also know that it was during the three years he spent there that he and Barnabas (who is not mentioned in the Acts after 15.36-41; but cp. Col. 4.10 and 1 Cor. 9.6) and Titus (who is not mentioned at all in the Acts, but is referred to only in Paul's letters[35]) went to Jerusalem to participate in the conference there in order to solve the Judaistic problem. And finally we know that all Paul's letters – with the exception of 1 and 2 Thess. – were written within a period of one year at the most (between February 54 and February 55). Some of them were written towards the end of his imprisonment in Ephesus, which was a result of his conflict with the Judaists, others were written shortly after; several of these letters reflect the confrontation with the Judaists, including the interpretation of the Mosaic law and Paul's attempt to deal with this problem.[36]

According to Acts 18.18, however, it was not in Ephesus, but in Cenchreae – before he went to Ephesus – that Paul had his hair cut off and took a Nazirite vow which could be fulfilled only in the temple of Jerusalem, and which therefore meant that he had to go to Judea immediately.[37] The author of the Acts

---

35 Paul first met Titus in Ephesus, and Titus had not been in Corinth (2 Cor. 7.14!) before Paul sent him there with the first letter to the Corinthians: see my *Die paul. Chronologie*, pp. 84-85 with n. 21, and pp. 96-98. See also n. 86 below.

36 See my *Chronologie*, in particular pp. 76-88: "Die Erwähnung von Titus im Galaterbrief".

37 Grundmann has explained the problem of the Nazirite vow as follows (Helikon 4 (1964), p. 50, n. 7): The hypothesis that Paul went to Jerusalem according to Acts 18.22 (see n. 3 above) is also supported by "the vow mentioned in Acts 18.18, which was taken by Paul, not Aquila; but the problem is that he should have had his hair cut off in Jerusalem; cf. Joseph. Bell. Jud. II 15, 1; Strack-Billerbeck, Kommentar zum NT aus Talmud und Midrasch II 747-751, whereas Luke says that he had his hair cut off in Cenchreae." I myself have always understood this passage to mean that although Paul had to fulfil the Nazirite vow in Jerusalem and must then have his hair cut again, he had it cut when he decided to take the vow, as a symbol of the vow and for practical reasons – he might not be able to have a haircut for a long time! Cf. Conzelmann, *Die Apostelgeschichte*, p. 108 (p. 155 in *Acts of the Apostles*): "Certainly nothing would have prevented having one's

---

does not explain why Paul had to go to Judea (Acts 18.22!), probably because he had already "used" the material for the Jerusalem Conference in Acts 15.4 ff., or because he did not know the reason. As far as the Judaists are concerned, the Acts never mentions them, except when they appear in Jerusalem: in Acts 15.1-2, 5 and 21.20-22. The first of these texts is notoriously suspect: for one thing, it refers to a gathering in Antioch which never took place,[38] for another, it is an obscure exposition of the following passage concerning the Jerusalem Conference.[39] And according to the latter text, there were many thousands of Judaists among the Jews – which brings F.C. Baur's famous and plausible conjecture to mind.[40] Baur's theory, which turns the Judaists, i.e. law-abiding Jewish Christians, into fanatical Jews, or "zealots",[41] is wrong and therefore unacceptable, because it is clearly the author's intention to emphasize the increasing number of *Christian* Jews; cf. Acts 1.15; 2.41; 4.4; 6.1, 7.[42] Whatever the case, the Acts' references to the Judaists are desultory and absolutely unreliable.[43] Furthermore, the author fails to explain the meaning of

---

hair cut before the vow as well. Luke, however, thinks of the cutting of the hair [Paul's haircut at Cenchreae] as an element of the vow itself." The reason for this misunderstanding and whether it should be blamed on Luke or the tradition before him remain open to discussion.

38 See n. 22 above.

39 See Lüdemann, *Das frühe Christentum*, p. 173.

40 The conjecture consists in deleting the words *tôn pepisteukóton*, Acts 21.20, so that the text refers to Jews, not Judaists: Baur, *Paulus* (see section 3.4 below), Stuttgart 1845, pp. 199-200 = 2nd ed., I, Leipzig 1866, pp. 227-228. According to Haenchen, *Die Apostelgeschichte*, p. 539, n. 3 (p. 608, n. 4 in *The Acts of the Apostles*), Baur had presented this theory as early as in 1829; it was presented again by Johannes Munck, *Paulus und die Heilsgeschichte* (Acta Jutlandica, XXVI, 1), Copenhagen 1954 (English translation: *Paul and the Salvation of Mankind*, London 1959), pp. 235-236 – this is one of the few points on which Baur and Munck agree with each other.

41 See section 2.1.2 above.

42 Cf. Lüdemann, *Das frühe Christentum*, p. 240. However, Lüdemann says about the basic tradition: "Many Jews who are zealous for the law belong to the Jerusalem community" (p. 242; p. 234 in *Early Christianity*); furthermore, he maintains that "the nomistic character of the Jerusalem community in the 50s" is a historical fact (p. 244; p. 326 in *Early Christianity*); but this conglomerate of editorial adaptation and tradition is not convincing. Walter Schmithals' analysis in *Paulus und Jakobus* (Forschungen zur Religion und Literatur des Alten und Neuen Testaments, 85), Göttingen 1963, pp. 70-80 (pp. 85-96 in *Paul and James*), is much better.

43 Cf. Schmithals, *Paulus und Jakobus*, p. 73.

the Nazirite vow in Acts 18.18, probably because he is unsure of his facts. It seems reasonable to assume that there is a genetic connection between the Nazirite vow in Acts 18.18 and the four Nazirites in Acts 21.23. Combined with the knowledge of the origins of the Judaistic movement we can acquire from Paul's letters, this assumption will, if proved right, contribute towards clarifying the extent and character of the author's editorial adaptation of the Acts.

As regards the Acts' inadequate information about the Judaists, it is important to note that Paul's letters clearly indicate that the Judaists first appear after Paul has come to Ephesus.[44] This is important because it contradicts the existence of a connection between "Hebrews" (Acts 6.1 ff.) and Judaists on one side, and "Hellenists" (Acts 6.1 ff.) and Paul on the other, a connection which researchers have been inclined to take for granted ever since F.C. Baur. The idea of such a connection has been – and still is – fundamental for our understanding of early Christianity, its history and development.[45] This idea has nothing to do with Paul's letters but is based entirely on the representation of the Acts, which is wrong on this point: there is no historical connection between the Judaists, whose first appearance in history is dated as late as the early fifties, and the "Hebrews"; nor is there any connection between Paul and the "Hellenists". The situation must have been far more complicated than this simplified picture will have us believe. It is therefore necessary to include Acts 6.1 ff. and the entire question of the Hebrews and Hellenists in the analysis of the Acts and the investigation as a whole in order to acquire a better understanding of the history of early Christianity.

In other words, such an investigation cannot be limited to the individual Pauline passages in the Acts; the first parts of the Acts, in this case Acts 6.1 ff., must also be included. This will be attempted in section 3.3 below.

To a certain extent, the same applies to the last parts of the Acts. After Acts 20.2-3, referring to the three months in Greece (i.e. Corinth, where Paul wrote his letter to the Romans), the representation of the Acts is no longer "covered" by Paul's letters. On the other hand, this passage marks the beginning of a narrative which appears to follow Paul's activities almost day by day until his

---

44 2 Cor. 7.14. See n. 35 above.
45 This view is represented by Martin Hengel, Zeitschrift für Theologie und Kirche 72 (1975), pp. 151-206 (see section 3.3 below) = id., *Between Jesus and Paul*, 1983 (see section 2.5), pp. 1-29. See also the passage referred to in n. 130, section 2.6.5.

arrival in Rome. This narrative also contains those parts of the Acts in which – apart from Acts 16.10-17 – we find the "we" passages: Acts 20.5-8, 20.13-15, 21.1-18 and 27.1-28.16. Let it be understood once and for all that these "we" passages come from one single narrative, which the author of the Acts must have adapted for his own purpose, cutting it into fragments and placing these where we find them now. This means that the "we" passages represent a "source" which deserves much attention, both for its own sake, and because the editorial adaptation of these passages can give us an impression of the way in which the author of the Acts adapted his material.

3.2 Disciples and apostles

Bibliography

J.B. Lightfoot: *Saint Paul's Epistle to the Galatians. A Revised Text with Introduction, Notes, and Dissertations*, London 1865 (later reprinted many times), pp. 92-101: "The name and office of an Apostle".

Adolf Harnack: *Die Lehre der Zwölf Apostel nebst Untersuchungen zur ältesten Geschichte der Kirchenverfassung und des Kirchenrechts* (Texte und Untersuchungen zur Geschichte der altchristlichen Literatur, II/1-2), Leipzig 1884.

Id.: *Die Mission und Ausbreitung des Christentums in den ersten drei Jahrhunderten*, first published in 1902, 4th ed. Leipzig 1924, pp. 332-379: "Die christlichen Missionare (Apostel, Evangelisten, Propheten, bzw. Lehrer; nicht-berufsmäßige Missionare)".

Karl Holl: *Der Kirchenbegriff des Paulus in seinem Verhältnis zu dem der Urgemeinde*, first published in 1921, in: id., *Gesammelte Aufsätze zur Kirchengeschichte*, II, Tübingen 1928, pp. 44-67 = K.H. Rengstorf, ed., *Das Paulusbild in der neueren deutschen Forschung* (Wege der Forschung, XXIV), Darmstadt 1964, 2nd ed. 1969, pp. 144-178.

Olof Linton: *Das Problem der Urkirche in der neueren Forschung. Eine kritische Darstellung* (Uppsala Universitets Årsskrift 1932), Uppsala 1932, pp. 69-101: "Die Apostel".

K.H. Rengstorf: art. "apostéllo, apóstolos", in: *Theologisches Wörterbuch zum Neuen Testament*, I, Stuttgart 1933, pp. 397-448.

Hans von Campenhausen, Der urchristliche Apostelbegriff, Studia Theologica 1 (1947-48), pp. 96-130.

Ferdinand Hahn: Der Apostolat im Urchristentum. Seine Eigenart und seine Voraussetzungen, Kerygma und Dogma 20 (1974), pp. 54-77.

Gerd Theißen: *Soziologie der Jesusbewegung. Ein Beitrag zur Entstehungsgeschichte des Urchristentums* (Theologische Existenz heute, 194), Munich 1977, 2nd ed. 1978 = id., *Jesusoverleveringen og dens sociale baggrund. Et sociologisk bidrag til den tidligste kristendoms historie*, translated by Geert Hallbäck, Copenhagen 1979.

Wilhelm Pratscher, *Der Herrenbruder Jakobus und die Jakobustradition* (Forschungen zur Religion und Literatur des Alten und Neuen Testaments, 139), Göttingen 1987.

3.2.1 The problem

In 1865, J.B. Lightfoot[46] presented a critical study of the "apostle" concept, a work which is still appreciated today. Among other things, he pointed out that the word "apostle", when it represents a person, does not mean a messenger (an "angel"), but a delegate who has the same authority and power as the one who sent him.

Lightfoot also explained that referring to the classical Greek use of the word is pointless: in classical Greek, "apostle" rarely means a person, but mostly "a naval expedition, a fleet despatched on foreign service". In the classical Greek literature, only Herodotus (5th century B.C.) has a couple of examples which show that the word could be used about a person; on this point, however, he seems to represent the popular idiom which is also used in the Greek translation of the Old Testament (LXX, Septuaginta), in the New Testament and in the contemporary official language of the Jews.

The Greek word *apóstolos* occurs only once in LXX (1 Kgs. 14.6, as a translation of the Hebrew past participle *shaluach*); otherwise it is used to describe the Jewish delegates whom the Jewish leaders in Palestine sent out to the Diaspora, for instance to deliver official letters (cf. Acts 28.21) or – until the temple was destroyed in A.D. 70 – to collect the annual temple tax. Although the existing evidence of this Jewish use of the word dates from a relatively late period, Lightfoot maintains that it represents the origin of its Christian meaning, including the fact that Jesus called his closest disciples "apostles". I shall return to this later in the book.

---

46   Joseph Barber Lightfoot (1828-89), Fenton John Anthony Hort (1828-92) and Brooke Foss Westcott (1825-1901) formed the famous Cambridge triumvirate; see e.g. Graham A. Patrick, *F.J.A. Hort. Eminent Victorian*, Sheffield 1987.

However, Lightfoot also emphasizes that when used in a Christian context, the name "apostle" was by no means limited to the twelve disciples. On the contrary, the disciples are rarely called "apostles" in the Gospels. In fact, this happens only once in the Gospel of Mark (Mk. 6.30), once in the Gospel of Matthew (Matt. 10.2), and never in the Gospel of John. The statement in Jn. 13.16 does not refer directly to the twelve disciples, but rather to the general principle that "a servant is not greater than his master, nor a messenger (Greek: *apóstolos*) than the one who sent him". In this case, the word has its normal meaning when used about a person: a delegate. Furthermore, although Luke uses the word to describe the twelve disciples in Lk. 6.13, the same author also uses the word in a wider sense when he calls Barnabas and Paul apostles (Acts 14.4, 14) – I shall also return to this below.

Paul himself, whose letters represent the earliest existing evidence of Christian usage, did not limit the use of the word to the twelve disciples alone. On the contrary, 1 Cor. 15.5, 7, which refer to "the Twelve" and "all the apostles" respectively, seem to show that "the apostles" included many more people than "the Twelve". Moreover, Lightfoot believes that James, Jesus' brother, was also an apostle (1 Cor. 15.7; Gal. 1.19), as were Silvanus (1 Thess. 2.6), Junia and Andronicus (Rom. 16.7).

It is difficult to define the exact meaning of the Christian "apostle" concept. There are several indications, however, that an apostle must have seen Christ after his resurrection (as Paul had; cf. 1 Cor. 9.1; 15.8) and must have been called by God (as Paul had been; cf. 1 Cor. 1.1). The more than 500 brothers who had seen Christ (1 Cor. 15.6) had apparently not been called and were therefore not apostles; and Timothy and Apollos were not apostles because they had not seen Christ.

Lightfoot's demonstration of the fact that the word "apostle" was not restricted to the twelve disciples is important, but it lacks precision. His observation that its meaning came from Jewish usage is also valuable, but why does he not draw the obvious conclusions that the functions of the apostles were linked to the communications between Palestine and the Diaspora, that Paul's apostolate was unusual in the sense that it went beyond these limits, and that Jewish origins were required for apostles? Finally, Lightfoot's observation that the word "apostle" occurs only once in LXX seems to prevent him from seeing other connections with Old Testament ways of thinking, for instance the

154

connection between the concept of prophet and the concept of apostle: after all, both the prophet and the apostle were God's messengers.

3.2.2 The discovery of the Didache

The Didache (or The Teaching of the Twelve Apostles) made a sensation when it was published in 1883 by Philotheos Bryennios (1833-1914). The document was soon included in the collection of "The Apostolic Fathers" and was believed to be very old, possibly even from the apostolic era. The community rules of the Didache indicated that although the ecclesiastical office did not yet hold the central position it later acquired, the charismatic church leaders were certainly regarded as the highest authorities, despite the fact that they did not hold official offices, though such offices are mentioned (bishops and deacons: Did. 15.1-2; cf. even Phil. 1.1). Among the charismatic church leaders were the travelling apostles. The passage about the travelling teachers, apostles and prophets (the same categories are mentioned in 1 Cor. 12.28 in this order: apostles, prophets, teachers) is quoted below (Did. 11.1-13.7):[47]

11.1 Whosoever then comes and teaches you all these things aforesaid, receive him. 2 But if the teacher himself be perverted and teach another doctrine to destroy these things, do not listen to him, but if his teaching be for the increase of righteousness and knowledge of the Lord, receive him as the Lord.

3 And concerning the Apostles and Prophets, act thus according to the ordinance of the Gospel [cf. Matt. 10.40; Lk. 10.16; Jn. 13.20]. 4 Let every Apostle who comes to you be received as the Lord, 5 but let him not stay more than one day, or if need be a second as well; but if he stay three days, he is a false prophet. 6 And when an Apostle goes forth let him accept nothing but bread till he reach his night's lodging; but if he ask for money, he is a false prophet [cf. Matt. 10.9-10 with parr.; Lk. 22.36].

7 Do not test or examine any prophet who is speaking in a spirit, "for every sin shall be forgiven, but this sin shall not be forgiven." 8 But not everyone who speaks in a spirit is a prophet, except he have the behaviour of the Lord. From his behaviour, then, the false prophet and the true prophet shall be known. 9 And no prophet who orders a meal in a spirit shall eat of it: otherwise he is a false prophet. 10 And every prophet who teaches the truth, if he do not what he teaches, is a false prophet. 11 But no prophet who has been tried and is genuine, though he enact a worldly mystery of the Church, if he teach not others to do what he does himself, shall be judged by you: for

---

47 English translation: *The Apostolic Fathers. With an English Translation by Kirsopp Lake* (The Loeb Classical Library), I, London – Cambridge (Mass.) 1912, pp. 325-329.

he has his judgment with God, for so also did the prophets of old. 12 But whosoever shall say in a spirit "Give me money, or something else", you shall not listen to him; but if he tell you to give on behalf of others in want, let none judge him. ...

13.1 But every true prophet who wishes to settle among you is "worthy of his food." 2 Likewise a true teacher is himself worthy, like the workman, of his food [Matt. 10.10; Lk. 10.7; 1 Cor. 9.14; 1 Tim. 5.18].[48]

The publication of Did. in 1883 had the effect of convincing people that the then prevalent view on the origins and development of the ecclesiastical office was right and even proved to be right. In the beginning, there were charismatic preachers who travelled from one place to another ("itinerant charismatics", as Gerd Theißen calls them); together with the resident local congregation, they represented the original organization. Later came the resident local church leaders, who obtained permanent (paid?) offices through the institutionalization of their power. Even if Did. was not a document from the apostolic era itself, but was written during the post-apostolic era, it indicated sufficiently clearly how things had developed, and the sceptic attitude to itinerant teachers, apostles and prophets that is reflected in the document seemed to confirm the view that Did. gave a true picture of the "original" situation as it was during the apostolic era.

It was largely on the basis of Did. that Harnack formed his opinion of the apostle concept, an opinion which had a considerable effect on the understanding of the following generations, because of Harnack's authority. Teachers, apostles and prophets were turned into one category of charismatic persons by "apostolizing" the teachers and prophets and "de-apostolizing" the apostles (in fact, the names "apostle" and "prophet" are interchangeable: Did. 11.6 – see the quotation above). Furthermore, Harnack pointed out that all three

---

48 See also Gerd Theißen, Wanderradikalismus. Literatursoziologische Aspekte der Überlieferung von Worten Jesu im Urchristentum, first published in 1973, in: id., *Studien zur Soziologie des Urchristentums* (Wissenschaftliche Untersuchungen zum Neuen Testament, 19), 2nd enlarged ed., Tübingen 1983, pp. 79-105 = The Wandering Radicals: Light Shed by the Sociology of Literature on the Early Transmission of Jesus Sayings, in: id., *Social Reality and the Early Christians: Theology, Ethics, and the World of the New Testament*, Minneapolis 1992, pp. 33-59; John Dominic Crossan, Itinerants and Householders in the Earliest Kingdom Movement, in: Elizabeth A. Castelli/Hal Taussig, eds., *Reimagining Christian Origins: A Colloquium Honoring Burton L. Mack*, Valley Forge 1996, pp. 113-129, especially pp. 117 ff.

categories had the same characteristic custom of travelling from one congregation to another.

It has been rightly maintained, however, that *travelling* is not in itself a decisive factor of the apostle concept, and that it is not synonymous with *having been sent*,[49] although this remains the central point of the original Christian apostle concept. You could also say: nothing in Paul's letters indicates that the apostle Paul travelled restlessly from one place to another; on the contrary, he used to stay a long time with the congregations he founded (he even established himself as an artisan: 1 Thess. 2.9; 2 Thess. 3.8; 1 Cor. 4.12; Acts 20.34) in order to ensure that they were able to stand on their own feet before he left.[50] However, the essential part of Harnack's apostle concept is the idea of charisma: like the teacher and the prophet, the apostle is personally, spiritually and morally endowed with a special "gift of grace" (Greek: *chárisma*: 1 Cor. 12.28; cf. Did. 11.7 ff.). This gives him an unlimited authority which is independent of any institution or office. This basically psychological point of view is very characteristic of the liberal theology represented by Harnack. On the other hand, he leaves the apostle concept unclarified because he has to bracket the apostle with the teacher and the prophet as a consequence of his theory that spiritual power is the decisive factor.

On the subject of "those who were apostles before Paul himself" (Gal. 1.17), Harnack gave the following explanation.

In addition to the original, charismatic apostolate, of which Paul was the principal representative, and which was unrestricted and unlimited in terms of numbers, there was, according to Harnack, another apostolate represented by a strictly limited number of apostles: the Jerusalem leaders themselves. In other words, Harnack distinguished between the *charismatic* apostolate (for instance Paul's apostolate) and the *traditionalistic* apostolate (for instance the apostolate of James, the Lord's brother). The traditionalistic apostolate originated in the Jewish apostle concept, according to which an "apostle" was a delegate entrusted with special tasks such as tax collection (cf. the discoveries of Lightfoot mentioned in section 3.2.1 above). This was a secular task and had nothing to do with preaching religion. At a certain point – according to Harnack, it was during the Jerusalem Conference: Gal. 2.10 – the charismatic

---

49   See Linton, *Das Problem der Urkirche*, pp. 78-79.
50   See section 3.1.4, the passages referred to in nn. 27-29.

apostolate encountered this traditionalistic apostolate. When this happened, the charismatic apostolate immediately took over the functions of the traditionalistic apostolate in the sense that it undertook the task of collecting tributes from the charismatically founded congregations on behalf of the leaders in Jerusalem. Harnack wrote: "The principle that from then on in history, the Twelve became the twelve *apostles*, or even just *the* apostles, was established by Paul, and he established it – paradoxically – in order to emphasize his own importance."[51]

This explanation – imaginative as it is – is not acceptable. In the first place, it is far from certain that it was decided at the Jerusalem Conference that the congregation in Jerusalem should impose a tax on the Gentile Christian congregations. Secondly, there is no evidence that the Jewish apostle concept represents the historical origin of the Jerusalem apostle concept; Lightfoot himself declared in 1865 that the Jewish material was of little importance when it came to explaining the Christian apostolate; on the other hand, he regarded it as a necessary – but not sufficient – explanation of the fact that Jesus appointed his twelve disciples apostles. In the third place, it is uncertain whether the leaders of the original Jerusalem congregation really represented a "traditionalistic" apostle concept as opposed to Paul's "charismatic" apostle concept. If the Jerusalem leaders had also experienced appearances or "visions" of Christ (1 Cor. 15.5 ff.), it is difficult to understand why they were not "charismatics" like Paul, for instance, unless there is a fundamental difference between "real" appearances of Christ on the earth and ecstatic visions of Christ.[52]

On these grounds, it must be concluded that Harnack did not succeed in explaining the relationship between Paul and the leaders of the original congregation. This is probably due to the fact that he was most interested in the "charismatic" apostle concept as he saw it represented by Paul and Did., while he could not find any convincing explanation of the Jerusalem apostle concept, which in his view must have been quite different.

---

51 Harnack, *Mission u. Ausbreitung*, p. 336.
52 Cf. Lindblom, *Gesichte u. Offenbarungen*, 1968 (see section 2.7 above), pp. 78-113: "Christophanien und Christusepiphanien".

3.2.3 "The Twelve" = "all the apostles"?

In his study from 1921, Karl Holl investigated the relationship between Paul's and the Jerusalem congregation's views on the apostolate and the church. In 1 Cor. 15.5 ff., he believed he had found a text that indicated the existence of two different views: v. 5, which is about the appearances of Christ to Cephas (i.e. Peter) and "the Twelve", and v. 7, which describes the appearances of Christ to James (the Lord's brother) and "all the apostles", are both seen in contrast to vv. 8-9, which is about Christ's appearance to Paul himself. The most obvious explanation of this text is that "the Twelve" and "all the apostles" represent two different groups. Holl avoids this explanation by maintaining that "all the apostles" are "the Twelve" *plus* James, the Lord's brother, who soon placed himself at the head of the group of apostles, and that in fact, Paul reported the two series of appearances loyally in 1 Cor. 15.5 and 15.7.[53] In other words, Holl rejects the view that had been generally accepted since Lightfoot, according to which "all the apostles" represented a larger group (including Paul himself, Barnabas, Andronicus, Junia and others), and maintains that the group of "all apostles" was a *closed* and *exclusive* circle.[54] Gal. 2.10, which refers to the collection for the poor in Jerusalem, also shows that the congregation in Jerusalem considered themselves entitled to exercise authority over all other congregations, and that Paul had to accept this. As regards Paul's own apostolate, he had joined an established and exclusive circle as a "latecomer" (1 Cor. 15.8) and was fully conscious of this (in this passage, Paul calls himself *éktroma*, "one who is prematurely born"). According to Holl, this was also reflected in the original apostles' lack of respect for him, which was a problem he had to fight for the rest of his life.

Holl saw all this as a confirmation of the view held by F.C. Baur and the Tübingen school: early Christianity was dominated by two incompatible wings, the Jerusalem wing and the Pauline wing.[55] Although Holl's view is reminiscent of Harnack's, it differs from it: Holl maintains that the *traditionalistic* apostolate ("the Twelve" plus James) did not develop gradually, but arose

---

53 Holl, in: *Paulusbild*, pp. 149 ff.

54 In spite of many differences, Holl's point of view is reminiscent of Harnack's. On the other hand, the 1924 edition of Harnack's *Mission u. Ausbreitung* is probably to some extent inspired by Holl; see also n. 55 below.

55 See Holl, in: *Paulusbild*, p. 164, on the subject of the collection: "The Tübingen school was on the right track in this matter, but they did not follow up their ideas in detail."

spontaneously, in the immediate vicinity of the source of events, the appearances of Christ,[56] and when Paul wanted his apostolate to be recognized, it was because his church concept was different from that of the original church.

However, Holl is wrong to interpret the fact that Paul called himself "(the) one who is born prematurely" (1 Cor 15.8) as an indication that he considered "all the apostles" (1 Cor 15.7) to be a closed and exclusive circle. Because in any circumstances, the name Paul gives himself here is "an enormous exaggeration".[57] And more important still, "all the apostles" (with or without James) cannot possibly mean "the Twelve". Presumably only a few of "the Twelve" were apostles; we only know for certain that Peter and Zebedee's sons, James – who according to Acts 12.2 suffered martyrdom as early as during the reign of Herod Agrippa (dead A.D. 44) – and John (Gal. 2.9), were apostles.

However, the assessment of both Harnack's and Holl's views on the Jerusalem and the Pauline apostle concept depends mainly on the still unanswered question of whether they had unconsciously let themselves be influenced by the twelve-man apostle concept we find in Lk.-Acts. This will be examined in the following section.

3.2.4 The historical origins of the apostle concept

In his study of the historical origins of the apostle concept, Lightfoot drew attention to the influence of the Jewish apostle institution. Harnack did the same when he defined the Jerusalemitic apostle concept as opposed to Paul's. On the other hand, Holl attached no importance to Jewish origins except in relation to the delegates who visited the Christian congregations (Phil. 2.25; 2 Cor. 8.23; cf. Acts 14.4, 14).

Since then, however, these Jewish origins have been investigated by others, including Karl Heinrich Rengstorf. Possibly as a result of these investigations, the Jewish apostle concept – a "delegate" who has been given authority by the one who sent him (cf. Jn. 13.16) – crystallized into a purely formal concept, the *content* of which was entirely determined by the one who had sent the delegate.

From this point of view, being an apostle is nothing in itself, but being the apostle of *Christ* is something very special. As Linton said in 1932: "If that is so ..., then the characteristics of Christ's apostles, and the *substance* of the

---

56 Cf. Linton, *Problem der Urkirche*, p. 89.
57 Linton, ib., p. 87.

apostolate, do not lie in the fact that they were apostles, but that they were the apostles of *Christ*."[58]

This view forms the basis of Hans von Campenhausen's epoch-making treatise from 1947-48 on the original Christian apostle concept. Moreover, he emphasized the necessity of referring to documents from the apostolic era itself in order to understand the importance of being an apostle of Jesus Christ – in other words, we have to use Paul's letters, which are the only existing Christian documents from the apostolic era.

Campenhausen was soon able to establish the fact that the idea of twelve apostles did not originate in the apostolic era (Paul mentioned "the Twelve", but not "the twelve apostles"; otherwise he would have excluded himself from being an apostle); it originated in the post-apostolic era, or to be more precise, in Lk.-Acts, in which "the Twelve (disciples)" are simply identified with the apostles, and Paul – a main character in the Acts! – is thus excluded from belonging to the circle of apostles: Lk. 6.13; Acts 1.15-26.[59] Admittedly, Barnabas and Paul (in this order!) are called "apostles" in Acts 14.4, 14, but in this context it means "congregation delegates", i.e. delegates from the congregation in Antioch (Acts 13.1-3, which refers to the "first missionary journey").[60]

Furthermore, it is true that "the Twelve (disciples)" are called "apostles" in Mark 6.30 and Matt. 10.2, when they are sent out by Jesus, but this can in no way be understood as a title: "Nobody would interpret this isolated instance of the use of *apóstolos* as a special title for the Twelve if Luke and the later tradition had not accustomed us to think of it as such."[61] As already mentioned, Jn. never uses the word "apostles" when referring to the disciples.

Paul's own use of the word "apostle" is clear: Besides himself (Rom. 1.1; 1 Cor. 1.1; 2 Cor. 1.1; Gal. 1.1 etc.), Paul also refers to "all the apostles" (1 Cor. 15.7), counting himself as one of them. He mentions this as an indisputable fact, but not as something he takes for granted. It is important to note that the other

---

58 Linton, *Problem der Urkirche*, p. 93; cf. Campenhausen, StTh 1 (1947-48), p. 103 with n. 2, which also quotes these words and rightly gives Linton the credit for having understood the fundamental importance of the relationship between form and content.

59 This is the reason why the author of Lk.-Acts cannot have been Paul's collaborator Luke the physician (Col. 4.14; Philem. 24), as already explained in section 3.1.2.

60 Campenhausen, StTh 1 (1947-48), p. 115.

61 Campenhausen, ib., p. 105.

apostles do not dispute Paul's position as Christ's apostle (on the contrary, they fully approved his and Barnabas' apostolates at the Jerusalem Conference: Gal. 2.7-9) any more than Paul disputes the other apostles' rank as Christ's apostles. If the situation may appear different (cf. e.g. Harnack and Holl), it is due to a misinterpretation of Paul's own statement in Gal. 1.1 ff. In this passage, Paul does not defend his apostolate against those who were apostles before him and who might have disputed his right to be an apostle; he makes it clear to his own Galatian congregations, who were exposed to the influence of the Judaists (see section 3.4 below), what it really means to be the apostle of Jesus Christ: "what Paul wants to point out is not the special rank which characterizes his apostolate, but simply the nature of the new Christian apostolate, whose authority cannot be challenged by any human authority, even from Jerusalem."[62] According to Campenhausen, there are no indications at all "that Paul, in all his conflicts with his rivals, defends his own apostolate. What matters to him is the question of his preaching, his spiritual power, his integrity and his belief in being an apostle, and also his rights as an apostle in certain congregations – but not his own apostolate as such."[63]

Paul's letters *from the apostolic era itself* had no essential influence on the apostle concept such as it was handed down to posterity – this was Harnack's theory.[64] On the contrary, it was Lk.-Acts *from the post-apostolic era* that formed the apostle concept which has prevailed ever since, i.e. that "the apostles" are "the Twelve (disciples)". As Campenhausen rightly points out: "Through him [the author of Lk.-Acts], the adapted tradition created the permanent future concept of the apostle, who is both a witness and a missionary. Only the twelve apostles of Jesus represent this concept in what you might call a symbolical, concentrated form."[65] Since the traditional assessment of the apostolic era is based on the Acts, it has proved difficult to disregard this basically unauthentic apostle concept, which has the undeniable advantage of being easy to handle from a theological point of view.

---

62 Campenhausen, ib., p. 104.
63 Campenhausen, ib., p. 108.
64 See n. 51 above. Campenhausen rightly rejects this theory, StTh 1 (1947-48), p. 118, n. 1: "Paul has nothing to do with this development, although the contrary view has been expressed time and again since Ad. Harnack."
65 Campenhausen, StTh 1 (1947-48), p. 118.

At this stage, it might be useful to review the similarities and the differences between Lightfoot's and Campenhausen's respective views on the apostle concept. Among the similarities is the fact that they both believed in a wider apostle concept: we do not know the number of apostles; perhaps it included James, the Lord's brother, and Barnabas, and perhaps others were included as well. Among the differences is the fact that while Lightfoot counted the twelve disciples among the apostles – Jesus himself had appointed them and called them apostles (Lk. 6.13!) – Campenhausen denied this: the idea that the twelve disciples were also apostles appears in Lk.-Acts, not before. There can be no doubt that Campenhausen is right in correcting Lightfoot's view on this point.

Others have studied the apostle concept after Campenhausen, e.g. Ferdinand Hahn (in 1974), but no important new elements have been added to what had already been discovered. However, Ferdinand Hahn deserves credit for pointing out the four groups of passages in Paul's letters in which the term "apostle" is used: 1) Phil. 2.25 and 2 Cor. 8.23 about congregation delegates with temporary tasks; 2) 1 Cor 9.5; 15.7; Gal. 1.17-19 about a permanent group of delegates who had regular apostolic functions and probably included Barnabas, the Lord's brother James, Andronicus and Junia; 3) Gal. 1.1, 11-12, 15-17; 2.6-9 and other passages about Paul's own position and functions as an apostle; and 4) 2 Cor. 11.5 and 12.11 about the "super-apostles", whom Hahn does not identify with the original apostles in Jerusalem, but with the "pseudo-apostles" (11.13), who masqueraded as apostles of Christ (also 11.13).[66]

Of these four groups, only No. 2 and No. 3 are interesting in the present context – plus No. 4, but only in as far as it is – at least to some extent – identical to No. 2. Apart from this, the attempts made by Hahn and others to clarify the problematics are relatively unimportant; unfortunately Hahn did not quite succeed in maintaining Campenhausen's discovery that "the twelve apostles" is a fictive concept invented by the author of Lk.-Acts or the tradition behind this authorship.

All things considered, we must conclude that "disciples" and "apostles" are two completely different concepts, and that these two groups are only, at the

---

66 With this interpretation, Hahn, KuD 20 (1974), p. 60, endorses the now prevalent opinion. Campenhausen has a different point of view, StTh 1 (1947-48), p. 107: "after all, it is possible that Paul is referring to the Jerusalem authorities." See also section 3.6 below.

most, partially identical: we only know for certain that Peter and Zebedee's two sons, James and John, were both disciples and apostles, but all the others of the twelve disciples have faded into obscurity.

This supports the theory that the apostle concept as such came into existence during the period after the death and resurrection of Jesus, not before. The church was founded by the apostles; and as its followers grew in number and spread over increasing geographical areas, it came to represent a new beginning based on the interpretation of the events connected with the life, death and resurrection of Jesus.

3.2.5 *James' special position*

There is one person who should in all probability be counted among the apostles: James, Jesus' brother (see Gal. 1.19; 2.9, 12; 1 Cor. 9.5; 15.7), despite the statement in Jn. that James and the other brothers had no faith in Jesus while he lived (Jn. 7.5). Only the fact that James was an apostle – and perhaps even more than that: see the paragraph below – can explain that he is mentioned separately in Gal. 1.19, and that he presided over the negotiations during the Jerusalem Conference as a matter of course. This meeting would then be a real *apostolic* meeting with James, Peter and John on one side of the table and the apostles Paul and Barnabas on the other (naturally Titus, who was also in Jerusalem: Gal. 2.1, 3, did not participate in the negotiations). According to Gal. 2.12, Peter immediately obeyed James when he spoke. Furthermore, it appears from the Acts that this James is the unchallenged leader of the congregation in Jerusalem (Acts 12.17; 15.13 ff.; 21.18 ff.), and in fact, Paul's letters also presents him as the leader of the apostles (Gal. 2.9; 1 Cor. 15.7). Of course James is also mentioned in the Gospels as the first of Jesus' brothers, i.e. the second son of the family (Mark 6.3 with parallel texts).

How did this happen?

Jesus' brother James is mentioned not only in the New Testament, but also in Josephus (died circa 100) and in Hegesippus (died circa 180). They both describe James' martyrdom: Josephus, Ant. Jud. XX, 199-203 (chapter 9.1), and Hegesippus in Eusebius, Hist. eccl. II, 23.4-18. The narratives are independent of each other, but each describes in its own way how James and other Jewish Christians were stoned to death, an event that has been dated to circa 62. Josephus refers to James as the brother of Jesus, who was called Christ.

As far as I can see, James' prominent position in the history of the earliest Christianity can be explained only by referring to his origins: he was the closest brother of the crucified Jesus and, as such, his earthly heir as far as the kingship is concerned; cf. sections 2.4, 2.5, 2.6 and 2.7 above.

The importance of the royal origins of Jesus' relatives is emphasized in a narrative by Hegesippus, in Eusebius, Hist. eccl. III, 19-20.6 and 32.5-6: because of their Davidic origins, two grandsons of Judas and a brother of Jesus (cf. Mk. 6.3), were brought before the emperor Domitian (81-96), who interrogated them about their properties and their political views. On the former subject, they explained that they had 9,000 denarii between them, and owned a plot of land which they cultivated themselves. To prove this, they had to show their hands to the emperor, who was immediately convinced that they were farmers. On the latter subject, they referred to the preaching of Jesus about the end of the world and the impending judgement. Once the emperor had satisfied himself that they were harmless people, they were allowed to go home and were, according to Hegesippus, entrusted with supervising the congregations.[67] Other passages in Hegesippus confirm that Davidic descent was regarded with much suspicion.[68]

We would undoubtedly be going too far if we regarded James' position as a primitive Christian "caliphate" or "papacy",[69] and there is no reason to do so. Both "caliph" and "pope" are misleading terms. On the other hand, we should remember that James was of Davidic and therefore royal descent. After the death of Jesus, James was the oldest representative of his family and the obvious candidate to assume what had previously been Jesus' kingship. This is the more evident as the disciples themselves had been entrusted with royal power: Lk. 22.28-30; Matt. 19.28,[70] and the Christians were to be kings and

---

67 Cf. Niels Hyldahl, Hegesipps Hypomnemata, Studia Theologica 14 (1960), pp. 70-113, see pp. 86-87.

68 Hyldahl, ib., pp. 89 ff.

69 For information on this subject, see Hans von Campenhausen, Die Nachfolge des Jakobus. Zur Frage eines urchristlichen "Kalifats", Zeitschrift für Kirchengeschichte 63 (1950-51), pp. 133-144; Martin Hengel, Jakobus der Herrenbruder – der erste "Pabst"? in: Erich Gräßer/Otto Merk, eds., *Glaube und Eschatologie. Festschrift für Werner Georg Kümmel zum 80. Geburtstag*, Tübingen 1985, pp. 71-104.

70 Cf. Gerd Theißen, NTSt 35 (1989), pp. 343-360 (see section 2.3.2 above).

priests and judges: 1 Cor. 6.3; 1 Pet. 2.1-10. Even the apostles had to defer to Jesus' brother James.

3.3 Hellenists and Hebrews

Bibliography

Niels Hyldahl: *Udenfor og indenfor. Sociale og økonomiske aspekter i den ældste kristendom* (Tekst & Tolkning, 5. Monografier udgivet af Institut for Bibelsk Eksegese), Copenhagen 1974, pp. 7-52: "Udenfor – Jødisk fattigforsorg på Jesu tid".

Martin Hengel: Between Jesus and Paul. The "Hellenists", the "Seven" and Stephen (Acts 6.1-15; 7.54-8.3), first published in German in 1975, in: id., *Between Jesus and Paul. Studies in the Earliest History of Christianity*, London 1983, pp. 1-29, with notes pp. 133-156 (see also above, sections 2.5 and 2.6.5, the passage referred to in n. 130).

Nikolaus Walter: Apostelgeschichte 6.1 und die Anfänge der Urgemeinde in Jerusalem, New Testament Studies 29 (1983), pp. 370-393.

Heikki Räisänen: The "Hellenists" – a Bridge Between Jesus and Paul? in: id., *The Torah and Christ. Essays in German and English on the Problem of the Law in Early Christianity/Deutsche und englische Aufsätze zur Gesetzesproblematik im Urchristentum* (Publications of the Finnish Exegetical Society, 45), Helsinki 1986, pp. 242-306 – with a comprehensive but not complete bibliography.

Edvin Larsson: Hellenisterna och urförsamlingen, in: Tryggve Kronholm and others, eds., *Judendom och kristendom under de första århundradena. Nordiskt patristikerprojekt 1982-85*, Vol. I, Stavanger – Oslo – Bergen – Tromsø 1986, pp. 145-164 = Die Hellenisten und die Urgemeinde, New Testament Studies 33 (1987), pp. 205-225.

Craig C. Hill: *Hellenists and Hebrews. Reappraising Division within the Earliest Church*, Minneapolis 1992.

3.3.1 The viewpoint to date

As already mentioned when discussing the question of the relationship between Paul's letters and the Acts (end of section 3.1.4), it is necessary to examine the question of the Hellenists and the Hebrews in Acts 6.1 ff. in order to gain an insight into the earliest history of Christianity and its relationship with early Judaism.

The fact is that for many years, New Testament exegetes have interpreted the question of the Hebrews and the Hellenists, and the conflict between them, as a profound disagreement in theology and ecclesiastical policy in the history of early Christianity. According to this interpretation, the division between the two wings, the Hebrews and the Hellenists, was seen as an immediate forerunner of the disagreement which, as we know from Paul's letters, existed between the Judaists and Paul himself in the middle of the century. I shall return to the question of the Judaists in the following section, but first I shall try to clarify the question of the Hellenists and the Hebrews.

The text in Acts 6.1-7 reads as follows:

1 During this period, when disciples[71] were growing in number, a grievance arose on the part of the Hellenists against the Hebrews; they complained that their widows were being overlooked in the daily distribution.[72] 2 The Twelve called the whole company of disciples together and said, "It would not be fitting for us to neglect the word of God in order to assist in the distribution. 3 Therefore, friends, pick seven men of good repute from your number, men full of spirit and of wisdom, and we will appoint them for this duty; 4 then we can devote ourselves to prayer and to the ministry of the word." 5 This proposal proved acceptable to the whole company. They elected Stephen, a man full of faith and of the Holy Spirit, along with Philip, Prochorus, Nicanor, Timon, Parmenas, and Nicolas of Antioch, who had been a convert to Judaism, 6 and presented them to the apostles, who prayed and laid their hands on them.

7 The word of God spread more and more widely; the number of disciples in Jerusalem was increasing rapidly, and very many of the priests adhered to the faith.

The text then proceeds to describe how Stephen was accused, interrogated and finally stoned to death (Acts 6.8-7.60). It says in Acts 8.1:

1 ... That day was the beginning of a time of violent persecution for the church in Jerusalem; and all except the apostles were scattered over the country districts of Judea and Samaria. ...

---

71 In the Acts, "disciples" are Christians in general: according to Lk.-Acts, "the twelve disciples" are identical to "the apostles", so the term "disciple" can be used to describe all Christians; cf. section 3.2.4 above.

72 The western text has the addition: "in the Hebrews' service", which correctly indicates that the Hebrews were responsible for the daily distribution; this addition does not represent the original text, but shows that it was understood correctly.

The following chapters describe how Christianity spread in Samaria and Syria, Paul's conversion near Damascus and his first visit to Jerusalem as a Christian, where he had a dispute with the Hellenists, who planned to kill him (Acts 9.29), for which reason he had to be sent away to Tarsus. Then it says, in Acts 11.19:

19 Meanwhile those who had been scattered after the persecution that arose over Stephen made their way to Phoenicia, Cyprus, and Antioch, ...

In Antioch, Christians from Cyprus and Cyrene began to preach the Gospel to the Greeks as well, so the Gentile mission had now become a reality (Acts 11.20),[73] but of course this does not mean that the Jewish mission had stopped.

Ever since F.C. Baur (1792-1860) published his book about Paul in 1845, New Testament research has been almost entirely dominated by the view that the narrative of the Hellenists and the Hebrews and the seven overseers of the poor in Acts 6.1 ff. reflected a profound theological disagreement between two parties or wings of earliest Christianity: on one side were the Hebrews, who were strictly law-abiding and did not differ from their Jewish contemporaries except in their belief in Jesus Christ; their leader was the apostle Peter, the head of the Twelve. On the other side were the Hellenists, led by Stephen, the head of the Seven, and they associated their belief in Christ with freedom from the obligation to observe the Mosaic law. Accordingly, it was the Hellenists, not the Hebrews, who alone suffered persecution after Stephen's martyrdom, and who spread the "law-free" Gospel among Gentile nations when they had been expelled from Jerusalem. Thus the contrast between the Judaistic movement and Paulinism, which has been more or less taken for granted since Baur, was based on the earliest history of the Jerusalem congregation.[74]

---

73 In Acts 11.20, there are two variants: "the Greeks" (Greek: *toùs hellénas*) and "the Hellenists" (Greek: *toùs hellenistás*). Unfortunately the latter variant has been accepted in Nestle-Aland, 26th ed., and in *The Greek New Testament*, 3rd ed., but it makes no sense and is the result of a misunderstanding. The old Nestle had chosen the right variant: "the Greeks". Otherwise the term "Hellenists" only occurs in Acts 6.1 and 9.29.

74 Baur, *Paulus, der Apostel Jesu Christi* (see section 3.4 below), 1845, pp. 38-41 = 2nd ed., I, 1866, pp. 45-49; cf. Goguel, *La naissance du christianisme*, 1946 (see section 3 above), pp. 190-201; Haenchen, *Die Apostelgeschichte*, 13th ed. 1961 (see section 3.1.2 above, n. 6), pp. 218-222 (pp. 264-269 in *The Acts of the Apostles*) – and many, many others. Baur says: "We must therefore presume that the first persecution of the Christians had the important consequence for the congregation in Jerusalem that the two parties, the

There is a common feature in the traditional interpretation of the narrative in Acts 6.1-7: although it is a well-known fact that several problems remain unsolved – including the question of the Hellenists and who they were, the Seven, the conflict situation as such – this knowledge does not prevent the assumption that the narrative covers a serious conflict in the original congregation in Jerusalem. It is just generally assumed that an opposition arose between two groups of the congregation at a very early stage. On a certain occasion, this opposition was exposed, materializing in the Hellenists' demand for participation in decision-making or – this has also been maintained – in the Hebrews' attempt to force the Hellenists out. According to this interpretation of the text, the conflict resulted in the establishment of a double organization: one branch belonging to the Twelve, with Peter as their leader, and another belonging to the Seven, with Stephen as their leader. Taking care of social problems was not the main task of the Seven; they were a parallel to the Twelve, and the contrast between the two groups was theological. Stephen's execution marked the beginning of the expulsion of the Hellenistic part of the congregation, and it was the Hellenists who founded the Gentile mission, which was so unpopular among the members of the other branch of the Jerusalemitic congregation. After the expulsion of the Hellenists, the Jerusalemitic congregation consisted of Hebrews alone, who were now free from any interference from the Hellenists, and free to pursue their zeal for the Mosaic law, cf. Acts 21.20.[75] Finally, Stephen's speech (Acts 7.2 ff.) appears to throw light on the Hellenists' theology, showing its critical attitude to the temple and the sacrificial cult in Jerusalem.

3.3.2 Open questions

It is possible, however, that this whole construction is based on a misinterpretation of Acts 6.1 ff., and is really the result of a circular argument. Without knowing it himself, Conzelmann makes this very clear. He writes: "The

Hebrews and the Hellenists, who had so far been close to each other in spite of certain differences, were now further separated. The fact that the Jerusalem congregation consisted of Hebrews alone made them adhere more closely to their strict Judaizing attitude, which eventually developed into a regular opposition to the freer Hellenistic Christianity" (p. 39 = 2nd ed., I, pp. 46-47). Baur even calls the Hellenist Stephen Paul's predecessor.

75 See the comments on this text in section 3.1.4, the passages referred to in n. 40 – n. 43.

actual events which lie behind this account of the selection of the seven can be perceived only vaguely, because Luke has radically reworked the material in order to avoid the impression of an internal crisis during the time of the apostles."[76] According to this statement, it is difficult to discover the real events behind the narrative because this is unclear, and by implication, the narrative is unclear because the real events were connected with a crisis which the narrative attempts to conceal. So the point to be proved, i.e. the existence of opposition between the Twelve and the Seven, between the Hebrews and the Hellenists, is used as evidence for the conclusion! During the interpretation of the narrative, which is the only source of information we have on this subject, both the historical reality and the narrative itself have been distorted by a constant preoccupation with the presumed historical events. The narrative must therefore be analysed on its own premises and interpreted regardless of the historical results – a requirement which a redaction-critical analyst like Hans Conzelmann ought to have acknowledged and satisfied in his own work.

If the traditional interpretation was correct, it would have led to several obviously unreasonable conclusions. In the first place, the increasing number of disciples mentioned in the introduction to the narrative would represent a cause of the conflict – but this would be inconsistent with the end of the narrative, where it says that after the conflict had been resolved, the number of disciples in Jerusalem was increasing rapidly, and that even many priests from the temple adhered to the faith. In other words, according to the traditional view, the increasing numbers of Christians would have exposed the history of the earliest Christianity to constant threats of collapse, but the text says nothing of this. Secondly, it would imply that the congregation's former economic and social organization with communal property managed by the apostles (e.g. Acts 4.34-35) had collapsed irredeemably, so that it had to be replaced by a completely new type of management of seven overseers of the poor in order to enable the congregation to function at all. Such a contradiction between Acts 2-5 and 6 could, of course, be explained away by suggesting that as from 6.1, the author of the Acts must have used a new source which he had not used in the preceding chapters; but in that case he must either have misunderstood his source or failed to observe how revealing it really was in relation to the narratives in chapters 2-5. Both alternatives are equally improbable.

---

76 Conzelmann, *Die Apostelgeschichte*, p. 43 (p. 44 in *Acts of the Apostles*).

3.3.3 A new viewpoint

Our sources of information are extremely limited when it comes to defining the meaning of the term "Hellenist" (Acts 6.1; 9.29), whereas the term "Hebrew" occurs more frequently (Acts 6.1; 2 Cor. 11.22; Phil. 3.5; the heading of Heb.). There is no reason to doubt, however, that both terms refer to a difference in languages: the Hellenists were Greek-speaking Jews, while the Hebrews spoke Aramaic. Moreover, Acts 6.9 strongly indicates that this difference in languages was linked to other differences in culture and sociology: the Hebrews were native Palestinian Jews, while the Hellenists were immigrants from the Diaspora now living in Palestine. There is general agreement on this central point. Both Hellenists and Hebrews were Jews.

On this basis, it is possible to establish a link to earlier parts of the Acts in which the exact terms "Hellenists" and "Hebrews" are not used. I am referring to the narrative concerning the day of Pentecost, Acts 2.1-13. In 1968, Bent Noack wrote: "The whole context makes it clear what the author wants to say, i.e. that the inhabitants of Jerusalem included both the people who were born and raised in the city, and Jews from the Diaspora who had settled in the holy city. This statement [i.e. Acts 2.5: "Now there were staying in Jerusalem devout Jews drawn from every nation under heaven"] is simply necessary in order to explain the list in vv. 9-11 and prevent it from being understood as a list of foreigners in general. In other words: when the reader comes to v. 6: "... a crowd of them gathered ...," he already knows that this "crowd" stands for the entire population of Jerusalem or at least a representative cross section of them, *both native inhabitants and newcomers, both Palestinian Jews and former Diaspora Jews.*"[77]

In fact, this already explains the meaning of the terms "Hebrews" and "Hellenists" in Acts 6.1: the population of Jerusalem, which consisted of native Palestinian Jews and newcomers who were former Diaspora Jews. We need look no further for a definition of "Hebrews" and "Hellenists" in the narrative – we need not even go as far as to assume that they were Christians, much less take this for granted.

---

77 Bent Noack, *Pinsedagen. Litterære og historiske problemer i Acta kap. 2 og drøftelsen af dem i de sidste årtier* (Københavns Universitets festskrift, marts 1968), Copenhagen 1968, p. 116 (the italics in the quotation are mine).

In 1924, Paul Billerbeck presented the material he had collected concerning the Jewish poor relief in Palestine at the time of Jesus.[78]

It appears from this that two categories of Jewish poor were entitled to financial relief from public funds: A) local poor people who lived permanently in their native city or town, and B) other poor people, mostly those staying temporarily in a city or town – for instance pilgrims in Jerusalem – but also Jews who had settled as newcomers and sunk into poverty for some reason.

A) Money for the local poor was collected from all local residents once a week in a special box (Hebr. *chupa*).[79] The distribution also took place once a week, usually on Fridays. Every poor person who was entitled to this form of relief received enough money for fourteen meals, i.e. two meals a day during the following week.

B) The local residents also had to contribute to the relief for foreigners; in this case the collection took place every day, and usually the contributions consisted of food, which was collected in a tray or dish (Hebr. *tamchuj*). The food was also distributed every day, one day's ration for each poor foreigner who was entitled to this form of relief.

None of the exegetes who knew the Jewish organization of poor relief from Billerbeck has been able to use his material in connection with the interpretation of Acts 6.1 ff. I am referring here to Joachim Jeremias, Kirsopp Lake, Ernst Haenchen, and others.[80]

Even Jeremias is unable to use the information, but maintains that the distribution mentioned in Acts 6.1 consisted of food supplies for one day at a time, and that it was concentrated in one place, Jerusalem; but strictly speaking these conclusions are not based on information from Billerbeck, but on Acts 6.1 itself.

---

78 (Hermann L. Strack and) Paul Billerbeck, *Kommentar zum Neuen Testament aus Talmud und Midrasch*, II, Munich 1924, pp. 643-647; and id., IV/1, Munich 1928, pp. 536-558: "Die altjüdische Privatwohltätigkeit". Cf. Hyldahl, *Udenfor og indenfor*, 1974, pp. 39 ff. (with further references); Schürer, *History*, II, 1979, p. 437 (very brief). See also the observation referred to in n. 55, section 1.2.1.

79 Cf. 1 Cor. 16.2!

80 Joachim Jeremias, *Jerusalem zur Zeit Jesu. Kulturgeschichtliche Untersuchungen zur neutestamentlichen Zeitgeschichte*, II A (Die sozialen Verhältnisse: Reich und arm), Leipzig 1924, p. 47; Kirsopp Lake, *Beginnings*, Part I, Vol. V, 1933, pp. 140-151: "The Communism of Acts II. and IV.-VI. and the Appointment of the Seven"; Haenchen, *Die Apostelgeschichte*, 1961, p. 215 (pp. 261-262 in *The Acts of the Apostles*).

In his work from 1933, Kirsopp Lake refers to Billerbeck and writes: "It is obvious that these facts throw a flood of light on the "daily ministration" of Acts vi. 1," but then he proceeds to draw the following conclusion: "and the natural explanation of the story is that the Christians formed a separate community in so far as they collected and distributed a "basket" and a "tray" independently of the rest of the Jewish population."[81] In this case, the problem of connecting the two categories of Jewish poor relief ("basket" and "tray") with Acts 6.1 ("the daily ministration") is avoided rather than solved, and the result is conjecture concerning a separate form of Christian poor relief organized "independently of the rest of the Jewish population" – a Christian poor relief, the existence of which is based on no other evidence whatsoever.

In 1961, the two kinds of poor relief are also mentioned by Haenchen, who knows them from Billerbeck, but like Jeremias and others too, Haenchen maintains that the daily distribution mentioned in Acts 6.1 corresponds neither to A) nor B) as described above. According to Haenchen, the daily distribution in Acts 6.1 was for the local poor and took place not once a week, but every day as in B). From this, Haenchen draws the same conclusion as Lake, i.e. that a Christian poor relief scheme for widows of Hellenists must have existed even before the conflict between the Hebrews and the Hellenists; this relief was similar but not identical to the Jewish relief system, and it did not become necessary until the Christians were no longer entitled to relief from the Jews. According to Haenchen, the Christian Jews in Jerusalem must therefore have been excluded from the Jewish society for rather a long time. In fact, Haenchen draws a number of very far-reaching conclusions from the presumed uselessness of the Jewish information: 1) Originally, the Jewish poor relief also included the Christian poor; 2) but soon the Christians were excluded from the Jewish society, so they established their own daily distributions to the congregation's poor, including widows of Hellenists, but organized by the Hebrew branch of the congregation; 3) at one point, because of theological and ecclesiastical disagreements between Hellenists and Hebrews, the latter deprived the Hellenistic widows of their share of the daily distributions; and 4) therefore the Hellenists established their own congregation in Jerusalem with their own poor relief organized by the Seven.

---

81 Lake, *Beginnings*, Part I, Vol. V, p. 149.

To this day, the prevalent view is that from the beginning, the earliest Christianity split up into two branches, one Hebrew and one Hellenistic, and that the Hellenists among the Christians were more progressive and were first to break away from the traditional Judaism, so that they represented the link with Paul and his view of Christianity.[82]

3.3.4 The application of Billerbeck's observations

In my opinion there can be no doubt that exegetes have been too hasty in deciding that the Jewish information which Paul Billerbeck brought to light could not be used for the purpose of clarifying the conflict situation in Acts 6.1. The argument that the daily distribution mentioned there must have been a separate Christian arrangement because it was organized for the benefit of local poor who would otherwise have been entitled to the Jewish weekly distribution, is both premature and untenable. The point is that the daily distribution mentioned in Acts 6.1 was organized for the benefit of the *Hellenistic* widows, as it says explicitly, and they were of course not local poor, but foreigners.

In the light of this fact, the picture that emerges of the conflict is this: In Jerusalem, the Hebrews – who as native inhabitants were naturally responsible for the management of both the weekly and the daily distributions – stopped the distributions to the widows who had come from the Diaspora. The consequences of this restriction were quite serious, so the Hellenists raised objections against the Hebrews and reproached them for failing to fulfil their duty to support these widows. Being relatively few in number, however, their objections were made in vain; the Hellenistic widows were still turned away from the tables during the daily distributions of the meals which they were otherwise entitled to receive from the Hebrews.

Thanks to its growth (Acts 6.1!), the Christian congregation had by then sufficient financial resources to step in and do what was necessary in this

---

82   Cf. Hengel, 1975; David Seccombe, Was there Organized Charity in Jerusalem before the Christians? Journal of Theological Studies 29 (1978), pp. 140-143; Räisänen, 1986; Larsson, 1986; Lüdemann, *Das frühe Christentum*, 1987, pp. 79-85, esp. p. 84. The only exception I know is Nikolaus Walter, 1983, whose understanding of Acts. 6.1 ff. is similar to, but independent of mine; see Walter, NTSt 29 (1983), esp. pp. 376 ff. However, Walter has not succeeded in explaining the connection between the distribution of food to the foreigners mentioned in Billerbeck and "the daily distribution" mentioned in Acts 6.1-2. See also Craig C. Hill, 1992.

situation: take over the support of the non-Christian widows among the Hellenistic Jews in Jerusalem by establishing a relief organization of Christian Hellenists; this initiative met with opposition from the Jews (Acts 6.8 ff.; 9.29), but that is a different matter.

As already mentioned, there must have been differences in language and culture between the Hebrews and the Hellenists, since the Palestinian Jews and the Jews from the Diaspora spoke different languages and had different cultural backgrounds. It is important to keep in mind, however, that the disagreement between them was a purely Jewish matter which had nothing to do with the Christians, so there is no reason to believe that there were any theological or even ecclesiastical problems involved in the situation; nor is there any reason to see the differences between Hebrews and Hellenists as a reflection of the contrast between the Judaistic movement and the "Paulinism" we know from Paul's letters from the middle of the first century. Above all, the difference in language can easily be overestimated: in Palestine too, most Jews spoke Greek,[83] and the apostle Peter himself spent some time in Antioch, the capital of Syria (Gal. 2.11 ff.), where few people can have spoken Aramaic.

The observation in Acts 8.1 that all Christians *except the apostles* were scattered because of the persecution that began after Stephen's martyrdom (cf. 11.19) is entirely due to the editorial adaptation of the tradition and cannot be used for drawing any conclusions about the historical truth. The idea that the apostles had to stay in Jerusalem to wait for the power from above (cf. Lk. 24.49) must have been so fixed in the mind of the author of Lk.-Acts that he could not imagine that they might not have stayed there; in fact, the observation in Acts 8.1 can only be used as an example to illustrate the redactional work of the author and his strong influence on the history of Christianity: to this day, the concept of "the twelve apostles" in Lk.-Acts remains fixed in most people's minds.

As mentioned above, it is important to distinguish between A) the weekly distribution of money to local poor, and B) the daily distribution of food to

---

83 Saul Liebermann, *Greek in Jewish Palestine. Studies in the Life and Manners of Jewish Palestine in the II-IV Centuries C. E.*, New York 1942; Johnson, *Purpose of the Biblical Genealogies*, 1969 (see section 2.4 above), p. 187: "It is well known that knowledge of Greek was common even among Aramaic-speaking peasants in Palestine, and especially among the upper and middle classes, including Palestinian Rabbis;" see also the documentation there, pp. 187 ff.

foreigners – a logical system, at least in theory. The question is whether the system functioned in the same way in practice at all times and in all places.

When it comes to the question of the historical truth behind Acts 6.1 ff., there is every reason to be sceptical. Having established the fact that the conflict between Hebrews and Hellenists did not take place within the earliest congregation in Jerusalem, but in the Jewish society, we have to decide whether the narrative itself can be taken at face value. On this point, we should recall that the Acts is a relatively late and secondary text compared to Paul's letters. Furthermore, it is reasonable to assume that it reflects mainly social conditions such as the author knew them from his own lifetime. The inscription from Aphrodisias in Asia Minor from circa A.D. 200 (see section 1.4.2 above) belonged to a Jewish "soup-kitchen", i.e. an institution that supplied food to the poor. This seems to indicate a poor relief of the kind described in category B) above, i.e. a daily distribution of food, rather than a weekly distribution of money as in category A). It is an inscription from a building, and one of the first words is the otherwise unknown Greek word *pátella*. One of the editors writes about this word: "The Mishnaic Hebrew word for "dish" [*tamchuj*] is used in the Mishnah and Tosephta and in both Talmudim as the name of the charitable institution, organized in Jewish communities for the daily collection (in a dish, in fact) and distribution of cooked food *gratis* to the poor and vagrants. ... *pátella*, we suggest, could stand for the distribution station for charity food – i.e. a community soup-kitchen."[84] If the author of the Acts gained his knowledge of the Jewish poor relief from the Jewish Diaspora, then Acts 6.1 ff. cannot be used as evidence of any conflict between Hebrews and Hellenists in Jerusalem in the first century, during the apostolic era itself, which means that all discussions concerning a conflict between two wings in the earliest Christianity must cease once and for all.

---

84 Robert Tannenbaum, in: Reynolds/Tannenbaum, *Jews and God-Fearers at Aphrodisias* (see section 1.4 above), p. 27. In addition to the texts mentioned in this section, I also refer to the Testament of Job; see Bent Noack, Om Jobs Testamente som kristent skrift, in: *Israel – Kristus – Kirken. Festskrift til professor, dr. theol. Sverre Aalen på 70-årsdagen den 7. december 1979* (Tillegshefte 5 til Tidsskrift for Teologi og Kirke), Oslo – Bergen – Tromsø 1979, pp. 27-40; Berndt Schaller, *Das Testament Hiobs*, in: *Jüdische Schriften aus hell.-röm. Zeit* (see section I above), III/3, 1979, pp. 301-387; Michael A. Knibb/Pieter W. van der Horst, eds., *Studies on the Testament of Job* (Society for New Testament Studies, Monograph Series, 66), Cambridge 1989.

3.4 The Judaists

Bibliography

Ferdinand Christian Baur: *Paulus, der Apostel Jesu Christi. Sein Leben und Wirken, seine Briefe und seine Lehre. Ein Beitrag zu einer kritischen Geschichte des Urchristenthums,* first published in Stuttgart 1845, 2nd ed. Leipzig, I-II, 1866-67, here esp. I, pp. 280-287: "Der Brief an die Galater".

Walther Schmithals: *Paulus und Jakobus* (Forschungen zur Religion und Literatur des Alten und Neuen Testaments, 85), Göttingen 1963 = *Paul and James* (Studies in Biblical Theology, 46), London 1965.

Philipp Vielhauer: Gesetzesdienst und Stoicheiadienst im Galaterbrief, in: Johannes Friedrich/Wolfgang Pöhlmann/Peter Stuhlmacher, eds., *Rechtfertigung. Festschrift für Ernst Käsemann zum 70. Geburtstag,* Tübingen – Göttingen 1976, pp. 543-555 = id., *Oikodome. Aufsätze zum Neuen Testament,* Band 2, ed. Günter Klein (Theologische Bücherei, 65), Munich 1979, pp. 183-195.

Gerd Lüdemann: *Paulus und das Judentum* (Theologische Existenz heute, 215), Munich 1983.

Jürgen Becker: *Paulus. Der Apostel der Völker,* Tübingen 1989, pp. 277-285: "Das antiheidenchristliche Judenchristentum".

3.4.1 The emergence of the Judaist movement

When dealing with the question of the Judaist movement, of which only Paul's letters, not the Acts, can give us a true picture, it is important to clarify both the chronological problem of its origins and the factual problem of its nature.

As far as the chronology is concerned, it has already been established (cf. section 3.1.4) that the Judaist movement can be traced back to Paul's three years in Ephesus, but no further. When he came to Ephesus – and not until then – Paul first met Titus, who was a "Greek", i.e. a Gentile (Gal. 2.3), and made him one of his collaborators. These facts are indicated by 2 Cor. 7.14. Before Paul sent Titus to the Corinthian congregation with 1 Cor. ("the tearful letter"), which was written in Ephesus (1 Cor. 16.8), and delivered by Titus himself (2 Cor. 2.13; 7.6-7, 15; 8.6, 10; 12.8), Titus had never been in Corinth, which Paul had just left; if Titus had been in Corinth before then, or perhaps even been a Corinthian himself,[85] Paul could not have written – as he did – that he had

---

85   This was suggested by e.g. Lüdemann, *Chronologie*, 1980, p. 199, n. 103, where Titus is identified as Titius Justus in Acts 18.7. This was an attempt to introduce Titus in the

Map of the Aegean territories at the time of Paul

expressed to Titus his pride[86] in the Corinthian congregation, and that his praise proved to be justified when Titus returned from Corinth. In other words: Paul did not meet Titus until he came to Ephesus in the province of Asia, after he had founded his Galatian, Macedonian and Greek congregations.

The fact that Paul brought Titus with him when he went to Jerusalem to participate in the Jerusalem Conference (Gal. 2.1, 3) makes it clear that the

---

Acts, in which he is otherwise not mentioned; I made the same mistake under the influence of Lüdemann: my *Galaterbrevet fortolket* (Bibelselskabets kommentarserie), 1982, p. 38. But see my *Chronologie*, 1986, p. 84, n. 20.

86 *"kekaúchemai* [2 Cor. 7.14], when Titus left for Corinth. At that time, he did not know the Corinthians," as Lietzmann rightly observes in *An die Korinther I/II* (Handbuch zum Neuen Testament, 9), 4th ed., ed. by W.G. Kümmel, Tübingen 1949, p. 133; Kümmel, ib., p. 208; Charles H. Buck, The Collection for the Saints, Harvard Theological Review 43 (1950), pp. 1-29, see pp. 6-7; my *Chronologie*, p. 84 with n. 21. Cf. section 3.1.4 above, the passage referred to in n. 35.

Conference took place *after* Paul's arrival in Ephesus, and *after* he had met Titus there.

From this we can draw the conclusions that the Jerusalem Conference (Gal. 2.1-10 = Acts 18.22) took place *relatively late* in his career as both a missionary and apostle of the Gentiles or, to be more precise, three years before he wrote 2 Cor. and that this journey to Jerusalem was only a short break during the three years he spent in Ephesus; in the absolute chronology, it can almost certainly be dated to A.D. 53, which is considerably later than traditional datings of this event (see also section 3.5.1 below).

Is this chronological fact of any special importance?

The answer is yes. It is important because it proves that the purpose of the Jerusalem Conference was to solve the problems which had arisen after the Gentile mission was founded, and as a consequence of this. Before this, these problems did not exist, although Acts 15 suggests the contrary. Accordingly, the Judaist movement emerged as a reaction against the establishment of the Gentile-Christian congregations, which were beyond Jewish jurisdiction and control. So the Jerusalem Conference was held in order to solve the problems that had arisen in connection with the emergence of the Judaist movement, and it took place years after the Gentile mission had been successfully established.

Furthermore, it sheds new light on the conflict in Antioch (Gal. 2.11 ff.), which broke out immediately after the Jerusalem Conference (Gal. 2.1-10). This conflict has often been overinterpreted as an intensification of the Judaist reaction against the Gentile-Christian congregations and seen as a reflection of a definitive schism between Paul and Jerusalem which made Paul leave the eastern territories and make his own way west to escape from the direct control of the Judaistic powers. The conflict in Antioch can hardly have been serious enough to justify such a drastic reaction; it was more likely just a temporary disagreement. After the Jerusalem Conference, Paul had to return to Ephesus in any case, and after the conflict he can hardly have seen himself as the loser in the battle, nor did he have any objective reasons to do so. On the contrary, after the Jerusalem Conference and the conflict in Antioch, Paul and Barnabas were soon working together again (Col. 4.10; 1 Cor. 9.6), probably on the collection for Jerusalem; in fact, there is no reason at all to suspect a schism between the two apostles for the Gentiles. Moreover, we have the obvious evidence of the Letter to the Galatians; this letter would hardly have been preserved for posterity if Paul had suffered defeat in relation to his Galatian congregations. And finally, there is every indication that the collection for Jerusalem (Gal. 2.10; 1 Cor. 16.1-4; 2 Cor. 8-9; Rom. 15.25-29) was carried out more or less according to plan.

On the basis of the chronological evidence, it can therefore be established that the Judaist movement did not emerge until after the middle of the first Christian century. This fact alone makes it extremely difficult to establish a connection between the Judaist movement and various phenomena in the earliest history of Christianity, such as the conflict between Hellenists and Hebrews (see section 3.3 above), although such a connection has often been suggested or even taken for granted.

Moreover, the relatively late emergence of the Judaist movement is confirmed in various ways by the Letter to the Galatians – and, what is more, not as part of Paul's apology, but as a fact which appears clearly from the letter itself.

First of all, it is important to note that Paul's teaching of justification by faith was first presented in writing, i.e. in his letters (Gal., 1 and 2 Cor., Rom.; see also Phil. 3.7 ff.); he had not done this verbally when he founded his congregations. Gerd Lüdemann has explained this very clearly: The reason why the Judaists were able to infiltrate Paul's Gentile-Christian congregations is simply that these congregations had not been forewarned; the Galatian congregations would have been much better prepared to defend themselves against the Judaists if Paul had taught them right from the beginning, when he founded these congregations, that they would be justified by faith, not by keeping the law; now Paul had to come to their rescue by sending them a letter they could use as a weapon against the Judaists.[87]

Secondly, Gal. 1.6-7 refers to the fast-spreading influence of the Judaist movement in the Galatian congregations: "6 I am astonished to find you turning away so quickly from him who called you by grace, and following a different gospel. 7 Not that it is in fact another gospel; ..." The words "so quickly" cannot mean shortly after Paul's foundation of the congregations in Galatia; otherwise Paul would have reacted much sooner. The words must refer to the short period

---

87 Lüdemann, *Paulus u. das Judentum*, p. 49, n. 74: "If the Galatians had known this [the teaching of justification by faith], they would have been better armed against the infiltrators."

which had elapsed since the emergence of the Judaist movement; however short it was, it must have been long enough for the Judaist movement to appear in the Galatian congregations and spread among their members. No sooner had the Judaists arrived than the Galatian congregations were ready and willing to follow them!

Thirdly, the Letter to the Galatians is Paul's first opportunity to inform his Galatian congregations of his participation in the Jerusalem Conference (Gal. 2.1-10); the precise purpose of this conference was to discuss the problems caused by the emergence of the Judaistic movement during the period that had elapsed since the Galatian congregations were founded. However obvious it appears once it is known, this fact has probably been the most difficult to establish, but also the most important. Admittedly, other Christians, including the Judaists themselves, may have informed the Galatians of the Jerusalem Conference before Paul wrote his letter, or at the same time; it is even probable that something of the kind really happened. But Paul himself cannot have informed them of the Jerusalem Conference before he wrote his letter (not, for instance, when he founded the Galatian congregations!). We know this because his description of the Jerusalem Conference is not an explanatory follow-up to a previous communication from Paul to the Galatians; it is really his first communication with them on this subject. This is also the best possible indication that the "new" Pauline chronology (Gal. 2.1 = Acts 18.22) is correct. So the fact remains that Paul cannot have informed the Galatian congregations of the Jerusalem Conference when he founded these congregations as early as in the 40s, but that he must have done this for the first time in his letter – which also represents his second "visit" to them (Gal. 4.13).[88] This again confirms the fact that the Judaist movement was a relatively new phenomenon; it simply did not exist at the time when the Galatian congregations were founded.

---

88 The fact that Gal. is a substitute for a visit and therefore becomes a "visit" itself, is explained in my *Chronologie*, pp. 79-80 with n. 9 and n. 10. Paul visited the Galatian congregations only once, i.e. when he founded them. Acts 18.23, which refers to another visit to "the Galatian country and Phrygia" is an editorial repetition of Acts 16.6 ("Phrygia and the Galatian country") which *may* be due to a misinterpretation of Gal. 4.13; see section 3.1.4, the passage referred to in n. 25.

3.4.2 The Judaist movement as a phenomenon

The Letter to the Galatians is by far our most important source of information on the nature of the Judaist movement. Also Phil. 3.2 ff., and possibly other texts as well (e.g. 2 Thess. 3.2 (?), but hardly 2 Cor. 10-13) undoubtedly refer to the Judaists. But without the Letter to the Galatians we would have been unable to say anything precise or decisive about the Judaist movement as such.

First of all, it is important to establish the fact that Gal.'s references to "actions dictated by law" and "circumcision" clearly indicate that syncretism and/or gnosticism were not involved in the conflict between Paul and his Galatian congregations. Yet it has been argued in modern times, e.g. by Wilhelm Lütgert, in 1919, and Walter Schmithals, in 1956, that the phenomenon which Paul attacked in his letter to the Galatians was syncretic and gnostic.[89] However, even if Schmithals is right that syncretism and gnosticism are of Jewish-Christian and therefore also Jewish origins, this argument only complicates the situation; furthermore, Philipp Vielhauer criticizes Schmithals in his treatise from 1976, in which he discusses Schmithals' argumentation and refuses to accept his conclusions.[90] Admittedly, 1 Cor. (and 2 Cor.?) seems to indicate the existence of a "gnosticism" in the Corinthian congregation which could explain several of the problems that existed in this congregation at the time when 1 Cor. was written, including the party quarrels and the barrier between "the strong" and "the weak". However, this gnosticism was most likely inspired by the Alexandrian-Jewish religious philosophy, which had probably been introduced in Corinth by Apollos (1 Cor. 1.12; 3.5-6, 22; 4.6; 16.12). I shall return to this later in this chapter.[91] It is important to understand, however, that the Corinthian gnosticism has nothing to do with the situation of the

---

89 Wilhelm Lütgert, *Gesetz und Geist. Eine Untersuchung zur Vorgeschichte des Galaterbriefes* (Beiträge zur Förderung christlicher Theologie, 22/6), Gütersloh 1919; Walter Schmithals, Die Häretiker in Galatien, first published in 1956, in: id., *Paulus und die Gnostiker. Untersuchungen zu den kleinen Paulusbriefen* (Theologische Forschung, 35), Hamburg – Bergstedt 1965, pp. 9-46. It is unusual to include Gal. among "the minor letters of Paul", as Schmithals does here. It is important to note that while Lütgert maintained that Paul was fighting on two fronts in the Galatian conflict, i.e. both against Judaists and Gnostics (cf. the title of his book), Schmithals knocked these two fronts into one: a Jewish-Christian gnosticism.

90 Cf. also Vielhauer, *Geschichte der urchristlichen Literatur*, Berlin – New York 1975 (see section 4.6 below), pp. 103-125.

91 See section 3.6 below.

Galatian congregations when Gal. was written, and that this gnosticism was certainly not Judaistic.

The observations on "actions dictated by law" and "circumcision" in Gal. clearly point to early Judaism as the frame of reference for the conflict in question. In other words, these observations refer to the Judaist movement, and today there appears to be general agreement on this point – again, I should say, for apart from Lütgert, Schmithals and others, this had been the prevalent view since Baur and the Tübingen School.

The Judaist movement is generally understood as a conception of Christianity according to which Christians, whether they were of Jewish or Gentile origins, were obliged to observe the Mosaic law, including the requirement of circumcision (Gen. 17.12; Lev. 12.3; cf. Lk. 1.59; Phil. 3.5). Naturally this conception of Christianity was opposed to Paul's view of Christianity. If it is true that both a "Judaist" movement and a "Pauline" movement existed in the earliest history of Christianity, as most New Testament exegetes still maintain, they must, therefore, have represented two different and incompatible wings. In recent years, Johannes Munck (1904-65) and a few others have attempted – justly but not very successfully – to dispute this well-established view.[92]

When discussing the general, traditional view of Judaism, we must keep in mind that our understanding of Judaism as a separate conception of Christianity does not come from Paul's letters, but from the Acts, where it says: "If you are not circumcised in accordance with Mosaic practice, you cannot be saved" (Acts 15.1). It is only apparently that Judaism, as it is reflected in the traditional view, represents a "historical" conception of Christianity, a conception which was later, during the post-apostolic era, dated back to the apostolic era. It cannot be proved, however, that the real historical Judaism was a phenomenon which was presented as true Christianity by any Christian individual or wing.

---

92 Johannes Munck, *Paulus und die Heilgeschichte*, 1954 (see section 3.1.4 above, n. 40). Strangely enough, in *Paulus u. Jakobus*, 1963, Walter Schmithals goes along with Munck, since Schmithals also maintains that there is no evidence at all of any "Judaist" movement; but this agreement between Munck and Schmithals (which Munck did not find flattering) is only due to the fact that Schmithals maintains that gnosticism was Paul's great opponent, and therefore refuses to accept the possible existence of a Judaist movement as well.

This does not imply that I deny the existence of various disagreements or conflicts during the early history of Christianity, such as the party conflicts in the Corinthian congregation (1 Cor. 1.12 ff.). But I do deny the existence of any evidence that the history of the earliest Christianity was dominated by a conflict between two incompatible wings, i.e. "Judaists" and "Paulinists". In fact, the history of early Christianity was dominated by a far more serious conflict: the conflict between Judaism and Christianity. As often happens in historical research and other areas, most people seem to have lost the ability to see the wood for the trees!

EXCURSUS: The Galatian situation – in the light of historical research
F.C. Baur saw the Galatian situation as a battle between Paulinism and the Judaist movement, and he saw the Judaist movement as an internal ecclesiastical reaction against the fact that Paul preached the Gospel to Gentiles; the Judaists, who were led by Peter, demanded that Gentiles should observe the Mosaic law, including the requirement of circumcision, in order to be saved by Christ. Similar battles developed between the Judaist and Pauline movements in other of Paul's congregations, especially in Corinth, so it seemed justifiable to refer to the existence of a kind of "pan-Judaist" movement (Leonhard Goppelt's characterization of Baur's view) in Paul's footsteps. Vielhauer is probably right in saying that the Judaistic hypothesis in Baur's classical version has no adherents today. For one thing, the history of early Christianity is too complex to justify the theory of a "pan-Judaist" movement, and it is also difficult to make Peter and Jesus' brother James directly responsible for an anti-Pauline opposition of the nature and importance suggested by Baur. Nevertheless, a modified version of the Judaist hypothesis has been the only tenable theory till now; cf. e.g. Vielhauer himself, 1975 and 1976.[93]

This is confirmed by the fact that when Lütgert attempted to present a different view of the Galatian situation in 1919, he did not completely reject the view held by Baur and his followers. On the contrary, Lütgert retained the Judaist hypothesis for certain parts of Gal., but for other parts of the letter, he suggested that Paul fought against a pneumatism or enthusiasm inspired by paganism – this applied especially to texts such as Gal. 4.8-11 and 5.2-6.10, but also the historical account in Gal. 1.13-2.14. Although J.H. Ropes reproduced Lütgert's view in 1929,[94] it gained little support; its weak point was the assumption that Paul was fighting on two fronts: against both the

---

93 Cf. the passage referred to in n. 90 above.
94 J.H. Ropes, *The singular Problem of the Epistle to the Galatians* (Harvard Theological Studies, XIV), Cambridge (Mass.) 1929.

Judaist movement and pneumatism, an assumption that was not supported by any indications of changes between the fronts of "law" and "spirit" in the letter itself.

In his book on Paul published in 1954,[95] Munck launched a frontal attack on Baur and the Tübingen School. Although the attack exposed important weaknesses in the enemy and sporadically indicated new angles of approach which might eventually reveal a new and different picture of Paul (and which are far more promising than German exegetes in general have been willing to admit), it represented no real threat to the traditional view of Paul. Admittedly, Munck was right in maintaining that according to the view of the Tübingen School, James, Peter and John must have treated Paul with "an incredible mildness" during the Jerusalem Conference (Gal. 2.1-10). However, this criticism only touched Baur and the Tübingen School itself, not the modified hypothesis, which does not make James and Peter directly responsible for the requirements of circumcision and observance of the Mosaic law in Paul's Gentile-Christian congregations. Moreover, Munck's explanation of the Galatian situation was unconvincing on several points, for instance in his attempt to prove – in agreement with the conservative Th. Zahn[96] – that the conflict in Antioch (Gal. 2.11-14) took place before the Jerusalem Conference (Gal. 2.1-10); this would imply that the showdown between Paul and Peter was not the final word in the relationship between the two apostles. Munck's attempt was also unconvincing when it came to the main point: his identification of the Galatian opponents. On this point, Munck followed a suggestion of Hirsch from 1930[97] concerning Gal. 6.13: the present participle *hoi peritemnómenoi* was supposed to mean "those who let themselves be circumcised", which could only apply to Gentile Christians – Jewish Christians did not "let themselves be circumcised", they had been circumcised on the eighth day after they were born. Munck maintains that it was Galatian Gentile Christians who in their misguided eagerness to imitate the Jerusalem apostles wanted to introduce circumcision and observance of the Mosaic law in the Galatian congregations as well. However, these conclusions are too far-reaching considering the doubtful premises; in Codex Vaticanus and P 46 on Gal. 6.13, for instance, we find the variant of the past participle *hoi peritetmeménoi*, "the circumcised". Munck also rejected Hirsch's own view that the historical origins of the Judaistic Gentile Christians were to be found in the situation described in Gal. 2.14, not in any misguided eagerness to imitate what they believed the Jerusalem apostles recommended – in Munck's view, there was no historical link at all between the Galatian "Judaists" and Jerusalem or Antioch.

---

95 See n. 92 above.
96 And Lüdemann, see section 3.1.2, the passage referred to in n. 11.
97 Emanuel Hirsch, Zwei Fragen zu Galater 6, Zeitschrift für die neutestamentliche Wissenschaft 29 (1930), pp. 192-197.

One detail in Munck's book deserves to be mentioned here: his interpretation of Gal. 2.12: *foboúmenos toùs ek tês peritomês*. According to Munck, this should not be understood in the sense that Peter was afraid of the Jewish Christians, whom he had no reason to fear; nor had he any particular reasons to fear "the messengers from James" (Schmithals is probably right that otherwise Paul would have used the personal pronoun *foboúmenos autoús*).[98] It was the Jews Peter feared, i.e. the non-Christian Jews. On this point, Munck is supported by e.g. Reicke, 1953, Schmithals, 1963, Nickle, 1966, Jewett, 1970-71, and Bauckham, 1979.[99]

In his treatise of 1956, Schmithals answered Lütgert's appeal for a new interpretation of Gal., but rightly criticized Lütgert for the assumption that Paul was fighting on two fronts, "law" and "spirit". However, Schmithals was wrong to opt in favour of the front of "spirit" and maintain that in Gal., Paul was fighting against Jewish-Christian Gnostics, who had a gnostic rather than a nomistic motivation for the requirement of circumcision: the ego's release from the restraint of the flesh, i.e. *sárx* (?!). In agreement with Lütgert, Schmithals understood from Gal. 5.3 and 6.13 that these Jewish-Christian Gnostics were lax in their observance of the Mosaic law, and that Paul had not understood their gnostic view at all, but wrongly believed them to be some kind of nomists – in fact, Schmithals' investigation is based on the assumption that Paul had misunderstood his opponents.

Schmithals' book *Paulus und Jakobus* from 1963 is more important than his treatise from 1956. In several respects, *Paulus und Jakobus* is inspired by Munck. Both Munck and Schmithals were against Baur and the Judaist movement, but apart from a few thought-provoking exegetic sections, Schmithals' book from 1963 is unacceptable: the purpose of the book is to prove that there was no "Judaist movement" before A.D. 70, but Schmithals' motive for this is simply to make room for the "pan-gnosticism" which could not otherwise be proved to have existed.

One detail deserves to be mentioned here; Schmithals first suggested it in his treatise of 1956, and then elaborated it further in his book of 1963: the idea that the intruders who had "sneaked in" (Gal. 2.4; cf. 2 Cor. 11.26) were non-Christian Jews, i.e. representatives of contemporary Judaism, who had gained entry to the Jerusalem

---

98 Schmithals, *Paulus u. Jakobus*, p. 54 (pp. 66-67 in *Paul and James*).
99 Bo Reicke, Der geschichtliche Hintergrund des Apostelkonzils und der Antiochia-Episode, Gal. 2,1-14, in: *Studia Paulina in honorem Johannis de Zwaan septuagenarii*, Haarlem 1953, pp. 172-187; Schmithals: see n. 98 above; K.F. Nickle, *The Collection. A Study in Paul's Strategy* (Studies in Biblical Theology, 48), London 1966, pp. 65-66; Robert Jewett, The Agitators and the Galatian Congregation, New Testament Studies 17 (1970-71), pp. 198-212; Vielhauer, *Geschichte* (see n. 90 above), pp. 122-123 with n. 23; Richard Bauckham, Barnabas in Galatians, Journal for the Study of the New Testament 2 (1979), pp. 61-70, esp. p. 69, n. 9.

186

Conference in order to find out what was going on. Although I used to be fascinated by this idea myself,[100] I must admit that it is hardly tenable. In my view, Schmithals' interpretation of Peter's fear of the non-Christian Jews is more important than his interpretation of Gal. 2.4; cf. Vielhauer.[101]

As far as Heinrich Schlier is concerned, I refer to the introduction to the 1965 edition of his commentary on the Letter to the Galatians,[102] although this was first published as early as in 1949. This is in order to demonstrate how much Schmithals has been able to shake or at least weaken the Judaist hypothesis, even in its modified form. In his introduction, Schlier lists four characteristics of the opponents in the Galatian congregations:

1) they insist on circumcision as a condition of salvation;
2) they insist on observance of a specific feast calendar (Gal. 4.10), but Schlier is uncertain whether this should be understood in the light of Jewish law-observance or pagan star-worship;
3) they represent a certain form of anti-nomism (Gal. 5.3 and 6.13), which expresses itself in enthusiasm and libertinism;
4) they carry on a controversy against Paul, blame him for inconsistency and opportunism (Gal. 5.11), and for his inferiority to the Jerusalem apostles, who had experienced revelations and had more authority.

However, the opponents did not accuse Paul of dependence on the apostles in Jerusalem, since such a dependence could not be used as an accusation, but would reflect badly on themselves; in order to carry any weight, it must be an accusation of apostasy on the part of Paul, and there is no indication of this. The question of the alleged dependence on Jerusalem will be discussed below.

It is characteristic of Schlier that he refuses to label the opponents as Judaists in the traditional sense of the word, or Jewish Christians, as Schmithals maintains. From a religio-historical point of view, however, Schlier agrees with Schmithals; this appears most clearly from his third point, anti-nomism as a characteristic of the Galatian opponents. Moreover, Schlier finally declares that the historical picture of the Galatian situation is not decisive for the interpretation of Gal., which he explains as follows: "No matter who his opponents were, and what individual beliefs they may have held, Paul sees them, according to the information he has received, as representatives of a Jewish-Christian nomism which is not consistent and ignores the essential requirement of the law, the *agape*. If a different version of a legalistic Jewish Christianity had

---

100 My *Udenfor og indenfor*, 1974, pp. 72-73; *Paulus' breve*, 1977, p. 96.
101 Cf. n. 99 above.
102 Heinrich Schlier, *Der Brief an die Galater* (Kritisch-exegetischer Kommentar zum Neuen Testament, VII), Göttingen 1965, pp. 15-24.

187

appeared among the Christian congregations in Galatia, the apostle would hardly have reacted differently, because his answer is based mainly on general principles" (p. 24). But how can the historical reality be completely unimportant for the interpretation of the text?! And is it really possible to interpret the text so independently of the historical facts?! Cf. Vielhauer, 1976, in his criticism of Schmithals: "if Paul had misunderstood his opponents so completely that he fought them as a movement that never existed, then he must have been in a worse mental state than Don Quixote was when he attacked the windmills."[103]

Compared to Lütgert's, Schmithals' and Schlier's views of the problem, Vielhauer's clear and matter-of-fact explanation feels like a relief. His precise criticism simply annihilates Schmithals' gnostic hypothesis. Faced with the alternatives of "law" and "spirit" – which *are* alternatives – Vielhauer resolutely opts for the "law" alternative: the Galatian opponents were proponents of a nomism with Judaistic features, and the attempt to prove that the Judaist movement did not exist has failed. Nevertheless, in Schmithals' treatise on Gal. from 1956,[104] there is one important point on which I agree with him (and not with Schlier, 1965, p. 19, or Vielhauer, 1975, p. 120): unlike in Acts 15.1, it says nowhere in Gal. that circumcision and observance were explicitly required as a condition of salvation; the Galatian opponents did not necessarily regard the Mosaic law as the road to salvation. I shall return to this subject later.

In my view, Vielhauer is right in maintaining that according to Gal. 4.8-11, the Galatians had no *stoicheîa* cult, either before they became Christians, or when they were prepared to submit to the requirement of law-observance and circumcision. When Paul uses the term *stoicheîa toû kósmou* (Gal. 4.3; cf. 4.9 – Vielhauer does not see any real analogy in Col. 2.8 and 2.20, whereas Schmithals and Schlier maintain that the passages in Gal. should be interpreted on the basis of Col.), he denounces both their former paganism and their present nomism: in the eyes of Christ, Judaism is no better than paganism.[105]

Vielhauer also maintains that Gal. 5.3 and 6.13 cannot support the weight of the interpretation which several exegetes, including Schmithals and Schlier, apply to them. These passages do not show that the opponents have failed to observe the Mosaic law, or that they were lax; otherwise the Pharisees and the scribes should also be denounced as libertinists (!) – cf. Matt. 23.3-4. According to Vielhauer, however, this is an example of a well-known polemic *topos*. To put it boldly: if the Galatians really want to observe the Mosaic law, they must follow its provisions to the letter as Paul himself did before his conversion (Gal. 1.13-14). Moreover, "the observance of the law was

---

103 Vielhauer, in: *Rechtfertigung*, p. 544.
104 Schmithals, *Paulus u. die Gnostiker*, 1965, p. 29.
105 Vielhauer, 1976; id., *Geschichte*, 1975, pp. 115-117.

not standardized even for pious Palestinians, it was not the same for Diaspora Jews as for Palestinian Jews, and Jewish missionaries who worked among Gentiles had to make certain concessions. It was simply impossible for former pagans and for people living outside Palestine to keep the letter of the law in the Pharisaic sense. The attitude which Paul denounces in 5.3 and 6.13 corresponds to the result which could be achieved through the normal relaxation of the rules imposed on former pagans and in Gentile territories, it is not moral laxity."[106] Vielhauer is certainly right in as far as Gal. 5.3 and 6.13 do not refer to morally suspect persons with libertinistic lifestyles. But Vielhauer's observation can be stated more precisely: With the words in Gal. 5.3 and 6.13, Paul explains that the Judaists in Galatia are hypocrites, since they do not observe the Mosaic law by conviction, but only to a certain extent, and only to make a good impression on others.

With his criticism, Vielhauer demonstrated that there is no evidence in the texts that anti-nomism was a characteristic of the Galatian opponents – Schlier's third characteristic, borrowed from Schmithals.

However, Vielhauer makes a point of emphasizing that in returning to the Judaist hypothesis, he does not imitate Baur, but modifies and reduces the traditional view:

1) it is still uncertain whether there were any personal and organizational links between the Judaist agitators in Galatia on one side and Jerusalem and Antioch on the other (Gal. 2.1-10, 11-14);
2) it has not yet been clarified whether the present participle *hoi peritemnómenoi* in Gal. 6.13 is sufficient evidence that the Judaistic agitators in Galatia were in fact Gentile Christians (if so, with historical links to Antioch, Gal. 2.14; cf. Hirsch);
3) it is still uncertain whether *ho tarásson hymâs* in Gal. 5.10 should be understood generically, or whether it should be understood individually as one of *hoi tarássontes hymâs* in Gal. 1.7;
4) it is still uncertain whether the Judaist agitators could rightly invoke support or consent from the "pillars" (Gal. 2.9) – Paul himself is loyal to these "pillars" and refers to no connection between them and the agitators.

As regards Vielhauer's modification and reduction of the Judaistic hypothesis in its traditional or classical form, I maintain that as long as the above-mentioned points (the precise points which modify and reduce the traditional hypothesis!) are unclarified, the Galatian situation as a whole remains unclarified. If these points are allowed to remain unclarified, then there is really no other difference between the

---

106 Vielhauer, *Geschichte*, 1975, pp. 114-115.

traditional and the modified hypothesis than the lack of clarification. This means that Vielhauer too has ended up in a dilemma.

In order to gain further insight, it is necessary to take a closer look at Paul's historical account in Gal. 1-2.

The account in Gal. 1.13-2.14 goes far back in time to the period before Paul's conversion, which suggests that Paul is trying to correct a general opinion which implied a number of accusations against him – in other words: in this passage, Paul presents an apologia in which he specifically refutes the accusation of being dependent on Jerusalem and the apostles there. The many denials (*"without* going up to Jerusalem ..."*, "I was still *unknown* by sight to ..."*, "Titus ... was *not* compelled"*, "they imparted *nothing* further to me ..."*, etc.) appear like so many denials of a number of specific allegations to the contrary, so these denials could possibly be used in an attempt to reconstruct the accusations made against Paul. It is obvious that once complete, such a reconstruction would shed new light on an important aspect of the Galatian situation and help to identify the opposition to Paul and the authorities it may have represented.

From this point of view, Paul's apologia would be important in itself – once the accusations had been rejected as false, Paul could move on to the next item on the agenda: the theological exposition of justification through faith in Gal. 3-4. It would then be useless to look for an organic connection between Gal. 1-2 and 3 ff., especially since the passage in Gal. 2.15-21 would represent a logical transition between the historical and the theological part of the letter. From an exegetic point of view, the interpretation of Gal. 1-2 would be successfully completed in so far as the historical reconstruction of the opponents' accusations had been made; furthermore, apart from Gal. 5.11 – to which I shall return – Gal. 1-2 constitutes the basis for Schlier's fourth point: the polemic against Paul as a characteristic of the Galatian opponents.

This idea was taken up by Olof Linton in his much discussed treatise of 1947.[107] It is a well-known fact that the accounts of Paul and the Acts in Gal. 1-2 and Acts 9 and 15 differ from each other on a number of points. Linton tries to explain these differences by referring to the *reconstructed* accusations against Paul which lie behind Gal. 1-2. Paul's account has often been compared with the account in Acts, and also with the reconstructed (Galatian) version, but the situation is different when it comes to a comparison between this reconstructed Galatian version and the account in Acts: here Linton finds a surprising agreement and concludes that Paul's own denial of the Galatian version had no impact, and that the account of the Acts is based on historical knowledge of the Galatian opposition to Paul – a knowledge which must still have been present and available when the Acts was written.

---

107 Olof Linton, En dementi och dess öde. Gal. 1 och 2 – Apg. 9 och 15, Svensk Exegetisk Årsbok XII (1947), pp. 203-219 = id., The Third Aspect. A Neglected Point of View. A Study in Gal. i-ii and Acts ix and xv, Studia Theologica 3 (1949), pp. 79-95.

Although Linton's thesis has often been quoted with approval, it is hardly tenable. For one thing, it is not absolutely certain that the accounts of Paul and the Acts are as utterly different as Linton assumes; in fact, it is quite possible that unlike Paul's account, the account of the Acts was considerably affected by various theological and editorial considerations. Moreover, the Galatian version is not identical with the account in Acts in every respect. However, Linton's treatise has the great virtue of demonstrating the real consequences of the traditional view when this is taken seriously: Paul is careless about the truth (in spite of Gal. 1.20!), and there is some substance in the Galatian view of Paul as a man who could not be trusted. Is Linton's thesis worth this price?[108]

Lütgert, who was the first to draw attention to the question of Paul's dependence on the Jerusalem leaders in Gal. 1.17-19, maintained that the Judaists could not have used such a dependence as an accusation against Paul: "In the view of the Judaists, the fact which Paul refers to in this context, namely his dependence on the original apostles, would be no reproach at all."[109] The only thing Paul could be reproached for in connection with the question of his dependence on Jerusalem would be a deviation from the Gospel of the Jerusalem leaders: "Only in connection with such a deviation could he have been questioned about his earlier dependency, though not in the sense of an accusation. However, Paul does not defend himself against the accusation of deviation, but against an insinuation of dependence which was not justified, and which was not reprehensible from the point of view of the Judaists. So Paul's entire argumentation does not correspond with the traditional interpretation of the letter."[110]

---

108 Christoph Burchard, *Der dreizehnte Zeuge*, 1970 (see section 3.1.3 above, n. 15), pp. 159-160, subjected Linton's explanation to a justified criticism: "This thesis, which is often quoted with sympathy or approval, is questionable in its present form. Linton's exegesis is more than sketchy, and his method is not very subtle. His "Galatian version" is the result of a simple inversion of Paul's statements in Gal. 1-2, and he compares this with the Acts without considering Luke's contribution. In my view, such a "Galatian version" has nothing in common with Luke's text. There is nothing in 9.26-30 [the text in Acts which Burchard discusses here] which hints at any allegations that Paul had gone to Jerusalem immediately or soon after his conversion (he goes there after "many days" and only because he has to), that he had stayed there for a long time (Luke says nothing about the duration), or that he had worked as a zealous pupil of the apostles (he did nothing of the kind, but preached in Jerusalem as he had done in Damascus, inspired by his vision of Jesus, independently of the apostles). If the tradition had "Galatian" features, Luke must have wiped them out. So Linton's thesis remains unproven on this point (and probably in general). Even so, there may be some truth in it. ..."

109 Lütgert, *Gesetz u. Geist*, p. 46.

110 Lütgert, ib., p. 46.

Referring to Lütgert, Schmithals also maintains that dependency on Jerusalem could not give rise to criticism from the Judaists: "Admittedly, this could be used to question his authority as an apostle, but certainly not to reject his gospel. Moreover, however much it might degrade Paul as an *apostle*, such an allegation would be a credit to his gospel. If a different gospel had come from Jerusalem because Paul's gospel was false, then it would have been logical to accuse Paul of undue independence in relation to the one and only true Gospel, but surely not for *dependence* on this."[111]

Both Lütgert and Schmithals conclude from this that Gal. 1.17-19 refers to an accusation against Paul for his dependence on Jerusalem, and that the accusation was not made by Judaists, but by pneumatics!

Günther Bornkamm also recognizes this difficulty: "But surely his Judaizing opponents would have been the last people to join battle with him on the issue of dependence on Jerusalem."[112] If they did accuse Paul, their accusation might have been phrased as follows: "The original apostles had set Paul right, but to his shame he had cut adrift from what he had been taught – that Law, circumcision, and salvation must always go together – arbitrarily watering it down, in order to give him an easier approach to the Gentiles (Gal. 1:10). His preaching therefore meant betrayal of the national heritage; they, on the other hand, stood in the true line of continuity and presented the legitimate gospel. In Galatians 1, Paul cuts this line of argument short by saying: Your very premises are wrong; the fact is that I had no relation whatsoever with Jerusalem, ... Thus, it all points not to Paul's opponents having held up dependence on Jerusalem against him, but to Paul's having contested and demolished what they regarded as indispensable, the connection between the gospel and Jewish tradition."[113]

As mentioned above, Schlier excludes dependence on Jerusalem from the accusations which the agitators in Galatia made against Paul: "If his opponents reproached him for this dependence in particular, they must in fact also have reproached him for having deviated from his teachers' gospel. There is no evidence in Gal. of such an accusation. Probably his opponents only reproached him for the fact that he had received no revelations of the Messiah, Jesus, and that he could therefore not compare with the authorities in Jerusalem."[114]

Vielhauer's argument is similar: "The usual answer that the accusation referred to dependence [on the authorities in Jerusalem] is inadequate in all its variants, as

---

111 Schmithals, *Paulus u. die Gnostiker*, 1965, p. 16.
112 Günther Bornkamm, *Paulus* (Urban-Bücher, 119), Stuttgart 1969, pp. 41-42 = *Paul*, Minneapolis 1995, p. 18.
113 Bornkamm, ib., p. 42 (p. 19 in *Paul*).
114 Schlier, *Der Brief an die Galater*, 1965, p. 22.

Schmithals rightly explained."[115] It therefore seems most probable that the Judaist agitators' accusation was based on the fact that unlike the leaders in Jerusalem, Paul had received no revelations and could therefore not compare with them – Schlier as quoted by Vielhauer.[116]

Lütgert and Schmithals succeeded in showing that Gal. 1.17 ff. does not refer to a Judaist accusation. But while Lütgert and Schmithals both maintain that Paul denies an accusation from pneumatics or gnostics, Bornkamm finds no accusation behind the statement, but understands this as a demonstrative expression of Paul's independence; Schlier and Vielhauer again simply exclude the question of independence of Jerusalem from the anti-Pauline polemic – at most, the opponents may have claimed that Paul could not compare with the leaders in Jerusalem, and Paul then maintained that his (!) gospel was independent of theirs. On this point, Vielhauer's concession to Schmithals is surprising, while Schlier's concession is really inconsistent: from an anti-nomistic and syncretistic point of view, Schlier's third characteristic, an accusation of dependence on Jerusalem would be quite logical.

I realize that this summary is rather confusing! Everybody agrees that there is no evidence of any Judaist accusation, including the proponents of the Judaist hypothesis (Bornkamm and Vielhauer). However, while some researchers maintain that it must be a gnostic accusation (Lütgert and Schmithals), others reduce the accusation to a mild criticism (Schlier and Vielhauer), and one (Bornkamm) says that there was no accusation, and that Paul was the aggressor in the conflict.

3.4.3 Clearing up the confusion

In order to clear up the confusion illustrated above, we must analyze both the form and content of Gal. 1-2, especially 1.13-2.14.

1) First of all, it might be useful to recall a fact which has already been established in connection with Hans von Campenhausen's definition of the apostle concept. When Paul emphasizes, in Gal. 1.1 ff., that he has received his apostolate from Christ himself without any human intervention, he is not trying to defend himself in relation to those who were apostles before him, because they, or others, may have questioned his right to be an apostle; he wants to make clear to his Galatian congregations, who were exposed to Judaist influence, what it means to be an apostle: "what Paul wants to point out is not the special rank which characterizes his apostolate, but simply the nature of the new Christian apostolate, whose authority cannot be challenged by any human

---

115 Vielhauer, *Geschichte*, 1975, p. 118.
116 Vielhauer, ib., p. 118.

authority, even from Jerusalem".[117] This immediately dispels the confusion as far as the question of dependence or independence on Jerusalem is concerned.

2) Paul begins his historical account in Gal. 1.13-2.14 by mentioning his former adherence to Judaism: 1.13-14. With a short reference to his conversion, he then proceeds to describe his new life as a believer in Christ, beginning with the words "But when ..." (Greek: *hóte dè* ...): 1.15-17. This is followed by a description of his work as a Christian, interrupted by two short visits to Jerusalem; this description falls into three parts, each beginning with the word "thereupon" (Greek: *épeita* ...): 1.18, 21; 2.1. Finally comes the relapse, signalized by the same wording as before: "But when ..." (Greek: *hóte dè* ...): 2.11 – a relapse into Judaism, not for Paul, but for Peter. The apostle Peter has, so to speak, returned to the starting point which he had formerly left behind him and given up: Judaism. This is the main issue of Gal.: the relationship between Judaism and Christianity.

3) The Letter to the Galatians reveals the motives behind the Judaist movement. First, cowardice: the apostle Cephas/Peter was afraid of the Jews, so he gave up taking his meals with the Gentile Christians in Antioch (Gal. 2.12). It was also cowardice that prompted those who tried to force circumcision on the Galatian Gentile Christians in Antioch, in order to escape persecution from the Jews (6.12). And just as Cephas's change of behaviour made him a hypocrite, i.e. made him act in a way which was against his convictions, it was also hypocrisy when "adherents" of circumcision tried to force circumcision on the Galatians: they did not even observe the law themselves, but hoped to save themselves from persecution by telling the Jews that they had persuaded the Galatians to be circumcised (6.13).

Persecution had always existed during the history of Judaism: just as the slave-woman Hagar's son Ishmael had persecuted the free woman Sarah's son Isaac, so it was now, in the Christian era (4.29). As for Paul himself, he could, from one moment to the next, save himself from persecution if he began to "preach circumcision". He writes (5.11): "if I am still advocating circumcision, then why am I still being persecuted?" In fact, persecution is a recurrent, yet

---

117 See section 3.2.4 above, the passage referred to in n. 62.

often neglected, theme in the letter: Gal. 1.13, 23; 4.29; 5.11; 6.12, and it also appears in connection with the Judaists.[118]

In this context, however, we must note that the Judaists are not guilty of persecution. On the contrary, they are threatened by persecution, i.e. by the Jews, and therefore try to escape this persecution by persuading the Gentile Christians to be circumcised.

Titus was *not* subjected to coercion or pressure in Jerusalem, as Paul triumphantly points out (Gal. 2.3). But Cephas used coercion on the Gentile Christians in Antioch when he pretended to practise "true Christianity" (2.14). Coercion was used to try to force the requirement of circumcision on the Galatian Gentile Christians, and the Judaists acted against their better judgement and conviction when they used despicable persuasion on the Galatian Gentile Christians – Paul writes (5.8): "This persuasion did not come from he who called you!"[119]

So the motive for the Judaist campaign against the Gentile Christians was not love of truth or a conviction that they represented "true Christianity" (cf. Gal. 2.14b); on the contrary, it was fear of the Jews (cf. 2.12) and the hope of being saved from their persecution by the Judaist propaganda among Gentile Christians (6.12-13).

---

118 On Gal. 5.11: see Lüdemann, *Chronologie* (see section 3.1.2 above, n. 2), p. 72, n. 40 (p. 116, n. 41 in *Paul, apostle to the Gentiles*). Unfortunately Lüdemann changed his mind in his book *Das frühe Christentum*, 1987, p. 183, and now maintains, like many others, that Paul admitted in Gal. 5.11 that he had "preached circumcision" – i.e. in the case of Timothy, whom Paul had circumcised before he took him on as a collaborator (Acts 16.1-3): "It is quite possible that the case of Timothy's circumcision was exploited by Paul's opponents in Galatia. As Gal. 5.11 shows, Paul was accused of occasionally having himself preached circumcision ... Perhaps too the conference called for circumcision of Titus by referring to Timothy" (p. 177 in *Early Christianity*). Of course Paul did not "preach circumcision" to his Gentile Christian congregations, least of all in Galatia! Unlike Titus (Gal. 2.3), Timothy was a Jew because his mother was a Jew. For information on the theme of persecution, see Ernst Baasland, Persecution: A Neglected Feature in the Letter to the Galatians, Studia Theologica 38 (1984), pp. 135-150.

119 The verb *anangkázein*, "to force" or "to compel" (Gal. 2.3; 2.14; 6.12) is also used by Josephus, Vita 113 (chapter 23) in his description of a Jewish attempt (which Josephus resisted) to force circumcision on a number of Gentiles during the Jewish-Roman war. See further Hengel, *Die Zeloten*, pp. 201-204: "Die Zwangsbeschneidung als Schutz für die Vorrechte Israels" (pp. 197-200 in *The Zealots*: "Compulsory Circumcision as a Protection of Israel's Privileges").

The hypocrisy of the Judaists (Gal. 2.13; cf. 6.13) reveals the fact that they were not themselves convinced that they represented the truth. This alone shows that the Judaist movement is inferior to Paul's preaching, which makes it relevant to raise the question of whether Munck and Schmithals were right after all when they denied the existence of any real "Judaist" movement.[120]

4) Even the word "Judaization" as the traditional name for the phenomenon which Paul denounces in Gal. is strange. Its meaning – the view of Christianity according to which Christians also had to observe the Mosaic law in order to be saved – comes from German theology (German: *Judaismus*), and with this in mind, it may be difficult to understand that the main issue of Gal. is the relationship between Judaism and Christianity, and *vice versa*. In order to overcome this difficulty, the word *Judaismus* must be analyzed.

Surprisingly, it emerges that even in Greek: *ioudaïsmós* (Gal. 1.13-14!) simply means Judaism, as in English, and in French: *Judaïsme*, i.e. true, traditional Judaism.

In other words: By introducing the word *Judaismus*, German theology turned the conflict into an internal ecclesiastical phenomenon, which concerned only Christianity and the various wings of Christianity. This mutation happened during later ecclesiastical history: the conflicts that existed in the modern church could be justified if they were seen as reflections of conflicts in the earliest history of Christianity, in the sense that disagreement was a natural characteristic of Christianity.

Actually, however, the conflict was a life-and-death conflict between Judaism and Christianity.

3.4.4 Conclusion

In the light of this essential fact, it is clear that the Judaist movement can no longer be considered as a Christian movement which was equal to "Paulinism" (!), only different from it. Now, however, another equally important question arises: What caused the emergence of the Judaist movement?

It was contemporary Judaism which for certain, unfortunately unknown, political reasons started the persecution of the Christians Jews, who came under the jurisdiction of the Jewish synagogue authorities. Of course the Jewish authorities had no jurisdiction over Christians of Gentile origins, but by

---

120 Cf. n. 92 above.

threatening the Christian Jews with persecution if they did not act according to instructions, the Jewish authorities could indirectly impose the requirement of circumcision on the Gentile Christians, who were "brothers" of the Jewish Christians. Through this cunning scheme, the Jews could infiltrate the Christian congregations and use them to spread what was really Judaism, not Christianity. It would no longer be possible to distinguish Christian mission from Jewish proselytism, and if the scheme was successfully carried out, the days of Christianity would be numbered.

3.5 The Jerusalem Conference and the conflict in Antioch

Bibliography

Hans Conzelmann: *Geschichte der Urchristentums* (see section 3 above), pp. 66-74: "Das Apostelkonzil".

Gerd Lüdemann: *Studien zur Chronologie*, 1980 (see section 3.1.2 above, n. 2), pp. 86-110.

Id.: *Das frühe Christentum* (see section 3 above), pp. 172-179: "Apostelgeschichte 15".

Geert Hallbäck: Jerusalem og Antiokia i Gal. 2. En historisk hypotese, Dansk Teologisk Tidsskrift 53 (1990), pp. 300-316.

Andreas Wechsler: *Geschichtsbild und Apostelstreit. Eine forschungsgeschichtliche und exegetische Studie über den antiochenischen Zwischenfall (Gal. 2,11-14)* (Beihefte zur Zeitschrift für die neutestamentliche Wissenschaft, 62), Berlin – New York 1991.

Bradley H. McLean: Galatians 2. 7-8 and the Recognition of Paul's Apostolic Status at the Jerusalem Conference: A Critique of G. Luedemann's Solution, New Testament Studies 37 (1991), pp. 67-76.

A. Schmidt: Das Missionsdekret in Galater 2.7-8 als Vereinbarung vom ersten Besuch Pauli in Jerusalem, New Testament Studies 38 (1992), pp. 149-152.

Nicholas Taylor: *Paul, Antioch and Jerusalem. A Study in Relationships and Authority in Earliest Christianity* (Journal for the Study of the New Testament, Supplement Series, 66), Sheffield 1992, pp. 96-122: "The question of the Law and the Jerusalem Conference", and pp. 123-139: "Peter and Paul at Antioch".

Niels Hyldahl: "For fjorten år siden": 2 Kor 12,2, in: Niels Peter Lemche/Mogens Müller, eds., *Fra dybet. Festskrift til John Strange i anledning af 60 års fødselsdagen den 20. juli 1994* (Forum for bibelsk eksegese, 5), Copenhagen 1994, pp. 109-118.

3.5.1 Observations on the Jerusalem Conference

On the basis of the observations made in the preceding sections, especially 3.1 and 3.4, and other observations, we can draw the following conclusions:

First, the reasons for holding the Jerusalem Conference (Gal. 2.1-10) are to be found in the emergence of the Judaist movement. The Judaist movement was a relatively late phenomenon in the history of earliest Christianity, since it can be traced no further back than the beginning of the 50s, and first located in Ephesus. According to the precise, absolute dating of the Jerusalem Conference that I have suggested, i.e. A.D. 53, the Judaist movement must have made its first appearance in Ephesus shortly before this, during the three years which Paul spent there, and presumably it soon spread to the Galatian congregations; it does not appear from Paul's warning in Phil. 3 whether it also reached Philippi, or whether he thought this was a potential danger which he wanted his letter to prevent.

At that time, Paul found himself in a very difficult situation. Immediately on his return to Ephesus after the Jerusalem Conference, he was arrested and imprisoned, so there was very little he could do. What would happen to his congregations?

Paul had decided to go to Jerusalem and make an agreement with the leaders there in an attempt to stop the Judaist influence on the Gentile-Christian congregations. The Judaists were Jewish-Christian missionaries (Greek: *ergátai*, "workers": Phil. 3.2; cf. 2 Cor. 11.13[121]), who were *not* responsible to Paul, but to the leaders in Jerusalem, so he needed an agreement with them in order to stop the Judaist propaganda – it was not an attempt to persuade the Judaists; Paul was hardly on speaking-terms with the Judaists and never spoke directly to them, not even in his letters, which were not addressed to them, but to his own congregations, whom he warned against the Judaists.

Secondly, it can be established that Paul took the initiative for the Jerusalem Conference – not the congregation in Antioch, as explained in Acts 15.1-2 (Paul and Barnabas did not go to Antioch before the Jerusalem Conference), and certainly not the "pillars" in Jerusalem, i.e. Jesus' brother James, Peter and Zebedee's son John. The revelation which Paul mentions in this connection (Gal. 2.1) without describing its nature, presumably indicates that he saw a

---

121 Cf. Matt. 10.10 = Lk. 10.7: "the worker (Gr. *ergátes*) deserves his keep"; cf. 1 Cor. 9.14; 1 Tim. 5.18.

possibility of solving the problems by approaching the "pillars". He took Barnabas with him, which shows that Barnabas was then working in the same place as Paul himself, in Ephesus or at least somewhere in the province of Asia; it also indicates that Barnabas had the same problems with the Judaists in his congregations as Paul had in his. At that time, Paul seems to have regarded Barnabas as his equal (cf. Gal. 2.9). While Paul had been founding his Galatian, Macedonian and Greek congregations, Barnabas had been establishing congregations in Colossae, Hierapolis, Laodicea in the country of Phrygia in the province of Asia (see Col. 4.10), and possibly also the Gentile-Christian part of the congregation in Ephesus itself – cf. Paul's observations about himself and Barnabas in 1 Cor. 9.6, which he wrote in Ephesus. The "schism" between Barnabas and Paul which is mentioned in Acts 15.36-41, and which has often, but hardly correctly, been identified as the "schism" after the conflict in Antioch (Gal. 2.11 ff.), *may* refer to the fact that their ways parted temporarily in central Asia Minor, where Paul was working in Galatia, and Barnabas in Phrygia, until they met again in Ephesus before the Jerusalem Conference.

Thirdly, the "false brothers" mentioned in connection with the Jerusalem Conference (Gal. 2.4; cf. 2 Cor. 11.26) had probably been operating in Paul's (and Barnabas') Gentile-Christian congregations, not in Jerusalem: they had "sneaked in" – or been smuggled in – "to spy on the liberty we [i.e. we who do not attach any importance to circumcision] enjoy in the fellowship of Christ Jesus, in order to bring us into bondage" (Gal. 2.4).[122] And where else could

---

122 Cf. Hans Lietzmann, *An die Galater* (Handbuch zum Neuen Testament, 10), 2nd ed., Tübingen 1923, p. 10: "This is a general reference to the fact that Judaist spies and agitators were operating in the Pauline congregations, for whose sake Paul is now defending his own right; it does not refer to a quarrel between *pseudádelfoi* and Paul in Jerusalem. Naturally *kataskopêsai* is also practised in the Pauline congregations;" cf. also Munck, *Paulus u. die Heilsgeschichte*, pp. 88-89; and William O. Walker, Why Paul Went to Jerusalem: The Interpretation of Galatians 2:1-5, Catholic Biblical Quarterly 54 (1992), pp. 503-510. In: Et paulinsk *annus mirabilis?* Dansk Teologisk Tidsskrift 52 (1989), pp. 21-40, Troels Engberg-Pedersen maintains, on p. 36, n. 5, that Paul must have met the false brothers in Jerusalem in connection with the Jerusalem Conference; cf. also Geert Hallbäck, DTT 53 (1990), p. 307. However, there is no reason to believe that Judaists were operating in Palestine, where their presence represented no threat to Christian freedom; when it says in Gal. 2.5: "but not for one moment did we yield to their dictation", this hardly means that Paul and Barnabas resisted the false brothers in a personal confrontation in Jerusalem, but rather that Paul and Barnabas made it clear to the Jerusalem leaders that they took a firm stand against the false brothers and their

they have been operating? There was nothing for them to do in Jerusalem and the whole of Palestine – unless, of course, the "false brothers" were not Judaists at all, but Jewish observers who had gained entry to the Jerusalem Conference, as Schmithals maintains;[123] but the "false brothers" are still "brothers", i.e. Christians, although they are false, i.e. unreliable. On these grounds, it must be concluded that they were Judaists who were operating in Paul's congregations – a conclusion which is clearly substantiated by the Letter to the Galatians.

In the fourth place, the Jerusalem Conference was held after Paul and Barnabas had been working for many years in the Gentile mission; their work is fully recognized by the Jerusalem leaders, and the agreement made at the meeting concerns a *future* division of the mission into a Jewish and a Gentile mission; but on the whole, this division only confirms the existing practice:[124] it is agreed that in the future, Paul and Barnabas will preach only among Gentiles, and James, Peter and John among Jews (Gal. 2.9). It can hardly be a geographical division of the mission, since at this time, the preaching of the Gospel among Jews in Palestine must already have been in progress for a long time. So it must have been a simple ethnographic division.[125] The division of the mission into a Jewish and a Gentile mission, which must, as already mentioned, have been practised for many years, was now formally adopted as a principle at the Jerusalem Conference. This corresponds completely with the impression given by the texts of 1 Thess. 1.9-10 and 1 Cor. 9.5-6.[126] It remains an open question whether this agreement was observed in practice, or whether the conflict in Antioch (Gal. 2.11 ff.) shows that the agreement was broken by the Jerusalem leaders themselves.

---

activities in the Pauline congregations. On the other hand, this does not of course exclude the possibility that representatives of the Judaists ("the false brothers who had sneaked in") were also present in Jerusalem and had pleaded their cause at the meeting there.
123 See section 3.4.2, the passage referred to in n. 100.
124 Cf. Hallbäck, DTT 53 (1990), pp. 306, 308 and others.
125 A different point of view is presented in Taylor, *Paul, Antioch and Jerusalem*, pp. 113 ff.
126 It is hardly possible or even imaginable that the Acts is right in saying again and again in its description of Paul's missionary work that he first approached the Jews in the places he visited, and only began to preach to the Gentiles when the Jews had turned their backs on him (cf. Acts 13.48 ff.; 17.2 ff.: 19.8 ff.) – this cannot be a true description of the situation even before the Jerusalem Conference (Acts 18.22!) and the formal agreement on the division of the mission.

On the other hand, it is hardly true that the formal acknowledgement of the Gentile mission, which Paul obtained during the Jerusalem Conference, made him look forward to an integration of the Jewish and the Gentile Christians, while the agreement made at the meeting was really nothing but a fragile compromise.[127] It is much more likely that from the outset, Paul aimed at an agreement which could guarantee him freedom from Judaist interference in his congregations.

In the fifth place, it was agreed that the Gentile-Christian congregations should help the poor in Jerusalem by collecting money for them (Gal. 2.10; cf. 1 Cor. 16.1-4; 2 Cor. 8-9; Rom. 15.25 ff.). This was not a tax or duty which the congregation in Jerusalem imposed on the Gentile-Christian congregations (contrary to Karl Holl, see section 3.2.3). It may not even have been a collection for the Jewish Christians, who were hardly any poorer than Paul's Gentile-Christian congregations (cf. 2 Cor. 8.2); it may have been a collection for indigent Jews during the period of scarcity which came during the sabbatical year 54-55;[128] apparently the money was not delivered to the Christian congregation in Jerusalem (Acts 21.17 ff.). Whatever the case, Paul – and probably Barnabas too – participated actively in the collection work, which was successfully carried out, although the Acts tells us little about it (see Acts 24.17). If the congregation in Jerusalem had refused to receive the money, this would imply not only that the money was intended for them, but also that Paul expresses fear of the congregation in Jerusalem in Rom. 15.31, and both assumptions are open to doubt – the people Paul feared in Jerusalem were the non-Christian Jews.

Geert Hallbäck made a critical analysis of Gal. 2 in his precise and clear study of the Jerusalem Conference and the conflict in Antioch. He sees a collision between two kinds of authority: Paul's charismatic authority and the traditional authority of the "pillars" in Jerusalem. While Paul's authority comes from a vision of Christ (Gal. 1.11-12), the Judaists derive their authority from Jerusalem and the leaders there. Even the fact that Paul went to Jerusalem could therefore undermine his own authority and make it look as if he had submitted to these leaders against his own will – which would be fatal to his argumentation in Gal. as a whole. Hallbäck writes: "The unusually convoluted

---

127 This seems to be the view of Geert Hallbäck: DTT 53 (1990), p. 308.
128 Cf. my *Chronologie*, pp. 124-127; see also section 3.7 below.

language in this passage reflects the fact that Paul tries to avoid this consequence while recognizing at the same time the *real* authority of Jerusalem and even *uses* this authority to strengthen his own position with the Galatians (he explains that he had brought the question of the Gentile mission before the congregation in Jerusalem "to make sure that the race I had run and was running should not be in vain" [Gal. 2.2], which shows that a repudiation from Jerusalem would have been fatal!). Vv. 6-9 are one long syntactic construction characterized by several parentheses, explanations and reservations. On the one hand, Paul wants to emphasize that "those of repute", i.e. the leading apostles in Jerusalem, have no precedence over him, for neither he nor God recognizes personal distinctions (2.6), and he takes great care to ensure that the meeting does not result in the Jerusalem leaders' *approval* of the Gentile mission, but in their *acknowledgement* of the fact that this mission has been sanctioned by God (2.7, 9). On the other hand, the main clauses of the construction emphasize that "those of repute" imposed nothing further on Paul (2.6); on the contrary, they accepted Paul and Barnabas as partners and "shook hands on the partner-ship"."[129]

In principle, all this is correct. It is important to note, however, that in Paul's view, the "pillars" had no authority over him. The "pillars" represented the Judaists' authority, and he could only do one thing to stop their propaganda in Paul's own congregations: to confront these "pillars", or "those of repute", "those reputed to be something", "those who are reputed to be pillars", as Paul characteristically calls them (Gal. 2.2, 6, 9), and persuade them to admonish the Judaists. That Paul succeeded in meeting with the "pillars" and making them accept his work was perhaps more due to good luck than careful planning on his part. In any case, however, the Judaists were now seen as people who had no support from the Jerusalem congregation. The "pillars" were *not* Judaists and did not support the Judaists' activities, either openly or secretly. In other words, the carpet had been pulled out from under the Judaists.

An interesting detail deserves to be mentioned here. It has often been mentioned as a strange fact that in Gal. 2.7-8, Paul calls the apostle Cephas by his Greek name, Peter. It has been suggested that Paul "quoted" from a written report of the Jerusalem Conference, but of course this cannot explain why Paul uses the name Peter in this context. However, Gerd Lüdemann has suggested

---

129 Hallbäck, DTT 53 (1990), pp. 307-308.

that Paul does this in order to recall the previous agreement between him and Peter during Paul's first visit to Jerusalem as a Christian (Gal. 1.18-19): Paul should be apostle for the Gentiles, while Peter should be responsible for the mission among the Jews. This agreement, which was many years old at the time of the Jerusalem Conference and known by the other "pillars" (James had been present) as well as by Paul's Gentile-Christian congregations in Galatia (where Peter's Greek name would have been used), was also the indisputable proof of Paul's status as the apostle of the Gentiles.[130] This also suggests the possibility that Paul's status as the Gentiles' apostle began with his famous ascension to the third heaven or Paradise fourteen years before he wrote his last letter to Corinth (2 Cor. 12.2-4), which should be compared with the Acts' strange account of Paul's vision of Christ in the temple during his first visit to Jerusalem as a Christian (Acts 22.17-21). According to this hypothesis, Paul's call to become an apostle for the Gentiles dates from that occasion and not from his conversion on the road to Damascus.

3.5.2 The conflict in Antioch

It was precisely the question of whether the agreement made at the Jerusalem Conference had been kept or broken that caused the conflict between Peter and Paul, which took place in Antioch immediately after the Jerusalem Conference (Gal. 2.11 ff., cf. Acts 18.22-23). From Paul's point of view, Peter's behaviour, i.e. the fact that he has stopped taking his meals with the Gentile Christians in Antioch and drawn all the other Jewish Christians with him into this hypocrisy, as Paul calls it, is a breach of the agreement that had just been made in Jerusalem, according to which Gentile-Christian congregations were under no obligation to observe the Mosaic law or "live like Jews" (Greek: *ioudaízein*, Gal. 2.14). To the Jerusalem leaders, however, a separation between Jewish and Gentile Christians seemed a natural consequence of the new agreement that the Jewish mission should be separated from the Gentile mission, which was the reason why the Jews had stopped taking their meals with the Gentiles.

---

130 Lüdemann, *Chronologie*, pp. 86-91: "Redaktion und Tradition in Gal. 2.7f", and pp. 91-94: "Gal. 2.7f als Bestandteil einer paulinischen Personaltradition vor dem Konvent"; Schmidt, NTSt 38 (1992), pp. 151-152.

But is Paul's description of the conflict in Antioch at all reliable? Might he not be trying to disguise his own defeat, and is it perhaps only in his own letter that he appears as the winner?

To understand what really happened in Antioch, we must first try to find out what made Peter stop taking his meals with the Gentile Christians as was normally the case. The key to this problem is the role of "the messengers from James" who came to Antioch (Gal. 2.12). Geert Hallbäck is right in suggesting that historio-critical exegetes should be able to discover the facts which Paul's description seems to disguise, and not allow themselves to be "blinded by a successful strategy" in his description of the course of events.[131] The arrival of James' messengers must have made a strong impression, since it immediately caused both Peter and Barnabas to change their previous practice. Apparently James is the guarantor of the agreement made at the Jerusalem Conference, and in this capacity he calls both Peter and the other Antiochene Jewish Christians to order through his messengers. James simply enforces the new agreement on the division of the mission, and Cephas and the other Jewish Christians except Paul loyally submit to his authority.

No doubt this is a correct observation which fully confirms James' strong position as the unchallenged leader of the congregation in Jerusalem;[132] there are good reasons for referring to him as the first among the "pillars" at the time when the Jerusalem Conference took place (Gal. 2.9). With Geert Hallbäck's view in mind, however, I find it important to point out that James hardly acted as he did because he believed the Judaist interpretation of Christianity to be "true". His action was motivated by his desire to free the Jewish Christians, who were his responsibility, from Jewish persecution: if James could guarantee to the Jewish authorities that Christian Jews would not conspire to undermine the authority of the Mosaic law, he had done his best.

While the Judaist movement – the attempt to persuade Gentile Christians to let themselves be circumcised and thus become Jews – is due to the threat of Jewish persecution of Jewish Christians (see sections 3.4.3 and 3.4.4 above), James' insistence on enforcing the agreement on the separation of Jewish Christians from Gentile Christians is paradoxically due to the same threat of Jewish persecution. So the same threat is the cause of both phenomena: the

---

131 Hallbäck, DTT 53 (1990), p. 311.
132 Cf. section 3.2.5 above.

infiltration of the Gentile Christians intended to turn them into Jews, and the isolation of the Jewish Christians intended to ensure that they remain Jewish.

James was far from being a Judaist, and during the Jerusalem Conference, he unconditionally accepted that Paul should continue his work as the apostle of the Gentiles, if only this did not mean that Jewish Christians had to give up their ethnic relationship with Judaism. So the price was an absolute separation between Jewish and Gentile Christians – a high price. Presumably Paul paid this price willingly, James only reluctantly.

Did Paul then suffer a defeat in Antioch – a defeat which he carefully tries to cover up in his description of the events? I do not think so, although this has often been maintained by others.[133] On the contrary, what Paul did by confronting Peter openly in Antioch was to *emphasize* his position: the Gentile Christians should not follow the Jewish Christians in observing the Mosaic law, including the requirement of circumcision. Moreover, it says nowhere that Paul was alone in this situation; naturally it was only the Jewish Christians – but not Paul himself! – who went along with Peter when he stopped taking his meals with the Gentile Christians in Antioch.[134]

---

133 By e.g. Hallbäck, DTT 53 (1990), pp. 311 and 314.

134 According to Acts 15.23 ff. (cf. 16.4; 21.25), it was also agreed at the Jerusalem Conference that Gentile Christians – either everywhere or only in Syria and Cilicia – should observe "the apostolic decree": they should abstain from meat that had been offered to idols, blood, anything that had been strangled (i.e. animals not slaughtered according to Jewish precepts) and from fornication. This apostolic decree is not mentioned in Paul's letters; on the contrary, Paul emphasizes that no obligations or restrictions were imposed on him apart from the decision concerning the collection for Jerusalem (Gal. 2.6-7). Furthermore, Paul's own warnings against fornication and idolatry in 1 Cor. 6.12 ff. and 8.1 ff. do not indicate that he knew of the decree, although they are not incompatible with it. Even if the apostolic decree is historical – and we do not know if it is – it hardly belongs in the context of the Jerusalem Conference. On the other hand, it is conceivable that it belongs in the context of the discussion on the relationship between Gentile Christians and Jewish Christians in mixed congregations, especially in Antioch, where the conflict between Peter and Paul took place. In that case, the decree must have been issued after Paul and Barnabas left Antioch (cf. the observation in Acts 21.25), but can hardly have been very important to the Gentile-Christian congregations which Paul and Barnabas had established in Asia Minor, Macedonia and Greece. For information on the apostolic decree and the Jerusalem Conference, see also the explanation in Klinghardt, *Gesetz und Volk Gottes*, 1988 (see section 2.4 above), pp. 207-224: "Der historische Ort des Aposteldekrets".

3.6 The situation in Corinth

Bibliography

Ferdinand Christian Baur: Die Christuspartei in der korinthischen Gemeinde, der
  Gegensatz des petrinischen und paulinischen Christenthums in der ältesten Kirche,
  der Apostel Petrus in Rom, Tübinger Zeitschrift für Theologie, 1831, Part 4, pp.
  61-206 = Klaus Scholder, ed., *Ferdinand Christian Baur, Ausgewählte Werke in
  Einzelausgaben*, Stuttgart – Bad Cannstadt 1963, I, pp. 1-146.
Eduard Golla: *Zwischenreise und Zwischenbrief. Eine Untersuchung der Frage, ob der
  Apostel Paulus zwischen dem Ersten und Zweiten Korintherbrief eine Reise nach
  Korinth unternommen und einen uns verlorengegangenen Brief an die Korinther
  geschrieben habe* (Biblische Studien, XX/4), Freiburg (Breisgau) 1922 (see
  section 3.1.4 above, n. 30).
Nils A. Dahl: Paul and the Church at Corinth according to 1 Corinthians 1:10-4:21, in:
  Christian History and Interpretation, 1967 (see section 3.1 above), pp. 313-335.
Niels Hyldahl: Den korintiske krise – en skitse, Dansk Teologisk Tidsskrift 40 (1977),
  pp. 18-30.
Josef Zmijewski: *Der Stil der paulinischen "Narrenrede". Analyse der Sprachgestal-
  tung in 2 Kor 11,1-12,10 als Beitrag zur Methodik von Stiluntersuchungen
  neutestamentlicher Texte* (Bonner Biblische Beiträge, 52), Cologne – Bonn 1978.
Gerhard Sellin: Das "Geheimnis" der Weisheit und das Rätsel der "Christuspartei" (zu
  1 Kor 1-4), Zeitschrift für die neutestamentliche Wissenschaft 73 (1982), pp. 69-
  96.
Id.: *Der Streit um die Auferstehung der Toten. Eine religionsgeschichtliche und
  exegetische Untersuchung von 1. Korinther 15* (Forschungen zur Religion und
  Literatur des Alten und Neuen Testaments, 138), Göttingen 1986.
Simone Pétrement: *Le Dieu séparé. Les origines du gnosticisme*, Paris 1984 = *A
  Separate God: The Christian Origins of Gnosticism*, San Fransisco 1990 – London
  1991.
Helmut Merklein: Die Einheitlichkeit des ersten Korintherbriefes, Zeitschrift für die
  neutestamentliche Wissenschaft 75 (1984), pp. 153-183.
Dieter Lührmann: Freundschaftsbrief trotz Spannungen. Zu Gattung und Aufbau des
  Ersten Korintherbriefes, in: Wolfgang Schrage, ed., *Studien zum Text und zur
  Ethik des Neuen Testaments. Festschrift zum 80. Geburtstag von Heinrich
  Greeven* (Beihefte zur Zeitschrift für die neutestamentliche Wissenschaft, 47),
  Berlin – New York 1986, pp. 298-314.
Niels Hyldahl: The Corinthian "Parties" and the Corinthian Crisis, Studia Theologica
  45 (1991), pp. 19-32.

Karl-Wilhelm Niebuhr: *Heidenapostel aus Israel. Die jüdische Identität des Paulus nach ihrer Darstellung in seinen Briefen* (Wissenschaftliche Untersuchungen zum Neuen Testament, 62), Tübingen 1992.

Niels Hyldahl: Paul and Apollos: Exegetical Observations to 1 Cor. 3.1-23, in: Per Bilde/Helge Kjær Nielsen/Jørgen Podemann Sørensen, eds., *Apocryphon Severini presented to Søren Giversen*, Århus 1993, pp. 68-82.

Raimund Bieringer/Jan Lamprecht: *Studies on 2 Corinthians* (Bibliotheca Ephemeridum Theologicarum Lovaniensium, CXII), Leuven 1994.

Bärbel Bosenius: *Die Abwesenheit des Apostels als theologisches Programm. Der zweite Korintherbrief als Beispiel für die Brieflichkeit der paulinischen Theologie* (Texte und Arbeiten zum neutestamentlichen Zeitalter, 11), Tübingen – Basel 1994.

Niels Hyldahl: Paul and Hellenistic Judaism in Corinth, in: Peder Borgen/Søren Giversen, eds., *The New Testament and Hellenistic Judaism*, Århus 1995, pp. 204-216.

Troels Engberg-Pedersen: 2. Korintherbrevs indledningsspørgsmål, in: Lone Fatum/Mogens Müller, eds., *Tro og historie. Festskrift til Niels Hyldahl* ... (Forum for bibelsk eksegese, 7), Copenhagen 1996, pp. 69-88.

3.6.1 The narrative in the Corinthian correspondence

As far as the Corinthian congregation was concerned, Paul soon found himself in a situation which was much more serious than the trouble he had had with the Galatian congregations. The date of Paul's first visit to Corinth remains a controversial question. Gerd Lüdemann has repeatedly maintained that this event occurred no later than in the early 40s. His argumentation is based on Acts 18.2, which says that Claudius had issued an edict that "all Jews should leave Rome." This edict is usually dated to A.D. 49, but Lüdemann maintains that it should be dated to the beginning of Claudius' reign (A.D. 41-54), and that Paul's arrival in Corinth should be dated accordingly. Lüdemann is probably right on the first point,[135] but hardly on the second point. It says in Acts 18.2 that when Paul came to Corinth, he met the Jewish Christian Aquila and his wife Priscilla, who "had recently arrived from Italy." But what does "recently" mean? Clearly it refers to Paul's arrival in Corinth, but considering

---

135 See Gerd Lüdemann, Das Judenedikt des Claudius (ApG 18,2), in: Claus Bussmann/Walter Radl, eds., *Der Treue Gottes trauen. Beiträge zum Werk des Lukas. Festschrift für Gerhard Schneider*, Freiburg – Basel – Wien 1991, pp. 289-298. Cf. section 4.3.2 below, the passage referred to in n. 27.

the relatively late date of the Acts' composition (this particular piece of information is not confirmed by any of Paul's letters from the same period!), it does not prove that Paul himself had arrived in Corinth as early as this. Nor is the Gallio inscription of any help when it comes to dating Paul's arrival in Corinth.[136]

All things considered, the traditional dating of Paul's arrival in Corinth to the autumn of A.D. 49 is probably correct; Paul then left Corinth eighteen months later (Acts 18.11), i.e. in the early summer of A.D. 51, and spent the next three years until Pentecost A.D. 54 in Ephesus, where he stayed all the three years, except for one visit to Jerusalem on the occasion of the Jerusalem Conference in A.D. 53.[137]

When discussing 1 Cor., the first thing I wish to point out is the very strong probability that this letter constitutes a literary entity. The many attempts that have been made to demonstrate that it was constructed by a later editor on the basis of several letters from Paul have all proved to be futile. The originators of these hypotheses will never be able to prove that 1 Cor. did not come from a single hand or mouth, Paul's, in essence just as we have the letter today in the New Testament (except, perhaps, for a few interpolations). If these modern fragmentation hypotheses were true – also for 2 Cor. – the number of letters which the Corinthian Christians received from Paul would have frightened even more hardy readers than those in Corinth, which shows that interpreters take their work too lightly if they use nothing but knives and scissors in their work on the text.

The next point I wish to make about 1 Cor. concerns its literary character and the identification of the "tearful letter" mentioned in 2 Cor. 2.3 ff. and 7.8 ff. To suggest that this tearful letter was a letter, now lost, which was written between 1 and 2 Cor. ("the intermediate letter"), or that the tearful letter is identical to 2 Cor. 10-13 ("the four-chapter letter") would be to operate with unknown factors or with hypotheses which again require the use of knives and scissors. There is no alternative to the old solution: to identify this tearful letter with 1 Cor. itself. Surprising as it may seem, this is nonetheless the simplest solution to the problem of the relationship between 1 and 2 Cor., but it requires

---

136 See Dixon Slingerland, JBL 110 (1991), pp. 439-449 (see section 3.1 above).
137 See my *Chronologie*, pp. 112-124.

that the reader is prepared to accept 1 Cor. as "a tearful letter", i.e. a letter which was written with tears in uncertainty as to its effect on the recipients.

The third point to be mentioned here concerns the number of journeys Paul made to Corinth. Assuming that the tearful letter is identical to 1 Cor., there can have been no "intermediate visit". Paul had visited Corinth only once, i.e. when he founded the congregation there (2 Cor. 1.19, 23), and even the visit after the composition of 2 Cor. was only his second visit to Corinth.[138]

The fourth point is that since it was Titus who delivered the tearful letter (2 Cor. 7.6 ff.; cf. 12.18), we can now conclude that 1 Cor. was brought to Greece by Titus; the reason why Titus is not mentioned in 1 Cor. itself is that he was unknown in Corinth at that time.[139] This may also explain the fact that Titus is not mentioned in the Acts; in this context, however, it is also interesting to note that the author of the Acts prevented himself from mentioning Titus (cf. Gal. 2.1, 3) in connection with the Jerusalem Conference (Acts 15.4 ff.) by bringing the description of this event forward by several chapters, contrary to the correct chronology.

The fifth point is that Titus, who delivered the letter to Corinth, could not of course have co-signed this letter. The co-signatory is Sosthenes (1 Cor. 1.1) – a person whom the Corinthians must have known. But why is Timothy not mentioned as a co-signatory of this letter, as in most of Paul's other letters? The answer is that he was not present when 1 Cor. was written, but had already set out on a journey on Paul's behalf – a journey which would take him from Ephesus to Corinth (1 Cor. 4.17; 16.10-11) – so he could not deliver the letter,

---

138 Cf. Golla, *Zwischenreise u. Zwischenbesuch*, pp. 35 ff.; my *Chronologie*, pp. 34 ff. and pp. 102-106: "Die Reise des Paulus nach Korinth". I interpret 2 Cor. 13.1-2 as follows: "This third time I will come to you [cf. 2 Cor. 12.14]: "every charge must be established on the evidence of two or three witnesses" [Deut. 19.15]. I said before [cf. 1 Cor. 4.19-21], and I am saying now – as if I were present for the second time, though I am absent now – to those who have sinned before [cf. 2 Cor. 12.21], and to all others, that when I come again [cf. 2 Cor. 2.1; 12.21], I will show no leniency [cf. 2 Cor. 1.23]." The "third time" refers to two other times when Paul did not come (or was not ready to come: 2 Cor. 12.14), i.e. the two times he wrote letters instead of coming: 1) the previous letter which was written during his imprisonment in Ephesus and is mentioned in 1 Cor. 5.9, and 2) 1 Cor. itself; contrary to the traditional interpretation, the words "as if I were present for the second time" do not refer to a previous, "intermediate" visit; as suggested by the words "absent now", they refer to the present moment when 2 Cor. is being written and therefore show that Paul's next visit to Corinth will only be his second visit there.

139 See n. 86 above.

and would not know its contents until later. On the other hand, Timothy was with Paul when 2 Cor. was written (2 Cor. 1.1), but as we know, it was not he, but Titus, who brought this letter to Corinth (2 Cor. 8.6, 16).

Paul wrote the tearful letter because he had promised the Corinthians that he would visit them (1 Cor. 4.18-21), but later decided to postpone the visit and to write 1 Cor. (the tearful letter) as a temporary substitute for a visit. 2 Cor. tells us why Paul decided to postpone the visit: he wrote the tearful letter in order to avoid a painful visit (2 Cor. 2.1 ff.; cf. 7.8 ff.). So something must have happened, not between 1 and 2 Cor. ("an intermediate event"), but before he wrote 1 Cor., something which can explain why Paul decided to postpone the visit he had promised the Corinthians. What can this have been?

There seems to be only one possible answer to this question: the arrival of Chloe's people in Ephesus and the rumours they had brought with them about the situation in Corinth (1 Cor. 1.11; cf. 5.1; 11.18). If this had not happened, Paul could have gone to Corinth as he had promised and met Timothy there, as agreed, before Timothy's departure from Ephesus (4.17, 18-21). Now, however, after Titus' unexpected arrival with the letter (16.11), Timothy was told to return to Ephesus, humiliated by his previous ignorance of the letter; later Timothy was rehabilitated through Paul's explicit references to him in the next letter (2 Cor. 1.1, 19).

Without yet revealing his intention to postpone the visit, Paul refers to his original travel plan in 1 Cor. 4.17 and 4.18-21, explaining that Timothy has already left for Corinth (he did not go there directly, since he would otherwise have arrived before the letter), and that Paul himself will come after him. Paul returns to this travel plan in 2 Cor. 1.15-16, according to which he originally planned to visit Corinth twice: once on his way to Macedonia and once again on his way back. This shows that Paul had agreed with Timothy that they should meet in Corinth and travel to Macedonia together; after the visit there, in Philippi, they would both return to Corinth. The correctness of this reconstruction of the original travel plan is fully confirmed by Phil. 2.19-23 and 2.24: Timothy will visit Philippi (on his way from Ephesus, through the province of Asia to Macedonia, and from there to Corinth), and Paul is convinced that he will soon visit Philippi personally (i.e. via Corinth, with

Timothy as his travelling companion). Result: 1 Cor. 4.17, 18-21 = 2 Cor. 1.15-16 = Phil. 2.19-23, 24.[140]

As already mentioned, the original travel plans were changed for both Paul and Timothy, a fact that Paul reveals at the end of 1 Cor., which was written during the spring (1 Cor. 5.7; 16.8) – but of course the fact that he wrote 1 Cor. suggests in itself that he might change the original travel plan. He does not reveal this until the end of the letter, where he says that he will not go directly to Corinth, but will visit Macedonia first and then go to Corinth and spend the next winter there (1 Cor. 16.5-9); therefore Timothy has to be told on his arrival in Corinth that he must return to Ephesus (16.10-11). The new travel plan was carried through, as we can see from 2 Cor.: Timothy had returned from Ephesus, and with him Paul went from Ephesus to Troas and then to Macedonia (2 Cor. 1.8 ff.; 2.12-13; 7.5 ff.). There, after Titus' arrival from Corinth (7.6 ff.), and in the presence of Timothy (1.1), he wrote the new letter, in which he renewed his old promise of a visit (12.14, 21; 13.1-2). By then it was autumn (8.10; 9.2), so the visit to Corinth would be a winter visit according to the revised travel plan (1 Cor. 16.6).

In 1 Cor. 5.9, Paul refers to a previous letter that he has written to the Corinthian Christians, who have in his view misunderstood or misinterpreted it, so that Paul himself has to clarify its meaning, which he does in Cor. 5.11 ff. The question is: who can have informed Paul of the misunderstanding or misinterpretation of this previous letter? There are several possibilities: 1) the Corinthian delegation, composed of Stephanas, Fortunatus and Achaicus, who visited Paul in Ephesus, and who are mentioned by Paul himself (1 Cor. 16.17; cf. 1.16); 2) the persons who delivered the Corinthian letter, with its many questions, to Paul (7.1 – see below); 3) Chloe's people (1.11); 4) Sosthenes and/or Apollos, who had both been to Corinth, but were now staying with Paul in Ephesus (1.11, 12; 3.4-23; 4.6; 16.12); or 5) the Corinthians' letter itself (7.1), with the questions it may have contained concerning Paul's previous letter.

In order to answer this question, we have to consider the possibility that Paul's previous letter may have something to do with the reason why he decided to postpone his visit and write 1 Cor. instead; this points to the third possibility

---

140 Cf. my *Chronologie*, pp. 18-26 and pp. 27-42; see also Golla, *Zwischenreise u. Zwischenbrief*, pp. 29 ff. See also the passage referred to in n. 33 above.

mentioned above, i.e. that Chloe's people had informed Paul that the Corinthians had misunderstood or misinterpreted the previous letter. However, in order to substantiate this hypothesis, we also have to consider the question of whom Paul could have sent to Corinth with the previous letter. Again, there are several possibilities: 1) the Corinthian delegation, when they returned to Corinth from Ephesus; 2) Chloe's people – but they had just arrived when 1 Cor. was being written; 3) Sosthenes – but Paul is unlikely to have sent him to Corinth, since he had recently returned from there and was staying with Paul when 1 Cor. was being written; and 4) Apollos – but there are no indications that Paul asked him to bring this letter to Corinth. It must therefore have been the Corinthian delegation who brought Paul's previous letter to Corinth when they returned after their visit to Paul in Ephesus.

In other words: Paul wrote the previous letter (1 Cor. 5.9) while Stephanas, Fortunatus and Achaicus were in Ephesus; they received it from Paul during their visit to him and delivered it when they returned to Corinth. We can therefore exclude the possibility that the Corinthians' letter (1 Cor. 7.1) contained questions about Paul's previous letter.

As far as the identification of the previous letter is concerned, there are two possibilities: 1) either it is lost, 2) or part of it is preserved in 2 Cor. 6.14-7.1. I am inclined to believe in the latter possibility, for the following reasons: a) 2 Cor. 6.14-7.1 clearly interrupts the coherence in 2 Cor. and must have been misplaced for some "technical" reason during the processes of manuscript transcription,[141] b) its content, which refers to believers and unbelievers,[142]

---

141 Different views are found in Gordon D. Fee, II Corinthians vi. 14-vii. 1 and Food offered to Idols, New Testament Studies 23 (1976-77), pp. 140-161; Margaret E. Thrall, The Problem of II Cor. vi. 14-vii. 1 in some recent discussions, New Testament Studies 24 (1977-78), pp. 132-148; Jerome Murphy-O'Connor, Relating 2 Corinthians 6. 14-7. 1 to its Context, New Testament Studies 33 (1987), pp. 272-275; G.K. Beale, The Old Testament Background in 2 Corinthians 5-7 and its Bearing on the Literary Problem of 2 Corinthians 6. 14-7. 1, New Testament Studies 35 (1989), pp. 550-581, esp. pp. 566 ff.; Raimund Bieringer, in: Bieringer/Lamprecht, *Studies on 2 Corinthians*, 1994, pp. 551-570: "2 Korinther 6,14-7,1 im Kontext des 2. Korintherbriefes. Forschungsüberblick und Versuch eines eigenen Zugangs"; now also Engberg-Pedersen, 1996, pp. 83-84.
142 A different view is found in G.W.H. Lampe, Church Discipline and the Interpretation of the Epistles to the Corinthians, in: *Christian History and Interpretation*, 1967 (see section 3.1 above), pp. 337-361, see p. 343. Lampe thought that 2 Cor. 6.14-7.1 might well be a part of a previous letter from Paul and referred to mixed marriages between believers and unbelievers (what then about 1 Cor. 7.12-16?), but that this part of the

corresponds surprisingly well with the context in 1 Cor. 5.1 ff., and c) at first sight, it can have been understood to mean that Paul asked the Corinthian Christians not to have anything to do with unbelievers.[143] However, this is not a very important question.

1 Cor. 7.1 shows that the Corinthians had written a letter to Paul, asking him a number of questions of importance to the congregation in Corinth. In 1 Cor., Paul answers some of these questions; he does not mean to answer all of them, but says that he will answer the rest of them when he comes to Corinth (11.34). Regarding the question of who had brought Paul this letter, it has often been maintained that the Corinthian delegation did this (just as they also brought 1 Cor. home – as if they were simply acting as postmen!). But this cannot be true. For one thing, the delegation is not mentioned in 1 Cor. 7.1, and moreover, the delegation could easily have presented the questions orally, since all three delegates, with Stephanas as their leader, would have been able to guarantee the correctness of both questions and answers. It is simply

---

previous letter is not mentioned in 1 Cor. 5.9 ff. because Paul explicitly explains that his previous instructions have nothing to do with the relationship between believers and unbelievers. This view is not convincing; cf. John M.G. Barclay, Thessalonica and Corinth: Social Contrasts in Pauline Christianity, Journal for the Study of the New Testament 47 (1992), pp. 49-74, see p. 59, n. 16 there.

143 Sellin believes that the previous letter (A) can still be reconstructed on the basis of texts in 1 Cor. itself: 11.2-34; 5.1-8; 6.12-20; 9.24-10.22 and 6.1-11; then came the Corinthians' letter with the questions about this previous letter, and then Paul's answering letter (B), "the theme letter": 5.9-13; 7.1-40; 8.1-9.23; 10.23-11.1 and 12.1-16.24; then came Paul's letter about the quarrels (C): 1.1-4.21. See Sellin, ZNW 73 (1982), p. 72 with n. 9; id., Auferstehung, pp. 49-53; id., Hauptprobleme des Ersten Korintherbriefes, in: Aufstieg und Niedergang der römischen Welt, II/25.4, Berlin – New York 1987, pp. 2940-3044, see pp. 2964 ff. It is clear that with this fragmentation hypothesis, Sellin must reject any idea that 2 Cor. 6.14-7.1 was a part of this previous letter. He therefore considers this text to be a non-Pauline interpolation (but compare 2 Cor. 6.16 with 1 Cor. 3.16-17!). The same applies to Joseph A. Fitzmyer, Qumran and the Interpolated Paragraph in 2 Cor. 6: 14-7: 1, Catholic Biblical Quarterly 23 (1961), pp. 271-280 = id., Essays on the Semitic Background of the New Testament, London 1971, pp. 205-217; Joachim Gnilka, 2 Kor 6,14-7,1 im Lichte der Qumranschriften und der Zwölf-Patriarchen-Testamente, in: J. Blinzler/O. Kuß/F. Mußner, eds., Neutestamentliche Aufsätze für Prof. Josef Schmid, Regensburg 1963, pp. 86-99; Hans Dieter Betz, 2 Cor 6:14-7:1: An Anti-Pauline Fragment? Journal of Biblical Literature 92 (1973), pp. 88-108; id., Galatians. A Commentary on Paul's Letter to the Churches in Galatia (Hermeneia. A Critical and Historical Commentary on the Bible), Philadelphia 1979, pp. 329-330.

inconceivable that Chloe's people brought the Corinthian letter to Ephesus, so this possibility can be ruled out. This leaves us with one possibility: it was Sosthenes who brought the letter with him when he went to Ephesus. Paul told the delegation that he intended to answer the questions himself as he thought he would soon be visiting Corinth; but the bad news which Paul received from Chloe's people forced him to postpone his visit to Corinth, so he wrote 1 Cor., in which he answers the most important of the questions asked in the Corinthians' letter. The argument that it was Sosthenes who brought the Corinthians' letter to Paul is supported by the fact that Sosthenes is mentioned as co-signatory of the letter which contains the answers to the most important of the questions the Corinthians had asked in their letter.

So the Corinthian delegation (1 Cor. 16.17-18) did not bring the Corinthians' letter to Ephesus (Sosthenes did); nor did they bring Paul's 1 Cor. back to Corinth (Titus did). On the other hand, they had brought Paul's short, previous letter (mentioned in 1 Cor. 5.9) back with them to Corinth. While they were staying with Paul in Ephesus, they had also been told that Timothy and Paul would come to Corinth soon (according to the original travel plan), and that Paul would then answer the questions asked in the Corinthians' letter; finally, they had been asked if the Corinthian congregation would contribute to the collection for Jerusalem – in fact, this collection was the main purpose of Timothy's and Paul's planned journeys.

Was the visit of the delegation from Corinth then really nothing but a courtesy visit? Far from it! They visited Paul because he was in prison, just like Epaphroditus was sent to Paul from Philippi during the same term of imprisonment in Ephesus (Phil. 2.25 ff.: 4.18). There is no doubt that this was the reason for the Corinthian delegation's visit.

In 1 Cor. 7.1, Paul begins to answer the questions the Corinthians had asked him in their letter. When they reached this passage in 1 Cor., if not before, the Corinthian readers must have understood that Paul intended to change the original travel plan he had mentioned to the delegation.

It is usually assumed that Paul's answer covers most of the rest of 1 Cor., including all the passages beginning with *perì dé*, i.e. 1 Cor. 7.1, 25; 8.1, 4; 11.2 (?); 12.1; 16.1, 12. This could then be used for the purpose of reconstructing the

Corinthians' letter and discovering the origins of 1 Cor. and Paul's previous letter.[144]

This assumption is not tenable, however. In 2 Cor. 9.1, the same *perì dé* construction is not used as an introduction to an answer to any question at all; the same applies to the three instances of this in 1 Thess. 4.9, 13 and 5.1 (and the *hypèr dé* passage in 2 Thess. 2.1, which refers to 1 Thess. 4.14).[145] The Corinthians would hardly have asked Paul in a letter if Apollos would visit them (1 Cor. 16.12). The delegation could of course have asked Paul about this, and he could have answered immediately; or perhaps his situation at that time would have prevented him from answering immediately? Whatever the case, a close reading of 1 Cor. 16.12 shows that it does not refer to any question the Corinthians might have asked about Apollos; Paul simply informs the Corinthians that Apollos will not be among the brothers who will come to Corinth and bring 1 Cor. with them.

Similarly, the Corinthians would hardly have asked a question in writing about the collection for Jerusalem (1 Cor. 16.1). If they had done so, it would have implied that before they wrote their own letter to Paul, somebody had already informed them of this future collection; of course Paul could have informed them of the collection in his previous letter, but as we have seen, this presumably short letter was not written until the Corinthian delegates had joined Paul in Ephesus. It follows from this that the Corinthians had not asked any questions about the collection, and that the text simply represents Paul's own instructions: it is Paul himself who raises this subject on the basis of the information he has already given to the delegation who have visited him in prison in Ephesus.

The subjects in 1 Cor. which can with certainty be identified as answers to questions asked in the Corinthians' letter are only: 1) marriage, divorce, etc. (1 Cor. 7.1-40), 2) meat consecrated to idols (8.1-11.1), and 3) charismatic achievements (12.1-14.40), with 4) the comments on women's participation in worship (11.2-16) as a remote possibility. It cannot be excluded, however, that

---

144 Cf. e.g. Hurd, *Origin*, 1965 (see section 3.1.2 above, n. 2), pp. 213-239: "The Contents of Paul's Previous Letter"; Sellin, *Auferstehung,* pp. 49 ff.

145 See also E. Baasland, Die *perí*-Formel und die Argumentation(ssituation) des Paulus, Studia Theologica 42 (1988), pp. 69-87; Margaret M. Mitchell, Concerning *perì dé* in 1 Corinthians, Novum Testamentum 31 (1989), pp. 229-256.

5) the admonitions about the Lord's Supper (11.17-34; cf. 10.16-21) also represent an answer to a question in the Corinthians' letter, especially when seen in the light of the observation in 11.34, and the fact that Chloe's people may have informed Paul of irregularities connected with the Lord's Supper does not exclude this possibility.

We have seen that Paul had been in prison in Ephesus before he wrote 1 Cor. during the spring;[146] probably he had spent the entire winter in prison and was now staying with Aquila and Priscilla (1 Cor. 16.19; cf. Rom. 16.3-4). After his release from prison, but before he wrote 1 Cor. and changed the original travel plan as explained above, Paul probably visited the congregations in the centre of the province of Asia – otherwise the greetings he sends from them (1 Cor. 16.19) are difficult to explain. Philem. 22, which was written during his imprisonment in Ephesus, confirms that Paul intended to go to Colossae (where Philemon lived), accompanied by Timothy (Philem. 1). This is where Gal. belongs. This letter shows that Titus was also with Paul when it was written (Gal. 2.3; cf. 1.2: "all the brothers now with me").[147] Paul's physical condition after his recent imprisonment (cf. Gal. 6.17) prevented him from going to Galatia, so he had to write a letter instead (cf. Gal. 4.13, 20). So Gal. was written in Colossae and brought to Galatia by Timothy and the brothers (note the anonymity of the "co-signatories", who were also bearers of the letter); they also instructed the Galatians orally about the collection for Jerusalem – there are no instructions about this collection in Gal. itself, only the reference to the decision made at the Jerusalem Conference (Gal. 2.10) – and reported on their visit on their return to Paul. Then Paul returned to Ephesus accompanied by Titus, while Timothy and the other brothers travelled on through Asia to Macedonia. In this context, the words in 1 Cor. 16.1 are important: "Now about the collection in aid of God's people: you should follow the instructions I gave (*diétaxa* – i.e. through the bearers of Gal.) to our churches in Galatia." These

---

146 See 1 Cor. 15.32 and 2 Cor. 1.8; it is important to note that in 2 Cor. 1.8, Paul does not inform the Corinthian Christians that he had been in prison (he mentions the "trouble in Asia" as something they already know); he describes the hardships of the imprisonment.

147 Cf. Udo Borse, *Der Standort des Galaterbriefes* (Bonner Biblische Beiträge, 41), Cologne 1972, pp. 44, 53 and 149, n. 587; my *Chronologie*, pp. 6 and 77.

words indicate that Gal. was written during the short period between Paul's release from the prison in Ephesus and the composition of 1 Cor. there.[148]

Finally, as regards Apollos, he must have had travelling companions on his journey to Corinth and back. It is important to note, however, that only Sosthenes, not Apollos, is mentioned as co-signatory of 1 Cor., and that there are no greetings from Apollos in the letter; this suggests a certain distance between Paul and Apollos at the time when the letter was written.[149] Later, in 2 Cor., Apollos is not mentioned at all, so he cannot be one of the two unnamed persons who accompanied Titus during his second visit to Corinth (2 Cor. 8.18 ff.). Nor did Apollos accompany Titus during the latter's first visit to Corinth (1 Cor. 16.12!), so he cannot be identified as the unnamed brother who had accompanied Titus the first time and is mentioned in 2 Cor. 12.18.

3.6.2 The Corinthian crisis

An antique letter is usually defined as one half of a dialogue; the modern reader, who cannot know the circumstances under which the letter was written, must then try to reconstruct the other half. Unfortunately those who study antique letters often neglect what is perhaps the most interesting fact, i.e. that the letter itself constitutes a link in the chain of events to which the letter refers.[150] When the addressee has received a letter, the world is not the same as it was before. It is essential for a historian to understand a letter as an event which has its own place among a number of events. A visit is postponed, and a letter is written instead, or perhaps as a temporary substitute for the visit. The postponement or cancellation of a visit, and the letter which is written instead, are events in themselves. What a loss it would have been for posterity if Paul had not postponed his visit to Corinth!

---

148 Cf. my *Chronologie*, pp. 64-75: "Paulus und die Galater"; Paulus' Galaterbrev i hans *annus mirabilis*, Dansk Teologisk Tidsskrift 52 (1989), pp. 106-109.

149 Cf. Pétrement, *Le Dieu séparé*, p. 374 (p. 272 in *A Separate God*): "When Paul speaks of Apollos' decision not to return immediately to Corinth, he speaks of it in the past, which seems to indicate that he did not meet him often ("It was not at all his will ...". If he met him often, would he not have said: "It is not at all his will ..."?)." However, this argumentation is uncertain, since the past tense in 16.12 might be a kind of "letter aorist".

150 See Norman R. Petersen, *Rediscovering Paul: Philemon and the Sociology of Paul's narrative World*, Philadelphia 1985, pp. 53-65: "On the Sociology of Letters"; Abraham J. Malherbe, *Ancient Epistolary Theorists* (Society of Biblical Literature Sources for Biblical Study, 19), Atlanta 1988.

The first observation to be made in this context is that despite his promise of a visit, Paul decides not to go to Corinth and confront the Corinthian crisis in person. On the contrary, he writes a letter, 1 Cor., in which he tries to solve the problems from a distance, with the disadvantage of not knowing whether he will succeed or not; he will not know the outcome until Titus returns from his visit to Corinth and meets him in Macedonia (2 Cor. 2.13; 7.5 ff.).

Paul's decision not to appear in person involves another disadvantage from his point of view: he may be seen as a man who lacks personal authority, a man who must admit to his Corinthian congregation, at least temporarily, that he is weak (1 Cor. 4.10; 2 Cor. 11.21, 30; 12.5, 9-10) and unable to control the situation. He has become "a spectacle to the world" (1 Cor. 4.9), and he knows it. What can he do to regain his authority?

It is hardly a coincidence that the passage in 1 Cor. in which Paul first mentions his promise to come and his original travel plan (1 Cor. 4.18-21) is also the passage in which he is on the point of revealing his intention of changing his travel plan and postponing his visit. When he wrote this, and while he was writing the whole letter, he had in fact already changed the travel plan. However, since he has to keep his readers waiting until they have read the rest of the letter, he does not mention the change of plan until towards the end of the letter (1 Cor. 16.5-9).

This means that Paul's reference to his promise of a visit – a promise that soon becomes a threat (1 Cor. 4.19) – and the reference to his travel plan are placed in an important part of the letter as a whole: at the end of the first part of the letter (1.10-4.21) and before the transition (5.1-6.20) to the part of the letter in which he begins to answer the questions the Corinthians had asked him in their own letter (7.1 ff.). Except for the first four chapters, Paul could have told the Corinthians everything in the letter face to face without too much trouble. But he could only tell them the contents of chapter 1-4 in writing, in a letter, and it would not be correct to maintain that this part of the letter is what Paul would have said if he had been present in person. It is not a substitute for his presence, but a compensation for his absence. In other words: 1 Cor. 4.18-21 marks the end of the part of the letter that describes the reason why he decided not to come but to write the letter instead. Obviously the reason is the divisions or rather division in the Corinthian congregation described to him by Chloe's people (1.10 ff.).

The form of this part of the letter corresponds with its content: "I appeal to you, my brothers, in the name of our Lord Jesus Christ ..." (1.10; cf. the almost identical words in 2 Cor. 10.1), which means that 1 Cor., at least in its first four chapters, assumes the character of a severe admonishment – it is certainly not a friendly letter (cf. the observations above concerning 1 Cor.'s character of a "tearful letter").

No other letter in *corpus Paulinum* is similar to 1 Cor. in form. It begins with admonishments and ends by announcing the postponement of a visit; there are no indications of any previous strategic arrangement of the contents in two parts: 1) theology, instruction or theory, and 2) application, admonition or practice, as we find in the Letter to the Romans (Rom. 1-8 or -11 and 12-15), or even in the Letter to the Galatians (Gal. 1-4 and 5-6), and also in Greek popular philosophy. On the contrary, Paul's strategy in 1 Cor. is a desperate strategy. When dealing with the Galatian crisis, Paul intended to come in person, although he was prevented from doing so. However, he dared not confront the Corinthian crisis in person until the Corinthians had submitted to his authority, and he had to write them two long letters before they did.

Just as 1 Cor. begins with a serious admonishment, 2 Cor. ends with another serious admonishment. And just as 1 Cor. 1.10-4.21 was not written as a substitute for Paul's presence, but as a compensation for the absence he found necessary in the circumstances, 2 Cor. 10.1-13.13 is written as a compensation for his necessary absence. This emerges clearly from the words at the end of the letter: "In writing this letter before I come, my aim is to spare myself, when I do come, any sharp exercise of authority – authority which the Lord gave me for building up and not for pulling down" (2 Cor. 13.10; cf. 10.8). Paul could hardly have expressed himself more clearly. However, he dared not show himself in Corinth until he was certain that he would not have to exclude a considerable part of the congregation and run the risk of eventually declaring the Corinthian congregation non-existent. So he did everything in his power to submit the Corinthians to his authority before his own arrival. Perhaps he hoped that Titus, who also took this letter to Greece, would be able to bring about the measure of reconciliation which Paul himself was unable to establish;[151] in any case, Titus and his two travelling companions probably acted as buffers between Paul's letters and the congregation in Corinth.

---

151 Cf. Petersen, *Rediscovering Paul*, p. 117.

As indicated by the literary form, the essential part of 2 Cor. is found in 2 Cor. 10.1-13.13. These last four chapters also constitute the part of the letter which describes the reason for writing the letter, and which could not be communicated by word of mouth, but only in writing. This is fully confirmed by the other parts of the letter. All 2 Cor. 1-7 is "only" a preamble or introduction and does not, in itself, constitute a complete letter.[152] Even when including 2 Cor. 8-9, the text cannot represent a complete letter, since it is obvious that a letter cannot possibly end with these two chapters concerning the collection for Jerusalem – especially when considering that they are preceded by chapters 1-7 as their preamble. The end of the letter can only be found in chapters 10-13.

On these grounds, it can be established that 1 and 2 Cor. constitute a literary entity. 1 Cor. 1-4 and 2 Cor. 10-13 contain the words which could not be said face to face, but only written in a letter. These parts of the two letters, the beginning of the first one and the end of the last one, correspond with each other in form and content as well as in literary strategy.

Since 1974, Gerd Theißen has attempted to prove in his studies that the division in the Corinthian congregation was caused by sociological problems.[153]

---

152 In many respects, 1 Thess. 1-3 is a parallel to 2 Cor. 1-7: 1) both are preambles to yet unfinished letters; 2) both take up more than half the volume of the letter; 3) in both cases, Paul uses the preamble to describe the historical development from the establishment of the congregation in question up to the moment when the letter is being written; 4) in both cases, Paul has sent a collaborator to represent himself; 5) in both cases, the collaborator returns with good news – in 1 Thess.: Timothy (1 Thess. 3.1-5, 6 ff.), in 2 Cor.: Titus (2 Cor. 7.6-7; cf. 8.6); compare especially 1 Thess. 3.6 and 2 Cor. 7.7. The correctness of this analysis is confirmed by Paul's use of the words "faith – love – hope" in 1 Thess. 1.3 (cf. Col. 1.4-5), interrupted in 3.6: "faith – love" (cf. 3.10: "whatever is lacking in your faith"), and 4.13: "who have no hope", but re-established in 5.8: "faith – love – hope". See my Auferstehung Christi – Auferstehung der Toten (1 Thess. 4.13-18), 1980 (cf. section 2.7 above), p. 123. Note that the well-known, but not original order: "faith – hope – love" in the New Testament is found only in 1 Cor. 13.13.

153 Gerd Theißen, *Studien zur Soziologie des Urchristentums* (see section 3.2.2 above, n. 48). See also id., *The Social Setting of Pauline Christianity: Essays on Corinth*, ed. and trans. John H. Schütz, Philadelphia – Edinburgh 1982; id., *Sociology of Early Palestinian Christianity*, trans. J. Bowden, Philadelphia 1978. I refer in particular to the following studies/essays: "Legitimation und Lebensunterhalt: ein Beitrag zur Soziologie urchristlicher Missionare", 1975 (pp. 201-230), "Soziale Schichtung in der korintischen Gemeinde. Ein Beitrag zur Soziologie des hellenistischen Urchristentums", 1974 (pp. 231-271), and "Die Starken und Schwachen in Korinth. Soziologische Analyse eines theologischen

He thought he could prove the existence of a conflict between the rich and the poor, between the socially strong and weak. Paul's statement in 1 Cor. 1.26 that there are not many "wise, powerful and noble" people among the Corinthian Christians is understood literally in the sense that there were few of these people, but the fact that they are mentioned indicates that they had considerable power and influence. In a passage in which Paul seems to address himself to the entire congregation, 4.9-13, he says that they are "sensible, powerful and honoured", but a close reading reveals the fact that these characteristics are almost the same as those mentioned earlier in the letter (1.26). According to Theißen, this shows that Paul is not speaking to the entire congregation, but only to "the wise, strong and noble", and that they are responsible for the division in the congregation.[154]

In other words, Paul's accentuation of the Corinthian Christians' low social status is given an almost opposite meaning and used to show that there were quite a few rich and influential Christians in Corinth;[155] according to Theißen, one of these was the quaestor Erastus, later to become aedile, who is known from a Corinthian inscription, and whom Theißen identifies as the Corinthian Erastus in Rom. 16.23.[156] The conflict between the weak (1 Cor. 8.7, 9, 11, 12; 9.22) and the strong (1.26; 4.10) is considered as a social conflict between the

---

Streites", 1975 (pp. 272-289), all of which have been translated into English in: *The Social Setting of Pauline Christianity.*

154 Theißen, *Studien zur Soziologie*, p. 228 (*The Social Setting of Pauline Christianity*, p. 56): "Yet in the matter of partisan allegiance, Paul addresses himself to the few who are wise, powerful and of noble birth (1:26). And when he contrasts his own social situation in 1 Cor. 4:9-13 with that of the Corinthians – more precisely, with that of the "wise", the "strong" and the "reputable" (RVS "held in honour") Corinthians (4:10) – it is not accidental that he mentions working with his hands, suggesting that among those whom he addresses are Christians who do not need to support themselves with their own labour. Meanwhile, the context (1 Cor. 3:18-4:9) makes it clear that Paul is speaking to those who are responsible for the party divisions."

155 Theißen, *Studien zur Soziologie*, p. 234 (p. 72 in *The Social Setting of Pauline Christianity*): "If Paul says that there were not many in the Corinthian congregation who were wise, powerful, and wellborn, then this much is certain: there were some." Cf. Dieter Säger, Die *dynatoí* in 1 Cor. 1.26, Zeitschrift für die neutestamentliche Wissenschaft 76 (1985), pp. 285-291: "the powerful" means "the rich".

156 Theißen, *Studien zur Soziologie*, pp. 236-245 (pp. 75-83 in *The Social Setting of Pauline Christianity*).

poor and the rich.[157] Only the rich owned houses where the believers could meet (11.22), and only the rich members of the congregation allowed themselves to eat meat consecrated to idols (8.4 ff.). The whole conflict was due to social differences and disagreements between members of the congregation.

There is no doubt that at the time when 1 (and 2) Cor. were being written, there was a serious conflict in the Corinthian congregation with apparently social implications, and that the delicate question of money was also involved, since money was needed both for the collection for Jerusalem which was being discussed in Corinth, for the financial support of Paul – which he refused to receive – and for the "super-apostles".

But there are at least four problems which have not been solved or even mentioned in Theißen's investigations. 1) Paul calls himself "weak" (1 Cor. 4.10; cf. 2.3) as opposed to the Corinthians. He does not contrast a strong and a weak wing in Corinth; he contrasts his own weakness with the strength of the Corinthians (see also 2 Cor. 11.21). 2) The division in the Corinthian congregation did not exist when Paul founded the congregation with Silvanus and Timothy as his collaborators (2 Cor. 1.19), and there was no division when he left Corinth. The division did not emerge until later; it had not existed from the beginning. 3) Apparently Stephanas and his household (1 Cor. 1.16; 16.15 ff.) belonged to the influential and relatively wealthy part of the congregation in Corinth. But Stephanas was, as Paul explicitly says, the first Christian convert in Corinth, and Paul himself had baptized him and his household (1.16; 16.15; cf. Rom. 16.5 concerning Epaenetus). Stephanas cannot therefore have been responsible for the division in Corinth, and the difference between "the rich" and "the poor" must have been visible from the beginning. 4) Paul uses the term "riches" (*ploûtos*: 1 Cor. 1.5; 4.8) in a special way, not in a material or financial sense, but in a "spiritual" sense. So it is more than doubtful whether the strong and influential persons who were responsible for the division in Corinth were also wealthy or even rich.

This sociological explanation of the Corinthian crisis is not tenable. Instead I point to the fact mentioned above, i.e. that the congregation in Corinth was not divided when it was founded by Paul. The divisions did not emerge until later. Paul planted the seed, he laid the foundation (1 Cor. 3.6, 10). Most of the people

---

157 Cf. Theißen, *Studien zur Soziologie*, pp. 272-289 (pp. 121-143 in *The Social Setting of Pauline Christianity*).

he converted were people of humble means, including both slaves and their masters, people from the workshops or the market street[158] whom he had won for the Christian faith, but more influential people like Stephanas, Gaius (see Rom. 16.23), Crispus and Sosthenes also found the way to Christianity through Paul. No serious social conflicts arose in the congregation while Paul himself was staying in Corinth. When he had left the city, Apollos and his collaborators arrived during his absence, and their missionary work in Corinth was surprisingly successful in terms of new converts,[159] who did not in every respect live up to Paul's expectations of Christians. For instance, the new Christians who had been converted by Apollos had some quite non-Pauline ideas of marriage, divorce and sexual behaviour, dealings with non-Christians and worship gatherings, including the Lord's Supper. First of all, they did not know Paul, whom they had never seen or met, and therefore did not recognize him as an apostle – a fact which is fully understandable from their point of view.[160]

These circumstances created a social – but not necessarily socio-economic – gap between Paul's and Apollos' people, and since the latter were in all probability more numerous and influential than Paul's people, Paul had to stay away until he had regained control and authority or had succeeded in gaining control and authority over Apollos' wing in the Corinthian congregation.

As already mentioned, there seems to have been a certain distance between Paul and Apollos. Apollos had simply refused to follow Paul's request that he should go to Corinth together with the brothers (1 Cor. 16.12). It is also significant that Paul and Apollos apparently never worked together in Corinth, and that Paul had not sent him there in the first place; in fact, Apollos worked in Corinth without Paul's consent, and when he arrived, Paul and his collaborators

---

158 Cf. Abraham J. Malherbe, *Paul and the Thessalonians: The Philosophic Traditions of Pastoral Care*, Philadelphia 1987, pp. 17-20: "Paul in the Workshop", which gives a convincing impression of Paul's missionary strategy both in Thessalonica and in Corinth.

159 This is probably the reason why Paul seems to belittle the importance of baptism in 1 Cor. 1.14 ff.; but see also Petersen, *Rediscovering Paul*, pp. 120 ff.

160 Cf. Petersen, *Rediscovering Paul*, p. 115: "Paul's role as the initiator of action is evident, even in the interesting case of Apollos, who may well be the exception which illustrates the rule. For despite Paul's questioning of this fellow worker's work in 1 Corinthians 1 – 4, Apollos apparently enjoyed a sufficient independence from Paul to decline his appeal (*parakalo*) that he visit Corinth (1 Cor. 16:12). If so, Paul's authority may not have been acknowledged by Apollos, and Paul's identification of him as a fellow worker in 3:5-23 may reflect Paul's attempt to get the Corinthians to view Apollos as *his* subordinate."

had already left the city. Paul's statement, "I planted the seed, and Apollos watered it" (3.6), also illustrates the chronological order of Paul's and Apollos' activities in Corinth.[161]

Several interpreters have recognized the fact that the Christians whom Paul opposes in 1 Cor. 1-4 were Apollos' Corinthian supporters. This emerges especially clearly from Gerhard Sellin's and Simone Pétrement's studies. They demonstrate convincingly that 1 Cor. 3.1-23 is aimed at Apollos' influence,[162] and not, as others have maintained, at Cephas' influence as well;[163] there are no indications that Paul has suddenly changed his target when he issues his warnings against the person or persons building on the foundation he laid himself. This is a significant observation, since the text in 3.1 ff. is inseparably linked to the preceding text, thereby ensuring the internal coherence in this central part of the letter.

Another observation is perhaps even more important: Paul is addressing Apollos and his collaborators when he sarcastically refers to "super-apostles" in 2 Cor. 10-13 (11.5; 12.11) or "pseudo-apostles" (11.13), which is the same.[164] It is clear that they have nothing to do with Jerusalem and the Judaists whom we know from Gal.: the "super-apostles" are *not* the apostles in Jerusalem, and the "pseudo-apostles" are *not* their delegates, as has often been assumed.

---

161 Cf. Hurd, *Origin*, 1965 (see section 3.1.1 above, n. 2), p. 98. See also section 3.1.4, the passage referred to in n. 34.

162 See also the quotation from Petersen in n. 160 above. In my opinion, Barclay's rejection of this view in JSNT 47 (1992) (see n. 142 above), p. 64, n. 29, is unreasonable and superficial.

163 E.g. Philipp Vielhauer, Paulus und die Kephaspartei in Korinth, New Testament Studies 21 (1974-75), pp. 341-352 (= id., *Oikodome. Aufsätze zum Neuen Testament*, 2, ed. G. Klein (Theologische Bücherei, 65), Munich 1979, pp. 169-182), especially pp. 347-348; Michael D. Goulder, *Sophía* in 1 Corinthians, New Testament Studies 37 (1991), pp. 516-534, deplores the fact that to his knowledge, no "Tübingen interpretation" of 1 Cor. has been presented since Wilhelm Lütgert's demonstration of its weaknesses in 1908, but apparently Goulder is not aware of Vielhauer's "Tübingen interpretation". See also my observations in DTT 40 (1977), pp. 23-24.

164 Cf. Pétrement, *Le Dieu séparé*, pp. 343-363: "Les "gnostiques" de Corinthe" (*The Separated God*, pp. 247-264: "The "Gnostics" at Corinth"); Hyldahl, StTh 46 (1991), pp. 27 ff. Petersen, *Rediscovering Paul*, pp. 122 ff., has rightly pointed out that in 1 Cor., Paul is the only person who is called an apostle in relation to the Corinthians (cf. 1 Cor. 12.28). The fact that competing apostles are active in Corinth when he is writing 2 Cor. indicates that Apollos and his collaborators have awarded themselves the title of apostle.

In 1831, F.C. Baur suggested on the basis of 1 Cor. 1-4 that a Pauline and a Petrine wing were fighting each other in Corinth, and that this fighting was still going on when 2 Cor. 10-13 was being written: the "super-apostles" with whom Paul compares himself were the leaders in Jerusalem, first of all Peter/Cephas and James, while the "pseudo-apostles" were their delegates. According to this hypothesis, Paul faced a massive Judaist influence in Corinth as well.[165] With a few minor differences, this view was in principle supported by Ernst Käsemann in 1942, and C.K. Barrett in 1971.[166] However, Käsemann and Barrett saw a new situation in 2 Cor., in as far as they both assumed that the Judaists did not appear until during the interval between 1 and 2 Cor. and therefore had nothing to do with the situation such as it was when 1 Cor. was being written; both Käsemann and Barrett explicitly referred to them as "intruders". (It is surprising to note how little influence Barrett's own assumption from 1963[167] had on his later analysis of 2 Cor., i.e. that Peter had been in Corinth already before 1 Cor. was written: if Peter – who, according to Barrett, was one of the Jerusalem "super-apostles", not one of their delegates – had really been in Corinth and thus acted as his own delegate, it would be extremely difficult to distinguish between the two kinds of "apostles".) Barrett refers to 2 Cor. 11.15: "servants of Satan" and 11.23: "servants of Christ", to show that these cannot possibly have been identical. But this argument is not convincing – who can believe that the servants of Christ (the Jerusalem "super-apostles") would have delegates who

---

165 Baur, Die Christuspartei ..., 1831; id., *Paulus, der Apostel Jesu Christi. Sein Leben ...*, 1845, pp. 259-332 = 2nd ed., I, 1866, pp. 287-343: "Die beiden Briefe an die Korinthier".

166 Ernst Käsemann, Die Legitimität des Apostels. Eine Untersuchung zu II Korinther 10-13, Zeitschrift für die neutestamentliche Wissenschaft 41 (1942), pp. 33-71 (= Libelli, 33, Darmstadt 1956); C.K. Barrett, Paul's Opponents in II Corinthians, New Testament Studies 17 (1970-71), pp. 233-254 (= id., *Essays on Paul*, Philadelphia – London 1982, pp. 60-86).

167 Charles Kingsley Barrett, Cephas and Corinth, in: Otto Betz/Martin Hengel/Peter Schmidt, eds., *Abraham unser Vater. Juden und Christen im Gespräch über die Bibel. Festschrift für Otto Michel zum 60. Geburtstag* (Arbeiten zur Geschichte des Antiken Judentums und des Urchristentums, 5), Leiden – Cologne 1963, pp. 1-12 (= Barrett, *Essays on Paul*, pp. 28-39). Cf. also Lietzmann, *An die Korinther I/II*, 1949 (see section 3.4.1 above, n. 86), p. 7.

proved to be servants of Satan (the "pseudo-apostles")? Barrett's own explanation of this paradox is not convincing.[168]

The Judaist hypothesis is disproved by the total absence of references to the requirement of circumcision and observance of the Mosaic law in 1 and 2 Cor.; it is insufficient just to say that the Judaists did not always insist on circumcision.

In 1947, Rudolf Bultmann criticized his own pupil Ernst Käsemann for having established an impossible distinction between "super-apostles" and "pseudo-apostles". In Bultmann's view, they were identical. However, he identified these opponents as Hellenistic gnostics who had, according to his interpretation of 1 and 2 Cor., been active in Corinth for a long time: they were provided with credentials (2 Cor. 3.1) and had been operating in Corinth (2 Cor. 12.11).[169] Apart from certain disparities, Bultmann's view was supported by Walter Schmithals in 1956 and – each in his own way – by Gerhard Friedrich in 1963 and Dieter Georgi in 1964; in 1984, Simone Pétrement supported Friedrich's view, though not uncritically.[170]

The gnostic hypotheses are untenable, since they do not help to explain the fact that the "apostles" who were active in Corinth at the time when 2 Cor. was being written, were of Jewish origins (2 Cor. 11.22). It is not sufficient to say that these gnostics were Jewish Christians.

On the basis of these positive and negative observations, it must be concluded that these people were neither Judaists nor gnostics. It is much more probable that they represented the Jewish-Hellenistic wisdom and philosophy of

---

168 Barrett, NTSt 17 (1970-71), p. 253 (= Barrett, *Essays on Paul*, p. 81): the "pseudo-apostles" were "unsatisfactory agents who misrepresented their principals, ... though the latter may also have been such as to give the former some excuse."

169 Rudolf Bultmann, *Exegetische Probleme des Zweiten Korintherbriefes* (Symbolae Biblicae Upsalienses, 9), Uppsala 1947; 2nd ed. Darmstadt 1963 = *Exegetica*, ed. Erich Dinkler, 1967 (see section 2.2 above), pp. 298-322.

170 Walter Schmithals, *Die Gnosis in Korinth* (Forschungen zur Religion und Literatur des Alten und Neuen Testaments, 48), Göttingen 1956; G. Friedrich, Die Gegner des Paulus im 2. Korinther, in: *Abraham unser Vater*, 1963 (see n. 167 above), pp. 181-215; Dieter Georgi, *Die Gegner des Paulus im 2. Korintherbrief. Studien zur religiösen Propaganda in der Spätantike* (Wissenschaftliche Monographien zum Alten und Neuen Testament, 11), Neukirchen-Vluyn 1964 (= *The Opponents of Paul in Second Corinthians. A Study of Religious Propaganda in Late Antiquity* (Studies of the New Testament and its World), Edinburgh 1987); Pétrement, *Le Dieu séparé*, pp. 358-363: "Sur quelques interprétations récentes" (*A Separate God*, pp. 259-264: "On some Recent Interpretations").

the type that existed in Alexandria, first of all represented by Philo. In Acts 18.24 ff., Apollos is described as an Alexandrian Jew, but this is less important than the information we find in 2 Cor. 11.22, i.e. that he and his collaborators were Hellenistic Jews of the type described by Sellin and Pétrement.

There are many points of agreement between 1 and 2 Cor.: the reference to Jeremiah 9.23 (1 Cor. 1.31; 2 Cor. 10.17); the question of "living on the Gospel" (1 Cor. 4.12; 9.4 ff.; 2 Cor. 11.7 ff.; 12.13 ff.); boasting (1 Cor. 4.7 etc.; 2 Cor. 11.12 etc.); conceit (1 Cor. 4.6, 18; 5.2; 8.1; 13.4; 2 Cor. 12.20); the uniqueness of "belonging to Christ" (1 Cor. 1.12; 3.23; 2 Cor. 10.7); *lógos* (1 Cor. 1.5; 2.4; 4.19-20; 2 Cor. 2.17; 10.10; 11.6); *pneûma* (1 Cor. 2.10 ff.; 15.44 ff.; 2 Cor. 3.6, 17); *gnôsis* (1 Cor. 1.5; 8.1; 13.2; 2 Cor. 11.6). I therefore agree with Bultmann, Pétrement and others that Paul's opponents are the same in 1 and 2 Cor.

Furthermore, I agree with Bultmann, Pétrement and others that the "super-apostles" (2 Cor. 11.5; 12.11) are identical to the "pseudo-apostles" (2 Cor. 11.13).

But here we face an important problem. How can Paul call the same persons "servants of Satan" (2 Cor. 11.15) *and* "servants of Christ" (11.23)? This seems impossible.

This is the reason why the text of 2 Cor. 11.22-23 is so important. Although this text has been analysed by Josef Zmijewski, in 1978, and Karl-Wilhelm Niebuhr, in 1992, its full importance has not been recognized. In my view, Paul says some absolutely essential things here.

In 2 Cor. 11.22-23, Paul asks not three, but four rhetorical questions and answers them himself, but his fourth answer differs dramatically from the first three answers: "Are they Hebrews? So am I. Israelites? So am I. Abraham's descendants? So am I. Are they servants of Christ? I am mad to speak like this, but I can outdo them!" With the first three questions, Paul is clearly saying that the Corinthian Christians should not ask strangers to give them what they have already got; cf. Phil. 3.4 ff. The "apostles" are Jews, but so is Paul, and the Corinthians can find everything they need in him.

But to the last question: Are they servants of Christ?, his answer is: No, but I am! In this respect, Paul *surpasses* them, and in his person, the Corinthians

227

have more than they will ever find among these strangers:[171] they are not even Christians.

So Apollos and the other competing "apostles" were Hellenistic Jews (2 Cor. 11.22), who represented a wisdom ideology based on philosophical principles (1 Cor. 1.17-3.23). One of the characteristics of the philosophy which Apollos brought to Corinth was its rhetorical form and style. Unlike Paul, as it may appear, he uses eloquence, *lógos*, to gain support. As far as the nature of his philosophy is concerned, we have no other sources of information than the indications in 1 Cor. 1-4. Apparently the allegation of achieving cognition, *gnôsis*, was an important element, and Apollos probably called his philosophy wisdom, *sophía*. According to this "wisdom", people were either pneumatics, psychics or sarcics (1 Cor. 2.10-16; 3.1-3), a distinction that refers to ontological differences between individuals; some were pneumatics, others phychics, while some were only sarcics. Sarcics were definitively lost and could never hope to achieve cognition and eventually reach the state of perfection and immortality; those who possessed the spirit were already gnostics, and psychics might either become pneumatics or sink to the level of the sarcics.

Admittedly, these few characteristics are insufficient to enable the interpreter to determine the details of Apollos' philosophy with any degree of certainty. On the other hand, they make it clear that his philosophy was related to the Alexandrian philosophy.

Few as they are, it is still remarkable that these characteristics do not even reveal whether Apollos was a Christian. Although Paul calls him "brother" (1 Cor. 16.12), he had probably not been baptized, but knew only John's baptism

---

171 Zmijewski, *Stil der paul. "Narrenrede"*, pp. 241-243, has analysed this passage in detail and suggests two alternative interpretations: 1) exclusively: "In this case, the answer to the question, "Are they servants of Christ?" should be understood to mean: They are not, but I am!" (p. 242), and: "The "exclusive" interpretation of *hypér* may then be justified by the following passage (from v. 23b), in which Paul stops making comparisons and speaks only of himself and his own fate as an apostle in such a way that any other apostolic claims seem impossible" (p. 242); 2) superlatively: "Paul refuses to compare himself ... with his opponents, ...: Whether these people are "servants of Christ" or not, *I* certainly am (because of the burden of trouble and suffering I have borne for the sake of Christ)!" (p. 242). While Zmijewski himself prefers the second alternative, Niebuhr, *Heidenapostel aus Israel*, p. 129 and pp. 132-133, appears to prefer the first alternative, since he refers to Paul's "exclusive superiority" (pp. 129 and 132); yet Niebuhr refers to Zmijewski on this subject.

(see section 2.3.3, above, n. 52). His knowledge of the Scriptures (Acts 18.24), i.e. the Greek Septuaginta, does not prove that he was a Christian, but it may subsequently explain why Paul feels compelled to launch a counter-attack – especially in his dismissive interpretation of Exod. 34 in 2 Cor. 3.4-18 – against those who see themselves as experts on the Scriptures, like Apollos and his followers; it may also explain why Paul can ultimately not regard these people as Christians.

With Apollos, a genuine branch of Hellenistic philosophy had found its way to Corinth and established itself in Paul's Christian congregation there. The Corinthian Christians were not prepared either to accept or reject this foreign thinking. If they had been prepared, they would probably have been less impressed by it than they appear to have been. The question is: how would Paul tackle the problem?

Clearly the gospel Paul had preached in Corinth was not a philosophy or a philosophical system. This observation is not based on Paul's words in 1 Cor. 2.1 ff. about his own preaching in Corinth, since these words are coloured by the situation in which he finds himself at the time when he is writing the letter, but the entire narrative in 1 and 2 Cor. makes it very clear that Paul was not a philosopher. On the other hand, Paul says explicitly in 1 Cor. 1.18 ff. that the Gospel is not a philosophy: unlike worldly wisdom, the Gospel is folly in the eyes of the world, and only to the truly perfect does the Gospel reveal itself as wisdom (2.6 ff.).

There can be no doubt that Paul framed his argumentation in 1 Cor. 1.18 ff. as a rejection of Apollos' wisdom. Of course Troels Engberg-Pedersen is right in pointing out that our most important task is to try to follow the line of thought in the text such as it is.[172] However, if this implies that we ignore or neglect Paul's narrative world, of which the text itself is only one element, then we do not follow his line of thought, or at least we do not try to follow it in the way his Corinthian readers must have done. The text is not a philosophical essay about the relations between theory and practice; it is Paul's desperate rejection of Apollos' influence in Corinth.

Consequently, the line of thought is *not* broken in 1 Cor. 2.6, the passage in which Paul maintains, in contrast to his previous observations on the Gospel as

---

172 Troels Engberg-Pedersen, The Gospel and Social Practice according to 1 Corinthians, New Testament Studies 33 (1987), pp. 557-584, see p. 564.

a folly, that there is after all a wisdom which belongs to the perfect. In saying this, Paul does not move from "faith" to "cognition": from faith as the only possible positive response to the word about the cross (1.18 ff.) to an understanding of its meaning that represents a special Christian wisdom (2.6 ff.), an understanding which becomes the theoretical basis of social practice, according to Engberg-Pedersen.[173] The wisdom Paul mentions here does not transcend faith; there is nothing "more" in Christian wisdom that can surpass Christian faith,[174] but according to Paul, Christian wisdom is folly in the eyes of those who have no faith, and who therefore do not represent Christianity, but only Hellenistic philosophy, i.e. Apollos and his followers.

The "rupture" in 1 Cor. 2.6 does not indicate that Paul moves from simple faith to intellectual understanding; it is a reaction provoked by Apollos' "wisdom". The message of the cross is folly in the eyes of the world. At the same time, however, it is also, precisely like the wisdom of God, the only true wisdom, which by far surpasses Apollos' so-called "philosophy". If this is a "rupture", then it must be a rupture with traditional Hellenistic philosophy, not with Paul's own logical thinking. However, Paul can hardly have realized that by presenting this polemic thesis, he became the initiator of an important movement in Christian thinking and theology: the concept of Christianity as the only true philosophy, only revealed to the true philosopher, is clearly the model for the Christian philosopher's gown worn by Justin (Dial. 1.1 ff.) and other Christian philosophers.

On the other hand, Paul certainly realized that since he had been upstaged for a time by Apollos' impressive wisdom, he had to subordinate this wisdom to the gospel he himself had preached. Paul's argumentation is more than a formalistic subordination of philosophy to Christianity, and his reaction against Apollos also represents a genuine rejection of the substance of Apollos' philosophical thinking. There are two important aspects to this: a sociological and an anthropological aspect.

As we have seen, Apollos divided humans into three types, pneumatics, psychics and sarcics. Paul refused to accept this categorization. In his own words, but with reference to Apollos' terminology, Paul declared that all three

---

173 Engberg-Pedersen, NTSt 33 (1987), p. 565.
174 Contrary to Engberg-Pedersen, ib.

types were really one and the same: they were all sarcics (1 Cor. 3.1 ff.). On the other hand, he defines the believer as a pneumatic (2.16; cf. 7.40).

Paul's rejection of Apollos' distinctions has important social consequences. Apollos' anthropological distinctions clearly reflected an élitist sociology based on the principle of superiority versus inferiority (cf. the reference to the pneumatics as "kings" in 1 Cor. 4.8). Paul's rejection of this sociology ("the kingdom of God is not a matter of words," 4.20) means that Apollos and his followers must either give up their philosophical sociology and anthropology and submit to Paul's "democratic" concept of a Christian congregation, or they must leave the congregation for ever.

3.7 Paul in Jerusalem

Bibliography

Johannes Munck: *Paulus und die Heilsgeschichte* (Acta Jutlandica, XXVI, 1) Copenhagen 1954, pp. 233-237: "Paulus' Besuch bei Jakobus".
Walter Schmithals: *Paulus und Jakobus*, 1963 (see section 3.4 above), pp. 70-80: "Der letzte Besuch des Paulus in Jerusalem" = *Paul and James*, 1965, pp. 85-96: "Paul's Last Visit to Jerusalem".
Gerd Lüdemann: *Das frühe Christentum*, 1987 (see section 3 above), pp. 238-245: "Apostelgeschichte 21.1-36" = *Early Christianity*, 1989, pp. 230-237: "Acts 21.1-36".

In accordance with the agreement made at the Jerusalem Conference (Gal. 2.10), Paul organized a collection of money for Jerusalem in his Gentile-Christian congregations. He delivered the money himself (cf. Rom. 15.25-28, 30-31), accompanied by a delegation of representatives of these congregations (cf. Acts 20.4; 21.29; 27.2); the narrative of this event is found in Acts 21.18-26:

21.18 Next day Paul paid a visit to James; we accompanied him, and all the elders were present. 19 After greeting them, he described in detail all that God had done among the Gentiles by means of his ministry. 20 When they heard this, they gave praise to God. Then they said to Paul: "You observe, brother, how many thousands of converts we have among the Jews,[175] all of them staunch upholders of the law. 21 Now

---

175 Cf. section 3.1.4 above, the passage referred to in n. 39.

they have been given certain information about you: it is said that you teach all the Jews in the gentile world to turn their backs on Moses, and tell them not to circumcise their children or follow our way of life. 22 What is to be done, then? They are sure to hear that you have arrived. 23 Our proposal is this: we have four men here who are under a vow; 24 take them with you and go through the ritual of purification together, and pay their expenses, so that they may have their heads shaved; then everyone will know that there is nothing in the reports they have heard about you, but that you are yourself a practising Jew and observe the law. 25 As for the gentile converts, we sent them our decision that they should abstain from meat that has been offered to idols, from blood, from anything that has been strangled, and from fornication." 26 So Paul took the men, and next day, after going through the ritual of purification with them, he went into the temple to give notice of the date when the period of purification would end and the offering be made for each of them.

In this context, it is significant that Acts 24.17 supplements this narrative by stating that during the later interrogation before the Roman procurator Felix in Caesarea, Paul said the following words:

24.17 After an absence of several years, I came to bring charitable gifts to my nation and to offer sacrifices.

The narrative in the Acts does not mention the presentation of the money from the collection; on the other hand, it makes it clear that Paul disposes of considerable amounts of money (21.24; 24.17, 26). It also says that James and the Jerusalem congregation are worried about Paul's arrival, which cannot be kept secret, and refers to the rumours which are said to be circulating about him: that he has told the Jews in the Diaspora not to circumcise their children or follow any of the provisions of the Mosaic law; furthermore, it says that there are thousands of keen or zealous upholders of the law among the Jewish Christians in Jerusalem. From a historical point of view, the latter statement must be regarded as unreliable, both as regards their number and their strict observance of the law. Moreover, the threat against Paul did not come from the Christian Jews (who must also have been fewer than indicated here), but from the non-Christian Jews; cf. Acts 21.27 ff.; Rom. 15.31. In other words, through his editorial adaptation of the material of the tradition, the author of Lk.-Acts presents the situation as if the problem arose from the number of Jewish Christians (cf. Acts 2.41: three thousand; 4.4: five thousand; 6.1, 7; 21.10: tens of thousands) and their strict observance of the law.

Actually, it was of course not the Jewish Christians who posed a problem, but the non-Christian Jews, who must in any circumstances have represented a large majority of the population. It may be true that the non-Christian Jews believed in such rumours about Paul as mentioned above, i.e. that he had told the Jews living in the Diaspora not to circumcise their children or follow Jewish customs, and if these rumours were believed, they must have represented an extremely serious threat. It would probably have been impossible to convince the non-Christian Jews that these rumours were false, simply by explaining how absurd they were; this would have required proof, and even proof might have failed to stop the rumours.

In this difficult situation, James, who is in charge of the proceedings, suggests that Paul should demonstrate his own observance of the Mosaic law in public by paying the expenses of four poor Nazirites' sacrifices to the temple – as we know, Paul himself had already taken a Nazirite vow,[176] so it was natural for him to join the four Nazirites, who must have been Jewish Christians like himself.

It must be assumed that the expenses of these sacrifices represented only a small part of the amount of money collected in the Gentile-Christian communities, and that the bulk of the money could be used for the intended purpose: distribution of food to the poor.

Two facts indicate that "the poor" were not members of the Christian congregation in Jerusalem, but poor non-Christian Jews in Palestine. Firstly, the delegation of Gentile Christians must have attracted considerable attention on their arrival, and these Gentile Christians would hardly have dared to show themselves in Jerusalem if the money had been intended for the Christian poor there; this would have been an unnecessary risk for them to take, and in that case, it would have been far wiser and safer to send the money to Jerusalem in a more discreet way, for instance by entrusting it to a few Jewish Christians, whose arrival would hardly be noticed, and certainly not attract much attention. Secondly, Paul had to visit the temple anyway – he was a Nazirite himself, and now he would be able to perform his duties there together with four other Nazirites. If the money was intended for the Jewish poor, the temple was the only place to which it could be delivered; it would not have been delivered to the Christian congregation, and there are no indications to support this idea. In

---

176 See section 3.8.2 below.

this connection, we must not forget that it was a sabbatical year, and that most of the money was intended for buying imported grain; the distribution of this grain would have to be entrusted to a central Jewish authority and went far beyond the normal Jewish relief for the poor mentioned in section 3.3.3 above.

We cannot know for certain that the money was delivered as intended, but we must assume that it was. However, Paul's presence in the temple precinct had fatal consequences for him: he was arrested by the commandant of Antonia.[177]

From a theological point of view, the important question is whether Paul betrayed the Gospel on this occasion by demonstrating his observance of the Mosaic law in public, and whether his act was really a counterpart to the act for which he had blamed Peter in Antioch. On that occasion too, James had been the provoking factor (Gal. 2.12), and now the same seemed to have happened to Paul himself (Acts 21.23 ff.). Was there really any difference? And did Paul not now reveal himself to be a hypocrite, a man who acted against his own conviction?

Bearing in mind that the Acts is our only source on this subject, I can say only this: There is at least one difference between Peter's act in Antioch and Paul's act in Jerusalem. In the former case, others could be led to believe that they should do the same, i.e. follow Jewish custom, while there was no such risk in the latter case. In the former case, Christianity was threatened by extinction; in the latter case, the purpose of the act was to save the Jewish-Christian congregation from persecution. Unfortunately it was not successful: a few years later, James himself was stoned to death by his own countrymen.[178] But there seems to be no reason to accuse Paul of hypocrisy.

3.8 The use of "we" in the Acts

Bibliography

Adolf Harnack: *Lukas der Arzt. Der Verfasser des dritten Evangeliums und der Apostelgeschichte. Eine Untersuchung zur Geschichte der Fixierung der urchristlichen Überlieferung* (Beiträge zur Einleitung in das Neue Testament, I), Leipzig

---

177 See section 1.2.1 above, the passage referred to in n. 62.
178 Cf. section 3.2.5 above.

1906, pp. 19-85: "Specielle Untersuchungen über den sog. Wir-Bericht der Apostelgeschichte".

Id.: *Neue Untersuchungen zur Apostelgeschichte und zur Abfassungszeit der synoptischen Evangelien* (Beiträge zur Einleitung in das Neue Testament, IV), Leipzig 1911, pp. 1-21: "Die Identität des Verfassers der Wirstücke der Apostelgeschichte mit dem Verfasser des ganzen Werks".

Julius Wellhausen: *Noten zur Apostelgeschichte* (Nachrichten der Gesellschaft der Wissenschaften zu Göttingen, philol.-hist. Kl., 1), Berlin 1907, pp. 1-21.

Id.: *Kritische Analyse der Apostelgeschichte* (Abhandlungen der kgl. Gesellschaft der Wissenschaften zu Göttingen, philol.-hist. Kl., N.F. XV, 2), Berlin 1914, in particular p. 32, pp. 41-43, pp. 53-55.

Eduard Norden: *Agnostos Theos. Untersuchungen zur Formengeschichte religiöser Rede*, first published in Stuttgart 1913, 2nd ed. 1923; repr. Darmstadt 1956, pp. 311-332: "Zur Komposition der Acta Apostolorum".

Jackson/Lake, in: id., eds., *Beginnings*, Part I, Vol. II, 1922, pp. 158-167: "The we-sections".

Henry J. Cadbury, in: Jackson/Lake, eds., *Beginnings*, Part I, Vol. II, 1922, pp. 498-510: "Commentary on the Preface of Luke".

Martin Dibelius: Stilkritisches zur Apostelgeschichte, first published in 1923, in: id., *Aufsätze zur Apostelgeschichte*, ed. Heinrich Greeven (Forschungen zur Religion und Literatur des Alten und Neuen Testaments, 42), Göttingen 1951, 5th ed. 1968, pp. 9-28, in particular pp. 12-17.

Id.: Die Apostelgeschichte im Rahmen der urchristlichen Literaturgeschichte, in: id., *Aufsätze zur Apostelgeschichte* (see above), pp. 163-174, in particular pp. 166-174.

A.D. Nock: Review of Martin Dibelius' *Aufsätze zur Apostelgeschichte*, 1951 (see above), Gnomon 25 (1953), pp. 497-506 = id., The Book of Acts, in: id., *Essays on Religion and the Ancient World*, Cambridge (Mass.) 1972, II, pp. 821-832.

Alf Kragerud: Itinerariet i Apostlenes gjerninger, Norsk teologisk Tidsskrift 56 (1955), pp. 249-272.

Ernst Haenchen: *Die Apostelgeschichte*, 13th ed. 1961 (see section 3.1.2 above, n. 7), pp. 76-78, pp. 428-431, pp. 515-522, pp. 530-531.

Id.: Das "Wir" in der Apostelgeschichte und das Itinerar, Zeitschrift für Theologie und Kirche 58 (1961), pp. 329-366 = id., *Gott und Mensch. Gesammelte Aufsätze*, Tübingen 1965, pp. 227-264.

Hans Conzelmann: *Die Apostelgeschichte*, 1963 (see section 3.1.2 above, n. 6), pp. 5-6, p. 90, pp. 146-147.

Eckhard Plümacher: Wirklichkeitserfahrung und Geschichtsschreibung bei Lukas: Erwägungen zu den Wir-Stücken der Apostelgeschichte, Zeitschrift für die neutestamentliche Wissenschaft 68 (1977), pp. 2-22.

Vernon K. Robbins: By Land and by Sea: The We-Passages and Ancient Sea Voyages, in: Charles H. Talbert, ed., *Perspectives on Luke-Acts* (Association of Baptist Professors of Religion, Special Studies Series, 5), Danville – Edinburgh 1978, pp. 215-242.

Robert Jewett: *A Chronology*, 1979 (see section 3.1.2 above, n. 2), pp. 10-17: "The Use of Oral and Written Materials in Acts".

Edvin Larsson: "Vi"-passager och itinerarer. Om traditionsunderlaget för Apg.s skildring av Paulus' missionsresor, Svensk Exegetisk Årsbok 51-52 (1986-87), pp. 127-136.

Susan Marie Praeder: The Problem of First Person Narration in Acts, Novum Testamentum 29 (1987), pp. 193-218.

Heinz Warnecke: *Die tatsächliche Romfahrt des Apostels Paulus* (Stuttgarter Bibelstudien, 127), Stuttgart 1987.

Jürgen Wehnert: *Die Wir-Passagen der Apostelgeschichte. Ein lukanisches Stilmittel aus jüdischer Tradition* (Göttinger Theologische Arbeiten, 40), Göttingen 1989.

Claus-Jürgen Thornton: *Der Zeuge des Zeugen. Lukas als Historiker der Paulusreisen* (Wissenschaftliche Untersuchungen zum Neuen Testament, 56), Tübingen 1991.

3.8.1 A dilemma in research history

Paul's last letter, the Letter to the Romans, was written at the end of the three months he spent during his winter in Corinth A.D. 54-55 (cf. 1 Cor. 16.5-7; Acts 20.2-3), so from this point, events are no longer covered by his letters, only by the Acts, at least as far as Paul is concerned.

As briefly mentioned in section 3.1.4 above, it has been established that the four "we" passages of the Acts constitute one coherent narrative, which the author of the Acts must have adapted and placed where we now find its four parts: I, Acts 16.10-17; II, 20.5-8, 13-15; III, 21.1-18, and IV, 27.1-28.16.[179] These four passages represent a "source" which we shall now examine in detail.

First of all, a few observations on the "we" passages in the light of research history:

The traditional view, which was already present in the early Church, is that Lk.-Acts was written by Paul's collaborator Luke (Col. 4.14; Philem. 24), and that Luke used the pronoun "we" to indicate the events in which he had been personally involved, and to which he was therefore an eyewitness. This simple and straightforward view, which is represented by Adolf Harnack, Robert

---

179 The reading in D to Acts 11.28, which has "we" in connection with the reference to the prophet Agabus – cf. Acts 21.10! – is generally considered to be secondary.

Jewett and several others, is untenable for a number of reasons I have already mentioned;[180] moreover, it does not explain why the author of Lk.-Acts, who is able to say "I" (Lk. 1.3; Acts 1.1), would say "we" when referring to himself, nor does it explain why this "we" seems to appear and disappear at random.

According to the literary critical hypothesis which was predominant in the nineteenth century, and was later revived by Wellhausen, the author of Lk.-Acts – whoever he was – had used a source from an eyewitness in the "we" passages and worked this source into his own representation of the historical events. However, this literary critical hypothesis is also untenable because it fails to explain why the author of Lk.-Acts kept the "we" of the source unchanged in his own representation; no parallel to this can be found in the entire literature of Antiquity. Furthermore, the style of the "we" passages does not differ in any way from the style of the other parts of the Acts. There are two possible explanations for this: 1) the "we" passages were written by the same author as the other parts of the Acts, which corresponds to the traditional view, or 2) the author of Lk.-Acts adapted the "we" passages so thoroughly that their own style disappeared – except for the characteristic "we".

The itinerary hypothesis, as represented by Dibelius in particular, suggests that when the author of the Acts wrote the passages about Paul, he used one or several of the travel journals in which people noted the names of way-stations and persons etc.; this itinerary was not limited to the "we" passages, but constituted a continuous narrative. This explanation is invalidated by the entirely hypothetical idea of an itinerary, and by the fact that it is no longer the occurrence of the "we" that indicates the use of the itinerary, but rather the contents of the passages themselves.

Another literary hypothesis has gained an increasing number of supporters during recent decades, among others Plümacher, Robbins and Wehnert, a fact which confirms the inadequacy of the previous explanations. It suggests that the "we" is a stylistic feature intended to animate the narrative by pretending that the author himself was an eyewitness. However, this explanation is equally inadequate, since there are no convincing parallels in the entire Greek, Latin and Jewish literature; moreover, it does not give a satisfactory explanation of the seemingly random appearances and disappearances of the "we" passages, even assuming that they are used as a stylistic feature.

---

180 See section 3.1.2 above, the passages referred to in nn. 4, 5 and 6.

In fact, the interpretation of the Acts is stranded in a painful dilemma; cf. most recently Susan Marie Praeder and Jürgen Wehnert, who were both unable to solve the problem.

3.8.2 A possible solution (provisional observations)

Without pretending to present a complete hypothesis concerning the "we" passages in the Acts, I suggest an explanation that may represent a further step on the way towards solving this problem. My attempt at an explanation is based on the following observations:

1) The occurrence of "we" is essential for determining the "we" passages, but the immediate contexts of these passages should also be taken into consideration.

2) The "we" passages are remarkable for describing almost nothing but events connected with sea voyages, and for their precise indications of individual places of call, dates of arrival and departure etc.

3) The characteristic "we" in these passages is anonymous and represents, by implication, a plurality of travelling companions, *not* including Paul himself or any other named travelling companions, such as the Seven mentioned in Acts 20.4, including Aristarchus, who is mentioned again in 27.2. It is therefore useless to attempt to identify this anonymous "we", although such attempts have been made, involving persons we know from other contexts, for instance Silas/Silvanus, who cannot of course represent a plurality and would be expected to use the pronoun "I" when referring to himself; there is a difference between saying "we" and "I"!

Regarding the individual "we" passages, the following facts should be taken into account:

4) Paul's speech in Miletus to the elders from Ephesus, Acts 20.27-38, is clearly a product of editorial adaptation and interrupts the coherent narrative of two "we" passages: II, 20.5-8; 20.13-15 and III, 21.1-18 – the contents of these two "we" passages indicate that they belong together. The idea that Paul should have taken his leave of the elders from Ephesus in Miletus is contradicted by the probability that Rom. 16 is a farewell letter, or at least part of a farewell letter, to the congregation in Ephesus; if this is the case, Paul had already said good-bye to them. On the other hand, Acts 20.3 states that Paul's singular decision to sail to Syria – and so to Palestine and Jerusalem – by the long

roundabout route via Macedonia is due to a plot laid against him by the Jews; if this is so, and if Rom. 16 is a farewell letter to Ephesus, this letter must have been written and dispatched before the plot was discovered. All things considered, however, it is hardly probable that Paul would have "taken his leave" of the elders from Ephesus in the way described by the Acts; even if Paul met with them on that occasion, it would have been for the specific purpose of receiving the money which the congregations in the province of Asia had collected for Jerusalem. This explanation would also provide a more reasonable motive for the Jewish plot.

5) As already mentioned (in section 3.1.4), Acts 18.18 is probably wrong in saying that Paul took his Nazirite vow in Cenchreae, the eastern port of Corinth, before departing for Ephesus:[181] Paul cannot have known while he was staying in Corinth that he would have to go to Jerusalem to attend the Jerusalem Conference; on the contrary, this was not decided until afterwards, when the Judaist movement appeared in Ephesus. He must therefore have taken the Nazirite vow before leaving Corinth/Cenchreae on the long journey to Syria mentioned in Acts 20.3, and the purpose of this journey was to deliver the money collected for Jerusalem. In this way, a genetic connection is established between Paul's Nazirite vow in Corinth/Cenchreae (18.18) and the four Nazirites in Jerusalem (21.23-26). On these grounds, we can conclude that Acts 18.18 belongs with II, Acts 20.5-8 and 20.13-15.

6) This leaves only the first "we" passage I, Acts 16.10-17,[182] which comes immediately after Paul's nocturnal vision in Troas, where he saw a Macedonian man who asked him to "cross over to Macedonia and help us" (Acts 16.9). In my view, this "we" passage was misplaced by the author of the Acts and rightly belongs in connection with 20.1, immediately before the second "we" passage of the Acts. So this means that the "we" passages I and II also belong together.

7) The two years mentioned in Acts 24.27 can hardly represent Paul's term of imprisonment in Caesarea, but rather the tenure of the procurator Felix; after two years' tenure, Felix was succeeded by Festus, according to e.g. Kirsopp Lake, Haenchen and Lüdemann. This means that the voyage to Rome described in "we" passage IV, 27.1 ff., did not take place two years later, but according to

---

181 See section 3.1.4 above, the passage referred to in n. 36.
182 Cf. Paul R. Trebilco, Paul and Silas – "Servants of the Most High God", Journal for the Study of the New Testament 36 (1989), pp. 51-73.

its content is closely connected with "we" passage III, 21.1-18, and constitutes an almost direct continuation of this, interrupted only by Paul's short visits to Jerusalem and Caesarea. Sadly, the interpreters who made this correct observation on 24.27 seem to have forgotten it when they come to 27.1-2 and its reference to Aristarchus.[183]

8) Wellhausen, Dibelius and others have no real evidence to support their theory that the long "we" passage IV, Acts 27.1-28.16, which describes the dramatic voyage on the Mediterranean, differs from the other "we" passages and is simply a literary loan from contemporary navigation literature, into which the author of the Acts has subsequently inserted the passages concerning Paul (27.9-11, 21-26, 31, 33-36, 43). On the contrary, an autobiographical narrative by Josephus[184] bears witness to the realistic character of the dramatic narrative. Through his analysis of Acts 27.1 ff., Wehnert has made a valuable contribution towards a better interpretation of this text.

Thus the entire narrative covers a period of more than eighteen months and describes Paul's last journey, which he made for the purpose of bringing the collection to Jerusalem, and his following journey to Rome. The places of call were: Ephesus (summer 54) – Troas – Neapolis – Philippi – Thessalonica[185] – Corinth (winter 54-55) – Cenchreae[186] – Philippi (Easter 55) – Troas – Assos – Mitylene – Samos – Miletus – Cos – Rhodes – Patara – Tyre – Ptolemais – Caesarea – Jerusalem (Pentecost and summer 55) – Caesarea – Sidon – Myra – Fair Havens (Crete, autumn 55) – Malta (winter 55-56) – Syracuse – Rhegium –

---

183 See Hyldahl, Derfor efterlod jeg dig på Kreta, Fønix 11 (1987), pp. 157-163, in particular pp. 160-161.

184 Josephus, Vita 14-16 (chapter 3), in which he describes a journey to Rome circa A.D. 61: "14 ... I reached Rome after being in great jeopardy at sea. 15 For our ship foundered in the midst of the sea of Adria [cf. Acts 27.27], and our company of some six hundred souls [cp. Acts 27.37] had to swim all that night. About daybreak, through God's good providence, we sighted a ship of Cyrene, and I and certain others, about eighty in all, outstripped the others and were taken on board. 16 Landing safely at Dicaearchia, which the Italians call Puteoli [cf. Acts 28.13], I formed a friendship with Aliturus, an actor ..." English translation by H.St. Thackeray, in: *Josephus. With an English Translation*, I, 1926, pp. 7-9.

185 Cf. Acts 20.2: "that region".

186 Cf. Rom. 16.1 and Acts 18.18.

Puteoli[187] – Forum of Appius – Three Taverns – Rome (spring 56 and the following two years).

However, as Susan Marie Praeder has also pointed out, it is very important to note that the final solution to the singular problems of the "we" passages in the Acts has not yet been found.

---

187 See n. 184 above!

4 THE POST-APOSTOLIC ERA

Bibliography

a) Sources

The New Testament, except for Paul's authentic letters.
The Apostolic Fathers. With an English Translation by Kirsopp Lake (The Loeb Classical Library), I-II, London – Cambridge (Massachusetts) 1912-1913.
De apostolske Fædre i dansk oversættelse med indledninger og noter, eds. Niels Jørgen Cappelørn, Niels Hyldahl og Bertil Wiberg, Copenhagen 1985.
Søren Giversen: *De apostolske Fædre i oversættelse med indledning og noter*, I-II, Copenhagen 1985.
Eusebius' Ecclesiastical History (see section 3 above).

b) General works

Emil Schürer: *History of the Jewish People* (see section 1 above), I, 1973, pp. 484-513: "The Great War with Rome A.D. 66-74(?)", and pp. 514-557: "From the Destruction of Jerusalem to the Downfall of Bar Kokhba".
Leonhard Goppelt: *Die apostolische und nachapostolische Zeit*, 1962 (see section 3 above), §§ 14-22.
Hans Conzelmann: *Geschichte des Urchristentums*, 1969 (see section 3 above), pp. 94-118: "XI.: Die Kirche bis zum Ende des ersten Jahrhunderts", "XII.: Die Kirche und die Welt", "XIII.: Das Judenchristentum nach dem Jüdischen Krieg".

4.1 The destruction of the temple and the synod in Jamnia

Bibliography

Bent Noack: *Om Fadervor*, Copenhagen 1969, pp. 178-194: "Jødiske bønner" (including the Eighteen Prayer in Danish translation).
Peter Schäfer: Die sogenannte Synode von Jabne. Zur Trennung von Juden und Christen im ersten/zweiten Jh. n. Chr., in: id., *Studien zur Geschichte und Theologie des rabbinischen Judentums*, Leiden 1978, pp. 45-55.
Gerd Lüdemann: *Paulus, der Heidenapostel. Band II: Antipaulinismus im frühen Christentum* (Forschungen zur Religion und Literatur des Alten und Neuen Testaments, 130), Göttingen 1983, pp. 265-285: "Die Nachfolger der Jerusalemer Urgemeinde. Analyse der Pella-Tradition" = id., in: E.P. Sanders, ed., *Jewish and Christian Self-Definition I: The Shaping of Christianity in the Second and Third Centuries*, London – Philadelphia 1980, pp. 161-173 and 245-254.

William Horbury: The Benediction of the *Minim* and Early Jewish-Christian Controversy, Journal of Theological Studies 33 (1982), pp. 19-61.

4.1.1 Two points of view

The Jewish-Roman war began in A.D. 66, during the reign of emperor Nero (54-68), and ended in A.D. 70, during the reign of emperor Vespasian (69-79). At the end of the war, Jerusalem was captured, and the temple was destroyed. As a result of the destruction of the temple, the Jewish priesthood was abolished for ever, and the end of the war also brought about the annihilation of the religious parties of both the Sadducees and the Essenes; only the Pharisees, some of the scribes and the Christians survived the year 70.

Judaism as it was in New Testament times, or rather during the period before A.D. 70, when the second temple was destroyed and the Jewish people lost even more of their independence, had emerged during the Seleucid period, between circa 175 B.C. and 63 B.C. Before that period, Judaism can hardly have existed as a conscious national identity that included the entire Jewish people and was committed heart and soul to the cause of preserving its own precious heritage; it was probably more in the nature of an inherited, more or less conscious, attachment to religious institutions such as the temple, religious customs such as circumcision, and Old Testament traditions (of course with the Book of Daniel from circa 165 B.C. as the single characteristic exception). What I am trying to explain is this: During Antiochus IV's reign of terror (175-164 B.C.), the Jewish religion was threatened by extinction. This forced the Jewish people to consider their own identity as a nation, and to decide whether religion and people belonged together or not, and if they did, then to determine the relationship between religion and people. In other words, did the religion really constitute the people's identity, or would the people perhaps be able to exist without their religion? If they were unable to do this, but considered their religion to be their fundamental law, this means in practice that Judaism was chosen by the Jewish people as their constitution when it came into existence during the years after the reign of Antiochus IV.

This is also consistent with the fact that the word "Judaism" (Greek: *ioudaïsmós*) first emerged during that period: 2 Macc. 2.21; 8.1 and 14.38.[1]

The conscious decision in favour of Judaism as the constituting factor of the Jewish people is the most important single characteristic of the period before A.D. 70. This immediately raises the question: What happened during the period after A.D. 70, the tannaitic period, when the Mishah, the Tosefta and the Midrashim on the last four books of the Pentateuch had been edited and finished? Was Judaism not still the constituting factor of the people during this period? No doubt it was. But there *is* a difference. The decision in favour of Judaism was not made after A.D. 70; it had already been made long before then. After A.D. 70, the Jews did not have to decide whether Judaism should be their religion (they had no other choice). What they had to decide was whether they still represented a people who could have Judaism as their constitution. After the catastrophe in A.D. 70, it makes no sense to say that the Jews had to decide for or against their religion, for that decision had already been made. On the contrary, what represented the threat to the Jews was now the existence of a religion without a people or nation. During the reign of Antiochus IV, the threat had been the existence of a people or nation without a religion. Before A.D. 70, we find a people who constitute themselves through their religion; after 70, we find a religion that constitutes itself through its people. This does not mean that there was no connection, or no continuity. It does mean, however, that there *was* a difference, a very important difference.

The general view among both Christian and Jewish exegetes has been that the rabbinic literature from the tannaitic period – the period between the destruction of the temple in A.D. 70 and the final revision of the Mishnah by R. Judah ha-Nasi circa A.D. 200 – is truly representative of Judaism as it was even before the destruction of the temple. The correctness of this assumption is the obvious *raison d'être* for two as yet unsurpassed works: Emil Schürer's History of the Jewish People in the Age of Jesus, and Paul Billerbeck's Commentary on the New Testament, which is based on the Mishnaic and Talmudic material. But the correctness of this assumption was perhaps even more obvious to the many Jewish exegetes who worked on the New Testament texts and Jewish history

---

1 Cf. Hengel, *Judentum u. Hellenismus*, 1973 (see section 1 above), p. 2 (p. 1-2 in *Judaism and Hellenism*). The word also occurs in 4 Macc. 4.26 and in Ignatius, Magn. 8.1. And of course also in Gal. 1.13 and 1.14 – see section 3.4.3 above.

and literature from before A.D. 70: according to them, the rabbinic literature went far back in history, and this was even confirmed by the literature itself – in the words from the Mishnah Tractate Aboth:[2] "Moses received the [oral] Law from Sinai and committed it to Joshua, and Joshua to the elders [Josh. 24.31], and the elders to the Prophets [Jer. 7.25]; and the Prophets committed it to the men of the Great Synagogue" – and then follows the entire succession of scribes according to the tradition, from Simeon the Just[3] to Simeon ben Gamaliel circa A.D. 70.[4] While most Christian exegetes have expressed a negative view of the rabbinic tradition's presumed continuity between the periods before and after A.D. 70 in order to emphasize the uniqueness of Christianity as opposed to Judaism, most Jewish exegetes have emphasized this continuity in order to identify the original Judaism from before A.D. 70 with the later rabbinic Judaism.

In my view, however, both viewpoints are wrong.

In 1874, Julius Wellhausen wrote his book on the Pharisees and Sadducees,[5] which is still worth reading after more than 120 years. One of the most remarkable features of this book is the fact that the author refrains from using rabbinic sources as a basis for his description of the period between 175 B.C. and A.D. 70. He says that he has read only a few parts of the talmudic literature (the reader would be well advised to take this statement with a grain of salt!); instead, he recommends the Greek texts as adequate sources of information on the period, i.e. the First and the Second Book of the Maccabees, Ecclesiasticus, Solomon's Psalms, Josephus' works – and last but not least – the New Testament itself. Naturally Wellhausen did not – in 1874 – know the Hebrew original of Ecclesiasticus or the Hebrew texts from Qumran, and if the original Hebrew text of the First Book of the Maccabees had been discovered, he would certainly have studied it with great interest and care.

What is at issue here is not the value of the rabbinic literature; it is the question of whether this literature is representative of the period before A.D. 70. The old traditions represented in the rabbinic literature passed through the eye

---

2 English translation: H. Danby, *The Mishnah* (see section 1 above), p. 446.
3 Cf. section 1.2.1 above, the passages referred to in nn. 48 and 49.
4 See also Peter Schäfer, Das "Dogma" von der mündlichen Torah im rabbinischen Judentum, in: id., *Studien zur Geschichte und Theologie des rabbinischen Judentums*, 1978 (see section 4.1 above), pp. 152-197.
5 See section 1 above.

of a needle when they survived the fall of Jerusalem and the destruction of the temple; therefore they must be used with the greatest care, and only exceptionally.

On the other hand, and contrary to the method recommended by Wellhausen, E.P. Sanders presented a strong defense of Judaism itself in his book from 1977 on Paul and Palestinian Judaism.[6] The main part of Sanders' book consists of a description of both the tannaitic literature and various Jewish texts from the period before A.D. 70: the Qumran documents, Ecclesiasticus, the First Book of Enoch, the Book of Jubilees, Solomon's Psalms and the Fourth Book of Ezra – although the latter is from the period after A.D. 70. Sanders is right on one point: There are no grounds for maintaining, as many New Testament exegetes have done, that the rabbinic literature represents a legalistic view of justification by action, not by faith. On the contrary, this literature represents Judaism as a religion which depends entirely on God's merciful election of Israel and has therefore drawn the natural conclusion that observance of God's commandments is a simple and relatively unproblematic duty. Sanders is also right in emphasizing the non-systematic character of tannaitic thinking: it represents no systematic soteriology; the commandments must be observed simply because this is God's will, not because man has to deserve God's mercy or prove himself worthy of a place in the next world – God's mercy was already given to his people when he elected them, and everyone who remains within the covenant is guaranteed a place in the next world.

Nevertheless, Sanders' explanation gives rise to serious objections.

First of all, there is an essential difference between Wellhausen and Sanders as regards the selection of Jewish literature from the period before A.D. 70. What is missing in Sanders' book is the historical literature from this period: the two Books of the Maccabees, Josephus' works and the New Testament, with their enormous amount of information on early Judaism and its history. Sanders gives us the impression that Judaism was both non-systematic and extremely theoretical, with no roots in history and without any historical development. On the subject of Matt. 23 with its exclamations of woe to the scribes and Pharisees, Sanders admits only that there *may* have been such Jews who wasted their efforts on trivialities and neglected vital issues, human nature being what it

---

6   See section 1 above.

is.[7] This is a most unsatisfactory explanation in a book that pretends to compare Judaism and Christianity, and if Sanders objects that he does not compare religions, but only "patterns of religion", the answer will be that the far-reaching conclusions he draws from such a comparison are not justified.

Secondly, Sanders follows Wellhausen's example in representing the fall of Jerusalem and the destruction of the temple as the dividing line between two different eras, but unlike Wellhausen, he fails to draw the necessary conclusions from this observation. Sanders categorically rejects the traditional view that the tannaitic literature originated from the Pharisees and carries the stamp of Pharisaism. According to Sanders, there was no continuity between the Pharisees before A.D. 70 and the Rabbis behind the tannaitic literature after A.D. 70, and except for certain fragments of the rabbinic material, practically no Pharisaic literature survived the catastrophe in A.D. 70. Sanders *may* be right on the latter point (although he would find it difficult to explain the survival of the well-known tradition of the oral law or the Sayings of the Fathers rendered in the Mishnah Tractate Aboth, for instance). But perhaps it would be safer to say that the catastrophe in A.D. 70 had a cathartic effect on the members of the Pharisaic party in the sense that they developed into responsible, devoted leaders of the Jewish people. In any circumstances, by adopting this particular view, Sanders has prevented himself from making a just and therefore convincing judgment, either negative or positive, of Judaism before A.D. 70. His book is above all an admirable monument to the tannaitic literature, but it says almost nothing about the history of Judaism and the historical development before the tannaitic period. Certainly, New Testament exegesis can no longer use the rabbinic literature as proof of its legalistic character. At the same time, however, Sanders' surprising refusal to look for any connection between the Pharisees and the tannaitic literature prevents him from including the Pharisees in his characterization of the rabbinic literature as non-legalistic. Perhaps the real reason for Sanders' silence on this subject is a well-founded feeling that this characterization cannot be applied to the Pharisees because it would not be convincing in every respect, and because Pharisaic legalism and justification by action existed right up to A.D. 70, when they were swept away by the catastrophe.

---

7   Sanders, *Paul and Palestinian Judaism*, p. 426.

On the basis of these observations, we can draw the following conclusions: Sanders is right in maintaining that the rabbinic literature shows no signs of legalism and justification by action and cannot therefore be used as evidence for the legalistic character of Judaism. On the other hand, Wellhausen is obviously right in maintaining that studies of Judaism during the period between circa 175 B.C. and A.D. 70 must be made on the basis of contemporary and truly representative source material; this ought to be self-evident. Wellhausen is therefore also right in giving priority to the contemporary Greek sources (which today also include the new Hebrew material that was unknown to him) – a view that is indirectly supported by Martin Hengel in his book from 1969 (2nd ed. 1973) on Judaism and Hellenism.

So we can establish the fact that there are considerable differences between Judaism such as it was during the period before A.D. 70 and the monolithic Judaism we find in the tannaitic literature. Furthermore, on two particular points, Judaism from the period between 175 B.C. and A.D. 70 also differed from its previous history.

Firstly, during this period, Judaism was an increasingly heterogeneous movement that split up into many incompatible factions, parties, wings and sects. The heterogeneity was so pronounced that – if I may put it this way – even Christianity could emerge in the midst of this pluralistic Judaism. This could have happened neither before nor after this particular period. In fact, it is difficult to imagine how heterogeneous this period really was: there were Hasideans, Essenes, Pharisees, Sadducees, Christians, Sicarii, *am-haares*, priests, Levites, scribes – plus the Jews from the Diaspora who visited Palestine or settled there, and the Jews who were living in the Diaspora.

Secondly, during the period between 175 B.C. and A.D. 70, the Jewish people were willing to use force or even resort to violence in order to protect and defend the religion they had adopted, or, to be more precise: the people considered the use of force or violence to be justified by the just cause they had decided to defend, and this just cause was Judaism itself. Under these circumstances, it is not surprising that the Maccabees' ideal (1 Macc. 2.26, 54) was the Old Testament figure Phinehas, son of Eleazar, with his *zêlos* for the law (Num. 25).[8] The same *zêlos*, with or without a tinge of nationalism, but always in religious colours, can be traced throughout the entire history of

---

8   Cf. sections 1.2.1 and 2.4.3 above.

Judaism, from the Maccabees to the fall of Jerusalem and the destruction of the temple to the period that came after, even in the zealous attitude of Paul before his conversion, and among the Judaists in his congregations (Gal. 1.14; 4.17; Phil. 3.6) – a *zêlos* which can be said to have certain parallels in the State of Israel today.

However heterogeneous and violent this Judaism was – and I am inclined to believe that these two features have been underestimated rather than overestimated by Jewish as well as Christian exegetes – the crucial question was always the question of the right application and practice of the law. The question of the law is a major characteristic of this complex period, and it is impossible to mention a single Jewish movement, including Christianity, which was not passionately interested in the question of the law, its application and practice.

4.1.2 The synod in Jamnia

During the disaster of A.D. 70, a number of Jewish scribes led by Yohanan ben Zakkai fled secretly from the besieged Jerusalem to a small town called Jamnia (or Jabne) on the Mediterranean coast, where Vespasian had allowed them to live; there they founded a centre of scholarship which assumed the functions of the previous council of elders (*gerousía*) and synedrium.

In about A.D. 90 – the exact date is not known – a synod was held in Jamnia. The two most important results of this synod were: 1) the establishment of the Hebrew Old Testament Canon, and 2) the revision of the Jewish prayer called Shemoneh 'Esreh (the "Eighteen Prayer").

Both these decisions reflect a segregation from the Gentile world which enabled the Jews to survive as a people with Judaism as their common identity.

By establishing the Hebrew Canon, the Jews separated themselves from others who also used the Old Testament texts as holy scriptures, first of all the the Greek-speaking Christians, who had been using the Greek translation, Septuaginta, LXX, for a long time. By recognizing only the Hebrew Bible (and new translations which conformed to the new orthodoxy), the Jews rejected LXX, which was from then on used almost exclusively by the Christians. This resulted in a historical and theological separation that proved to have fatal consequences.

The inclusion of a curse on all *minim*, i.e. sectarians, in the "Eighteen Prayer" served to protect and defend Jewish orthodoxy; combined with the establishment of the Hebrew Canon, this measure resulted in a further separation from all others, including the Christians.

The question is whether traces of this new Jewish attitude to the outside world can be found in the Christian literature from this period.

If this is so, it is an obvious idea to compare the facts with the situation indicated by the revision of the "Eighteen Prayer". I am referring to the twelfth *berakah*, or "blessing", *birkath-haminim*, here quoted from the Palestinian text found by S. Schechter in the Cairo geniza and published in 1898:

> And for apostates let there be no hope; and may the insolent kingdom be quickly uprooted, in our days. And may the Nazarenes and the heretics perish quickly; and may they be erased from the Book of Life; and may they not be inscribed with the righteous. Blessed art thou, Lord, who humblest the insolent.[9]

It is important to note and emphasize that we do not know for certain whether this particular text is the original or authentic text adopted by the Synod in Jamnia. The text tradition was and remained fluid, as Peter Schäfer correctly points out. But it can be said with certainty that the twelfth *berakah* was formulated in Jamnia towards the end of the first century, which means that it must be as old as the Johannine literature.

The documentation of *birkath-haminim* in the Fathers of the Church is relatively late, from the third or fourth century, and the earliest evidence – if it is evidence – is found in Justin in his Dialogue with the Jew Trypho, written in about 160. Justin does not explicitly mention a "curse" on the Christians in the Jewish synagogue congregations, but refers to a defamation of Christ, and possibly he does not refer to *birkath-haminim*. Nevertheless, it seems likely that some kind of curse on the Christians has been used in practice, with the effect of excluding them from Judaism.

It is perhaps even more important to try to define the precise relationship between Judaism and Christianity. In his book of 1913 on Jewish worship,[10] Elbogen maintained that *birkath-haminim* was created in order to separate the

---

9   Cf. Schürer, *History*, II, 1979, p. 461.
10 I. Elbogen, *Der jüdische Gottesdienst in seiner geschichtlichen Entwicklung*, 3rd ed., Frankfurt a.M. 1931 = Hildesheim 1967, pp. 36 ff. and 51-52 (pp. 31 ff. and 45-46 in: id., *Jewish Liturgy. A Comprehensive History*, Philadelphia – New York 1993).

two religions, as he calls them, namely Christianity and Judaism. A Jewish Christian who participated in the "Eighteen Prayer" in the synagogue congregation would call down the curse on himself as a heretic if he said "Amen" to the twelfth *berakah*, or he would have to be expelled from the synagogue community. In his careful and very cautious investigation from 1978,[11] Peter Schäfer questioned this widespread view. According to Schäfer, *birkath-haminim* is not primarily aimed at Christians, but at heretics in general and especially the Roman rulers, who were heartily hated by the Jewish people after A.D. 70: those who maintain that *birkath-haminim* was aimed at the Christians in particular overestimate the role and importance of the Christians. Furthermore, Schäfer argues, contrary to Elbogen, that *birkath-haminim* was not introduced in order to separate two religions, but rather to clarify and solve internal Jewish problems. This means, according to Schäfer, that *birkath-haminim* has little or nothing to do with Christianity and the Christians. Schäfer also maintains that Christianity had already established itself as a religion which was independent of Judaism.

I do not believe that this is correct.[12] During the period in question, Judaism and Christianity had not yet become two different religions, as Schäfer maintains: this is Jewish apologetics. Furthermore, his reference to the Romans is irrelevant; it is true that *birkath-haminim* includes the wish that the Roman empire may be "quickly uprooted", but this wish has nothing to do with the curse on *minim*, heretics. It is closer to the truth to say that Christianity originated from the midst of Judaism with one aim in view: to be the true Israel. Tragically, the story ended with the development of what may be called two religions: Judaism and Christianity. It would be even more tragic, however, if the Christians ever forgot the historical origins they share with the Jewish people and the fact that the Christians' sole wish was to be the true representatives of Judaism.

---

11 See section 4.1 above.
12 Cf. Horbury, JThSt 38 (1982), pp. 19-61, who carefully investigates and discusses all relevant texts, both Jewish, New Testament and Patristic, and arrives at the conclusion I have tried to summarize here; especially his criticism of Schäfer corresponds to mine.

4.2 The Johannine literature and the question of Christ

Bibliography

Adolf Harnack: *Über den dritten Johannesbrief* (Texte und Untersuchungen, XV, 3), Berlin 1897.

Walter Bauer: *Rechtgläubigkeit und Ketzerei im ältesten Christentum* (Beiträge zur historischen Theologie, 10), first published in 1934, 2nd ed. edited by Georg Strecker, Tübingen 1964, pp. 95-98.

Christian Lindskrog: *Fortolkning til Første Johannesbrev*, Copenhagen 1941.

Id.: Problemet i 1. Johannesbrev, Dansk Teologisk Tidsskrift 4 (1941), pp. 27-44.

Ernst Käsemann: Ketzer und Zeuge. Zum johanneischen Verfasserproblem, first published in 1951, in: id., *Exegetische Versuche und Besinnungen*, I, Göttingen 1960, pp. 168-187.

Id.: *Jesu letzter Wille nach Johannes 17*, Tübingen 1966.

W.C. van Unnik: The Purpose of St. John's Gospel, in: *Studia Evangelica* (Texte und Untersuchungen, 73), Berlin 1959, pp. 382-411.

John A.T. Robinson: The New Look on the Fourth Gospel, in: *Studia Evangelica*, 1959 (see above), pp. 338-350 = id., *Twelve New Testament Studies* (Studies in Biblical Theology, 34), London 1962, pp. 94-106.

Id.: The Destination and Purpose of the Johannine Epistles, first published in 1960-61, in: id., *Twelve New Testament Studies*, 1962 (see above), pp. 126-138.

J.C. O'Neill: *The Puzzle of First John. A New Examination of Origin*, London 1966.

J. Louis Martyn: *History and Theology in the Fourth Gospel*, New York 1968; 2nd ed. Nashville 1979.

Niels Hyldahl: *Udenfor og indenfor*, 1974 (see section 3.3 above), pp. 87-103: "Den johannæiske kreds".

Klaus Wengst: *Bedrängte Gemeinde und verherrlichter Christus. Der historische Ort des Johannesevangeliums als Schlüssel zu seiner Interpretation* (Biblisch-Theologische Studien, 5), Neukirchen-Vluyn 1981, 2nd ed. 1983; 3rd. ed. (revised), Munich 1990, with the title: *Bedrängte Gemeinde und verherrlichter Christus. Ein Versuch über das Johannesevangelium.*

Birger Olsson: The History of the Johannine Movement, in: Lars Hartman/Birger Olsson, eds., *Aspects on the Johannine Literature. Papers presented at a conference of Scandinavian New Testament exegetes at Uppsala, June 16-19, 1986* (Coniectanea Biblica, New Testament Series, 18), Uppsala 1987, pp. 27-43.

Id.: Kringresande bröder, in: Peter Wilhelm Bøckman/Roald E. Kristiansen, eds., *Context. Festskrift til Peder Johan Borgen / Essays in Honour of Peder Johan Borgen* (Relieff. Publikasjoner utgitt av Religionsvitenskapelig institutt, the University of Trondheim, No. 24), Trondheim 1987, pp. 153-166.

Hans-Josef Klauck: *Die Johannesbriefe* (Erträge der Forschung, 276), Darmstadt 1991.
John Ashton: *Understanding the Fourth Gospel*, Oxford 1991.
P.M. Casey: *From Jewish Prophet to Gentile God*, 1991 (see section 2.5 above), pp. 23-40: "God Incarnate – Jesus in the Johannine Community", and pp. 156-159: "Deity, Incarnation and the Johannine Community".
Walther Schmithals: *Johannesevangelium und Johannesbriefe. Forschungsgeschichte und Analyse* (Beihefte zur Zeitschrift für die neutestamentliche Wissenschaft, 64), Berlin – New York 1992.

4.2.1 Indirect evidence

When studying the New Testament texts written after the fall of Jerusalem, we have to base our investigations on indirect evidence. The Evangelists' descriptions of the life and work of Jesus refer to the period of about A.D. 30, Paul's letters were all written in the 50s, and the Acts go no further than Paul's two years of imprisonment in Rome during the reign of emperor Nero. None of the other New Testament texts are "historical" in the sense of providing information on historical events in a way that can be compared to the Gospels, Paul's letters or the Acts.

This does not mean, however, that we have no knowledge of the history of Christianity during this period, i.e. the three last decades of the first century and the first decades of the second century. We do have indirect evidence, but it is difficult to use because of the problems of method it involves, and it is hardly justifiable to use indirect evidence except when it is supported by other sources or generally recognized arguments.

According to John A.T. Robinson's book from 1976 on redating the New Testament texts,[13] all 27 texts of the New Testament were written before A.D. 70, except the Revelation, which was written close to this date. If we were to believe this, the New Testament could tell us nothing, even indirectly, about the last decades of the first century, and our only sources for the history of Christianity during this period would be the texts written at the end of the century: the oldest parts of the Apostolic Fathers, namely Clement's first letter from circa A.D. 96 and Ignatius' letters from about A.D. 110. However,

---

13 John A.T. Robinson, *Redating the New Testament*, London 1987; but see also Olof Linton, Om datering af nytestamentlige skrifter. I anledning af John A.T. Robinson, Redating the New Testament, London 1976, Dansk Teologisk Tidsskrift 41 (1978), pp. 145-160.

everything indicates that Robinson is wrong in his early dating of the New Testament texts. There is hardly any doubt that the Gospels – with Mark as the single possible exception – were written after A.D. 70; this dating also applies to Jn. and Acts. All the other New Testament texts were also written during the last decades of the century or the first decades of the next century; the most important of these are: Jas., 1 Pet., 1, 2 and 3 Jn., the Pastoral Letters: 1 and 2 Tim. and Ti., and Rev.; in this context, I leave Eph., Heb., 2 Pet. and Jude out of account.

This is a sufficient amount of material, especially Jn. and 1, 2 and 3 Jn. This Johannine literature will be examined on the following pages, beginning with 1 Jn.

4.2.2 The Johannine literature
In 1 Jn. 2.18-19 it says:

> 18 Children, this is the last hour! You were told that an antichrist was to come. Well, many antichrists have already appeared, proof to us that this is indeed the last hour. 19 They left our ranks, but never really belonged to us; if they had, they would have stayed with us. They left so that it might be clear that none of them belong to us.

This text has usually been understood as a warning against the influence of heretics or sectarians who had at one stage separated themselves from the Johannine community, but continued to represent a threat to the orthodox Christians who had so far remained loyal to the true Christian faith. This is the first time these heretics or schismatics are mentioned in the letter, and their true identity is not revealed in this passage, but in the later parts of the text. A large majority of interpreters have maintained that the heterodoxy in question is of a Christological nature: the heretics did not share the orthodox Christians' view of Christ, but were unwilling to believe and accept that Christ had "become a man" or "had come in the flesh", as it says in 1 Jn. 4.2. In their view, Christ was so divine that he had only apparently, not really, come to the world; this happened when he was baptized, and he had then left the world again before his death. This type of heresy is called docetism (from Greek: *dokeîn*, "to appear") and belongs to the branch of dogmatics called Christology.

According to this interpretation, the heterodoxy denounced by the Johannine scriptures existed within the congregation or the Church itself (even if the heretics had separated themselves from the orthodox Christians), because the heterodox teachers also believed in Christ, but in their own way. According to this view, the relationship between loyal and schismatic Christians therefore reflected internal ecclesiastical problems, and it only remained to be seen which of them would prevail in the end.

But is this a true picture of the situation? I do not think so. Because who were the "antichrists" mentioned in 1 Jn. 2.18? Were they really people who did not believe in the incarnation of Christ? Is it not more likely that the words in 1 Jn. 4.2-3 imply that "antichrists" were people who did not believe that Jesus was Christ, come in the flesh? At least, this is the view of O'Neill.[14] Why not assume that the term "antichrists" simply stands for people who denied that Jesus was Christ? In 2.22-23, the author says: "22 Anyone who denies that Jesus is the Christ is nothing but a liar. *He* is the antichrist, for he denies both the Father and the Son: 23 to deny the Son is to be without the Father; to acknowledge the Son is to have the Father too."

But who were the people in the contemporary world who denied that Jesus was Christ, if not the Jews who did not believe in Christ? Who were the people who claimed to have the Father, but denied the Son, if not the orthodox Jews? This point of view changes the picture completely: instead of ecclesiastical, Christological disagreements, we now see a conflict between Judaism and Christianity.

It could be argued that this conflict need not take up the interpreter's attention, since it is apparently just another manifestation of the usual disagreement between Jews and Christians – a disagreement caused by the fact that the Jews did not believe in Christ as the Christians did. Is it not just a triviality to be noted in passing?

No, for in this case, the Christians who are involved in the conflict are Jews themselves, as we know from a passage in 3 Jn.

3 Jn. is a narrative of a number of missionaries who have set out for a journey "for the name's sake", that is, for the sake of Christ, but who refuse to accept anything from Gentiles; therefore the author of the letter and his fellow-Christians are obliged to support and help them (3 Jn. 5-8). In my view, missionaries who refused to accept anything from Gentiles can only have been

---

14 O'Neill, *Puzzle of First John*, p. 48, who translates 1 Jn. 4.2 like this: "Every spirit that confesses Jesus to be Messiah come in the flesh is from God." However, this translation must be considered to be extremely uncertain.

Jewish-Christian missionaries, and if so, this shows that the Johannine letters originate from Jewish-Christian communities – probably not in Palestine, but in the Diaspora; as is well known, the ecclesiastical tradition says that the Johannine literature originated from Ephesus, the capital of the province of Asia.

It was probably for the very same reason that the Jewish-Christian Gentile apostle Paul and his collaborator, Barnabas, refused to accept support from the Gentile-Christian congregations he founded, although Jesus' word that the worker deserves his pay ought to apply to them as well (1 Cor. 9.14).[15]

3 Jn. also refers to a controversy between the author of the letter and a man called Diotrephes, who is known from this letter only. According to the author, Diotrephes wants to be the leader of the congregation and "wants to have nothing to do with us" (3 Jn. 9). "So when I come," it says in the letter, "I will draw attention to the things he is doing: he lays nonsensical and spiteful charges against us; not content with that, he refuses to receive fellow-Christians himself, and interferes with those who would receive them, and tries to expel them from the congregation" (3 Jn. 10).

Many theories have been presented on the relationship between the author of the letter and this Diotrephes. In this context, I shall confine myself to two of these theories, one presented by Adolf Harnack in 1897, the other by Ernst Käsemann in 1951.

Harnack believed that the controversy between the author of the letter and Diotrephes was caused by organizational problems and had nothing to do with doctrine, theology or heterodoxy. According to Harnack, Diotrephes was the monarchical bishop of the congregation in question – "monarchical" bishop in the sense we know from the second century and meet for the first time in Ignatius' letters from circa A.D. 110. The author of the letter himself was in charge of the missionary work in the region of the congregation in question and did not want the monarchical bishop to interfere with his work.

---

15 See section 3.5.1 above, n. 121. On the subject of 3 Jn. 7, Casey is right in writing (*From Jewish Prophet to Gentile God*, p. 158): "The elder, who wrote 2 and 3 John, uses the description "Gentiles" as a reference to an outside group (3 Jn 7): however assimilated he was, he must have retained his Jewish self-identification;" according to Casey, the same applies to 1 Jn., which never refers to "the Jews" in a hostile way (p. 158).

257

Against the view of Harnack, it must be argued that 1) the monarchical episcopate we know from the second century was established for the purpose of controlling gnosticism, not to control Christian missionaries, 2) this monarchical episcopate had not yet been introduced in the congregations in Asia and Macedonia even at the time of Ignatius, and 3) the author of the letter was not a missionary leader, but had only supported some missionaries who had arrived at his place during their journey.

In his treatise on the author of the Johannine literature as a "heretic and a witness", Käsemann agrees with Harnack in so far as he also believes that Diotrephes was a monarchical bishop. But unlike Harnack, Käsemann maintains that the controversy between the author and Diotrephes was theological and doctrinal: the author of the letter – and of the entire Johannine literature – represented the exact Christological heresy which most interpreters of 1 Jn. have identified as the doctrine denounced by the letter, namely docetism.[16] This theory is so far-fetched that it is understandable that Käsemann has found few adherents.

My own view may seem equally far-fetched: Diotrephes was not a bishop, much less a monarchical bishop; but the principal or *rosh* of the local Jewish synagogue congregation, most of the members of which had become Christians. Naturally Diotrephes did everything he could to stop this development, and made full use of all his power and authority to do this; expulsion or excommunication from the synagogue or, as it says in the letter: *ekbállein*, "to expel" (3 Jn. 10).

In his book on the Gospel of Matthew, Bent Noack wrote that "it was in regions with numerous and old Jewish congregations that the Jewish Christianity behind the Gospel of Matthew gained a foothold. In these congregations, people could immediately start living a congregational life within relatively well-established limits because a congregation or a number of congregations already existed, people who had a common ethnic identity and could jointly constitute a Christian congregation that remained an ethnic, i.e. Jewish, community. This transition from orthodox Judaism to Christian Judaism took place in groups, not through the conversion of individuals: at least individual conversion was not the characteristic and principal factor of the process. A synagogue congregation developed into a Christian congregation. It

---

16   This view is first presented clearly in Käsemann's book *Jesu letzter Wille*, 1966.

was really a multiple conversion that resulted in the fact that the increasing majority of Christians took over the synagogue or detached themselves from it and established their own."[17]

The exact expression used in 3 Jn. 10 to indicate expulsion from the synagogue recurs in Jn. itself, in the narrative about the healing of the blind man by the pond of Siloam: this man, who had been blind from birth, was "expelled" or "excommunicated" (Jn. 9.34-35). Earlier in the same narrative, it says that the Jewish authorities had decided that anyone who acknowledged Jesus as Christ (cf. 1 Jn. 2.23) should be *aposynágogos*, "banned from the synagogue" (Jn. 9.22), an expression that recurs in Jn. 12.42 and 16.2; a similar expression, *aforízein*, "to exclude", is used in Lk. 6.22.

These observations seem to indicate that those interpreters are right who maintain that the Johannine literature, including the three letters and the Gospel itself, is not only of Jewish-Christian origins, but also belongs in a Jewish-Christian environment, and that "the Johannine community" was therefore Jewish Christian. The conflict was far from academic. It was a conflict within Judaism itself, between Jews who believed that Jesus was Christ, and other Jews who refused to believe this. That the Word "became flesh", as it says in the prologue to the Gospel, simply means that Christ had come, in the person of Jesus, and it is hardly accidental that of all the authors of the New Testament, John is the only one who uses the Hebrew word for Christ, "Messiah" (Jn. 1.41; 4.25).

Having said that, it is important to point out that the interpretation of the Johannine literature, Jn. and 1, 2 and 3 Jn., has been much debated during recent decades: interpreters disagree on the question of whether all four texts were written by one and the same author; most interpreters believe that Jn. was written by one person, and 1 Jn. by another, later (or earlier!) than Jn.; furthermore, there is disagreement as to whether 2 and 3 Jn. were also written by the person who wrote 1 Jn. This lack of consensus has resulted in the formation of the concept of a Johannine "community" or "school".

The general picture is further complicated by the fact that most interpreters consider the genesis of Jn. to have been extremely complex. Walter Schmithals

---

17 Bent Noack, *Matthæusevangeliets Folkelighed*, Copenhagen 1971, p. 138. Cf. Robinson, *Redating the New Testament*, p. 103, on Matt.: "At this stage all kinds of questions of organization, ministry and liturgy, doctrine and discipline, law and finance, present themselves afresh, as a "society" or "synagogue" takes on the burden of becoming a 'church'."

maintains, for instance, that Jn. was founded on a "basic gospel"; as a reaction against the decision made by the synod in Jamnia, this basic text emphasized that Jesus was Christ, and denounced the non-Christians among the author's Jewish countrymen. Later, this "basic gospel" was used by the Evangelist; with many additions of his own, he turned it into a gospel scripture which denounced the teachers of heterodoxy who represented a docetic Christology and therefore maintained that Christ was Jesus. According to Schmithals, 1, 2 and 3 Jn. were written at this stage of the literary genesis of Jn., and like the revised "basic gospel", they also denounced the docetic heterodoxy. So Schmithals' analysis represents a view which is completely different from the views of both Bultmann and Käsemann. Klaus Wengst understands Jn. and 1 Jn. from a historical point of view: while the letter denounces the docetic heterodoxy, the gospel text itself belongs in a Jewish context and reflects the situation in northern Palestine and the surrounding territories (not Ephesus!), where the Christian Jews were hard pressed by their non-Christian countrymen; Jn. represents a Jesus tradition that is no less genuine than that of the synoptic gospels. John Ashton interprets Jn. on purely, if complex, Jewish premises and maintains that the text can be understood only in the light of the synod in Jamnia and the subsequent expulsion of Christian Jews from the synagogue community; on this point, his view is in line with that of Schmithals and his reconstructed "basic gospel". P.M. Casey criticizes the hypothetical literary theories; yet he uses the gospel text to reconstruct the genesis of the Johannine congregation: from the beginning, it was a mixed congregation of Jews and Gentiles, and the Jewish members were Jews who had assimilated Hellenistic culture; after the synagogue community of Christian and non-Christian Jews had ceased to exist in about A.D. 90, the Christian Jews approached the Gentile Christians, and the final result of this development was a Christology which was incompatible with Jewish monotheism. According to Casey, Jn. represents a distinctly Gentile self-identification ("your law": Jn. 8.17), while, oddly enough, 1, 2 and 3 Jn. express a Jewish identity (3 Jn. 7!); whether the gospel text and the letters belong to the same "Johannine Community" remains an open question.

So the total picture is anything but clear, and it is doubtful whether a clarification can be expected.

It is important to note that the "lytic" docetism (according to which the unity of Jesus and Christ was unreal, since it began with his baptism and ended before his death) was abandoned when the reading *lýei* in 1 Jn. 4.3 was dropped; at the most, what remains is the fundamental docetism (according to which the human life of Christ was an illusion). This implies, however, that the Johannine literature takes no position on the question of the "unity" of Jesus and Christ: at the most, it can only be assumed that the Johannine literature represents Jesus Christ as a man of flesh and blood; according to Käsemann, Jn. differs from the synoptic gospels on this point.

260

It is also important to note that the baptism and the confession of belief in Christ play an important part in Jn. and 1 Jn.; this appears for instance from 1 Jn. 2.20 and 2.27 (*chrîsma*); 3.9 (*spérma*) and 3.24 (*pneûma*), and from Jn. 3.5 and 13.10; the latter passage can hardly be taken to mean that baptism must not be repeated, but rather that one baptism is sufficient; cf. 1 Jn. 2.27. In this context, it is also interesting to note that the well-known passage in 2 Jn. 9 about "anyone who goes beyond the teaching of Christ" can hardly refer to heretics or gnostics with a docetic Christology, but rather to people who have abandoned the belief in Christ; *proágein*, "to go beyond", or "leave", is here opposed to *ménein*, "remain" (in the teaching of Christ).

So far, the question of the theological points of contact between the Johannine literature and the Pauline theology also remains unclarified; however, the teaching of freedom from sin in 1 Jn. 3.6 and 3.9 can hardly be understood except in the light of Paul's teaching of justification.

Finally, it is also important to consider how the Johannine literature could be transferred to the Gentile-Christian Church if it was of Jewish-Christian origin as maintained above. This question also remains unclarified; does Jn. 19.25-27 with the words about Jesus' mother Mary and the favourite disciple perhaps indicate a concession on the part of the Gentile Christians?

The above-mentioned passage in 1 Jn. 2.18-19 has the words: "They [the antichrists] left our ranks, but never really belonged to us; if they had, they would have stayed with us." As I said above, these very harsh words do not refer to heretic or schismatic Christians, who could have been persuaded to return to the true faith, if they just had a different, Christological belief. On the contrary, these words are aimed at unbelieving Jews, and in the view of the author of the letter, the fact that they are unbelievers shows that they no longer represent the true Israel, which is now represented by the Christians (cf. Phil. 3.3). The non-Christian Jews have left the path of God.

It goes without saying that this literature does not reflect the situation as it was at the time of Jesus, although Jn. pretends that it does. It is far more probable, as the Johannine letters themselves indicate, that it reflects the situation during the last decades of the first century or perhaps even later, so the opinions and attitudes we find in the Johannine literature must belong to the post-apostolic era.

4.3 Roman rule and the Christians

Bibliography

Theodor Mommsen: *Römische Geschichte*, V, 5th ed., Berlin 1904, pp. 487-552: "Judäa und die Juden" = 7 (dtv-bibliothek 6059), Munich 1976, pp. 188-250.
Id.: Der Religionsfrevel nach römischem Recht, Historische Zeitschrift 64 (1890), pp. 389-429 (also in: id., *Gesammelte Schriften*, IV, Berlin 1907).
Id.: Die Rechtsverhältnisse des Apostels Paulus, Zeitschrift für die neutestamentliche Wissenschaft 2 (1901), pp. 81-96.
Maurice Goguel: *La naissance du christianisme*, 1946 (see section 3.1), pp. 545-592: "Le christianisme et l'état romain".
Gerd Lüdemann: *Das frühe Christentum* (see section 3.1 above), pp. 249-250: "Zum römischen Bürgerrecht des Paulus" = *Early Christianity*, pp. 240-241: "On Paul's Roman citizenship".
Wolfgang Stegemann: War der Apostel Paulus ein römischer Bürger? Zeitschrift für die neutestamentliche Wissenschaft 78 (1987), pp. 200-229.
Carsten Breengaard: *Kristenforfølgelser og kristendom – fra Nero til Ignatios af Antiokia* (Institut for Religionshistorie, the University of Copenhagen), Copenhagen 1990 (first published in 1986; new ed. with the title: *Kristenforfølgelser og kristendom. Fra sekt til statskirke*, Copenhagen 1992).
Niels Willert: Apologetiske og indignatoriske tendenser i Lukasskrifterne, Dansk Teologisk Tidsskrift 50 (1987), pp. 221-236.
Gerd Lüdemann: Das Judenedikt des Claudius (Apg 18,2), 1991 (see section 3.6.1 above, n. 135).

4.3.1 The Gentile-Christian congregations

As mentioned above (in section 4.2.1), only the authentic Pauline letters belong to the apostolic era, while all the other scriptures of the New Testament, with Mark as a possible exception, were created in the post-apostolic era. I shall now proceed to examine the First Letter of Peter and the scriptures of Luke as evidence of the relationship between the Roman authorities and the Christians during the post-apostolic era.

Unlike the Johannine scriptures mentioned in section 4.2.2, these texts are representative of Gentile-Christian communities and do not originate from communities which were under the direct influence of Judaism. It must be assumed that the emergence and propagation of Christianity among the Jews attracted little attention from the Romans, and that Jewish Christians were

262

generally allowed to live without any interference from the Roman authorities; the persecution they suffered originated mainly from the Jews themselves, not the Romans (cf. 1 Thess. 2.14; Gal. 1.13, 22-23).[18]

The situation was different for Christians of Gentile origins and Gentile-Christian congregations. No matter where they lived, Gentile Christians and their congregations would always differ from their Gentile neighbours because of the fact that they were neither Gentiles nor Jews according to their religion; nor were they protected by the privileges which the Jews, including the Jewish Christians, had enjoyed since the Romans' assumption of power: permission to observe their own traditional customs, and exemption from Roman military service. Therefore the Gentile Christians could not live unnoticed by the Roman authorities; the persecution they suffered came from Gentiles, not Jews (cf. again 1 Thess. 2.14) – even on the occasions when Jews had alerted the Roman authorities to the presence of Gentile Christians.

Several facts should be taken into consideration in order to clarify the situation.

Firstly, it is remarkable how few traces the destruction of the temple at the end of the Jewish-Roman war in A.D. 70 left in the New Testament texts from the post-apostolic era; this event is barely recorded (see 1 Pet. 5.13; Lk. 21.20 ff.). This indicates that the temple was of relatively little importance to the Gentile-Christian congregations. In other words, the Jewish-Roman war in 66-70 (-74?), Jerusalem's temple and its priests played no essential role from the point of view of the Gentile-Christian congregations. Admittedly, we have no evidence that the destruction of the temple was regarded as a major disaster by the Jewish-Christian communities either. Of course this may be due to lack of source material, but we must also bear in mind that in the view of these communities, the prospect of seeing a statue of the Roman emperor set up in the Jerusalem temple during the reign of emperor Caligula (37-41) had represented a far greater disaster;[19] this explanation is even more convincing if the tradition

---

18 When Jesus' relatives were brought before Domitian, it was not because they were Christians, but because they were of Davidic and therefore royal descent; see section 3.2.5, the passages referred to in nn. 67 and 68.

19 See Gerd Theißen, *Lokalkolorit u. Zeitgesch.*, 1989 (see section 2.3 above), pp. 133-176: "Die große Endzeitrede und die Bedrohung des Jerusalemer Tempels im Jahre 40 n.Chr." = "The Great Eschatological Discourse and the Threat to the Jerusalem Temple in 40 C.E.", in: id., *The Gospels in Context*, 1992 (see section 2.3 above), pp. 125-165.

is right in saying that the Palestinian Christians had really emigrated to Pella before the Jewish-Roman war in 66 ff.[20]

Secondly, as mentioned in section 3.5, the Christian mission had already been divided into a Jewish and a Gentile mission during the apostolic era, and this division had been formally adopted during the Jerusalem Conference. Hardly any Christian congregation, with the single possible exception of the congregation in Antioch (the situation in Rome is described below), was mixed, i.e. composed of both Jewish and Gentile Christians; the congregations were either Jewish-Christian or Gentile-Christian, like those of Paul. Whenever Christianity became visible in the Greek-Roman world, it was really the Gentile-Christian congregations that became visible. The sociological effect of this cannot be overestimated.

Thirdly, the separation between the Jewish-Christian and Gentile-Christian congregations meant that the mutual influence between the two kinds of congregations became negligible, and that the Gentile-Christian congregations relatively soon acquired independence and self-identity (cf. even Rom. 11.20 ff.). This eventually resulted in a theological division between Jewish Christianity and Gentile Christianity, so that each of them gradually developed its own character. Unfortunately this theological division also involved the risk that Gentile Christians might support the general anti-Semitism of this era,[21] betray Christianity's origins in Judaism and leave the Jewish-Christian congregations, of which we know but little, to their own fate. Later we shall see (in section 4.5.3) that this risk was anything but theoretical.

Fourthly, the end of the apostolic era coincided with the discontinuation of the Gentile-Christian congregation's relationship with the Jewish-Christian leaders. Characteristically, the apostles who had founded the Gentile congregations during the apostolic era were of Jewish origins;[22] Paul was the shining example of this. Moreover, the collection for Jerusalem had constituted another link with the Jewish world; during the apostolic era, the Gentile-Christian congregations recognized the importance of this, if reluctantly. With the beginning of the post-apostolic era, however, this link between the Jewish

---

20 See the reference to Lüdemann in section 4.1.
21 On the emergence of anti-Semitism: see section 1.1.2 above, the passage referred to in n. 14.
22 See section 3.2 above on disciples and apostles.

264

cultural world and the Gentile-Christian congregations was broken, paving the way for the final self-dependence of the Gentile-Christian congregations.

4.3.2 The edict of Claudius

The first confrontation between the Christians and the Roman authorities took place as early as during the reign of emperor Claudius (41-54), in the apostolic era. It says in Acts 18.2:

> There [in Corinth] he [Paul] met a Jew named Aquila, a native of Pontus, and his wife Priscilla; they had recently arrived from Italy because Claudius had issued an edict that all Jews should leave Rome.

The Jewish couple Aquila and Priscilla were Christians like Paul himself, and had probably become Christians in Rome, where Christianity had been introduced at a very early stage (cf. Acts 2.10), although we do not know how this had occurred. However, the text does not say that Claudius expelled the Jews from Rome because they were Christians, and the Roman authorities can hardly have known much about Christianity anyway. We have to consult another source in order to ascertain that the expulsion from Rome had anything to do with Christianity. In the work of the historian Suetonius, Claudius 25, it says:

> [Claudius] Iudaeos impulsore Chresto assidue tumultuantes Roma expulit, i.e.: "Since the Jews constantly made disturbances at the instigation of Chrestus, he [Claudius] expelled them from Rome."[23]

There is no room for doubt that this "Chrestus" is really "Christ": the text refers to an uprising among the Jews caused by the question of Christ.[24] In other words: at one point, the question of whether Jesus was Christ, or Messiah, had divided the Roman Jews and set off a conflict among them, and this conflict had then become so serious that the imperial Roman authorities decided to intervene.

According to Acts 18.2, all Jews were expelled; although this is not contradicted by Suetonius, who simply refers to "the Jews", it is contradicted by

---

23 J.C. Rolfe, ed., Suetonius, *Caesares* I-II (Loeb Classical Library), Cambridge (Mass.) 1914, vol. II, p. 53.

24 This is questioned by the atheistic historian Theodor Mommsen, *Röm. Gesch.*, V, p. 523, n. 20 = 7, p. 222, n. 20.

historical probability. Probably only the Jews who had been involved in the conflict were expelled from Rome; in other words, Rome's Christian Jews (including Aquila and Priscilla) were expelled because they had instigated the disturbances.

There is another piece of information which at first sight seems to refer to the same disturbances, as maintained by Gerd Lüdemann. It is a narrative from the historian Dio Cassius' Roman History, 60, 6.6, for the year A.D. 41; unlike Suetonius and Acts 18.2, however, it does not refer to any expulsion of Jews; they are only forbidden to hold meetings:

> As for the Jews, who had again increased so greatly that by reason of their multitude it would have been hard without raising a tumult to bar them from the city, he [i.e. Claudius] did not drive them out, but ordered them, while continuing their traditional mode of life, not to hold meetings.[25]

Gerd Lüdemann maintains that only some Jews were expelled from Rome, and that the Roman authorities tried to prevent political disturbances among the remaining Jews by forbidding them to hold meetings. The characteristic feature of Lüdemann's view is this combination of information from Suetonius and Dio Cassius, on the basis of which he dates Claudius' edict to the beginning of his reign and brings the date of Aquila's and Priscilla's arrival in Corinth forward accordingly.[26] In doing so, Lüdemann disregards the traditional date of the edict, A.D. 49. As already mentioned, Lüdemann may be right on this point,[27] but in the present context, a final answer to this question is not required.[28]

---

25 English translation: C. Cary, *Dio's Roman History* (Loeb Classical Library), VII, Cambridge (Mass.) 1961, pp. 382-384.
26 Lüdemann, *Chronologie*, 1980, pp. 183-195: "Das Judenedikt des Claudius".
27 See section 3.6.1 above, n. 135.
28 For further information on Claudius' edict and the Roman congregation during the period that followed, see also Peter Lampe, *Die stadtrömischen Christen*, 1989 (see section 4.5 below), pp. 4-8: "Die Ereignisse rund um das "Claudiusedikt"", pp. 53-63: "Juden- und Heidenchristen", and pp. 63-65: "Nachrichten aus Paulus' Römerbrief sowie Apg 28,30f". On p. 8, Lampe categorically rejects Lüdemann's combination of Suetonius' and Dio Cassius' information: Dio Cassius' information does not refer to Claudius' edict, which should still be dated to A.D. 49; it refers to Hist. Rom. 57, 18, which says that the Jews were expelled from Rome during the reign of emperor Tiberius because of their large number; unlike Tiberius, Claudius did not expel the Jews because they had grown numerous again, but only forbade them to hold meetings.

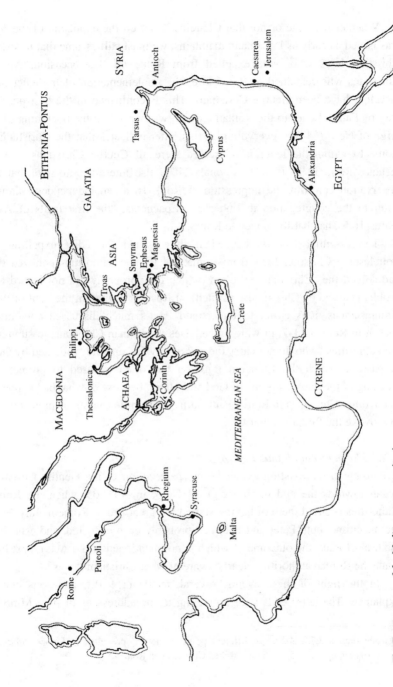

The Eastern part of the Mediterranean territories

267

Whether it is true or not that Claudius' edict on the expulsion of the Jews was issued as early as Lüdemann maintains, we must still assume that it was the Christian Jews who were expelled from Rome on that occasion. All the Christians who remained in Rome after the implementation of the edict must therefore have been Gentile Christians. This is confirmed in the best possible way by Paul's Letter to the Romans, which was written at the beginning of the reign of Nero (54-68): everything in this letter indicates that the Christians in Rome to whom the letter is addressed were all Gentile Christians; see for instance Rom. 11.13 ff. In this context, it is also interesting to note that this observation confirms the impression of Rom. 16 as an independent farewell letter to the congregation in Ephesus:[29] Epaenetus, "the first fruits of Asia" (Rom. 16.5), had hardly moved to Rome!

The essential fact is that when they issued the edict expelling the troublesome Christian Jews from Rome, the Roman authorities believed they had solved the "Christian" problem (which they probably did not regard as a problem caused by Christianity as such), at least for a time. In the light of these circumstances, it is easier to understand Paul's much discussed admonitory speech in Rom. 13.1-7, in which he advises the Roman Christians to submit to the authorities "who do not carry the sword in vain" and are "ordained by God" (a passage which the Lutheran tradition has often misused to promote its teaching of the double regime of God and State): because of what had happened to the other Christians in Rome, Paul warns the Gentile Christians in the city not to provoke the Roman authorities.

4.3.3 The persecution under Nero

According to the existing evidence, the persecution of the Gentile Christians began towards the end of the reign of Nero, in A.D. 65, when the Roman authorities accused them of having started the great fire of Rome in July 64. In the meantime, both Peter and Paul had probably been executed, and especially the trial of Paul (the outcome of which is not mentioned in the Acts) must have made the Roman authorities clearly aware of what Christianity was.

In the light of these events, several details in 1 Pet. and Acts can be explained. The letter ends with a greeting to the addressees in Asia Minor (1

---

29 See section 3.7.2 above. A different point of view is presented in Lampe, *Stadtröm. Christen*, pp. 124-153: "Die römischen Christen von Röm. 16".

Pet. 1.1) from "the chosen [congregation or sister][30] in Babylon" (5.13). "Babylon" can only mean Rome, and the fact that the Roman capital is called "Babylon" must be a reference to the Babylonians' capture of Jerusalem and the fall of the first temple in 587 B.C.[31] In other words: 1 Pet. must have been written after A.D. 70, when the Romans captured Jerusalem and destroyed the second temple, and therefore cannot have been written by the apostle Peter.[32]

The same letter also refers explicitly to the Christians by using the term *christianoí*, "Christianians", or "Christians" (1 Pet. 4.16). On this point, 1 Pet. is in agreement with the Acts, according to which "it was in Antioch that the disciples first got the name of Christians" (Acts 11.26; cf. 26.28). The precondition for calling people Christians is that they are Christians of Gentile origins who live in a Gentile environment and differ both from Jews and Gentiles: as Gentiles, they cannot hide themselves among the Jews, and as Christians, they have separated themselves from other Gentiles. So they are left unprotected in a hostile world. It says in 1 Pet. 4.12 ff.:

12 ... do not be taken aback by the fiery ordeal which has come to test you, as though it were something extraordinary. 13 On the contrary, in so far as it gives you a share in Christ's sufferings, you should rejoice; and then when his glory is revealed, your joy will be unbounded. 14 If you are reviled for being Christians, count yourselves happy, because the Spirit of God in all his glory rests upon you. 15 If you do suffer, it must not be for murder, theft, or any other crime, nor should it be for meddling in other people's business. 16 But if anyone suffers as a Christian, he should feel it no disgrace, but confess that name to the honour of God.

In other words, it is a Gentile Christian's fate to be exposed to humiliation and suffering for the sake of the Christian name. A Christian should neither avoid nor seek out humiliation and suffering, and like Paul in Rom. 13.1 ff., 1 Pet. 2.17 recommends obedience to "the king", i.e. the Roman emperor and the Roman authorities.

At first sight, there seems to be a difference between 1 Pet. and Acts. While the Acts makes no secret of the fact that the Jews are the great "enemy" who

---

30   Cf. 2 Jn. 1, 5, 13.
31   Cf. the references to Rome as "Babylon the great" in Rev., e.g. 14.8 and 16.19.
32   Contrary to Carsten Breengaard, *Kristenforfølgelser*, pp. 56 ff., which dates 1 Pet. to the 60s and considers it to be authentic. However, before A.D. 70, it would have made no sense to call Rome "Babylon". Breengaard's rejection of this argument, p. 56, n. 14, is unjustified.

always threatens the lives of the Christians, it suggests that there is peace and harmony between the Christians – i.e. the Gentile Christians – and the Roman authorities. In fact, the author of the Acts describes the relationship with the Roman authorities in an apologetic way, and tries to present the Christians as politically and socially harmless and even useful citizens. This "idealized" description reveals in itself that the relationship had a different character. Paul could have been acquitted if he had not appealed to the imperial court, as it says explicitly in Acts 26.32, but the author of the Acts knows the end of the story: Paul was executed (cf. Acts 20.25).

4.3.4 Legislation against the Christians?

As explained above, the First Letter of Peter and the Acts are concurrent testimonies of the Gentile Christians' situation in relation to the Roman authorities during the post-apostolic era. This raises a legal question: Did the authorities regard the Gentile Christians' profession of their faith as a crime? In other words, were the Christians accused *ob nomen*, "for the [Christian] name's sake", or must they be charged with real criminal acts, at least as a pretext, before the authorities could intervene?

This question is difficult to answer. In fact, we do not know if Christianity was criminalized as early as during the reign of Nero. The fact that Rome's Christians were made scapegoats of the city's fire, and that their alleged guilt was used as a pretext for punishing them seems to indicate that no prohibition had been issued against Christianity as such.

This argumentation is not contradicted by the fact that Christian leaders like Peter and Paul were accused and executed for being Christians, in fact *ob nomen*; in such cases, the authorities could always maintain that they were leaders of a subversive and politically suspect movement, while ordinary Christians would generally be treated more leniently.

This view is supported by the epoch-making investigation published in 1890[33] by Theodor Mommsen (1817-1903). Mommsen was also unable to find any historical evidence that Christianity in itself was forbidden. Instead, he suggested that the Roman authorities used the municipal police regulations called *ius coërcitionis* as the legal basis for taking action against the Christians. From the Romans' point of view, the legal procedure was therefore formally

---

33 Mommsen, Hist. Zeitschrift 64 (1890), pp. 389-429.

correct, which is also in keeping with Mommsen's own view of the Roman State; but from the Christians' point of view, it must have seemed arbitrary and unjust.

The theory that there was no anti-Christian legislation in the early apostolic era is also supported by another important fact. There are certain vague indications of persecution of Christians during the reign of emperor Domitian (81-96),[34] but a regular legal ban on Christianity was first introduced during the reign of emperor Trajan (98-117) and remained in force for many years. The evidence of the introduction of this ban is found in an exchange of letters from about A.D. 110 between Pliny the Younger, governor of the province of Bithynia-Pontus in Asia Minor (cf. 1 Pet. 1.1), and Trajan. These two letters, of which Trajan's letter had legal effect, are so important that I quote them here:[35]

In Pliny's letter, Ep. X. 96.1-10, it says:

1 ... In investigations of the Christians I have never taken part; hence I do not know what is the crime usually punished or investigated, or what allowances are made. 2 So I have had no little uncertainty whether there is any distinction of age, or whether the very weakest offenders are treated exactly like the stronger; whether pardon is given to those who repent, or whether a man who has once been a Christian gains nothing by having ceased to be such; whether punishment attaches to the mere name [nomen ipsum] apart from secret crimes, or the secret crimes connected with the name. Meanwhile this is the course I have taken with those who were accused before me as Christians. 3 I asked them whether they were Christians, and if they confessed, I asked them a second and third time with threats of punishment. If they kept to it, I ordered them for execution; for I held no question that whatever it was that they admitted, in any case obstinacy and unbending perversity deserve to be punished. 4 There were others of the like insanity; but as these were Roman citizens, I noted them down to be sent to Rome [cf. Paul in Acts].

Before long, as is often the case, the mere fact that the charge was taken notice of made it commoner, and several distinct cases arose. 5 An unsigned paper was presented, which gave the names of many. As for those who said that they neither were nor ever had been Christians, I thought it right to let them go, since they recited a prayer to the gods at my dictation, made supplication with incense and wine to your

---

34 See e.g. 1 Clem. 1.1: "the sudden and repeated misfortunes and calamities which have befallen us" (Kirsopp Lake, *The Apostolic Fathers*, vol. I, p. 9).
35 Translation (though with a minor change in 96.10): J. Stevenson, ed., *A New Eusebius. Documents illustrative of the history of the Church to A.D. 337*, London 1957, reprinted 1968, pp. 13-14 and 16.

statue, which I had ordered to be brought into the court for the purpose together with the images of the gods, and moreover cursed Christ – things which (so it is said) those who are really Christians cannot be made to do. 6 Others who were named by the informer said that they were Christians and then denied it, explaining that they had been, but had ceased to be such, some three years ago, some a good many years, and a few even twenty. All these too both worshipped your statue and the images of the gods, and cursed Christ.

7 They maintained, however, that the amount of their fault or error had been this, that it was their habit on a fixed day to assemble before daylight and recite by turns a form of words to Christ as a god; and that they bound themselves with an oath, not for any crime, but not to commit theft or robbery or adultery, not to break their word, and not to deny a deposit when demanded. After this was done, their custom was to depart, and to meet again to take food, but ordinary and harmless food, and even this (they said) they had given up after the issue of my edict, by which in accordance with your commands I had forbidden the existence of clubs [*hetaeriae*]. 8 On this I considered it the more necessary to find out from two maiden-servants who were called deaconesses [*ministrae*, Greek: *diákonoi*, cf. Rom. 16.1], and that by torments, how far this was true; but I discovered nothing else than a perverse and extravagant superstition [*superstitio prava et immodica*]. I therefore adjourned the case and hastened to consult you. 9 The matter seemed to me worth deliberation, especially on account of the number of those in danger, for many of all ages and every rank, and also of both sexes are brought into present or future danger. The contagion of that superstition has penetrated not the cities only, but the villages and country; yet it seems possible to stop it and set it right. 10 At any rate it is certain enough that the almost deserted temples begin to be resorted to, that long disused ceremonies of religion are restored, and that sacrificial meat finds a market, whereas buyers till now were very few. From this it may easily be supposed what a multitude of men can be reclaimed, if there be a place of repentance [*paenitentia*].

According to this letter, Trajan has already issued a ban on religious "clubs", *hetaeriae*, and Pliny has duly implemented this ban in his own province. But it is clear that Pliny needs specific rules he can apply to Christians; in particular, it remains an open question whether the name "Christian" alone, *ipsum nomen*, is sufficient as evidence, or whether it has to be supplemented with evidence of committed crimes. Pliny even finds it necessary to defend his punishment (execution) of those who have refused to abjure their faith by referring to the Christians' "obstinacy and unbending perversity".

This proves that no legal basis for proceeding against the Christians existed prior to Pliny's letter to Trajan.

In his answering letter, Ep. X. 97.1-2, Trajan writes:

1 You have adopted the proper course, my dear Secundus, in your examination of the cases of those who were accused to you as Christians, for indeed nothing can be laid down as a general ruling involving something like a set form of procedure. 2 They are not to be sought out; but if they are accused and convicted, they must be punished – yet on this condition, that whoso denies himself to be a Christian, and makes the fact plain by his actions, that is, by worshipping our gods, shall obtain pardon on his repentance [*paenitentia*], however suspicious his past conduct may be. Papers, however, which are presented unsigned ought not to be admitted in any charge, for they are a very bad example and unworthy of our time.

It appears from Trajan's answer that he fully approves Pliny's procedure, but on two points he gives detailed instructions: people who are suspected of being Christians shall not be sought out; they shall only be accused if they are brought before the court by others; and anonymous accusations shall be rejected – anybody who wants a Christian to be convicted must bring him before the court himself.

On this occasion – and not before – Christianity was officially criminalized.

4.3.5 The extent of the persecution

The preceding observations are based on a distinction between Jewish-Christian and Gentile-Christian congregations, of which only the latter appear to have been exposed to punitive measures on the part of the Roman authorities, while Jewish Christians, except prominent leaders like Peter and Paul, were ignored by the Romans. This distinction has not been made by many other researchers, but in my view, it is essential for understanding the history of early Christianity and its relationship with contemporary Judaism.

With the exception of Nero's persecution of the Gentile Christians in Rome, which was probably limited to the capital itself, real mass persecutions are unlikely to have occurred during the post-apostolic era. Not even the dramatic representation in Revelation suggests this: only one martyr, Antipas, is mentioned by name (Rev. 2.13; but see also 6.11 and 20.4). According to Rev., anybody who believes in Christ and remains loyal to the faith is a "witness"

(Greek: *mártys*). Yet increasing numbers of Christians were accused and executed because of their faith.

This was probably one of the factors that widened the gap between Jewish and Gentile Christians; it must also have had an indirect effect on the Jewish Christians, who had to make a difficult choice: either they must confess that they were Christians and expose themselves to persecution from both their Jewish compatriots and the Roman authorities, or they must keep their faith secret and suffer the same fate as the Jewish people in general: to belong to a people who had been defeated in the Jewish-Roman war.

If there is any substance in these observations, they emphasize the fact that Christianity was preserved for posterity by the Gentile-Christian congregations in the Greek-Roman world – not by the Jewish Christians. This is not surprising in as far as there had been more Gentile than Jewish Christians even during the apostolic era, if we are to believe Paul's own observations on the subject (Rom. 11.1 ff.). On the other hand, it is truly surprising that the Gentile Christians were able to preserve Christianity at all in a world that was hostile to them in every respect, especially since they could not expect any moral support from the Jewish Christians, much less from the traditional Judaism from which the Christian faith originated – the Jews had problems enough of their own. If we look for an explanation for the amazing success and viability of the Gentile-Christian congregations, we can probably find it in their social community, which took care of every Christian, and their intellectual freedom that allowed every Christian to have his own opinion on any subject connected with the outside world. These advantages must have been important enough to compensate for all the hardships the Christians must suffer in order to acquire them.

4.4 The First Letter of Clement; the Pastoral Letters; Ignatius' letters. The Ministry

Bibliography

Maurice Goguel: *L'église primitive*, 1947 (see section 3 above), pp. 110-164: "Les ministères".

Hans von Campenhausen: *Kirchliches Amt und geistliche Vollmacht in den ersten drei Jahrhunderten* (Beiträge zur historischen Theologie, 14), Tübingen 1953, 2nd ed. 1963.

Gustav Brøndsted: Evangelier og Evangelium, in: id., *Historie og Evangelium. Afhand-linger, Foredrag og Udkast* (Kirkehistoriske Studier, II. 23), ed. Niels Thomsen, Copenhagen 1966, pp. 135-204, especially pp. 189-201.

Id.: Ignatius fra Antiochia, ib., pp. 527-541.

Bent Noack: Pastoralbrevenes "troværdige tale", Dansk Teologisk Tidsskrift 32 (1969), pp. 1-22.

Hermann von Lips: *Glaube – Gemeinde – Amt. Zum Verständnis der Ordination in den Pastoralbriefen* (Forschungen zur Religion und Literatur des Alten und Neuen Testaments, 122), Göttingen 1979.

Reinhart Staats: Die katholische Kirche des Ignatius von Antiochien und das Problem ihrer Normativität im zweiten Jahrhundert, Zeitschrift für die neutestamentliche Wissenschaft 77 (1986), pp. 126-145 and 242-254.

G. Schöllgen: Monepiskopat und monarchischer Episkopat. Eine Bemerkung zur Terminologie, Zeitschrift für die neutestamentliche Wissenschaft 77 (1986), pp. 146-151.

Michael Wolter: *Die Pastoralbriefe als Paulustradition* (Forschungen zur Religion und Literatur des Alten und Neuen Testaments, 146), Göttingen 1988.

4.4.1 The Jewish origins of Christianity

In his book *Théologie du Judéo-Christianisme* of 1958, the Catholic ecclesiastical historian Jean Daniélou maintains that Christian theology is as old as Christianity itself, and did not first develop in the middle of the second century, when Christianity encountered Greek philosophy in the works of the apologists.[36] Of course Daniélou is right in this. He is also right in maintaining that before its encounter with Greek philosophy, theology had a "Semitic structure". However, by calling this theology from the period before the encounter with Greek philosophy "an early theology of Semitic structure",[37] he reveals that he regards this theology as provisional, and believes that the true theology was the theology that succeeded it (i.e. the Roman Catholic theology!) and changed its Semitic structure into a non-Semitic structure.

---

36   Jean Daniélou, *Théologie du Judéo-Christianisme. Histoire des doctrines chrétiennes avant Nicée*, Vol. I (Bibliothèque de Théologie), Tournai 1958. In his next book, *Message évangélique et Culture hellénistique aux IIe et IIIe siècles. Histoire des doctrines chrétiennes avant Nicée*, Vol. II (Bibliothèque de Théologie), Tournai 1961, Daniélou discusses Christian theology after the encounter with Greek philosophy.

37   Daniélou, ib., p. 1.

The problem presented by Daniélou is intriguing. The Christian literature he discusses in his book and considers to be expressive of Jewish Christianity and Jewish-Christian theology does not include the New Testament literature; he refers mainly to the literature known under the name of "The Apostolic Fathers", which includes such texts as Barnabas' letter, Hermas' "The Shepherd", Ignatius' letters and the First Letter of Clement. Daniélou calls this literature and its theology "Jewish-Christian", irrespective of whether its authors were of Jewish origin or not; in fact, the "Semitic structure" is his criterion for determining whether the literature is Jewish-Christian or not. However, if Daniélou had used his own criterion consistently, he would also have included the New Testament scriptures among the Jewish-Christian documents, but he dared not do this: according to his explanation, the New Testament is not a Jewish-Christian collection of texts; it is part of the Christian Bible. In fact, the only Christian scriptures which Daniélou calls "Jewish-Christian" are documents which belong neither to the New Testament Canon nor to the later Church. They do not represent true theology, but exist in a kind of grey zone.

This view is unacceptable. It is justifiable to maintain that a *Semitic structure* was characteristic of Christian literature and theology prior to the encounter with Greek philosophy in the middle of the second century. But then the same Semitic structure must also be attributed to all the New Testament scriptures. On the other hand, it would not be reasonable to describe the New Testament scriptures and The Apostolic Fathers as *Jewish-Christian documents*. Jewish Christianity must be distinguished from Gentile Christianity: it is simply the Christianity professed by Christians of Jewish origins. Paul, the apostle of the Gentiles, was a Jewish Christian, and the Pauline theology is therefore a Jewish-Christian theology – but this does not mean that the Gentile-Christian congregations he founded were Jewish-Christian! However, very little is known about the Jewish-Christian congregations, including those in Palestine, and any description of them must be based on documents that originate from Jewish-Christian communities and provide information about them, such as the Johannine scriptures (see section 4.2.2 above). Otherwise, any attempt to reconstruct "Jewish Christianity" and "Jewish Christian theology" is a pipedream with no historical foundation.[38]

As mentioned above, it is realistic to maintain that a Semitic structure was characteristic of all Christian literature and theology until the middle of the second century, but it is misleading to describe the same literature and theology as "Jewish-Christian".

The problem presented by Daniélou should therefore be seen from a different point of view. The question we should ask ourselves is: Why does the Christian literature and theology of Gentile-Christian origin that developed during the post-apostolic era (which lasted until the encounter with Greek philosophy) have a Semitic structure? The answer is really quite simple: because Christianity itself is of Jewish origin and was spread across the world by Christian preachers of Jewish origin.

The peculiarity of early Christian literature as compared to Patristic literature – the scriptures of the Fathers of the Church – will be discussed in section 4.6 below.

4.4.2 The First Letter of Clement

The first Letter of Clement can be dated to the end of the first century with a high degree of certainty.[39] It is a real letter, written on behalf of the Roman congregation to the congregation in Corinth, and the reason for writing it was the fact that the leaders of the Corinthian congregation, the elders, had been deposed and replaced by other people. As we already know, there had always been trouble in the Corinthian congregation (see section 3.6 above), and the letter from the Roman congregation requests that the deposed congregation leaders be reinstated in their offices as elders, "presbyters".

The letter itself does not mention the author's name, but according to the tradition, it was written by a man called Clement. From Hermas' "The Shepherd" (2 Vis. 4.3), we know that a man called Clement was responsible for

---

38 In my opinion, this applies for instance to Hans-Joachim Schoeps, *Theologie und Geschichte des Judenchristentums*, Tübingen 1949. A much more realistic view is presented in Johannes Munck, Jewish Christianity in Post-Apostolic Times, New Testament Studies 6 (1959-60), pp. 103-116 = Dansk Teologisk Tidsskrift 22 (1959), pp. 193-208 = Svensk Exegetisk Årsbok 25 (1960), pp. 78-96.

39 English translation: Kirsopp Lake, *The Apostolic Fathers. With an English Translation*, I, 1912, pp. 9-121.

277

correspondence with foreign congregations. So Clement was not a bishop, but must have held a prominent position in the Roman congregation. 1 Clem. was delivered to the Corinthian congregation by a delegation of three persons: Claudius Ephebus, Valerius Vito and Fortunatus (1 Clem. 65.1); one cannot help thinking of the three-man delegation the Corinthian delegation had sent to the imprisoned Paul about forty years earlier (1 Cor. 16.17-18), especially since one of the members of that delegation was also called Fortunatus! No doubt the bearers of the letter made sure that the letter was duly read to the entire Corinthian congregation, and did not return to Rome until the Roman congregation's request had been fulfilled.

The Roman congregation knows the history of the Corinthian congregation from Paul's 1 Cor. (there are no indications that 2 Cor. was also known in Rome), and can remind the Corinthian Christians of both Peter's and Paul's martyrdoms (1 Clem. 5.3-7) and the – as the author sees it – relatively less serious conflict that had then existed in the Corinthian congregation concerning the parties of Paul, Cephas and Apollos (1 Clem. 47.1-4; cf. 1 Cor. 1.10 ff.). The present conflict is much more serious: "It is a shameful report, beloved, extremely shameful, and unworthy of your training in Christ, that on account of one or two persons, the steadfast and ancient church of the Corinthians is being disloyal to the presbyters" (1 Clem. 47.6). The historical knowledge of the past and its connection with the present time is evident.

It is tempting to see the Roman congregation's intervention in the situation of the Corinthian congregation as the beginnings of a papacy, since the Roman congregation considered themselves entitled to intervene in the internal affairs of another congregation. However, this interpretation of the situation would be wrong. The letter from the Roman congregation is not a verbal attack on the congregation in Corinth, but a brotherly admonition, and a warning of the danger which the conflict in Corinth represents in relation to the non-Christian surroundings (1 Clem. 47.7). Moreover, Clement's letter was written long before the Roman congregation acquired sufficient power and authority to intervene in the affairs of other congregations.

The situation should be seen in the light of the organization of the congregations. Both the Roman and the Corinthian congregation were organized on the basis of democratic principles inspired by the Greek popular assembly, *ekklesía*. Each congregation was governed by a democratically elected collective leadership (cf. Acts 6.5 concerning the seven overseers of the poor) composed of a number of elders, *presbýteroi*, so no single person was entrusted with the leadership of the congregation. Some passages in the letter refer to "the bishops" and "the episcopate" (1 Clem. 42.4; 44.1, 4), but this does not mean that there were other offices than that of the elders: bishops (*epískopoi*) and elders are just different terms for the same positions. Even Paul's letter to the Philippians mentions both bishops and deacons in one and the same congregation (Phil. 1.1), and the Acts, which presupposes the existence of a presbyterial leadership of all congregations (Acts 11.30; 14.23; 20.17) refers to bishops too (Acts 20.28). As in the Pastoral Letters (see 1 Tim. 3.1; 5.17; Ti. 1.5, 7), bishops are the same as elders.

Polycarp's letter to the congregation in Philippi from circa A.D. 110 also takes it for granted that this congregation was still at that time, as in Paul's own time, governed by a collective leadership of elders (Polyc. praescr.; 6.1; 11.1). This is the more remarkable as Polycarp was already familiar with the completely new type of episcopate represented by Ignatius: the monarchical episcopate (see below).

1 Clem. also describes a theology of ministry founded on historical facts; naturally this is included in the letter with a view to the special situation of the Corinthian congregation. The letter states (1 Clem. 42.1-44.5):[40]

42.1 The Apostles received the Gospel for us from the Lord Jesus Christ, Jesus the Christ was sent from God. 2 The Christ therefore is from God and the Apostles from the Christ. In both ways, then, they were in accordance with the appointed order of God's will. 3 Having therefore received their commands, and being fully assured by the resurrection of our Lord Jesus Christ, and with faith confirmed by the word of God, they [i.e. the Apostles] went forth in the assurance of the Holy Spirit preaching the good news that the Kingdom of God is coming. 4 They preached from district to district, and from city to city, and they appointed their first converts, testing them by the Spirit, to be bishops and deacons [cf. Phil. 1.1] of the future believers. 5 And this was no new method, for many years before had bishops and deacons been written of; for the scripture says thus in one place, "I will establish their bishops in righteousness, and their deacons in faith."[41] ... 44.2 ..., since they [i.e. the Apostles] had received

---

40   Translation: Kirsopp Lake, *The Apostolic Fathers*, vol. I, pp. 79-85.
41   Isa. 60.17; the last part of the quotation, on the deacons, is not part of the Old Testament text, and the first part of the quotation does not refer to bishops, but to the authorities of the people.

perfect knowledge, they appointed those who had been already mentioned, and afterwards added the codicil that if they should fall asleep, other approved men should succeed to their ministry. 3 We consider therefore that it is not just to remove from their ministry those who were appointed by them, or later on by other eminent men, with the consent of the whole Church, and have ministered to the flock of Christ without blame, humbly, peaceably, and disinterestedly, and for many years have received a universally favourable testimony. ... 5 Blessed are those Presbyters who finished their course before now [i.e., have died in their office], and have obtained a fruitful and perfect release in the ripeness of completed work, for they have now no fear that any shall move them from the place appointed to them.

What we read here is a historically founded *successio apostolica*, or rather even more than this: the apostles themselves had been appointed by Christ, who had been sent by God. The apostles went out to preach the Gospel, and in every new place they came to, they appointed their first converts (cf. Rom. 16.5 and 1 Cor. 16.15 concerning Epaenetus and Stephanas respectively) bishops (i.e. elders, cf. 1 Clem. 44.5) and deacons when they had tested and approved them. Furthermore, the apostles stipulated that other approved and respected men should be appointed as successors to those who died in their office – but always "with the consent of the whole Church" (1 Clem. 44.3).

In this historical retrospection, the author of 1 Clem. explains what the apostles, for instance Paul, had foreseen and decided in advance: the appointment of more elders if the first died in their office. The author refers to at least three generations: 1) the apostles, 2) the first converts, who were appointed bishops and deacons, and 3) the later appointed elders. In *retrospect*, the author knows what the apostles had *foreseen* by virtue of their foreknowledge. This temporal aspect has to be taken seriously, for according to 1 Clem., it is the reason why the ministry of the elders is inviolable (it was established by the apostles themselves); at the same time, it expresses the democratic election of the congregation, which is equally inviolable.

A parallel is found in the Pastoral Letters, though with a significant difference. 1 Clem. looks back into history, describing what the apostles had foreseen and explaining the origins and inviolability of the ministry. In the almost contemporary Pastoral Letters, which have the character of testamentary farewell letters (especially in 2 Tim. 4.6 ff.), Paul looks into the future and decides in advance how the ministry is to be organized after his own demise (Ti. 1.5 ff.):

280

My intention in leaving you behind in Crete was that you should deal with any outstanding matters, and in particular should appoint elders in each town in accordance with the principles I have laid down ...

This passage also refers to at least three generations: 1) the apostle Paul, 2) Timothy/Titus, and 3) the elders appointed by them.

It is important to note that neither 1 Clem. nor Past. yield to the temptation of arguing for entrusting the congregation leadership to one person, although the situation (the division of the congregation in Corinth and the threat of heterodoxy in the congregations addressed in Past.) clearly seems to call for the introduction of a non-democratic form of leadership.

4.4.3 Ignatius' letters

A new situation is reflected in Ignatius' letters from about A.D. 110, in which we meet the monarchical episcopate for the first time. The bishop is now the "monarch", or supreme ruler, of the congregation.[42] The historical origins of the monarchical episcopate are unknown, but since it is represented by Ignatius, but had not yet been introduced in the western congregations in Asia Minor, Macedonia, Greece or Rome in his time, we must assume that the monarchical episcopate was first introduced in Syria, perhaps under the influence of Jewish-Christian congregations; it may even have been inspired by the reorganization of the Jewish society after the catastrophe in A.D. 70, possibly not quite independently of the decisions made by the synod in Jamnia in about A.D. 90 (see section 4.1.2 above).

Ignatius was bishop of the congregation in Antioch, the capital of the province of Syria, so he represented the historical link with the apostolic era. We do not know what had happened to the mixed congregation in Antioch since the conflict between Peter and Paul in this city (Gal. 2.11 ff.). Only one, very important fact can be established with a high degree of certainty: Ignatius himself and his Antiochene congregation were Gentile Christians, not Jewish Christians. There are no indications at all that Ignatius and the congregation in Antioch were Jewish Christians; at the time when Ignatius himself was arrested, wrote his letters and was taken to Rome, the congregation in Antioch suffered

---

42 On this subject, I follow the traditional view; a different view is found in Schöllgen, ZNW 77 (1986), pp. 146-151.

persecution, but their persecutors were Gentiles, not Jews (see section 4.3.1 above).

As the leader of his congregation, Ignatius had been arrested by the Roman authorities, and guarded by ten "leopards" (Ign. Rom. 5.1), i.e. soldiers, he was taken through Asia Minor to Rome, where the Roman authorities intended to execute him by throwing him to the wild animals in the arena.

On their way through Asia Minor, the travellers stopped in Philadelphia, Smyrna and Troas; from there they sailed to Neapolis, the port of Philippi.[43] We know from Polycarp's letter to Philippi that Ignatius really passed through Philippi (Polyc. 13.1-2). In Philadelphia, representatives of the congregations in Ephesus, Magnesia and Tralles came to see him, and in Smyrna, he wrote letters to these congregations in which he told them about his impending martyrdom in Rome and enjoined them to pray for his persecuted congregation in Antioch. He also wrote a letter to the congregation in Rome, entreating them not to try to prevent his martyrdom, and like 1 Clem. 5.3-7, he also referred to Peter's and Paul's martyrdoms (Ign. Rom. 4.3). In Troas, Ignatius wrote letters to the two congregations in Philadelphia and Smyrna that he had met during his journey, asking them to send messengers to Antioch with his congratulations to the congregation there on the occasion of the fact that this persecution had now stopped. He also wrote a letter to the "bishop" of Smyrna, Polycarp, whom he had met during his stay in Smyrna.[44]

There is only a limited overlap between the addressees of Ignatius' seven letters (*Ephesus*, Magnesia, Tralles, Rome, *Philadelphia*, *Smyrna*, Polycarp) and the addressees of the seven letters in Rev. 2-3 to the congregations in Asia Minor (*Ephesus*, *Smyrna*, Pergamum, Thyatira, Sardis, *Philadelphia*, Laodicea), but together the two collections of letters constitute a solid documentation of

---

43 The same route was followed by Paul: 2 Cor. 2.12-13; Acts 16.8 ff.; 20.5 ff.
44 The complicated critical reconstruction of Ignatius' letters was made by J.B. Lightfoot (see section 3.2.1 above): *The Apostolic Fathers, Part II. S. Ignatius, S. Polycarp. Revised Texts with Introductions, Notes, Dissertations, and Translations*, 2. ed., Vol. I-III, London 1889. The later attempts to question Lightfoot's reconstruction: J. Rius-Camps, *The Four Authentic Letters of Ignatius, the Martyr* (Pontificum Institutum Orientalium Studiorum), Rome 1979, and Robert Joly, *Le Dossier d'Ignace d'Antioche* (Éditions de l'Université de Bruxelles), Brussels 1979, are not convincing; see C.P. Hammond Bammel, Ignatian Problems, Journal of Theological Studies 33 (1982), pp. 62-97.

the large number of Christians and Christian congregations in western Asia Minor in about A.D. 100.

Especially Ignatius' two letters to the congregations in Philadelphia and Smyrna give us an insight into the internal affairs of the congregations in Asia Minor. Ignatius had met these congregations and can therefore be more explicit in his letters to them. These letters indicate that Ignatius warns the Christians against two kinds of heterodoxy: Judaism and docetism – at least this appears to be the case. But the question is whether his warning really refers to two kinds of heterodoxy, or, as it has also been suggested, it is aimed at one and the same (syncretistic?) phenomenon.

In Philad. 6.1, it says:[45]

6.1 But if anyone interpret Judaism [*ioudaïsmós*] to you, do not listen to him; for it is better to hear Christianity [*christianismós*] from the circumcised than Judaism from the uncircumcised. But both of them, unless they speak of Jesus Christ, are to me tombstones and sepulchres of the dead, on whom only the names of men are written.

Cf. Magn. 8.1-9.2, in which Ignatius also warns the Christian congregation against Judaism.

In 1 Smyrn. 1.1 ff., it says:[46]

1.1 ... our Lord, that he is in truth of the family of David according to the flesh, God's son by the will and power of God [cf. Paul, Rom. 1.3-4], truly born of a Virgin, baptised by John that "all righteousness might be fulfilled by him" [cf. Matt. 3.15], 2 truly nailed to a tree in the flesh for our sakes under Pontius Pilate and Herod the Tetrarch (and of its fruit are we from his divinely blessed Passion) that he "might set up an ensign" [cf. Isa. 5.26] for all ages through his Resurrection, for his saints and believers, whether among Jews, or among the heathen, in one body of his Church. 2.1 For he suffered all these things for us that we might attain salvation, and he truly suffered even as he also truly raised himself, not as some unbelievers say, that his Passion was merely in semblance, – but it is they who are merely in semblance, and even according to their opinions it shall happen to them, and they shall be without bodies and phantasmal. 3.1 For I know and believe that he was in the flesh even after the Resurrection. ...

Cf. Trall. 9.1-11.2, in which Ignatius also warns against a docetic Christology or a similar phenomenon.

---

45 Kirsopp Lake, *The Apostolic Fathers*, vol. I, p. 245.
46 Kirsopp Lake, *The Apostolic Fathers*, vol. I, pp. 253-255.

So Ignatius' warnings appear to be aimed at Judaism in the former case, and at docetism in the latter case.[47] Scholars inspired by the Religio-historical School have attempted to demonstrate that these two aspects had merged into one spiritual movement that was allegedly characteristic of the period in question: a syncretistic mixture of Jewish Christianity and gnosticism, or in other words, a gnosticism of Jewish-Christian character and origins.[48]

However, this religio-historical view is questionable for two reasons. Firstly, opinions are still divided on the definition of "gnosticism". How can we define a phenomenon as gnosticism when we have no evidence of a more or less fully developed gnostic system, but can only identify a few sporadic features that recur in the later gnostic systems from the middle of the second century and the following period? And is it an established fact, as maintained by the Religio-historical School, that gnosticism had pre-Christian origins and can therefore have influenced even parts of the New Testament scriptures? The uncertainty that surrounds these questions argues for a negative rather than a positive answer.

Secondly, it has never been proved that the Jewish Christianity whose existence during the post-apostolic era is documented had any syncretistic and gnostic characteristics. On the contrary, if we examine the texts that are known with certainty to be scriptures from Jewish-Christian congregations or communities, i.e. the Gospel of Matthew and the Johannine literature,[49] we find no indications of any gnostic or syncretistic influence.

To this must be added the simple observation that neither in Magn. nor in Philad. does Ignatius warn the Christians against any kind of Jewish Christianity, but only against Judaism.

There is only one course to take for those who wish to maintain that Ignatius' warnings against what appears to be two different dangers are really aimed at one single danger which he believes threatens the Christian congregations: they must also see a warning against Judaism in his warnings in

---

47 For information on docetism as a Christological heterodoxy, see section 4.2.2 above.
48 Notably Heinrich Schlier, *Religionsgeschichtliche Untersuchungen zu den Ignatiusbriefen* (Beiheft zur Zeitschrift für die neutestamentliche Wissenschaft, 8), Gießen 1929.
49 For information on the Johannine literature (i.e. Jn. and 1, 2 and 3 Jn.), see section 4.2.2 above.

Trall. and Smyrn. against what appears to be docetism.[50] When Ignatius emphasized so strongly that Christ *really* lived and died, it was not necessarily because other people maintained that Christ had only *apparently* lived as a man, and had only *apparently* died a human, i.e., real death. It is more reasonable to assume that other people maintained that *Christ* had never really lived and therefore never really died, and that Christ existed only in the imagination of the Christians. In other words: Ignatius' warnings refer to the same Jewish rejection of the Christian faith we know from the Johannine literature, but with one significant difference: the Johannine literature denounces the anti-Christianity that existed in Jewish-Christian communities, while Ignatius' letters warn against the danger of anti-Christianity in Gentile-Christian communities, whose members were exposed to the Jewish argumentation that Jesus was not Messiah, or Christ.

In Philad. 7.1 ff., Ignatius reports parts of a debate in which he must have participated when he was passing through Philadelphia:[51]

7.1 I cried out while I was with you, I spoke with a great voice, – with God's own voice, – "Give heed to the bishop, and to the presbytery and deacons." 2 But some suspected me of saying this because I had previous knowledge of the division of some persons: but he in whom I am bound is my witness that I had no knowledge of this from any human being, but the Spirit was preaching, and saying this, "Do nothing without the bishop, keep the flesh as the temple of God, love unity, flee from divisions, be imitators of Jesus Christ, as was he also of his Father." 8.1 I then did my best as a man who was set on unity. But where there is division and anger, God does not dwell. The Lord then forgives all who repent, if their repentance leads to the unity of God and the council of the bishop. I have faith in the grace of Jesus Christ, and he shall loose every bond from you. 2 But I beseech you to do nothing in factiousness, but after the teaching of Christ. For I heard some men saying, "if I find it not in the charters [*en toîs archeîois*, i.e, in the Old Testament] I do not believe in the Gospel," and when I said to them that it is in the Scripture, they answered me, "that is exactly the same question." But to me the charters are Jesus Christ, the inviolable charter is his cross, and death, and resurrection, and the faith which is through him; – in these I desire to be justified by your prayers.

---

50 If these two fronts are simply joined together to form a single front, there are no limits to the number of strange and sensational early Christian heresies the 20th century's researchers will be able to construct at their desks!

51 Kirsopp Lake, *The Apostolic Fathers*, vol. I, pp. 245-247 (with a slight modification in 8.2).

This important text from Ignatius' letters brings together the three elements that characterize Ignatius: 1) he denounces Judaism and its reference to the Old Testament as the only true canon, according to which even Christianity is judged and rejected; 2) he denounces "docetism" as a false doctrine and invokes the true canon: the cross, death and resurrection of Jesus Christ; and 3) he refers to the monarchical episcopate with its subordinates, namely presbyters and deacons, as the only ecclesiastical authority that is able to keep the Christian congregations united.

If this view of Ignatius' letters can be accepted, these texts will no longer be regarded as a number of incompatible elements accumulated in a confusing disorder; on the contrary, they will be seen to represent a theological and ecclesiastical conception of unity which is consistent and in agreement with the period during which these letters were written, and the situation in which they were conceived.

4.4.4 Conclusion

There is not necessarily an absolute opposition between Ignatius' episcopal church organization and the presbyterial church organization that characterized the western congregations in his time. As explained above, however, Ignatius' monarchical episcopate was connected with the struggle against contemporary Judaism, whereas the corresponding introduction of the monarchical episcopate in the West appears to have been connected with the struggle against gnosticism.[52] However, the latter phenomenon did not become a real threat to Christianity until the middle of the second century, at the end of the post-apostolic era.

4.5 Marcion

Bibliography

Adolf Harnack: *Marcion. Das Evangelium vom fremden Gott. Eine Monographie zur Geschichte der Grundlegung der katholischen Kirche* (Texte und Untersuchungen zur Geschichte der altchristlichen Literatur, 45), first published in 1921, 2nd ed. Leipzig 1924 = *Marcion. The Gospel of the Alien God*, Durham (North Carolina) 1990. Repr. (together with the following investigation) Darmstadt 1960.

---

52 See section 4.2.2, concerning Harnack's and Käsemann's theories on Diotrephes in 3 Jn.

Id.: *Neue Studien zu Marcion* (Texte und Untersuchungen zur Geschichte der altchristlichen Literatur, 44,4), Leipzig 1923.

Id.: Die Neuheit des Evangeliums nach Marcion, first published in 1929, in: id., *Aus der Werkstatt des Vollendeten*, Berlin 1930, pp. 128-143.

Emil Schürer: *The History of the Jewish People* (see section 1 above), I, 1973, pp. 514-557: "From the Destruction of Jerusalem to the Downfall of Bar Kokhba".

Peter Schäfer: *Der Bar Kokhba-Aufstand: Studien zum zweiten jüdischen Krieg gegen Rom* (Texte und Studien zum Antiken Judentum, 1), Tübingen 1981.

Niels Hyldahl: Kampen om skriftforståelsen i det andet århundrede, in: Tryggve Kronholm and others, eds., *Judendom och kristendom under de första århundradena*, Vol. 2, 1986 (see section 3.3 above), pp. 65-76, especially pp. 71-72.

Peter Lampe: *Die stadtrömischen Christen in den ersten beiden Jahrhunderten. Untersuchungen zur Sozialgeschichte* (Wissenschaftliche Untersuchungen zum Neuen Testament, 2, 18), 2nd ed., Tübingen 1989, pp. 203-219: "Marcion".

Gerd Lüdemann: *Ketzer. Die andere Seite des frühen Christentums*, Stuttgart 1995, pp. 154-174: "Der Erzketzer Markion und seine Zeit".

4.5.1 The Bar Kokhba revolt

In the present context, where we are studying the history of early Christianity in the light of early Judaism and its history, it may seem irrelevant to refer to Marcion and his view of Christianity – but not if we consider the date of Marcion's first appearance: circa A.D. 144.

The Jews suffered another defeat in their last great revolt against the Romans, the Bar Kokhba revolt, which took place in 132-135, towards the end of the reign of emperor Hadrian (117-138). The new revolt was severely quashed. The temple had been captured in A.D. 70; now Jerusalem was razed to the ground. A Roman colony called *Colonia Aelia Capitolina* was founded on the site of the city, and a temple for Jupiter was built in the place where the old temple had stood. The Jews who were still living in the city were expelled and replaced by non-Jewish colonists. A ban on circumcision (which the Romans regarded as castration) had already been issued before the revolt, but it was not aimed at the Jews in particular. Now it was strictly enforced, and any infringement of the ban was punished with death; as far as the Jews were concerned, the ban was not revoked until during the reign of the emperor Antoninus Pius (138-161), Hadrian's successor.

Emil Schürer writes: "The total paganisation of Jerusalem was the fulfilment of a scheme long before attempted by Antiochus Epiphanes. In another respect, too, the measures adopted by Hadrian resembled his. The ban on circumcision ... was now unquestionably maintained."[53] This observation is correct in as far as the Romans' destruction of Jerusalem and the Jewish religion is strongly reminiscent of Antiochus IV's treatment of the Jewish people when he imposed martial law on them in 168 B.C.[54] The Jews had revolted, and the Jewish people had to suffer the punishment inflicted upon them as rebels.

The reorganization of Jerusalem's status had the indirect effect of permitting Gentile Christians to settle in the city as colonists, so from then on, none of the Christians in Jerusalem were of Jewish origin, since all Jews were forbidden to enter the city.

4.5.2 Marcion

This was the situation when Marcion first appeared in the Christian congregation in Rome. He was a wealthy shipowner from Sinope on the Black Sea coast of Asia Minor, and came to Rome in about A.D. 140, gave the Roman congregation two hundred thousand sesterces, and expressed his wish to change their view of Christianity to suit his own.

In July 144, the Roman congregation refused to have anything to do with Marcion, gave the money back to him and expelled him from the church. Marcion then founded his own church; it still existed in the fourth century and had many congregations, though some of its members later joined the Manicheans.

Since Marcion's own scriptures are lost, our knowledge of his teaching comes from the later Patristic representations and rejections of his teaching. His own scriptures included his Antitheses (cf. the antitheses of the Sermon on the Mount, Matt. 5.21-48), and his New Testament canon.

As far as the New Testament is concerned, Marcion acknowledged only ten of the thirteen letters attributed to Paul: he rejected Past., but acknowledged Rom., 1 and 2 Cor., Gal., Eph., Phil., Col., 1 and 2 Thess., and Philem. This selection of Paul's letters indicates an impressive critical sense and is very close, or even identical, to modern theories on the authenticity of Paul's letters. As far as we know – we do not know Marcion's text of Paul in detail – Marcion

---

53 *History*, I, p. 555.
54 See section 1.1.2 above.

288

removed certain parts of Paul's text on the assumption that it had been subjected to Jewish interpolations and additions.

In addition to the "apostle" (Paul's letters), Marcion also acknowledged one "gospel", namely Lk., but "purged" it of its alleged Jewish additions, including the narrative of Jesus' birth and childhood in Lk. 1-2. Possibly Marcion chose Lk. because he believed its author to be identical to Paul's collaborator, Luke the physician (Col. 4.14), but he may also have attached importance to the fact that Lk. is the only gospel text written by a Gentile Christian. So his choice of Lk. confirms the impression of Marcion's critical sense.

The Antitheses are a kind of confession scripture for Marcion's adherents and express Marcion's view of Christianity. They are quoted here according to the selection made by Adolf Harnack in his book on Marcion;[55] the references in square brackets are my own.

I. The demiurge [the creator of this world, the God of the Old Testament] was known to Adam and the following generations, but the Father of Christ is unknown, as Christ himself said of him, "No one has known the Father but the Son" [cf. Lk. 10.22].

II. The demiurge did not even know where Adam was, so he called, "Where art thou?" [Gen. 3.9] Christ, on the other hand, knew even the thoughts of men [e.g. Lk. 5.22].

III. Joshua conquered the country with violence and cruelty; but Christ forbade all violence and preached mercy and peace.

IV. The Creator-God did not cause blind Isaac to see again [Gen. 27.1], but our Lord, because he is good, opened the eyes of many blind persons.

V. Moses intervened in the dispute of the brothers without being invited and rebuked the offender: "Why are you smiting your neighbor?" He, in turn, rebuked Moses: "Who made you a teacher and judge over us?" [Exod. 2.11 ff.] Christ, however, when a man demanded of him that he arbitrate the dispute with his brother over their inheritance, refused to take part in even so fair a cause – because he was the Christ of the good God, and not of the God who is a Judge – and said: "Who made me a judge over you?" [Lk. 12.13-14]

VI. Upon the exodus from Egypt the Creator-God gave Moses the charge, "Be ready, girded, shod, staff in hand, sacks on shoulders, and carry away with you gold and silver and all that belongs to the Egyptians" [Exod. 12.11 ff.]. But our Lord, the Good One, upon sending his disciples out into the world, said to them, "Have no shoes on your feet, no sack, no change of garments, no money in your purses!" [Lk. 9.3]

---

55 Harnack, *Marcion*, 2nd ed. 1924 = 1960, pp. 89-92 (*Marcion. The Gospel of the Alien God*, pp. 60-62).

VII. The prophet of the Creator-God, when the people were locked in battle, climbed to the top of the mountain and stretched forth his hands to God, that he might kill as many as possible in the battle [Exod. 17.10 ff.]; our Lord, the Good, stretched forth his hands (scil., on the cross) not to kill men but to save them.

VIII. In the law it is said, "An eye for an eye, a tooth for a tooth" [Exod. 21.24], but the Lord, the Good, says in the gospel, "If anyone strikes you on one cheek, turn to him the other also" [Lk. 6.29].

IX. In the law it is said, "Clothing for clothing," but the good Lord says, "If anyone takes from you your coat, let him have your cloak also" [Lk. 6.29].

X. The prophet of the Creator-God, in order to kill as many as possible in the battle, had the sun to stand still that it might not go down until the adversaries of the people were utterly annihilated [Josh.10.12 ff.]; but the Lord, the Good, says, "Let not the sun go down upon your wrath" [Eph. 4.26].

XI. At the reconquest of Zion the blind opposed David, and he had them killed [2 Sam. 5.6 ff.]; but Christ of his own accord came to help the blind [Lk. 18.35 ff.].

XII. At the request of Elijah the creator of the world sent down fire [2 Kgs. 1.10 ff.]; but Christ forbade his disciples to call down fire from heaven [Lk. 9.52 ff.].

XIII. The prophet of the Creator-God commanded the bears to come out of the thicket and to eat the children [2 Kgs. 2.23-24]; but the good Lord says, "Let the children come to me, and do not forbid them, for of such is the kingdom of heaven" [Lk. 18.15 ff.].

XIV. Out of the many lepers in Israel, Elisha, the prophet of the creator of the world, cleansed only one, Naaman the Syrian [2 Kgs. 5.1 ff.]; Christ, though he was "the alien", healed an Israelite whom his Lord (the creator of the world) had not been willing to heal [Lk. 5.12 ff.]. Elisha needed to use a material, water, for healing, and it had to be applied seven times [2 Kgs. 5.10 ff.]; Christ, however, healed by means of one single, simple word, and it was done at once. Elisha healed only one leper, but Christ healed ten, and these in disregard of the legal requirements; he simply told them to go their way, to show themselves to the priests, and on the way he cleansed them – without contact and without a word, by means of silent power, by his will alone [Lk. 17.12 ff.].

XV. The prophet of the world's creator says, "My bows are drawn, and my arrows are sharpened against them" [Isa. 5.28]; but the apostle says, "Put on the armour of God, that you may be able to quench the fiery darts of the wicked one" [Eph. 6.13 ff.].

XVI. The world-creator says, "You are not (any longer) to hear me with your ears," but Christ on the contrary says, "He who has ears to hear, let him hear" [Lk. 8.8].

XVII. The world-creator says, "Cursed is anybody who hangs upon the tree" [Deut. 21.23]; but Christ suffered death on the cross.

290

XVIII. The Christ of the Jews was destined by the creator of the world exclusively to lead the Jewish people back from the Dispersion; our Christ, however, has been entrusted by the good God with the liberation of the whole human race.

XIX. The good God is good toward all, but the creator of the world promises salvation only to those who are obedient to him ... the good God redeems those who believe in him but does not judge those who are disobedient toward him; the creator of the world, however, redeems those who believe in him and judges and punishes the sinners.

XX. *Maledictio* characterizes the law, and *benedictio* characterizes faith (the Gospel).

XXI. The creator of the world commands us to give to our brothers; but Christ simply says to give to give to all who ask.

XXII. In the law the creator of the world said, "I make the rich and the poor." Christ, however, blesses (only) the poor [Lk. 6.20].

XXIII. In the law of the righteous God, good fortune is given to the rich and misfortune to the poor; in the gospel this is reversed.

XXIV. In the law, God (the creator of the world) says, "You shall love the one who loves you and hate your enemy." But our Lord, the Good One, says, "Love your enemies and pray for those who persecute you" [Lk. 6.27-28].

XXV. The creator of the world ordained the Sabbath [Gen. 2.2-3]; but Christ takes it away [Lk. 6.1 ff.].

XXVI. The world-creator rejects the publicans as non-Jewish and profane men; Christ accepts the publicans [Lk. 5.27 ff.; 19.2 ff.].

XXVII. The law forbids the touching of a woman who has an issue of blood; Christ not only touches them but heals them as well [Lk. 8.43 ff.].

XXVIII. Moses permitted divorce [Deut. 24.1 ff.]; Christ forbade it [Lk. 16.18].

XXIX. The Christ of the Old Testament promised the Jews the restoration of the earlier state of things by the return of their land to them, and after death, in the underworld, a refuge in Abraham's bosom. Our Christ will establish the kingdom of God, an eternal and heavenly possession.

XXX. With the creator of the world, the place of punishment and the place of refuge both are situated in the underworld for those who are in the bondage of the law and the prophets; but Christ and the God to whom he belongs have a heavenly resting place and haven which the creator of the world never proclaimed.

The lack of identity between the Creator and the unknown God who is the Father of Jesus clearly indicates that Marcion was influenced by contemporary gnosticism in this respect. The god of the Jews is an evil, ignorant, just, strict and jealous god, and before Christ came, nobody had heard of the unknown and good God who appears in the preaching of Christ.

This fundamental principle is characteristic of many or even most of the gnostic systems from the second century and therefore not an exclusive feature of Marcion's teaching. It is no accident that this principle emerged during the period in question, immediately after the Jewish defeat in the Bar Kokhba revolt in A.D. 135. By describing the Jewish god, the God of the Old Testament, as an evil and ignorant god who must be rejected by every sensible person, the gnostics supported the general anti-Semitism of the period and ensured their own "safety".[56] The Roman congregation and the Christian Church did well to immediately reject both gnosticism, and Marcion and his teaching; in doing so, they confirmed that the Christian God was the same as the God of the Jews, and that the Old Testament was also the Christians' Bible.

It has often been suggested that Marcion with his canon composed of a gospel (= Lk.) and an apostle (= the ten Pauline letters) rejected the Old Testament, and that this forced the Church to elaborate its own canon, but this assumption is wrong, both from a theological and historical point of view.

In the first place, Marcion's choice of gospel and apostle presupposes the existence of New Testament scriptures with canonical validity from which he could select the texts he acknowledged. In any case, Lk. and Paul's letters were not made canonical by Marcion.

Secondly, Marcion did not "reject" the Old Testament. On the contrary, he saw the Old Testament as a revelation book of great value, but only gnostics, who possessed *gnôsis*, "insight", were able to interpret it and understand its meaning. Marcion's Antitheses simply make no sense except in the light of his admittedly negative reading and interpretation of the Old Testament.

Marcion's teaching might be seen as a kind of ultra-Paulinism in as far as Marcion did the things Paul had wanted to do, but had been prevented from doing. But such a view is basically false: Paul never doubted that the God of the Old Testament was also the Father of Jesus Christ and the God of the Christians

---

56 Lampe, *Stadtröm. Christen*, pp. 204 and 209-10, ascribes Marcion's view of the demiurge to his experiences during the reign of emperor Trajan (98-117): "These two demiurgical characteristics (belligerence; inconstancy/self-contradiction) reflect the experiences of a shipowner [sc. Marcion, who was a shipowner] during the reign of Trajan" (p. 209, italicized). This explanation of Marcion's theology is psychologizing and unconvincing; moreover, it does not even explain the anti-Semitic attitude.

– this is written on every page of his letters. Only the postulate of Jewish interpolations made it possible for Marcion to convince himself and his adherents that his teaching was identical to Paul's own teaching. The precise difference between Paul and Marcion is that Paul was a Jew, and Marcion was not.

It is essential for us to understand that Marcion's teaching was gnostic,[57] and that no gnostic systems existed – and Marcion's teaching *was* a system – until *after* the suppression of the Bar Kokhba revolt and the final and complete humiliation of the Jewish people.

4.5.3 Conclusion

In his book on Marcion, Adolf Harnack (1851-1930) wrote: "the rejection of the Old Testament in the second century [ascribed to Marcion] was a mistake which the great church rightly avoided; to maintain it in the sixteenth century [during the Reformation] was a fate from which the Reformation was not yet able to escape; but still to preserve it in Protestantism as a canonical document since the nineteenth century is the consequence of a religious and ecclesiastical crippling."[58]

These words are fantastic – and so is their ambiguity: Harnack does not wish to reject the Old Testament itself, only its canonical authority![59] This is nothing but a game of words. Today the canon concept has already been abandoned as a theological concept, Judaism and Christianity can be defined only from a historical point of view, and theology can no longer be defended as a branch of scholarship by referring to a theologically obsolete canon concept, which is not even acknowledged by theologians. Under these circumstances, a rejection of the Old Testament as "canonical evidence in Protestantism" is an

---

57 This is contrary to Harnack's view; also Lampe, *Stadtröm. Christen*, pp. 203 ff., seems to support Harnack's view of Marcion as a non-gnostic – gnostics are first mentioned on pp. 251 ff. in Lampe's book.

58 *Marcion*, 2nd ed., 1924, p. 217 = id., *Marcion. The Gospel of the Alien God*, p. 134 (italicized); this passage is also quoted in section 2.5.1 above, n. 101.

59 See Harnack, *Marcion*, p. 223 (p. 138 in *Marcion. The Gospel of the Alien God*): "... rejection [of the Old Testament] is not in the picture today at all. Rather, this book will be everywhere esteemed and treasured in its distinctiveness and its significance (the prophets) only when the *caconical authority* to which it is not entitled is withdrawn from it."

ambiguous and false statement, which implies a rejection of the Jewish people as inferior to the exclusive "Protestantism".

It has been suggested that a certain connection existed between Adolf Harnack's *Marcion* and Adolf Hitler, who could send six million Jews to the gas chambers without provoking any serious reaction from the representatives of theology and the Church. Of course theologians must be conscious of their responsibility as theologians, and of course it is essential to recognize and maintain what theology is – even the fact that theology exists at all. Having said that, I hasten to emphasize that the above-mentioned allegation is entirely unfounded and has nothing to do with reality.[60]

Christianity wanted to be true Judaism, the Church wanted to be the true Israel (cf. Phil. 3.3). The rejection of the humiliated and generally despised Jewish people which is so strongly reflected in theology and history alike finally made it possible for the Church to proclaim itself the new Israel – not "new" in the qualitative and eschatological sense of the word we know from the Old Testament, Paul's letters and the Revelation of John (i.e. Jer. 31.31; 2 Cor. 5.17; Rev. 21.1), but "new" in a quantitative sense: a "different" or "alienated" religion that rejects and denounces its own past.

Whenever this happens – as for instance in Marcion and his teaching of an unknown god who is not Abraham's, Isaac's and Jacob's God, but a new, strange god whom nobody knows – the Jewish people are deprived of their place in the history of Christianity, and theology no longer deserves to be called by its name.

4.6 Hegesippus' Hypomnemata; the Papias Fragments.
The beginnings of the Patristic Literature

Bibliography

Franz Overbeck: Über die Anfänge der patristischen Literatur, Historische Zeitschrift 48 (1882), pp. 417-472; republished in: Libelli, XV, Darmstadt 1954.

Id.: Über die Anfänge der Kirchengeschichtsschreibung. Programm zur Rektoratsfeier der Universität Basel, Basel 1892; republished in: Libelli, CLIII*, Darmstadt 1965.

---

60 See Friedrich Wilhelm Kantzenbach, art. "Harnack", in: *Theologische Realenzyklopädie*, XIV, Berlin – New York 1985, pp. 450-458, see p. 456.

Niels Hyldahl: Hegesipps Hypomnemata, Studia Theologica 14 (1960), pp. 70-113.

Philipp Vielhauer: Franz Overbeck und die neutestamentliche Wissenschaft, Evangelische Theologie 10 (1950-51), pp. 193-207 = in: id., *Aufsätze zum Neuen Testament* (Theologische Bücherei, 31), Munich 1965, pp. 235-252.

Id.: art. "Overbeck, Franz Camille", in: *Religion in Geschichte und Gegenwart*, 3rd ed., IV, Tübingen 1960, col. 1750-1752.

Id.: *Geschichte der urchristlichen Literatur. Einleitung in das Neue Testament, die Apokryphen und die Apostolischen Väter* (de Gruyter Lehrbuch), Berlin – New York 1975, repr. 1978, pp. 757-765: 'Papias von Hierapolis, "Auslegung von Herrenworten"'; pp. 765-774: 'Hegesipp, "Hypomnemata"'.

U.H.J. Körtner: *Papias von Hierapolis. Ein Beitrag zur Geschichte des frühen Christentums* (Forschungen zur Religion und Literatur des Alten und Neuen Testaments, 133), Göttingen 1983.

Martin Rese: Fruchtbare Mißverständnisse. Franz Overbeck und die neutestamentliche Wissenschaft, in: Rudolf Brändle/Ekkehard W. Stegemann, eds., *Franz Overbecks unerledigte Anfragen an das Christentum*, Munich 1988, pp. 211-226.

Martin Henry: *Franz Overbeck: Theologian? Religion and History in the Thought of Franz Overbeck* (European University Studies, 23), Frankfurt a.M. 1995.

4.6.1 Franz Overbeck and Patristic literature

Marcion came to Rome in about A.D. 144. The Christian apologist Justin wrote his Apologia[61] in Rome in about A.D. 150, during the reign of the emperor Antoninus Pius (138-161), when Quintus Lollius Urbicus was urban prefect of Rome (144-160). In about A.D. 160, Justin wrote his Dialogue with the Jew called Trypho. Justin was executed in Rome as a Christian in about A.D. 165, during the reign of Marcus Aurelius, the emperor and philosopher (161-180), when Junius Rusticus was urban prefect of Rome (163-168).

With such writings, intended for non-Christian readers, Christian literature had entered the cultural universe of its own time, and Patristic literature – the literature of the Fathers of the Church – had come into existence.

---

61 According to the existing editions, there are two apologias (or one apologia with an appendix); but in fact it is one and the same text which has been divided into two parts by mistake or misconception. See, for instance, my *Philosophie und Christentum. Eine Interpretation der Einleitung zum Dialog Justin* (Acta Theologica Danica, IX), Copenhagen 1966, pp. 14-16; H. Hermann Holfelder, *Eusébeia kaì philosophía*. Literarische Einheit und politischer Kontext von Justins Apologie, Zeitschrift für die neutestamentliche Wissenschaft 68 (1977), pp. 48-66 and pp. 231-251.

Patristic literature succeeded primitive Christian literature at the end of the apostolic era, in the middle of the second century. Patristics have been the subject of many deliberations and discussions, and many attempts have been made to determine their literary genre. Franz Overbeck (1837-1905) argued strongly in favour of the view that the literature that existed prior to the Patristics, including the New Testament scriptures, should be called "Christian primitive literature" rather than "primitive Christian literature".[62] Christian primitive literature was not "real" literature in the same sense as Patristic literature, which was also intended for other readers than Christians. According to Overbeck, Christian primitive literature was "in a strict and exclusive sense rooted in Christianity and nourished by the interests of the Christian congregations, independently of any outside influence."[63]

In 1950, Philipp Vielhauer provoked a sort of Overbeck renaissance in New Testament exegesis, but probably he overinterpreted Overbeck's own observations. For instance, Vielhauer maintained that Overbeck was the original initiator of form-critical analysis of New Testament literature (see section 2.2.2 above), especially the Gospel texts.

It is true that during the years after the First World War, when form critics, especially Martin Dibelius, began to speak of New Testament literature as "minor literature", they referred to Overbeck's view of "Christian primitive literature" as opposed to the Patristic literature. However, as Martin Rese has demonstrated, it was never Overbeck's intention to define the literary genres of the New Testament texts, as the form critics did, so Vielhauer's view of Overbeck as the pioneer of form criticism is hardly justified. Furthermore, Overbeck's intention in writing his treatise on the beginnings of Patristic literature was to determine the *transition* between the two literary phases, and for this purpose he concentrates on two texts which he could assign neither to Christian primitive literature nor to Patristic literature itself: Papias'

---

62 It has been maintained that I have misunderstood Overbeck's term by referring to "primitive Christian literature"; cf. Vielhauer, *Geschichte*, p. 767, n. 5. I therefore find it surprising that Vielhauer, who is a strong supporter of Overbeck's view, called his own book *Geschichte der Urchristlichen Literatur* [History of Primitive Christian Literature]. In spite of the criticism, I do not mind being mentioned together with Franz Overbeck: Vielhauer, p. 767.

63 Overbeck, *Geschichte der Literatur der alten Kirche*, quoted from Vielhauer, *Geschichte*, p. 770, which supports Overbeck's definition.

interpretations of the words of the Lord from circa A.D. 140,[64] and Hegesippus' Hypomnemata from circa A.D. 170. According to Overbeck, these two texts, which we know only from fragments preserved mainly by the ecclesiastical historian Eusebius, do not belong to Patristic literature, but represent transitional forms of this, although Hegesippus' work itself was written during the period after the appearance of the first Patristic works, the scriptures of the earliest apologists.

4.6.2 The end of the post-apostolic era

In this context, it is not my intention to discuss these works in detail or define their precise literary genre, but there is one aspect I must point out. Irrespective of our attitude to the literary peculiarity and genre of these two works, both of them are and claim to be historical documents in one sense or another. This does not appear from their titles – which should perhaps not even be regarded as regular book titles. For instance, as far as Hegesippus' *hypomnémata* is concerned, its name should not be understood to mean the same as *apomnemoneúmata* – the title of Xenophon's *Memorabilia* (memoirs) about Socrates. (In deference to the prevailing cultural taste, the apologist Justin also applies this title to the Gospels, as if they were "Memoirs of the Lord", which suggests the idea that Jesus was a new and better Socrates!) Such a misinterpretation of the "title" would invariably turn Hegesippus' text into a work on ecclesiastical history, which it is not. The word *hypomnémata* is simply the Greek equivalent to the Latin word *commentarii* (notes), the name which is also used for Caesar's famous "Gallic Wars". Similarly, the "title" of Papias' *exegéseis* is hardly informative; admittedly, it is a work of no less than five volumes, and its rhetorically formulated prologue reveals Papias' literary ambitions regarding the publication of his work, but tells us almost nothing about its literary genre.

Papias' and Hegesippus' works are "historical" in the sense that both authors themselves indicate that they have looked for and discovered old traditions, which they have then written down. In this respect, they are both reminiscent of Lk.-Acts, a work in two parts with an ambitious literary prologue

---

64 Körtner, *Papias*, dates the text to circa A.D. 110; cf. the justified objections in Wehnert, *Die Wir-Passagen der Apostelgeschichte*, 1989 (see section 3.8 above), pp. 57-59 with n. 43 (on p. 215).

(Lk. 1.1-4) similar to that of Papias.[65] In Papias' work, the "historical" aspect is also reflected in the prologue's description of his working method: he listened to the elders and wrote down what they told him:

3 But I will not hesitate also to set down for thy benefit [cf. Lk. 1.3], along with the interpretations, all that I ever carefully learnt and carefully recalled from the elders [*presbýteroi*], guaranteeing its truth. For I did not take delight, as most men do, in those who have much to say, but in those who teach what is true; not in those who recall foreign commandments, but in those who recall the commandments given by the Lord to faith, and reaching us from the truth itself. 4 And if anyone chanced to come who had actually been a follower of the elders [*presbýteroi*], I would enquire as to the discourses of the elders [*presbýteroi*], what Andrew or Peter said, or what Philip, or what Thomas or James, or what John or Matthew or any other of the Lord's disciples said; and the things which Aristion and John the elder, disciples of the Lord, say. For I supposed that things out of books did not profit me so much as the utterances of a voice "which liveth and abideth" [1 Pet. 1.23].[66]

Irrespective of the subject matter of this text, whose rhetorical form should not mislead us into thinking that the text is a (real) polemic against certain scriptures, including the Gospels, it is clear that Papias is very much aware of the historical tradition he has discovered and describes. In this respect, his attitude to Christian history is similar to that of the author of Lk.-Acts, and also reminiscent of the method adopted by the author of 1 Clem. (see section 4.4 above). The same applies to Hegesippus. During the journeys he made to study the existence of the apostolic tradition, he visited both Corinth and Rome. He makes the following observations on his visit to Rome:

2 ... With them I associated on my voyage to Rome, and I abode with the Corinthians many days, during which we were refreshed together in the true doctrine. 3 But when I came to Rome, I made for myself a succession-list [*diadoché*] as far as Anicetus, whose deacon was Eleutherus. Anicetus was succeeded by Soter, and after him came Eleutherus. And in every succession [*diadoché*] and in every city, that which the Law and the Prophets and the Lord preach is faithfully followed.[67]

---

65 On Lk.-Acts, see also C.F. Evans, as quoted in section 3.1.3 above, n. 19.
66 Eusebius, Hist. eccl. III, 39.3-4; English translation: Lawlor/Oulton, *Eusebius* (see section 3 above), vol. I, p. 99.
67 Eusebius, Hist. eccl. IV, 22.2-3; English translation: Lawlor/Oulton, *Eusebius*, vol. I, p. 127.

Although it is difficult to understand in detail, the text is really quite simple; Peter Lampe describes its contents as follows: "Hegesippus focused his interest on the *true teaching* (4,22,2), such as had been handed down from the Apostles to his own contemporaries. During his journey, Hegesippus convinced himself that this had happened in the various cities of the world, and satisfied himself that it had also happened in Rome. In other words, his aim was not to establish a succession-list of *monarchical* bishops. What he saw in his mind's eye was a succession of representatives of the true faith, and this was also what he looked for and found in Rome. That is all."[68]

Both Papias' and Hegesippus' works are characterized by a historical awareness of the unbroken connection between their own time and the Christian past. Combined with a high level of ambition in form and content, this indicates the same desire for culture expressed by the uncontested representatives of Patristic literature, such as Justin, Irenaeus, Clement of Alexandria, and others. The existence of scriptures such as Lk. and Acts contradicts Franz Overbeck's theory of a barrier between Christian "primitive literature" and Patristic literature: the transition between them is far too fluid to justify such a theory. Following in Overbeck's footsteps, Philipp Vielhauer persists in arguing for this questionable theory, for instance by referring to Hegesippus' Hypomnemata as nothing but "a fossil of Christian primitive literature in a time when a "real" Christian literature was just beginning to flourish."[69]

But if Overbeck's distinction between "Christian primitive literature" and Patristic literature is untenable and inaccurate, how should we then define the end of the post-apostolic era?

We can try to do this by observing the Christians' social status and cultural development: we know, for instance, that precisely in the middle of the second century, the Christians – especially in Rome, the capital – were able to attract even wealthy people, who provided housing (and tombs!) for the poor. This development came from a strong community spirit and great cultural ambitions, a heritage from Judaism, in which Christianity still had its roots, in spite of its awareness of its own distinctive character. The ecclesiastical office manifested

---

68 Lampe, *Stadtröm. Christen* (see section 4.5 above), p. 342. For information on the monarchical episcopate, which was introduced *after* Hegesippus' time, see section 4.4.1 above.

69 Vielhauer, *Geschichte*, p. 770.

itself mainly on a social level, and through their organization, their congregations, the Christians proved to possess a capacity to survive and support each other that must have surpassed anything which secular society could offer in terms of human resources. A bishop (Greek: *epískopos*), "supervisor", is a person whose main responsibility is to "supervise" others, take care of their social welfare and help them in general.[70] This stage in the history of Christianity coincides with the end of the Bar Kokhba war (132-135 – see section 4.5.1 above), after which the Christians are completely independent of Judaism.

---

70 See Lampe, *Stadtröm. Christen*, pp. 337-338.

INDEX

Authors

Texts

315